Contents

Chemistry 2

Chemistry 3

How to use this book

Learning Objectives

- These tell you exactly what you need to learn, or be able to do, for the exam.

- There's a specification reference at the bottom that links to the AQA specification.

Examples

These are here to help you understand the theory.

How Science Works

- How Science Works is a big part of GCSE Chemistry. There's a whole section on it at the front of the book.

- How Science Works is also covered throughout the book wherever you see this symbol.

Chemistry 1   1.4 Crude Oil and Fuels

1. Fractional Distillation of Crude Oil

Crude oil is a fossil fuel that is formed deep underground from the remains of plants and animals. Loads of useful products can be made from crude oil using a technique called fractional distillation.

What is crude oil?

Crude oil is a **mixture** of many different compounds. A mixture consists of two (or more) elements or compounds that aren't chemically bonded to each other. Most of the compounds in crude oil are **hydrocarbon** molecules. Hydrocarbons are basically fuels such as petrol and diesel. They're made of only carbon and hydrogen.

Properties of mixtures

There are no chemical bonds between the different parts of a mixture, so the different hydrocarbon molecules in crude oil aren't chemically bonded to one another. This means that they all keep their original properties, such as their boiling points (the temperature at which they turn from a liquid into a gas). The properties of a mixture are just a mixture of the properties of the separate parts.

Separating mixtures

Because the substances in a mixture all keep their original properties, the parts of a mixture can be separated out by physical methods.

> **Example**
>
> Crude oil can be split up into its separate fractions by fractional distillation. Each fraction contains molecules with a similar number of carbon atoms to each other.

Fractional distillation

Crude oil can be split into separate groups of hydrocarbons using a technique called fractional distillation. The crude oil is pumped into piece of equipment known as a fractionating column, which works continuously (it doesn't get switched off). This fractionating column has a temperature gradient running through it — it's hottest at the bottom and coldest at the top.

Learning Objectives:
- Know that crude oil is a mixture of lots of different compounds.
- Know that the substances in a mixture are not chemically bonded to each other.
- Know that most of the compounds in crude oil are hydrocarbons.
- Know that the properties of substances are not changed when the substance is in a mixture.
- Know that mixtures can be separated using physical methods such as distillation.
- Understand how fractional distillation is used to separate crude oil into fractions.

Specification Reference
C1.4.1, C1.4.2

Figure 1: A fractionating column.

Chemistry 1.4 **Crude Oil and Fuels**   61

Advantages and disadvantages of emulsifiers

You need to know the advantages and disadvantages of using emulsifiers.

Advantages

- Emulsifiers stop emulsions from separating out and this gives them a longer shelf-life.

- Emulsifiers allow food companies to produce food that's lower in fat but that still has a good texture.

Disadvantages

- Some people are allergic to certain emulsifiers. For example, egg yolk is often used as an emulsifier — so people who are allergic to eggs need to check the ingredients very carefully.

Tip: Low fat margarines contain less fat and more water than normal margarines. Emulsifiers help them to keep a nice spreadable texture. Otherwise you'd end up with a gunky mess of separated water, oils and hard fats.

Practice Questions — Fact Recall

Q1 Do oils dissolve in water?

Q2 a) Draw a simple diagram showing an oil-in-water emulsion.

    b) Give one way that the physical properties of an oil-in-water emulsion will be different to the properties of either oil or water.

Q3 a) Name two food products that are emulsions.

    b) Name one non-food product that is an emulsion.

Q4 a) What job does an emulsifier do?

    b) Give one advantage and one disadvantage of using emulsifiers in food products.

Q5 a) Draw and label an emulsifier molecule.

    b) Explain how emulsifier molecules stop an emulsion separating.

Practice Questions — Application

Q1 Kevin has 30 ml of olive oil and 10 ml of vinegar. He wants to make them into an emulsion to use as a salad dressing.

    a) Describe how Kevin could prepare the emulsion.

    Anna is also making a salad dressing. She has the same amount of oil and vinegar as Kevin, but she decides not to mix them.

    b) Which method will make a better salad dressing? Explain your answer.

Q2 Polysorbate 80 is a commonly used emulsifier. What does this tell you about the structure of a molecule of Polysorbate 80?

Exam Tip
Make sure you can remember how to make an emulsion — it's a simple little detail, but it might just come up.

Tips and Exam Tips

- There are tips throughout the book to help you understand the theory.

- There are also exam tips to help you with answering exam questions.

Practice Questions

- There are a lot of facts to learn for GCSE Chemistry — fact recall questions test that you know them.

- Annoyingly, the examiners also expect you to be able to apply your knowledge to new situations — application questions give you plenty of practice at doing this.

- All the answers are in the back of the book.

Higher Exam Material

- Some of the material in this book will only come up in the exam if you're sitting the higher exam papers.

- This material is clearly marked with boxes that look like this:

- If you're sitting the foundation papers, you don't need to learn it.

Section Checklist

Each section has a checklist at the end with boxes that let you tick off what you've learnt.

Glossary

There's a glossary at the back of the book full of all the definitions you need to know for the exam, plus loads of other useful words.

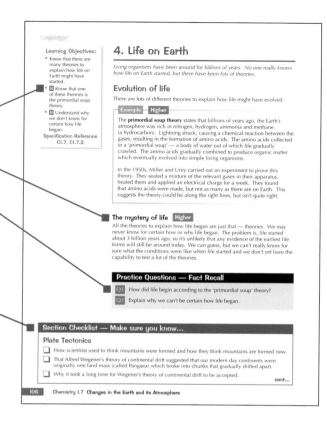

Learning Objectives:
* Know that there are many theories to explain how life on Earth might have started.
* **H** Know that one of these theories is the primordial soup theory.
* **H** Understand why we don't know for certain how life began.
Specification Reference C1.7, C1.7.2

4. Life on Earth

Living organisms have been around for billions of years. No one really knows how life on Earth started, but there have been lots of theories.

Evolution of life

There are lots of different theories to explain how life might have evolved.

Example **Higher**

The **primordial soup theory** states that billions of years ago, the Earth's atmosphere was rich in nitrogen, hydrogen, ammonia and methane (a hydrocarbon). Lightning struck, causing a chemical reaction between the gases, resulting in the formation of amino acids. The amino acids collected in a 'primordial soup' — a body of water out of which life gradually crawled. The amino acids gradually combined to produce organic matter which eventually evolved into simple living organisms.

In the 1950s, Miller and Urey carried out an experiment to prove this theory. They sealed a mixture of the relevant gases in their apparatus, heated them and applied an electrical charge for a week. They found that amino acids were made, but not as many as there are on Earth. This suggests the theory could be along the right lines, but isn't quite right.

The mystery of life **Higher**

All the theories to explain how life began are just that — theories. We may never know for certain how or why life began. The problem is, life started about 3 billion years ago, so it's unlikely that any evidence of the earliest life forms will still be around today. We can guess, but we can't really know for sure what the conditions were like when life started and we don't yet have the capability to test a lot of the theories.

Practice Questions — Fact Recall

Q1 How did life begin according to the 'primordial soup' theory?

Q2 Explain why we can't be certain how life began.

Section Checklist — Make sure you know...

Plate Tectonics

- [ ] How scientists used to think mountains were formed and how they think mountains are formed now.
- [ ] That Alfred Wegener's theory of continental drift suggested that our modern day continents were originally one land mass (called Pangaea) which broke into chunks that gradually drifted apart.
- [ ] Why it took a long time for Wegener's theory of continental drift to be accepted.

cont...

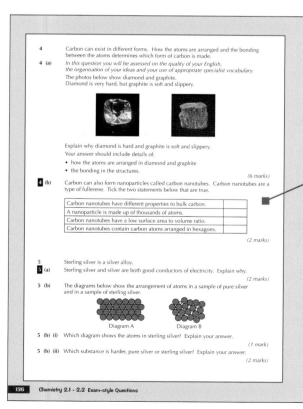

4   Carbon can exist in different forms. How the atoms are arranged and the bonding between the atoms determines which form of carbon is made.

4 (a)   *In this question you will be assessed on the quality of your English, the organisation of your ideas and your use of appropriate specialist vocabulary.*
The photos below show diamond and graphite.
Diamond is very hard, but graphite is soft and slippery.

Explain why diamond is hard and graphite is soft and slippery.
Your answer should include details of:
• how the atoms are arranged in diamond and graphite
• the bonding in the structures.
(6 marks)

4 (b)   Carbon can also form nanoparticles called carbon nanotubes. Carbon nanotubes are a type of fullerene. Tick the two statements below that are true.

Carbon nanotubes have different properties to bulk carbon.	
A nanoparticle is made up of thousands of atoms.	
Carbon nanotubes have a low surface area to volume ratio.	
Carbon nanotubes contain carbon atoms arranged in hexagons.	

(2 marks)

5   Sterling silver is a silver alloy.

5 (a)   Sterling silver and silver are both good conductors of electricity. Explain why.
(2 marks)

5 (b)   The diagrams below show the arrangement of atoms in a sample of pure silver and in a sample of sterling silver.

Diagram A   Diagram B

5 (b) (i)   Which diagram shows the atoms in sterling silver? Explain your answer.
(1 mark)

5 (b) (ii)   Which substance is harder, pure silver or sterling silver? Explain your answer.
(2 marks)

Exam-style Questions

- Practising exam-style questions is really important — there are some testing you on material from every section.

- They're the same style as the ones you'll get in the real exams.

- All the answers are in the back of the book, along with a mark scheme to show you how you get the marks.

- Higher-only questions are marked like this:

Controlled Assessment and Exam Help

There are sections at the back of the book stuffed full of things to help you with the controlled assessment and the exams.

Learning Objectives:

- Know what a hypothesis and a prediction are and understand their roles in developing scientific ideas.
- Understand that scientists try to explain observations using evidence collected in investigations.
- Understand the importance of carrying out fair tests and collecting repeatable, reproducible and valid results.
- Understand why some decisions relating to science are not just based on scientific evidence but take other factors into account.

Specification Reference
How Science Works

Tip: Investigations include lab experiments and studies.

1. The Scientific Process

Science is all about finding things out and learning things about the world we live in. This topic is all about the scientific process — how a scientist's initial idea turns into a theory that is accepted by the wider scientific community.

Hypotheses

Scientists try to explain things. Everything. They start by observing something they don't understand — it could be anything, e.g. planets in the sky, a person suffering from an illness, what matter is made of... anything.

Then, they come up with a **hypothesis** — a possible explanation for what they've observed. The next step is to test whether the hypothesis might be right or not — this involves gathering evidence (i.e. data from investigations).

The scientist uses the hypothesis to make a **prediction** — a statement based on the hypothesis that can be tested. They then carry out an investigation. If data from experiments or studies backs up the prediction, you're one step closer to figuring out if the hypothesis is true.

Testing a hypothesis

Other scientists will use the hypothesis to make their own predictions, and carry out their own experiments or studies. They'll also try to reproduce the original investigations to check the results. And if all the experiments in the world back up the hypothesis, then scientists start to think it's true.

However, if a scientist somewhere in the world does an experiment that doesn't fit with the hypothesis (and other scientists can reproduce these results), then the hypothesis is in trouble. When this happens, scientists have to come up with a new hypothesis (maybe a modification of the old hypothesis, or maybe a completely new one).

Tip: Sometimes it can take a really long time for a hypothesis to be accepted. Have a peek at the story of Alfred Wegener's theory of continental drift on pages 96-98 for a perfect example of this.

Accepting a hypothesis

If pretty much every scientist in the world believes a hypothesis to be true because experiments back it up, then it usually goes in the textbooks for students to learn. Accepted hypotheses are often referred to as **theories**.

Our currently accepted theories are the ones that have survived this 'trial by evidence' — they've been tested many, many times over the years and survived (while the less good ones have been ditched). However... they never, never become hard and fast, totally indisputable fact. You can never know... it'd only take one odd, totally inexplicable result, and the hypothesising and testing would start all over again.

Over time scientists have come up with different hypotheses about the structure of the atom.

About 100 years ago we thought atoms looked like this.

Then we thought they looked like this.

And then we thought they looked like this.

Tip: The different hypotheses on what an atom looks like are called different <u>models</u>. A model is a simplified description or a representation of an object or a concept.

Tip: There's lots more about the structure of the atom on page 17.

Collecting evidence

If a hypothesis is going to get accepted, there needs to be good evidence for it. The way evidence is gathered can have a big effect on how trustworthy it is.

Results from experiments in laboratories are great. A lab is the easiest place to control variables so that they're all kept constant (except for the one you're investigating). This makes it easier to carry out a **fair test**. For things that you can't investigate in the lab (e.g. climate) you conduct scientific studies. As many of the variables as possible are controlled, to make it a fair test.

Old wives' tales, rumours, hearsay, "what someone said", and so on, should be taken with a pinch of salt. Without any evidence they're not scientific — they're just opinions.

Tip: See page 7 for more on fair testing and variables.

Sample size

Data based on small samples isn't as good as data based on large samples. A sample should be representative of the whole population (i.e. it should share as many of the various characteristics in the population as possible) — a small sample can't do that as well.

The bigger the sample size the better, but scientists have to be realistic when choosing how big.

Figure 1: A scientist doing a laboratory experiment.

If you were studying the health effects of adding chlorine to drinking water it'd be great to study everyone in the UK (a huge sample), but it'd take ages and cost a bomb. Studying a thousand people would be more realistic.

Tip: See pages 224 and 225 for more about the addition of chlorine to drinking water.

Quality of evidence

You can have confidence in the results if they can be repeated (during the same experiment) and other scientists can reproduce them too (in other experiments). If the results aren't **repeatable** or **reproducible**, you can't believe them.

Figure 2: Stanley Pons and Martin Fleischmann — the scientists who allegedly discovered cold fusion.

Example

In 1989, two scientists claimed that they'd produced 'cold fusion' (the energy source of the Sun but without the big temperatures). It was huge news — if true, it would have meant free energy for the world forever. However, other scientists just couldn't reproduce the results, so they couldn't be believed. And until they are, 'cold fusion' isn't going to be accepted as fact.

If results are repeatable and reproducible, they're said to be **reliable**.

Getting valid evidence

Evidence also needs to be **valid**. Valid means that the data answers the original question.

Example

Do power lines cause cancer?

Some studies have found that children who live near overhead power lines are more likely to develop cancer. What they'd actually found was a **correlation** (relationship) between the variables "presence of power lines" and "incidence of cancer". They found that as one changed, so did the other.

But this evidence is not enough to say that the power lines cause cancer, as other explanations might be possible. For example, power lines are often near busy roads, so the areas tested could contain different levels of pollution from traffic. So these studies don't show a definite link and so don't answer the original question.

Tip: See page 14 for more on correlation.

Communicating results

Once evidence is collected it can be shared with other people. It's important that the evidence isn't presented in a **biased** way. This can sometimes happen when people want to make a point, e.g. they overemphasise a relationship in the data. (Sometimes without knowing they're doing it.) And there are all sorts of reasons why people might want to do this.

Examples

- They want to keep the organisation or company that's funding the research happy. (If the results aren't what they'd like they might not give them any more money to fund further research.)

- Governments might want to persuade voters, other governments, journalists, etc.

- Companies might want to 'big up' their products. Or make impressive safety claims.
- Environmental campaigners might want to persuade people to behave differently.

There's also a risk that if an investigation is done by a team of highly-regarded scientists it'll be taken more seriously than evidence from less well known scientists. But having experience, authority or a fancy qualification doesn't necessarily mean the evidence is good — the only way to tell is to look at the evidence scientifically (e.g. is it repeatable, valid, etc.).

Issues created by science

Scientific knowledge is increased by doing experiments. And this knowledge leads to scientific developments, e.g. new technologies or new advice. These developments can create issues though. For example, particular scientific developments might be ignored if they could create political issues, or emphasised if they help a particular cause.

Example

Some governments were pretty slow to accept the fact that human activities are causing global warming, despite all the evidence. This is because accepting it means they've got to do something about it, which costs money and could hurt their economy. This could lose them a lot of votes.

Tip: See page 68 for more on global warming.

Scientific developments can cause a whole host of other issues too.

Examples

- **Economic issues:** Society can't always afford to do things scientists recommend (e.g. investing heavily in alternative energy sources) without cutting back elsewhere.

- **Social issues:** Decisions based on scientific evidence affect people — e.g. should fossil fuels be taxed more highly (to invest in alternative energy)? Should alcohol be banned (to prevent health problems)? Would the effect on people's lifestyles be acceptable?

- **Environmental issues:** Chemical fertilisers may help us produce more food — but they also cause environmental problems.

- **Ethical issues:** There are a lot of things that scientific developments have made possible, but should we do them? E.g. clone humans, develop better nuclear weapons.

Figure 3: *Dolly the sheep — the first mammal to be cloned. A great scientific advance but some people think that cloning animals is morally wrong.*

Science has taught us an awful lot about the world we live in and how things work — but science doesn't have the answer for everything.

Questions science hasn't answered yet

We don't understand everything. And we never will. We'll find out more, for sure — as more hypotheses are suggested, and more experiments are done. But there'll always be stuff we don't know.

Examples

- Today we don't know as much as we'd like about the impacts of global warming. How much will sea level rise? And to what extent will weather patterns change?
- We also don't know anywhere near as much as we'd like about the Universe. Are there other life forms out there? And what is the Universe made of?

These are complicated questions. At the moment scientists don't all agree on the answers because there isn't enough repeatable, reproducible and valid evidence. But eventually, we probably will be able to answer these questions once and for all. All we need is more evidence. But by then there'll be loads of new questions to answer.

Figure 1: *The night sky. We can use high powered telescopes to observe the Universe but we still have little idea what it's made from or how it was formed.*

Questions science can't answer

There are some questions that all the experiments in the world won't help us answer — the "should we be doing this at all?" type questions.

Example

Think about new drugs which can be taken to boost your 'brain power'. Some people think they're good. Or at least no worse than taking vitamins or eating oily fish. They could let you keep thinking for longer, or improve your memory. It's thought that new drugs could allow people to think in ways that are beyond the powers of normal brains — in effect, to become geniuses.

Other people say they're bad. Taking them would give you an unfair advantage in exams, say. And perhaps people would be pressured into taking them so that they could work more effectively, and for longer hours.

Tip: It's important that scientists don't get wrapped up in whether they <u>can</u> do something, before stopping to think about whether they <u>should</u> do it. Some experiments have to be approved by ethics councils before scientists are allowed to carry them out.

The question of whether something is morally or ethically right or wrong can't be answered by more experiments — there is no "right" or "wrong" answer. The best we can do is get a consensus from society — a judgement that most people are more or less happy to live by. Science can provide more information to help people make this judgement, and the judgement might change over time. But in the end it's up to people and their conscience.

3. Designing Investigations

Learning Objective:
- Know how to design fair investigations that allow good quality data to be collected.

Specification Reference
How Science Works

To be a good scientist you need to know how to design a good experiment. That's what this topic is all about — how to make your experiment safe and how to make sure you get good quality results.

Making predictions from a hypothesis

Scientists observe things and come up with hypotheses to explain them (see page 1). To figure out whether a **hypothesis** might be correct or not you need to do an investigation to gather some evidence. The evidence will help support or disprove the hypothesis.

The first step is to use the hypothesis to come up with a **prediction** — a statement about what you think will happen that you can test.

Example

If your hypothesis is "eating a diet containing a large amount of saturated fat causes a high blood cholesterol level", then your prediction might be "people who eat large amounts of saturated fats will have a high level of cholesterol in their blood".

Investigations are used to see if there are patterns or relationships between two variables. For example, to see if there's a pattern or relationship between the variables 'amount of saturated fats eaten' and 'blood cholesterol level'. The investigation has to be a **fair test** to make sure the evidence is **valid**.

Tip: Sometimes the words 'hypothesis' and 'prediction' are used interchangeably.

Tip: See page 4 for more on valid evidence.

Ensuring it's a fair test

In a lab experiment you usually change one variable and measure how it affects the other variable. To make it a fair test everything else that could affect the results should stay the same (otherwise you can't tell if the thing you're changing is causing the results or not — the data won't be valid).

Tip: A variable is just something in the experiment that can change.

Example

You might change only the temperature of a chemical reaction and measure how this affects the rate of reaction. You need to keep the concentration of the reactants the same, otherwise you won't know if any change in the rate of reaction is caused by the change in temperature, or a difference in reactant concentration.

Figure 1: Students measuring the rate of a chemical reaction.

The variable you change is called the **independent variable**. The variable you measure is called the **dependent variable**. The variables that you keep the same are called **control variables**.

Example

In the rate of reaction example, temperature is the independent variable, the rate of the reaction is the dependent variable and the concentration of reactants and volume of reactants are control variables.

Tip: A study is an investigation that doesn't take place in a lab.

Controlling variables in a study

It's important that a study is a fair test, just like a lab experiment. It's a lot trickier to control the variables in a study than it is in a lab experiment though. Sometimes you can't control them all, but you can use a **control group** to help. This is a group of whatever you're studying (people, plants, lemmings, etc.) that's kept under the same conditions as the group in the experiment, but doesn't have anything done to it.

Example

If you're studying the effect of pesticides on crop growth, pesticide is applied to one field but not to another field (the control field). Both fields are planted with the same crop, and are in the same area (so they get the same weather conditions).

The control field is there to try and account for variables like the weather, which don't stay the same all the time, but could affect the results.

Figure 2: Crops being sprayed with pesticides.

Trial runs

It's a good idea to do a **trial run** (a quick version of your experiment) before you do the proper experiment. Trial runs are used to figure out the range of variable values used in the proper experiment (the upper and lower limit). If you don't get a change in the dependent variable at the lower values in the trial run, you might narrow the range in the proper experiment. But if you still get a big change at the upper values you might increase the range.

Example

For a rate of reaction experiment, you might do a trial run with a temperature range of 10-50 °C. If there was no reaction at the lower end (e.g. 10-20 °C), you might narrow the range to 20-50 °C for the proper experiment.

Tip: If you don't have time to do a trial run, you could always look at the data other people have got doing a similar experiment and use a range and intervals similar to theirs.

Trial runs can also be used to figure out the interval (gaps) between the values too. The intervals can't be too small (otherwise the experiment would take ages), or too big (otherwise you might miss something).

Example

If using 1 °C intervals doesn't give you much change in the rate of reaction each time you might decide to use 5 °C intervals, e.g 20, 25, 30, 35, 40, 45, 50 °C...

Trial runs can also help you figure out whether or not your experiment is repeatable.

Tip: Consistently repeating the results is crucial for ensuring that your results are repeatable. See page 10 for more on this.

Example

If you repeat it three times and the results are all similar, the experiment is repeatable.

Ensuring your experiment is safe

A **hazard** is something that can potentially cause harm. Hazards include:

- Microorganisms: e.g. some bacteria can make you ill.
- Chemicals: e.g. sulfuric acid can burn your skin and alcohols catch fire easily.
- Fire: e.g. an unattended Bunsen burner is a fire hazard.
- Electricity: e.g. faulty electrical equipment could give you a shock.

Tip: You can find out about potential hazards by looking in textbooks, doing some internet research, or asking your teacher.

Scientists need to manage the risk of hazards by doing things to reduce them.

Example

- If you're working with sulfuric acid, always wear gloves and safety goggles. This will reduce the risk of the acid coming into contact with your skin and eyes.
- If you're using a Bunsen burner, stand it on a heatproof mat. This will reduce the risk of starting a fire.

Figure 3: *Scientists wearing safety goggles to protect their eyes during an experiment.*

Learning Objectives:
- Know how to collect good quality data, taking repeatability, reproducibility, accuracy, precision and equipment selection and use into account.
- Understand what random errors, systematic errors and anomalous results are.

Specification Reference
How Science Works

Tip: For more on means see page 12.

Tip: Sometimes, you can work out what result you should get at the end of an experiment (the theoretical result) by doing a bit of maths. If your experiment is accurate there shouldn't be much difference between the theoretical results and the result you actually get.

4. Collecting Data

Once you've designed your experiment, you need to get on and do it. Here's a guide to making sure the results you collect are good.

Getting good quality results

When you do an experiment you want your results to be **repeatable**, **reproducible** and as **accurate** and **precise** as possible.

To check repeatability you need to repeat the readings — you should repeat each reading at least three times. To make sure your results are reproducible you can cross check them by taking a second set of readings with another instrument (or a different observer). Checking your results match with secondary sources, e.g. other studies, also increases the reliability of your data.

Your data also needs to be accurate. Really accurate results are those that are really close to the true answer. Collecting lots of data and calculating a mean will improve the accuracy of your results. Your data also needs to be precise. Precise results are ones where the data is all really close to the mean (i.e. not spread out).

Example

Look at the data in this table. Data set 1 is more precise than data set 2 because all the data in set 1 is really close to the mean, whereas the data in set 2 is more spread out.

Repeat	Data set 1	Data set 2
1	12	11
2	14	17
3	13	14
Mean	13	14

Choosing the right equipment

When doing an experiment, you need to make sure you're using the right equipment for the job. The measuring equipment you use has to be sensitive enough to measure the changes you're looking for.

Example

If you need to measure changes of 1 ml you need to use a measuring cylinder that can measure in 1 ml steps — it'd be no good trying with one that only measures 10 ml steps, it wouldn't be sensitive enough.

The smallest change a measuring instrument can detect is called its **resolution**. For example, some mass balances have a resolution of 1 g, some have a resolution of 0.1 g, and some are even more sensitive.

Figure 1: *Different types of measuring cylinder and glassware — make sure you choose the right one before you start an experiment.*

Also, equipment needs to be calibrated so that your data is more accurate.

> **Example**
>
> Mass balances need to be set to zero before you start weighing things.

Tip: Calibration is a way of making sure that a measuring device is measuring things accurately — you get it to measure something you know has a certain value and set the device to say that amount.

Errors

Random errors

The results of your experiment will always vary a bit because of **random errors** — tiny differences caused by things like human errors in measuring. You can reduce their effect by taking many readings and calculating the mean.

Systematic errors

If the same error is made every time, it's called a **systematic error**.

> **Example**
>
> If you measured from the very end of your ruler instead of from the 0 cm mark every time, all your measurements would be a bit small.

Figure 2: A mass balance that has been set to zero.

Just to make things more complicated, if a systematic error is caused by using equipment that isn't zeroed properly it's called a **zero error**. You can compensate for some systematic and zero errors if you know about them though.

Tip: A zero error is a specific type of systematic error.

> **Example**
>
> If a mass balance always reads 1 gram before you put anything on it, all your measurements will be 1 gram too heavy. This is a zero error. You can compensate for this by subtracting 1 gram from all your results.

Tip: Repeating the experiment in the exact same way and calculating an average won't correct a systematic error.

Anomalous results

Sometimes you get a result that doesn't seem to fit in with the rest at all. These results are called **anomalous results** (or outliers).

> **Example**
>
> Look at the data in this table. The entry that has been circled is an anomalous result because it's much larger than any of the other data values.
>
> | Experiment | A | B | C | D | E | F |
> |---|---|---|---|---|---|---|
> | Rate of reaction (cm³/s) | 10.5 | 11.2 | 10.8 | (85.4) | 10.6 | 11.1 |

Tip: There are lots of reasons why you might get an anomalous result, but usually they're due to human error rather than anything crazy happening in the experiment.

You should investigate anomalous results and try to work out what happened. If you can work out what happened (e.g. you measured something totally wrong) you can ignore them when processing your results.

Learning Objectives:
- Know why data is often organised into tables and understand the limitations of using tables to organise data.
- Be able to calculate ranges and means.
- Be able to select and draw an appropriate graph to display the data collected in an investigation.

Specification Reference
How Science Works

5. Processing and Presenting Data

Once you've collected some data, you might need to process it, and then you'll need to present it in a way that you can make sense of.

Organising data

It's really important that your data is organised. Tables are dead useful for organising data. When you draw a table use a ruler, make sure each column has a heading (including the units) and keep it neat and tidy.

Annoyingly, tables are about as useful as a chocolate teapot for showing patterns or relationships in data. You need to use some kind of graph for that.

Processing your data

When you've done repeats of an experiment you should always calculate the **mean** (average). To do this add together all the data values and divide by the total number of values in the sample.

You might also need to calculate the **range** (how spread out the data is). To do this find the largest number and subtract the smallest number from it.

Tip: You should ignore anomalous results when calculating the mean and the range.

Example

Look at the data in this table. The mean and range of the data for each test tube has been calculated.

Test tube	Repeat (g) 1	2	3	Mean (g)	Range (g)
A	28	37	32	(28 + 37 + 32) ÷ 3 = 32.3	37 − 28 = 9
B	47	51	60	(47 + 51 + 60) ÷ 3 = 52.7	60 − 47 = 13
C	68	72	70	(68 + 72 + 70) ÷ 3 = 70.0	72 − 68 = 4

Plotting your data on a graph

One of the best ways to present your data after you've processed it is to plot your results on a graph. There are lots of different types of graph you can use. The type of graph you use depends on the type of data you've collected.

Tip: Categoric data is data that comes in distinct categories, for example, type of fuel, metals.

Bar charts

If either the independent or dependent variable is **categoric** you should use a bar chart to display the data.

You also use a bar chart if one of the variables is **discrete** (the data can be counted in chunks, where there's no in-between value, e.g. number of people is discrete because you can't have half a person).

There are some golden rules you need to follow for drawing bar charts:

- Draw it nice and big (covering at least half of the graph paper).
- Leave a gap between different categories.
- Label both axes and remember to include the units.
- If you've got more than one set of data include a key.
- Give your graph a title explaining what it is showing.

Tip: These golden rules will make sure that your bar chart is clear, easy to read and easy to understand if someone else looks at it.

Have a look at Figure 1 for an example of a pretty decent bar chart.

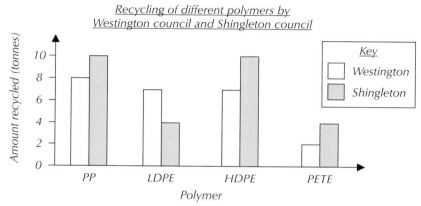

Figure 1: An example of a bar chart.

Line Graphs

If the independent and the dependent variable are **continuous** (numerical data that can have any value within a range, e.g. length, volume, temperature) you should use a line graph to display the data. Here are the golden rules for drawing line graphs:

- Draw it nice and big (covering at least half of the graph paper).
- Put the independent variable (the thing you change) on the x-axis (the horizontal one).
- Put the dependent variable (the thing you measure) on the y-axis (the vertical one).
- Label both axes and remember to include the units.
- To plot the points, use a sharp pencil and make a neat little cross.
- Don't join the dots up. You need to draw a line of best fit (or a curve of best fit if your points make a curve). When drawing a line (or curve), try to draw the line through or as near to as many points as possible, ignoring anomalous results.
- If you've got more than one set of data include a key.
- Give your graph a title explaining what it is showing.

Exam Tip
You could be asked to draw a bar chart or a line graph in your exam. If so, make sure you follow the golden rules or you could end up losing marks.

See Figure 2 for an example of a pretty good line graph.

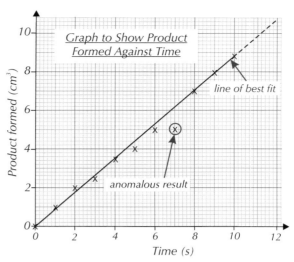

Figure 2: An example of a line graph.

Tip: If you're not in an exam, you can use a computer to plot your line graph and draw your line of best fit for you.

Scatter graphs

Tip: Scatter graphs can also be called scattergrams or scatterplots.

Scatter graphs are very similar to line graphs but they often don't have a line of best fit drawn on them. Like line graphs, scatter graphs can be used if the independent and dependent variables are continuous.

Correlations

Line graphs and scatter graphs are used to show the relationship between two variables (just like other graphs). Data can show three different types of **correlation** (relationship):

Tip: If all of the points are very close to the line of best fit then it's said to be a strong correlation. If there is a general trend but all the points are quite far away from the line of best fit it's a weak correlation.

Positive correlation
As one variable increases the other increases.

Negative correlation
As one variable increases the other decreases.

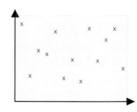

No correlation
There's no relationship between the two variables.

You also need to be able to describe the following relationships on line graphs.

Tip: On this graph the lines show positive linear relationships, but you can get linear relationships that show negative correlation too.

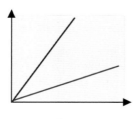

Linear
The graph is a straight line.

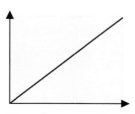

Directly proportional
The graph is a straight line where both variables increase (or decrease) in the same ratio.

6. Drawing Conclusions

Learning Objectives:
- Be able to draw conclusions based on the data available.
- Understand the difference between correlation and causation, and the possible reasons for correlation.
- Be able to evaluate investigations.

Specification Reference
How Science Works

So... you've planned an amazing experiment, you've done the experiment, collected some data and have processed and presented your data in a sensible way. Now it's time to figure out what your data actually tells you.

How to draw conclusions

Drawing conclusions might seem pretty straightforward — you just look at your data and say what pattern or relationship you see between the dependent and independent variables.

But you've got to be really careful that your conclusion matches the data you've got and doesn't go any further. You also need to be able to use your results to justify your conclusion (i.e. back up your conclusion with some specific data).

Example

This table shows the rate of a reaction in the presence of two different catalysts.

The conclusion of this experiment would be that catalyst B makes this reaction go faster than catalyst A.

Catalyst	Rate of reaction (cm^3/s)
A	13.5
B	19.5
No catalyst	5.5

Tip: There's more on catalysts on page 159.

The justification for this conclusion is that the rate of this reaction was 6 cm^3/s faster using catalyst B compared with catalyst A.

You can't conclude that catalyst B increases the rate of any other reaction more than catalyst A — the results might be completely different.

Correlation and causation

If two things are correlated (i.e. there's a relationship between them) it doesn't necessarily mean that a change in one variable is causing the change in the other — this is really important, don't forget it. There are three possible reasons for a correlation:

Tip: Causation just means one thing is causing another.

1. Chance

Even though it might seem a bit weird, it's possible that two things show a correlation in a study purely because of chance.

Example

One study might find a correlation between the number of people with breathing problems and the distance they live from a cement factory. But other scientists don't get a correlation when they investigate it — the results of the first study are just a fluke.

Tip: Lots of things are correlated without being directly related. E.g. the level of carbon dioxide (CO_2) in the atmosphere and the amount of obesity have both increased over the last 100 years, but that doesn't mean increased atmospheric CO_2 is causing people to become obese.

2. They're linked by a third variable

A lot of the time it may look as if a change in one variable is causing a change in the other, but it isn't — a third variable links the two things.

> **Example**
>
> There's a correlation between water temperature and shark attacks. This obviously isn't because warmer water makes sharks crazy. Instead, they're linked by a third variable — the number of people swimming (more people swim when the water's hotter, and with more people in the water you get more shark attacks).

3. Causation

Sometimes a change in one variable does cause a change in the other.

> **Example**
>
> There's a correlation between smoking and lung cancer. This is because chemicals in tobacco smoke cause lung cancer.

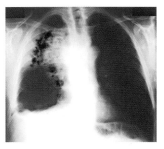

Figure 1: *A coloured chest X-ray of a smoker who has lung cancer.*

You can only conclude that a correlation is due to cause when you've controlled all the variables that could, just could, be affecting the result. (For the smoking example this would include things like age and exposure to other things that cause cancer).

Evaluation

This is the final part of an investigation. Here you need to evaluate (assess) the following things about your experiment and the data you gathered.

- **Repeatability**: Did you take enough repeat readings of the measurements? Would you do more repeats if you were to do the experiment again? Do you think you'd get similar data if you did the experiment again?

- **Reproducibility**: Have you compared your results with other people's results? Were your results similar? Could other scientists gain data showing the same relationships that are shown in your data?

- **Validity**: Does your data answer the question you set out to investigate?

Once you've thought about these points you can decide how much confidence you have in your conclusion. For example, if your results are repeatable, reproducible and valid and they back up your conclusion then you can have a high degree of confidence in your conclusion.

1. Atoms and Elements

Atoms and elements are the basis of all of chemistry. So you really need to know what they are. Luckily, these pages are here to help out with that...

The structure of the atom

Atoms are the tiny particles that everything is made up of. There are quite a few different (and equally useful) models of the atom — but chemists tend to like the nuclear model best. The nuclear model shows atoms as having a small **nucleus** surrounded by **electrons** (see Figure 1). You can use the nuclear model to explain pretty much the whole of chemistry.

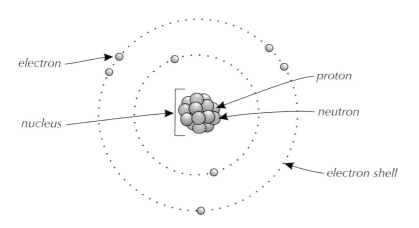

electron

nucleus

proton

neutron

electron shell

Figure 1: *The nuclear model of the atom.*

The nucleus

The nucleus is in the middle of the atom. It contains **protons** and **neutrons**. Protons are positively charged. Neutrons have no charge (they're neutral). So the nucleus has a positive charge overall because of the protons. But size-wise it's tiny compared to the rest of the atom.

The electrons

The electrons move around the nucleus. They're negatively charged. They're tiny, but they cover a lot of space. They occupy shells around the nucleus. Figure 2 shows the relative electrical charges of protons, neutrons and electrons.

Particle	Proton	Neutron	Electron
Charge	+1	0	−1

Figure 2: *The relative charges of protons, neutrons and electrons.*

Learning Objectives:

- Know that everything is made up of atoms.
- Know the structure of an atom.
- Know the relative charges of protons, neutrons and electrons.
- Know that the number of electrons in an atom is the same as the number of protons, and that this means atoms are neutral.
- Know that an element is made up of only one type of atom.
- Recall that there are roughly 100 known elements.
- Understand that the atoms of an element contain the same number of protons and that atoms of different elements contain different numbers of protons.

Specification Reference
C1.1.1

Tip: A <u>shell</u> is just an area where electrons are found. At GCSE you'll usually see them drawn as circles around the nucleus. Shells are sometimes called <u>energy levels</u>.

Electrical charge

Atoms have no charge overall. They are neutral. The charge on the electrons (–1) is the same size as the charge on the protons (+1) — but opposite. This means the number of protons always equals the number of electrons in an atom.

Tip: Don't worry about the way the electrons are arranged in the shells for now. You do need to know this stuff but it's all covered for you on pages 23-24.

Example

This atom has 7 protons. Each proton has a charge of +1, so the total charge of the nucleus is +7 (neutrons have no charge, remember).

The atom doesn't have a charge overall, so the total charge of the electrons must be –7, to cancel out the charge from the protons. As each electron has a charge of –1, this means there must be 7 electrons around the nucleus.

If some electrons are added or removed, the atom becomes charged and is then an ion. (See page 26 for more on ions.)

Elements

Atoms can have different numbers of protons, neutrons and electrons. It's the number of protons in the nucleus that decides what type of atom it is.

Tip: Protons, neutrons and electrons are all types of <u>sub-atomic particle</u>.

Examples

An atom with one proton in its nucleus is hydrogen.

An atom with two protons is helium.

If a substance only contains one type of atom it's called an **element**.

Example

Tip: Atoms of an element will also have the same number of electrons as each other, but it's the number of <u>protons</u> that's important — that's what determines what the element is.

Lithium is an element. It's made up of lithium atoms only. Each lithium atom contains 3 protons.

Lithium is an element...

...made of lithium atoms.

Each lithium atom has the same number of protons.

There are about 100 different elements — quite a lot of everyday substances are elements. For example, copper, iron, aluminium, oxygen and nitrogen are all elements. The important things to remember are...

- All the atoms of a particular element (e.g. nitrogen) have the same number of protons.

- Different elements have atoms with different numbers of protons.

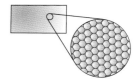
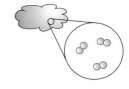

Figure 3: Copper (top) and nitrogen (bottom) are both elements. Copper is made up of copper atoms only and nitrogen is made up of nitrogen atoms only.

Practice Questions — Fact Recall

Q1 Describe the structure of an atom. Use the terms 'proton', 'neutron', 'electron', 'nucleus' and 'shell' in your answer.

Q2 What is the relative charge of...

a) a proton?

b) a neutron?

c) an electron?

Q3 What feature of an atom determines what type of atom it is?

Q4 What is an element?

Q5 Approximately how many elements are there?

Practice Questions — Application

Q1 Neon is an element. How many types of atom does neon contain?

Q2 An atom of silver contains 47 protons. How many electrons does an atom of silver contain?

Q3 An atom of selenium contains 34 electrons. How many protons does an atom of selenium contain?

Q4 Look at the diagrams of Atom A and Atom B. Are they atoms of the same element or different elements? Explain your answer.

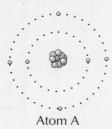
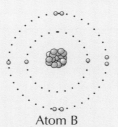

Atom A   Atom B

Q5 A particle contains 17 protons, 17 neutrons and 18 electrons.

a) What is the total charge of the nucleus?

b) What is the overall charge on the particle?

c) Is the particle an atom? Explain your answer.

Learning Objectives:
- Know that chemical symbols are used to represent atoms of different elements.
- Know what the periodic table is.
- Know where metals and non-metals are in the periodic table.
- Be able to work out the number of protons, electrons and neutrons in an atom from its atomic number and mass number.
- Know that elements in a group have the same number of electrons in their outer shell and so have similar properties.
- Know that Group 0 elements (the noble gases) have a full outer shell of electrons and that this makes them unreactive.

Specification Reference
C1.1.1, C1.1.2

2. The Periodic Table

The periodic table is a chemist's best friend. At first glance it might seem a bit intimidating but it's got loads of useful information in it. These pages will help you get a grip on exactly what that information is.

Chemical symbols

Atoms of each element can be represented by a one or two letter symbol — it's a type of shorthand that saves you the bother of having to write the full name of the element.

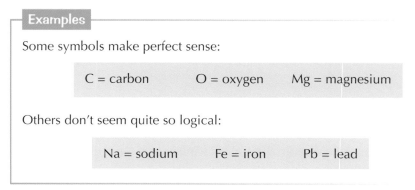

Examples

Some symbols make perfect sense:

C = carbon   O = oxygen   Mg = magnesium

Others don't seem quite so logical:

Na = sodium   Fe = iron   Pb = lead

What is the periodic table?

The **periodic table** is a table that contains all the known elements (about 100). The elements are represented by their symbols. The table is laid out so that elements with similar properties form columns. These vertical columns are called **groups**.

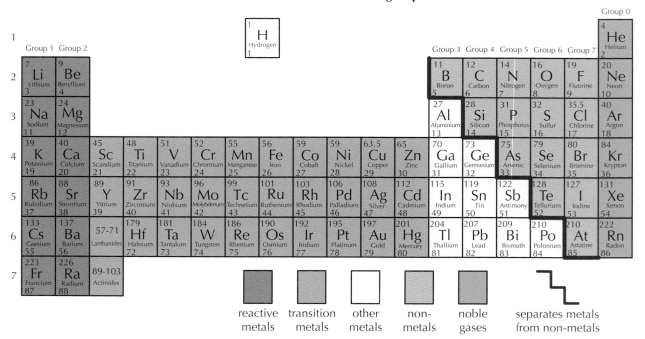

Figure 1: *The periodic table of the elements.*

Atomic numbers and mass numbers

Each symbol in the periodic table has two numbers by it. The smaller (bottom) number is the **atomic number**. This is the number of protons, which conveniently also tells you the number of electrons. The larger (top) number is the **mass number**. This is the total number of protons and neutrons.

Tip: The atomic number is sometimes called the proton number.

Example

The symbol tells you the element is magnesium.

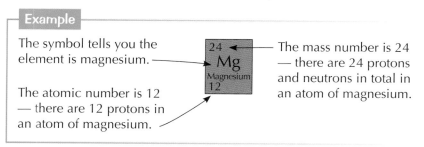

The mass number is 24 — there are 24 protons and neutrons in total in an atom of magnesium.

The atomic number is 12 — there are 12 protons in an atom of magnesium.

You can use the mass number and atomic number to work out the number of neutrons in an atom of an element. All you have to do is subtract the atomic number from the mass number.

Tip: Sometimes the mass number isn't a whole number. For example, the mass number of chlorine is 35.5. This is because atoms of an element can have different numbers of neutrons, and an average number of neutrons is used in the mass number. There's more on this on page 138.

Example

The symbol tells you the element is titanium.

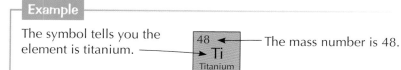

The mass number is 48.

The atomic number is 22.

Number of protons in an atom of titanium = 22.

The total number of protons and neutrons in an atom of titanium is 48, so the number of neutrons = 48 − 22 = 26.

The number of electrons in an atom is equal to the number of protons, so the number of electrons in an atom of titanium is 22.

Exam Tip
You could be asked to calculate the number of protons, neutrons or electrons in an atom from its atomic number and mass number. So make sure you know how to do it.

Groups in the periodic table

All of the elements in a group have the same number of electrons in their outer shell. This is why elements in the same group have similar properties. So, if you know the properties of one element, you can predict properties of other elements in that group.

Example 1

The Group 1 elements are Li, Na, K, Rb, Cs and Fr.

They all have one electron in their outer shell.

They're all metals and they react the same way. For example:

- They all react with water to form an alkaline solution and hydrogen gas.
- They all react with oxygen to form an oxide.

Figure 2: *Lithium, sodium and potassium are all in the same group so have similar properties. For example, they are all metals that are shiny when cut.*

Figure 3: *Group 0 elements are all unreactive. This property means that helium can be safely used in balloons (top), and neon is safe to use in neon signs (bottom).*

Example 2

The Group 0 elements (the **noble gases**) are He, Ne, Ar, Kr, Xe and Rn.

They all have eight electrons in their outer shell, apart from helium (which has two).

This means that they have a stable arrangement of electrons, which makes them unreactive.

Practice Questions — Fact Recall

Q1 What information does an atomic number give you?

Q2 What information does a mass number give you?

Q3 Why do elements in the same group of the periodic table have similar chemical properties?

Q4 How many electrons do Group 1 elements have in their outer shell?

Q5 What is another name for the Group 0 elements?

Q6 Why are Group 0 elements unreactive?

Practice Questions — Application

Use the periodic table on the back cover to answer the questions below.

Q1 Name three metals and three non-metals.

Q2 Name all the elements in Group 2 of the periodic table.

Q3 What is the chemical symbol used to represent:

   a) sulfur?   b) chlorine?   c) potassium?

Q4 Give the atomic number of the following elements:

   a) calcium   b) copper   c) boron

Q5 Give the mass number of the following elements:

   a) bromine   b) potassium   c) helium

Q6 a) How many protons does an atom of sodium contain?

   b) How many electrons does an atom of sodium contain?

   c) How many neutrons does an atom of sodium contain?

Q7 a) How many protons does an atom of iron contain?

   b) How many electrons does an atom of iron contain?

   c) How many neutrons does an atom of iron contain?

Q8 Nitrogen (N) has 5 electrons in its outer shell. How many electrons does Arsenic (As) have in its outer shell?

3. Electron Shells

So, you know that electrons are found in shells around the nucleus. The next thing you need to know is how they're arranged in these shells. Read on...

How are the electrons arranged in atoms?

Electrons always occupy **shells** (sometimes called **energy levels**). The electron shells with the lowest energy are always filled first — these are the ones closest to the nucleus. Only a certain number of electrons are allowed in each shell — see Figure 1.

Shell	Maximum number of electrons
1st	2
2nd	8
3rd	8

Figure 1: *Table showing how many electrons each electron shell can hold.*

Atoms are much happier when they have full electron shells — like the noble gases in Group 0. In most atoms the outer shell is not full and this makes the atom want to react to fill it.

Electronic structures

The **electronic structure** of an element is how the electrons are arranged in an atom of that element. You need to know the electronic structures for the first 20 elements (things get a bit more complicated after that). But they're not hard to work out. You just need to follow these steps:

1. Find the number of electrons in an atom of the element (using the periodic table).

2. Draw the first electron shell and add up to two electrons to it.

3. Draw the second electron shell and add up to eight electrons to it.

4. If you need to, draw the third electron shell and add up to eight electrons.

5. As soon as you've added enough electrons, stop.

Learning Objectives:

- Know that electrons are found in shells, also known as energy levels.
- Know that electrons fill the shells closest to the nucleus first.
- Know how many electrons each shell can hold.
- Be able to draw and write out the electronic structures of the first 20 elements of the periodic table.

Specification Reference
C1.1.1

Tip: Sometimes you'll see electrons drawn as dots (like on pages 17-18), other times you'll see them drawn as crosses. It doesn't matter which is used — they all represent electrons.

Example

Draw the electronic structure of nitrogen.

1. The periodic table tells us nitrogen has seven protons... so it must have seven electrons.

2. Draw the first electron shell and add 2 electrons.

3. Draw the second shell and add the remaining five electrons.

4. Nitrogen only has seven electrons so you don't need to draw a third shell.

Tip: You'd usually draw the first four electrons in each shell spread out around the shell. Then the next four electrons are drawn next to them to make pairs of electrons. But you don't need to worry about this for GCSE — just make sure you've got the right number of electrons in each shell.

Drawing an atom is one way of showing its electronic structure, but you can also write out the electronic structure using numbers.

Examples

1. You can show the electronic structure of nitrogen using a diagram like this...

...or you can write it out like this.

2, 5

This shows that there are two electrons in the 1st shell...

...and 5 in the 2nd.

2. Argon has 18 electrons. Two can go in the first shell and eight can go in the second. That leaves eight to go into the third electron shell. So the electronic structure of argon is... 2, 8, 8.

Potassium and calcium

Beyond the third electron shell (after argon in the periodic table) things get a bit complicated. You could get asked for the electronic structures of potassium and calcium. All you need to know is that potassium has one electron in the fourth shell and calcium has two. So the electronic structure of potassium is 2, 8, 8, 1 and the electronic structure of calcium is 2, 8, 8, 2.

Practice Questions — Fact Recall

Q1 What is another name for an electron shell?

Q2 How many electrons can go in the first electron shell?

Q3 How many electrons can go in the second electron shell?

Q4 How many electrons can go in the third electron shell?

Q5 Which shell fills with electrons first?

Practice Questions — Application

Q1 This diagram shows the electronic structure of an element. Which element is it?

Q2 Which element has the electronic structure 2, 4?

Q3 Which element has the electronic structure 2, 8, 6?

Q4 Draw the electronic structure of oxygen.

Q5 Draw the electronic structure of boron.

Q6 Write out the electronic structure of phosphorus.

Q7 Write out the electronic structure of magnesium.

4. Compounds

Elements are substances that are made up of just one type of atom. If a substance is made up of more than one type of atom then it might be a compound — and that's what these pages are about.

What are compounds?

When different elements react, atoms form **chemical bonds** with other atoms to form **compounds**. It's usually difficult to separate the two original elements out again. Making bonds involves atoms giving away, taking or sharing electrons (there's more on bonding on page 27). If the different atoms aren't bonded together then it's not a compound — it's a mixture (see Figure 1).

An element.

A compound.

A mixture.

Figure 1: *Diagrams to represent the atoms in an element, a compound and a mixture.*

Properties of compounds

The properties of a compound are totally different from the properties of the original elements.

Example

If iron (a lustrous magnetic metal) and sulfur (a nice yellow powder) react, the compound formed (iron sulfide) is a dull grey solid lump, and doesn't behave anything like either iron or sulfur.

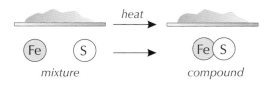

mixture $\longrightarrow$ compound

Compounds can be small **molecules** or great big structures called lattices (when I say big I'm talking in atomic terms).

Example

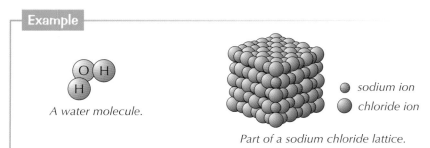

A water molecule.

○ *sodium ion*
○ *chloride ion*

Part of a sodium chloride lattice.

Learning Objectives:

- Know that elements can react to form compounds.
- Know that compounds are formed when electrons are shared or transferred between atoms.
- Know that when metals react with non-metals a compound made of ions is formed.
- Know that when non-metals react with other non-metals a compound made of molecules is formed.
- Know that the atoms in a molecule are held together by covalent bonds.

Specification Reference C1.1.3

Figure 2: *Iron sulfide (bottom) is a compound of iron (top) and sulfur (middle).*

Tip: <u>Ions</u> are made when atoms lose or gain electrons — there's more on ions on the next page.

Ions

A compound which is formed from a metal and a non-metal consists of **ions**. Ions are charged particles. They are made when atoms lose or gain electrons. Metal atoms lose electrons to form positive ions and non-metal atoms gain electrons to form negative ions.

Tip: You can work out whether an element is a metal or a non-metal by its position in the periodic table (see page 20).

Tip: The formation of ions is covered in more detail on pages 111-115.

Example 1

Metal atoms form positive ions

A sodium atom has 11 protons and 11 electrons. Protons have a relative charge of +1 and electrons have a relative charge of –1, so the atom has no overall charge.

total charge of protons → $11 - 11 = 0$ ← *overall charge* — *total charge of electrons*

If a sodium atom loses an electron it will only have 10 electrons, but it will still have 11 protons. So the sodium will have an overall charge of +1, and is said to be a positively charged ion.

total charge of protons → $11 - 10 = +1$ ← *overall charge* — *total charge of electrons*

Example 2

Non-metal atoms form negative ions

A chlorine atom has 17 protons and 17 electrons, so has no overall charge.

total charge of protons → $17 - 17 = 0$ ← *overall charge* — *total charge of electrons*

If a chlorine atom gains an electron it will have 18 electrons, but it will still only have 17 protons. So it will have an overall charge of –1, and is said to be a negatively charged ion.

total charge of protons → $17 - 18 = -1$ ← *overall charge* — *total charge of electrons*

Tip: Ions can be represented using chemical symbols, but the charge on the ion needs to be shown as well. For example, a chloride ion is written as Cl^- and a sodium ion is written as Na^+.

Ionic bonding

Ions with opposite charges (positive and negative) are strongly attracted to each other. This is called **ionic bonding**.

Example

Sodium (a metal) reacts with chlorine (a non-metal) to form the compound sodium chloride.

| *A sodium atom has 1 electron in its outer shell.* | *A chlorine atom has 7 electrons in its outer shell.* | *The sodium atom gives its outer electron to the chlorine atom. A sodium ion and a chloride ion are formed* |

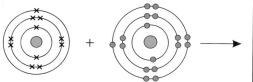 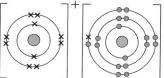

Tip: The + sign by the electronic structure of the sodium ion shows that it has a positive charge of 1 (+1). The – sign by the electronic structure of the chloride ion shows that it has a negative charge of 1 (–1).

The sodium and chloride ions are oppositely charged and so are attracted to each other. This is ionic bonding, and results in the formation of the stable compound sodium chloride.

Covalent bonding

A compound formed from non-metals consists of molecules. Each atom shares an electron with another atom — this is called a **covalent bond**. Each atom has to make enough covalent bonds to fill up its outer shell.

Tip: A <u>compound</u> is two or more atoms of different elements held together by chemical bonds. A <u>molecule</u> is two or more atoms held together by <u>covalent</u> bonds. The atoms can be of the same element or different elements — it's the covalent bond that makes it a molecule.

Example

Hydrogen and chlorine (both non-metals) react together and share an electron to form a molecule of hydrogen chloride. The molecule is made up of two different types of atom, so it's a compound.

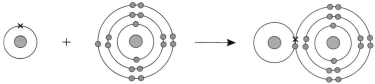

| *A hydrogen atom has 1 electron in its outer shell.* | *A chlorine atom has 7 electrons in its outer shell.* | *The atoms share a pair of electrons. This is a covalent bond, and holds the atoms together as a molecule.* |

Both the hydrogen atom and the chlorine atom now have full outer shells of electrons. This makes the molecule stable.

Tip: Diagrams showing covalent bonding like this are called <u>dot and cross diagrams</u>. You don't need to be able to draw these diagrams for your Unit 1 exam though.

Formulae

A formula shows what atoms are in a compound.

> **Examples**
>
> Carbon dioxide is a compound formed from a chemical reaction between carbon and oxygen. It contains one carbon atom and two oxygen atoms, so the formula is CO_2.
>
> The formula of sulfuric acid is H_2SO_4. So, each molecule contains two hydrogen atoms, one sulfur atom and four oxygen atoms.
>
> There might be brackets in a formula. For example, calcium hydroxide is $Ca(OH)_2$. The little number outside the bracket applies to everything inside the brackets. So in $Ca(OH)_2$ there is one calcium atom, two oxygen atoms and two hydrogen atoms.

Tip: 'Formulae' is just the plural of 'formula'. You may sometimes see it written as 'formulas'.

Practice Questions — Fact Recall

Q1 What is an ion?

Q2 Do metal atoms form positive ions or negative ions?

Q3 Do non-metal atoms form positive ions or negative ions?

Q4 If a compound is formed from a metal and a non-metal, what type of bonding will be present in the compound?

Q5 What type of bonding holds the atoms in a molecule together?

Practice Questions — Application

Q1 The formula of carbon monoxide is CO. What atoms are in a molecule of carbon monoxide?

Q2 The formula of nitric acid is HNO_3. What atoms are in a molecule of nitric acid?

Q3 Look at diagrams A, B, C and D. Which one shows a compound?

Q4 Will bromine form positive or negative ions?

Q5 Will potassium lose or gain electrons to form ions?

Q6 Will lithium form positive or negative ions?

Q7 Will oxygen lose or gain electrons to form ions?

Q8 Magnesium oxide is made from the reaction between magnesium and oxygen. What type of bonding exists in magnesium oxide?

Q9 Sulfur dioxide is made from the reaction between sulfur and oxygen. What type of bonding exists in sulfur dioxide?

Tip: You can use the periodic table to help you work out if an atom is a metal or a non-metal. There's a periodic table on the inside back cover of the book.

5. Equations

Equations crop up again and again in chemistry. You need to know what they show and how to write them.

Word equations and symbol equations

Word equations and symbol equations show what happens in a chemical reaction. They show the **reactants** (the substances that react together) and the **products** (the substances that are made in a reaction).

Example

Magnesium and oxygen react to form magnesium oxide. This can be represented by a word equation or a symbol equation.

Word equation: magnesium + oxygen → magnesium oxide

Balanced symbol equation: $2Mg + O_2 → 2MgO$

Magnesium and oxygen are the reactants in this reaction. Magnesium oxide is the product.

Conservation of mass

During chemical reactions, things don't appear out of nowhere and things don't just disappear. You still have the same atoms at the end of a chemical reaction as you had at the start. They're just arranged in different ways.

Balanced symbol equations show the atoms at the start (the reactant atoms) and the atoms at the end (the product atoms) and how they're arranged.

Example

Balanced symbol equation: $2Mg + O_2 → 2MgO$

The same atoms are present at the end of the reaction as at the start — they're just rearranged.

Because atoms aren't gained or lost, the mass of the reactants equals the mass of the products. This is called conservation of mass. You can use this fact to work out the mass of individual reactants and products in a reaction.

Learning Objectives:

- Know that word equations and symbol equations can be used to represent reactions.
- Be able to write word equations.
- Understand why the mass of the products of a reaction is the same as the mass of the reactants.
- Be able to calculate the mass of a product or a reactant from the masses of other substances involved in the reaction.
- Understand symbol equations.
- **H** Be able to write balanced symbol equations.

Specification Reference C1.1.3

Tip: You can think of the 2 before the Mg as meaning that there are two magnesium atoms. The 2 before the MgO means that there are two lots of MgO.

1. 6 g of magnesium completely reacts with 4 g of oxygen.
    What mass of magnesium oxide is formed?

    The total mass of the reactants is 4 + 6 = 10 g, so the mass of the
    product (magnesium oxide) must be 10 g.

2. 30 g of magnesium oxide is formed from 18 g of magnesium.
    How much oxygen reacted?

    The total mass of the product is 30 g, so the total mass of the reactants
    must be 30 g. The mass of the magnesium is 18 g, so the mass of the
    oxygen must be 30 – 18 = 12 g.

Exam Tip
You could be asked to
work out the mass of
a product formed, or
the mass of a reactant
used. Just remember
— the total mass of the
products is exactly the
same as the total mass of
the reactants.

Balanced equations

There must always be the same number of atoms of each element on both
sides of an equation — they can't just disappear. If there aren't the same
number on each side then the equation isn't balanced.

Example

Sulfuric acid (H_2SO_4) reacts with sodium hydroxide (NaOH) to give sodium
sulfate (Na_2SO_4) and water (H_2O). To write the symbol equation start by
writing out the formulae in an equation:

$$H_2SO_4 \; + \; NaOH \; \rightarrow \; Na_2SO_4 \; + \; H_2O$$

The formulas are all correct but the numbers of some atoms don't match up
on both sides (e.g. there are three Hs on the left, but only two on the right).
So the equation isn't balanced.

Method for balancing equations `Higher`

You balance the equation by putting numbers in front of the formulas
where needed. All you do is this:

Tip: You <u>can't</u> change
the small numbers inside
formulas (like changing
H_2O to H_3O). You can
only put numbers in
front of formulas (like
changing H_2O to $3H_2O$).

1. Find an element that doesn't balance and pencil in a number to try and
    sort it out.

2. See where it gets you. It may create another imbalance — if so, just
    pencil in another number and see where that gets you.

Tip: The more you
practise balancing
equations, the quicker
you'll get...

3. Carry on chasing unbalanced elements and it'll sort itself out pretty
    quickly.

In this equation we're short of H atoms on the right-hand side — there are three H atoms on the left and only two on the right.

$$H_2SO_4 + NaOH \rightarrow Na_2SO_4 + H_2O$$

The only thing you can do about that is make it $2H_2O$ instead of just H_2O:

$$H_2SO_4 + NaOH \rightarrow Na_2SO_4 + 2H_2O$$

But now you have too many H atoms and O atoms on the right-hand side, so to balance that up you could try putting $2NaOH$ on the left-hand side.

$$H_2SO_4 + 2NaOH \rightarrow Na_2SO_4 + 2H_2O$$

And suddenly there it is! Everything balances. There are four H, one S, six O and two Na on each side of the equation.

Exam Tip
If you're asked to write a symbol equation you always have to make sure it's balanced. If it's not balanced it's not a correct equation.

In this equation we're short of Cl atoms on the left-hand side.

$$Al + Cl_2 \rightarrow AlCl_3$$

Try making it $3Cl_2$ instead of just Cl_2.

$$Al + 3Cl_2 \rightarrow AlCl_3$$

That causes too many Cl atoms on the left-hand side, so balance up the Cls by putting 2 before the $AlCl_3$.

$$Al + 3Cl_2 \rightarrow 2AlCl_3$$

Now you can balance the Al atoms by adding a 2 in front of the Al.

$$2Al + 3Cl_2 \rightarrow 2AlCl_3$$

Everything is now balanced. There are two Al atoms on each side and six Cl atoms on each side.

Tip: If you made it '$2Cl_2$', you'd have four Cl on the left-hand side. There isn't a whole number that you could put in front of $AlCl_3$ to also give you four Cl on the right-hand side. So it's best to try $3Cl_2$.

Symbol equations show how many atoms of one element there are compared to the number of atoms of other elements. So it's fine to double, or triple, or quadruple the number of atoms in a balanced equation, as long as you do the same to every term in the equation.

Balanced equation to show the reaction of aluminium and chlorine. $\longrightarrow$ $2Al + 3Cl_2 \rightarrow 2AlCl_3$

The numbers added to the equation to balance it have all been doubled. The equation is still balanced. $\longrightarrow$ $4Al + 6Cl_2 \rightarrow 4AlCl_3$

Q1   Copper sulfate and iron react to form iron sulfate and copper.

    a) What substances are the products in this reaction?

    b) What substances are the reactants in this reaction?

    c) Write a word equation for the reaction of copper sulfate and iron.

Q2   127 g of copper reacts with 32 g of oxygen to form copper oxide.

    a) Write a word equation for this reaction.

    b) What is the mass of copper oxide formed?

Q3 $N_2 + 3H_2 \rightarrow 2NH_3$ is the equation for the reaction between nitrogen (N_2) and hydrogen (H_2) to form ammonia (NH_3). 56 g of nitrogen are used in the reaction. 68 g of ammonia are formed. What is the mass of hydrogen that reacts?

Q4   Sodium hydroxide reacts with hydrochloric acid to give sodium chloride and water.

    a) Write a word equation for this reaction.

    b) 80 g of sodium hydroxide completely reacts with 73 g of hydrochloric acid. 36 g of water is formed. What is the mass of sodium chloride produced?

Q5   Balance the following equations:

    a) $Cl_2 + KBr \rightarrow Br_2 + KCl$

    b) $HCl + Mg \rightarrow MgCl_2 + H_2$

    c) $C_3H_8 + O_2 \rightarrow CO_2 + H_2O$

    d) $Fe_2O_3 + CO \rightarrow Fe + CO_2$

Q6   Sulfuric acid (H_2SO_4) reacts with lithium hydroxide (LiOH) to form lithium sulfate (Li_2SO_4) and water (H_2O). Write a balanced symbol equation for this reaction.

Exam Tip
Always check your equation is balanced properly. It's easy to make a mistake, so once you think you've balanced it correctly go back and count up again.

Section Checklist — Make sure you know...

Atoms and Elements

☐ That everything is made up of tiny particles called atoms.

☐ The structure of the atom, including the arrangement of protons, neutrons and electrons.

☐ The relative charges of protons (+1), neutrons (0) and electrons (–1).

☐ That atoms are neutral (have no overall charge) as they have equal numbers of protons and electrons.

☐ That an element is a substance made up of only one type of atom.

☐ That atoms of an element have the same number of protons.

☐ That atoms of different elements have different numbers of protons.

cont...

The Periodic Table

☐ That elements can be represented by symbols, e.g. C for carbon, Na for sodium, O for oxygen.

☐ That the periodic table contains all the known elements.

☐ Where the metals and non-metals are found in the periodic table.

☐ How to use the periodic table to find the atomic number and mass number of an element.

☐ What atomic number and mass number tell you about an element.

☐ How to work out the number of protons, neutrons and electrons in an element from its atomic number and mass number.

☐ That elements in a group of the periodic table have the same number of electrons in their outer shells and that this gives them similar chemical properties.

☐ That elements in Group 0 of the periodic table are called the noble gases.

☐ That the noble gases don't react with other elements because they have a full outer shell of electrons.

Electron Shells

☐ How to work out the electronic structure of the first 20 elements of the periodic table.

Compounds

☐ That a compound is formed when atoms of different elements react together and form chemical bonds.

☐ That when metals react with non-metals, the metal atoms give up electrons and form positively charged ions and the non-metal atoms gain electrons to become negatively charged ions.

☐ That oppositely charged ions are attracted to each other and that this attraction is known as ionic bonding.

☐ That when non-metals react together their atoms share pairs of electrons. These shared electrons hold the atoms together in a molecule. This is called covalent bonding.

Equations

☐ That word equations and symbol equations are used to show the reactants and products of a chemical reaction.

☐ How to write word equations for reactions.

☐ That the mass of the products of a reaction is equal to the mass of the reactants, because no atoms are gained or lost during a chemical reaction.

☐ How to work out the mass of a certain reactant or product when you're given the masses of the other substances involved in the reaction.

☐ That a symbol equation gives you information about the number of atoms of each element involved in a reaction.

☐ H How to balance symbol equations.

Exam-style Questions

1   Carbon monoxide (CO) and carbon dioxide (CO_2) both contain carbon atoms and oxygen atoms.

1 (a)   Draw a ring around the correct words to complete these sentences.

1 (a) (i)   Carbon and oxygen are both

> non-metals.
>
> metals.
>
> noble gases.

(1 mark)

1 (a) (ii)   Carbon monoxide and carbon dioxide are both

> elements.
>
> compounds.
>
> noble gases.

(1 mark)

1 (b)   This is the symbol equation for the reaction of carbon monoxide and oxygen.

$$2CO \ + \ O_2 \ \rightarrow \ 2CO_2$$

1 (b) (i)   Write a word equation for the reaction of carbon monoxide with oxygen.

(1 mark)

1 (b) (ii)   Using the symbol equation, describe the reaction of carbon monoxide and oxygen in terms of the number of molecules of each substance involved.

(3 marks)

1 (c)   Complete this diagram so that it shows the electronic structure of carbon.

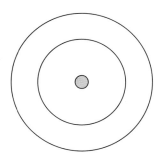

(2 marks)

2   Aluminium is a metal element that is used to make foil for cooking.

2 (a)   This table contains information about the atomic structure of aluminium.
Complete the table.

Atomic number	
Mass number	27
Number of protons	13
Number of electrons	
Number of neutrons	

(3 marks)

2 (b) (i)   Aluminium reacts with hydrochloric acid to form aluminium chloride and hydrogen.
Balance the symbol equation for this reaction.

......Al + ...HCl   →   ......AlCl$_3$ + ...H$_2$

(2 marks)

2 (b) (ii)   135 g of aluminium reacted with 547.5 g of hydrochloric acid to make 667.5 g of
aluminium chloride. What mass of hydrogen was produced?

(2 marks)

2 (b) (iii) Name the type of bonding that exists within hydrogen (H$_2$).

(1 mark)

2 (c)   Aluminium chloride can also be formed by reacting aluminium with chlorine.

2 (c) (i)   What group of the periodic table is chlorine in?

(1 mark)

2 (c) (ii) The reaction of aluminium and bromine is similar to the reaction of
aluminium and chlorine. Explain why.

(1 mark)

2 (c) (iii) Aluminium does not react with argon (Ar). Explain why not.

(2 marks)

1. Limestone and Other Carbonates

Limestone is a type of rock made from calcium carbonate.
Like other carbonates, it reacts in a number of different ways.

Limestone

Limestone is quarried out of the ground and made into blocks that can be used for building. Lots of old buildings like cathedrals are made from it. Limestone is mainly calcium carbonate — $CaCO_3$.

Thermal decomposition of metal carbonates

Thermal decomposition is when one substance chemically changes into at least two new substances when it's heated. Limestone thermally decomposes to make calcium oxide and carbon dioxide. Here's the equation for the reaction...

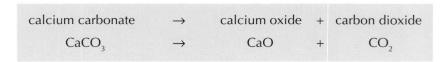

calcium carbonate	$\rightarrow$	calcium oxide	+	carbon dioxide
$CaCO_3$	$\rightarrow$	CaO	+	CO_2

When magnesium, copper, zinc and sodium carbonates are heated, they decompose in the same way.

> **Example**
>
> Magnesium carbonate breaks down to form magnesium oxide and carbon dioxide when it's heated.
>
> magnesium carbonate $\rightarrow$ magnesium oxide + carbon dioxide
>
> $MgCO_3$ $\rightarrow$ MgO + CO_2

You might have difficulty doing some of these reactions in class — a Bunsen burner can't reach a high enough temperature to thermally decompose some carbonates of Group 1 metals.

Metal carbonates and acid

Calcium carbonate also reacts with acid to make a calcium salt, carbon dioxide and water. This reaction means that limestone is damaged by acid rain (see page 67).

Calcium carbonate reacts with acid as shown in this word equation:

calcium carbonate + acid → calcium salt + carbon dioxide + water

The type of salt produced depends on the type of acid used.

Examples

If calcium carbonate reacts with sulfuric acid, a sulfate is produced.

calcium carbonate + sulfuric acid → calcium sulfate + carbon dioxide + water

$$CaCO_3 + H_2SO_4 \rightarrow CaSO_4 + CO_2 + H_2O$$

If calcium carbonate reacts with hydrochloric acid, a chloride is produced.

calcium carbonate + hydrochloric acid → calcium chloride + carbon dioxide + water

$$CaCO_3 + 2HCl \rightarrow CaCl_2 + CO_2 + H_2O$$

Other carbonates that react with acids are magnesium, copper, zinc and sodium. In these reactions carbon dioxide and water are always produced, but the salt formed depends on which carbonate and which acid react.

Example

When zinc carbonate reacts with sulfuric acid, zinc sulfate is formed.

zinc carbonate + sulfuric acid → zinc sulfate + carbon dioxide + water

$$ZnCO_3 + H_2SO_4 \rightarrow ZnSO_4 + CO_2 + H_2O$$

Exam Tip
You might be asked to write equations for the reactions of different carbonates with different acids, so make sure you can work them out. Remember, with sulfuric acid you always get a sulfate and with hydrochloric acid you always get a chloride.

Reaction of calcium oxide with water

When limestone (mainly $CaCO_3$) is broken down, calcium oxide (CaO) can be formed. When you add water to calcium oxide you get calcium hydroxide. The word and symbol equations for this reaction are...

calcium oxide + water → calcium hydroxide

$$CaO + H_2O \rightarrow Ca(OH)_2$$

Calcium hydroxide has two important uses:

1. Calcium hydroxide is an alkali which can be used to neutralise acidic soil in fields. Powdered limestone can be used for this too, but the advantage of calcium hydroxide is that it works much faster.

2. Calcium hydroxide can also be used in a test for carbon dioxide. If you make a solution of calcium hydroxide in water (called **limewater**) and bubble gas through it, the solution will turn cloudy if there's carbon dioxide in the gas (see Figure 1). The cloudiness is caused by the formation of calcium carbonate. The equation for this reaction is:

$$\text{calcium hydroxide} + \text{carbon dioxide} \rightarrow \text{calcium carbonate} + \text{water}$$
$$Ca(OH)_2 + CO_2 \rightarrow CaCO_3 + H_2O$$

Figure 1: A test tube containing limewater. It has turned cloudy due to the presence of CO_2 in the gas being bubbled through it.

Practice Questions — Fact Recall

Q1 Which compound does limestone mainly consist of?

Q2 Write the word and symbol equations for the thermal decomposition of calcium carbonate.

Q3 What are the products of the reaction between a metal carbonate and an acid?

Q4 When calcium carbonate reacts with sulfuric acid, which salt is produced?

Q5 Which compound reacts with water to form calcium hydroxide?

Q6 Describe how calcium hydroxide can be used to test for carbon dioxide. Include the symbol equation for the reaction involved.

Practice Questions — Application

Q1 Write a word equation for the thermal decomposition of zinc carbonate.

Q2 a) What salt is produced when magnesium carbonate reacts with hydrochloric acid?

   b) Balance the following equation:

   $$MgCO_3 + HCl \rightarrow MgCl_2 + CO_2 + H_2O$$

2. Using Limestone

Limestone is a really useful building material and necessary for the production of cement and concrete. The downside is that digging it up and processing it into cement and concrete causes a few problems...

Limestone as a building material

Limestone is a widely available building material and is cheaper than granite or marble. It's also a fairly easy rock to cut, which means it's pretty straightforward to make into different shapes, such as blocks. Limestone is also very hard-wearing.

Limestone can also be used to make other building materials. For example...

- Powdered limestone is heated in a kiln with powdered clay to make cement.

- Cement can be mixed with sand and water to make mortar. (Mortar is the stuff you stick bricks together with.)

- To make concrete you mix cement with sand and aggregate (water and gravel).

Limestone, concrete and cement have lots of qualities that make them great as building materials. They don't rot when they get wet like wood does. They can't be gnawed away by insects or rodents either. And to top it off, they're fire-resistant too.

Concrete can be poured into moulds to make blocks or panels that can be joined together. It's a very quick and cheap way of constructing buildings. Concrete also doesn't corrode like lots of metals do.

Other uses and benefits of limestone

Limestone is a key material for providing things that people want — like houses, roads and even schools... but it's also useful in other ways.

- Limestone is used to make chemicals that are used in making dyes, paints and medicines.

- Limestone products are used to neutralise acidic soil. Acidity in lakes and rivers caused by acid rain is also neutralised by limestone products.

- Limestone is also used in power station chimneys to neutralise sulfur dioxide, which is a cause of acid rain.

- Limestone quarries and associated businesses provide jobs for people and bring more money into the local economy. This can lead to local improvements in transport, roads, recreation facilities and health.

Figure 1: *Concrete being poured at a building site.*

Exam Tip
For the exam you only need to know about the properties of limestone building materials. But you might be given information about other building materials and asked to make comparisons.

Problems of using limestone

Quarrying limestone

HOW SCIENCE WORKS

Digging limestone out of the ground can cause environmental problems:

Figure 2: A limestone quarry where limestone rock is extracted from the ground.

- Quarrying involves making huge ugly holes which permanently change the landscape.

- Quarrying processes, like blasting rocks apart with explosives, make lots of noise and dust in quiet, scenic areas.

- Quarrying destroys the habitats of animals and birds.

- The limestone needs to be transported away from the quarry — usually in lorries. This causes more noise and pollution.

- Waste materials produce unsightly tips.

Thankfully it's normally a requirement of the planning permission that once quarrying is complete, landscaping and restoration of the area are carried out.

Limestone products

Figure 3: Air pollution from a cement factory.

The production and use of limestone causes problems too.

- Cement factories make a lot of dust, which can cause breathing problems for some people.

- Energy is needed to produce cement. The energy is likely to come from burning fossil fuels, which causes pollution.

- Concrete is a hideously unattractive building material. It also has fairly low tensile strength and can crack — it can be reinforced with steel bars to make it much stronger though.

Practice Questions — Fact Recall

Q1 Describe how you make...

a) Cement

b) Mortar

c) Concrete

Q2 Describe two benefits of using concrete as a building material.

Q3 Limestone can be used as a building material.
Give two other uses of limestone.

Q4 Limestone is extracted from the ground by quarrying.

a) Give three problems associated with quarrying limestone.

b) Describe two ways in which a quarry can benefit the local area.

Q5 Give one drawback of using concrete as a building material.

Q1 Richard is choosing materials for the floors of his conservatory and garage. Use the data in this table to answer the questions.

	Concrete	Wood	Marble
Cost (per m²)	£8.50	£25	£60
Appearance	Unattractive	Attractive	Attractive
Durability	Very hardwearing	Quite hardwearing	Very hardwearing

a) Suggest which material Richard should use in his garage and give reasons to support your choice.

b) Suggest which material Richard should use in his conservatory and give reasons to support your choice.

Section Checklist — Make sure you know...

Limestone and Other Carbonates

☐ That limestone is mostly calcium carbonate ($CaCO_3$) and is quarried from the ground.

☐ That thermal decomposition of calcium carbonate produces calcium oxide and carbon dioxide.

☐ That magnesium, copper, zinc and sodium carbonates thermally decompose to produce a metal oxide and carbon dioxide.

☐ That some Group 1 carbonates can't be decomposed in the school lab by a Bunsen burner.

☐ How to write word equations for the thermal decomposition of metal carbonates.

☐ That the reaction of calcium carbonate with acid produces a calcium salt, carbon dioxide and water.

☐ That limestone is damaged by acid rain.

☐ That magnesium, copper, zinc and sodium carbonates react with acids to produce a metal salt, carbon dioxide and water.

☐ How to write word equations for the reactions of metal carbonates with acids.

☐ That when calcium oxide reacts with water, calcium hydroxide is formed.

☐ That calcium hydroxide can be used to neutralise acidic soil.

☐ How calcium hydroxide in solution (limewater) can be used to test for carbon dioxide.

Using Limestone

☐ How cement, mortar and concrete are made from limestone.

☐ The advantages and disadvantages of using limestone, cement and concrete as building materials.

☐ The benefits of quarrying for limestone.

☐ The problems associated with limestone quarrying and manufacturing limestone building materials.

Learning Objectives:

- Know that a few unreactive metals are found in the earth as elements.

- Know that the majority of metals are found as compounds in a metal ore and that these ores are mined.

- Know that ores are rocks that contain enough of a metal to make it worthwhile to extract it.

- Understand that whether or not it is economical to extract a metal can change over time.

- Know that some ores are concentrated before the metal is extracted.

Specification Reference C1.3.1

1. Metal Ores

To get hold of most metals you start by digging them out of the ground. Sometimes it's as simple as that, but it's usually a bit more complicated...

Extracting metals from ores

A few unreactive metals like gold are found in the Earth as the metal itself, rather than as a compound. The rest of the metals we get by extracting them from **metal ores**, which are mined from under the ground. A metal ore is a rock which contains enough metal to make it profitable to extract the metal from it. In many cases the ore is an oxide of the metal. For example, the main aluminium ore is called bauxite — it's aluminium oxide (Al_2O_3).

Most metals need to be extracted from their ores using a chemical reaction. The economics (profitability) of metal extraction can change over time.

Examples

If the market price of a metal drops a lot, it could cost more to extract than the price it's sold for. In this situation the metal wouldn't be worth extracting because there would be no profit to be made. If the market price increases a lot then it might be worth extracting more of it.

As technology improves, it becomes possible to extract more metal from a sample of rock than was originally possible. So it might now be worth extracting metal that wasn't worth extracting in the past.

Chemical methods of extraction

A metal can be extracted from its ore chemically — by **reduction** (see page 44) or by **electrolysis** (splitting with electricity, see page 44). Occasionally some metals are extracted from their ores using **displacement reactions** (see page 46). Some ores may have to be concentrated before the metal is extracted — this involves getting rid of the unwanted rocky material.

Figure 1: *A sample of bauxite, the main ore of aluminium.*

Practice Questions — Fact Recall

Q1 What is a metal ore?

Q2 Explain why a change in the market price of a metal could affect how much of that metal is extracted from its ores.

Q3 Name two chemical methods of extracting metals from their ores.

2. Extracting Metals from Rocks

There are two main methods of extracting metals from metal ores. Which one to use is determined by how reactive the metal is...

The reactivity series

The **reactivity series** is a list of metals that are arranged in order of how reactive they are. The most reactive metals are at the top and the least reactive are at the bottom.

The position of each metal in the reactivity series is important. Whether a metal is higher or lower than carbon (the only non-metal in the series) determines the method that is used to extract it from its ore.

Even though carbon is a non-metal, it's included in the series so you can compare where metals are in relation to it.

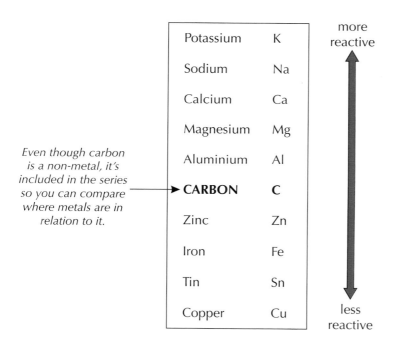

Figure 1: *The reactivity series of metals.*

The reactivity series and extracting metals

Metals that are below carbon in the reactivity series are less reactive than it. This means they can be extracted from their oxides by reduction using carbon (see next page).

Metals that are higher than carbon in the reactivity series are more reactive than carbon. They have to be extracted from their oxides using electrolysis (see next page), which is expensive.

Learning Objectives:
- Know that metals that are less reactive than carbon are extracted from their ores by reduction with carbon.
- Know that iron is extracted from its ore by reduction with carbon in the blast furnace.
- Understand what reduction is.
- Know that metals that are more reactive than carbon are extracted from their ores using electrolysis.
- Know that aluminium and titanium are examples of metals which can't be extracted by reduction with carbon.
- Understand why the extraction of aluminium and titanium from their oxides is expensive.

Specification Reference C1.3.1

Exam Tip
You don't need to worry about remembering the reactivity series. A copy of it will be given to you in the exam. Just remember what it shows and what that means for extracting metals.

Tip: Remember, the ore of a metal is usually the metal oxide.

Extraction by reduction with carbon

Tip: During a reduction reaction, oxygen is removed from the ore and the ore is said to be reduced.

A metal below carbon in the reactivity series can be extracted from its ore by reacting it with carbon. The reaction that takes place is called a **reduction reaction**, which is where oxygen is removed from the metal ore.

> **Example**
>
> Iron oxide (the ore of iron) is reduced in a blast furnace to make iron. Iron is less reactive than carbon so when iron oxide and carbon react the oxygen is removed from the iron ore, leaving iron metal.
>
> | $2Fe_2O_3$ | $+$ | $3C$ | $\rightarrow$ | $4Fe$ | $+$ | $3CO_2$ |
> |---|---|---|---|---|---|---|
> | iron(III) oxide | $+$ | carbon | $\rightarrow$ | iron | $+$ | carbon dioxide |

Extraction by electrolysis

Metals that are more reactive than carbon, such as aluminium, can't be extracted using carbon. So different processes, such as electrolysis have to be used. These processes are much more expensive than reduction with carbon because they have many stages and use a lot of energy.

Tip: Titanium isn't extracted by reduction with carbon or by electrolysis but all you need to know is that (like aluminium) it can't be extracted by reduction with carbon.

> **Example**
>
> Electrolysis can be used to extract aluminium from its oxide ore. A high temperature is needed to melt the aluminium oxide so that the aluminium can be extracted — this takes lots of energy, making it an expensive process.

Practice Questions — Fact Recall

Q1 Name the method used to extract a metal if it is...

　a) ...above carbon in the reactivity series.

　b) ...below carbon in the reactivity series.

Q2 Is an element at the top of the reactivity series more or less reactive than the elements below it?

Q3 When a metal ore is reduced by carbon, what is removed from it?

Q4 Why are other processes of extraction more expensive to carry out than reduction with carbon?

Tip: Have a look at the reactivity series on page 43 to help you with Q5.

Q5 Give two examples of metals that are extracted using electrolysis.

Practice Question — Application

Q1 What process is required to extract each of these metals from their metal oxides? Use the reactivity series on page 43 to help you.

　a) Tin
　b) Calcium

　c) Zinc
　d) Potassium

3. Extracting Copper

Copper is a really important metal and you need to know about the different ways that it can be extracted.

Extracting copper from copper-rich ores

Copper extraction using carbon

Copper can be easily extracted by reduction with carbon. The ore is heated in a furnace — this is called **smelting**. However, the copper produced this way is impure so electrolysis is used to purify it.

Copper purification by electrolysis

Electrolysis is the breaking down of a substance using electricity. It requires a liquid to conduct the electricity, called the **electrolyte**. Electrolytes are often metal salt solutions made from the ore (e.g. copper sulfate) or molten metal oxides. The electrolyte has free ions — these conduct the electricity and allow the whole thing to work.

In electrolysis there are two electrodes — one is positive and the other is negative. Electrons are lost or gained at the two electrodes — this allows ions to be formed at the positive electrode and atoms to bond at the negative electrode.

Here's how electrolysis is used to get copper:

1. The positive electrode is made of impure copper. Electrons are pulled off copper atoms at the positive electrode, causing them to go into solution as Cu^{2+} ions.

2. Cu^{2+} ions move towards the negative electrode, gain electrons and turn back into copper atoms.

3. The impurities are dropped at the positive electrode as a sludge, whilst pure copper atoms bond to the negative electrode.

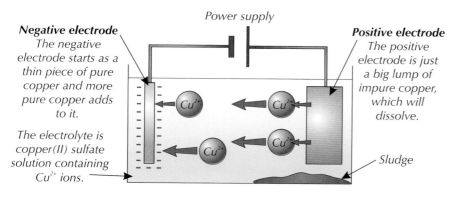

Negative electrode
The negative electrode starts as a thin piece of pure copper and more pure copper adds to it.

The electrolyte is copper(II) sulfate solution containing Cu^{2+} ions.

Power supply

Positive electrode
The positive electrode is just a big lump of impure copper, which will dissolve.

Sludge

Figure 1: *A diagram to show how electrolysis can be used to purify copper.*

Learning Objectives:
- Know that smelting is a process whereby copper is extracted from copper-rich ores by heating in a furnace.
- Know how electrolysis can be used to purify copper.
- Know that there is a limited supply of copper-rich ores and that traditional methods of extraction are damaging to the environment.
- Know that new ways of extracting copper from low-grade ores include bioleaching and phytomining.
- Know that copper can be extracted from solution using a displacement reaction involving scrap iron.

Specification Reference C1.3.1

Tip: You could extract copper straight from its ore by electrolysis if you wanted to, but it's more expensive than using reduction with carbon. A company will always pick the cheapest way unless there's a good reason not to.

Exam Tip
It's important to remember how the ions move in electrolysis — positive ions move towards the negative electrode, where they gain electrons and become copper atoms.

Extracting copper from low-grade ores

The supply of copper-rich ores is limited and the demand for copper is growing — this could lead to shortages in the future. To help with this, scientists are looking into new ways of extracting copper from low-grade ores (ores that only contain small amounts of copper) or from the waste that is currently produced when copper is extracted. Using traditional methods to extract copper from these low-grade ores is very expensive. Examples of new methods to extract copper from low-grade ores are **bioleaching** and **phytomining**.

Tip: It's important to recycle as much copper as possible because supplies of copper-rich ores are limited.

Bioleaching

Bioleaching uses bacteria to separate copper from copper sulfide. The bacteria get energy from the bond between copper and sulfur, separating out the copper from the ore in the process. The leachate (the solution produced by the process) contains copper, which can be extracted, e.g. by filtering.

Phytomining

Phytomining involves growing plants in soil that contains copper. The plants can't use or get rid of the copper so it gradually builds up in the leaves. The plants can be harvested, dried and burned in a furnace. The copper can be collected from the ash left in the furnace.

Figure 2: Bioleaching of copper sulfide ores at a copper mine.

Bioleaching and phytomining — pros and cons

Tip: Being able to weigh up the advantages and disadvantages of new techniques is an important skill for scientists to have.

Traditional methods of copper mining are pretty damaging to the environment (see page 48). These new methods of extraction are cheap and have a much smaller environmental impact. For example, they require less energy which is good for the environment because energy use often contributes to climate change and other environmental problems. Phytomining is also more carbon neutral than traditional methods — even though carbon dioxide is released when the plants are burned, they only release the same amount of carbon dioxide as they absorbed when they were growing. The disadvantage of these new extraction methods is that they're slow. For example, in phytomining it takes a long time for plants to grow and take up copper.

Copper extraction by displacement

More reactive metals react more vigorously than less reactive metals. If you put a reactive metal into a solution of a dissolved metal compound, the reactive metal will replace the less reactive metal in the compound — this is a **displacement reaction**. This happens because the more reactive metal bonds more strongly to the non-metal bit of the compound and pushes out the less reactive metal.

Copper can be extracted from a solution using a displacement reaction.

One way this can be done is by using scrap iron. This is really useful because iron is cheap but copper is expensive. If some iron is put in a solution of copper sulfate, the more reactive iron will "kick out" the less reactive copper from the solution. You end up with iron sulfate solution and copper metal. The equation for this reaction is:

copper sulfate + iron → iron sulfate + copper

If a piece of silver metal is put into a solution of copper sulfate, nothing happens. The more reactive metal (copper) is already in the solution.

Practice Questions — Fact Recall

Q1 What is the name given to the extraction of copper using a furnace?

Q2 Copper can be purified by electrolysis.

a) At which electrode do copper atoms go into solution as copper ions?

b) How are the copper ions formed?

c) Which electrode do the copper ions move towards?

Q3 a) Name two methods for extracting copper from low-grade ores.

b) Give one advantage of these methods over traditional methods.

Q4 Copper can be extracted from a solution of copper sulfate by adding scrap iron.

a) What type of reaction does this involve?

b) Give a benefit of using scrap iron in this reaction.

c) What are the two products of this reaction?

Learning Objectives:
- Understand that the process of metal extraction has negative environmental impacts and these must be balanced against the social and economic benefits that extracting metal brings.
- Understand why it is important to recycle metals.

Specification Reference
C1.3, C1.3.1

4. Impacts of Extracting Metals

Metals are used in all sorts of different ways so it's important that we have good supplies of them. But getting hold of metals uses lots of energy and negatively affects the environment.

What are the impacts of metal extraction?

People have to balance the social, economic and environmental effects of mining metal ores. Most of the issues are exactly the same as those to do with quarrying limestone on page 40.

Positive impacts

Mining metal ores is good because it means that useful products can be made. It also provides local people with jobs and brings money into the area. This means services such as transport and health can be improved.

Negative impacts

Mining ores is bad for the environment. It causes noise and increased levels of traffic due to lorries visiting the mine. Mining destroys habitats, scars the landscape and leaves deep mine shafts that can be dangerous for a long time after the mine has been abandoned. The process of mining produces lots of solid waste (such as bits of rock that aren't ores) which can be an eyesore.

Mining and extracting metals also takes lots of energy, most of which comes from burning fossil fuels. Burning fossil fuels releases gases such as carbon dioxide and sulfur dioxide into the atmosphere which contribute to acid rain and climate change (see pages 67 and 68).

So, mining for metals has its benefits and drawbacks. It's likely that not many people would be against the jobs and other economic benefits that a mine brings, but these positives have got to be weighed up against the negative aspects of mining, such as increased pollution and habitat destruction.

Tip: It's important to be able to weigh up the social, environmental and economic consequences of processes such as metal mining and extraction.

HOW SCIENCE WORKS

Recycling metals

It's important to recycle metals. Here are some reasons why:

- Recycling metals only uses a small fraction of the energy needed to mine and extract new metal. For example, recycling copper takes 15% of the energy that's needed to mine and extract new copper. This is good for the environment because using energy usually has negative environmental impacts. Using less energy also helps to conserve fossil fuels — this is important as they are a non-renewable resource which is running out.

- Energy doesn't come cheap, so recycling saves money too.

Figure 1: *Compacted cans ready to be recycled at a recycling plant.*

- There's a finite amount of each metal in the Earth. Recycling conserves these resources.

- Recycling metal cuts down on the amount of rubbish that gets sent to landfill. Landfill takes up space and pollutes the surroundings. If all the aluminium cans in the UK were recycled, there'd be 14 million fewer dustbins to empty each year.

Practice Questions — Fact Recall

Q1 Give one social or economic benefit of mining for metals.

Q2 Give two environmental impacts of mining.

Q3 Explain how mining can contribute to acid rain, global dimming and climate change.

Q4 a) How does recycling metal save energy?

b) State three other benefits of recycling metals.

Practice Question — Application

Q1 This table shows the amount of metal a council sent to landfill in two separate years. It costs the council £115 for every tonne of waste they send to landfill.

	Tonnes of waste metal to landfill	Cost (£)
Year 1	15 000	
Year 2	12 000	

a) i) Work out the cost of sending the waste metal to landfill each year.

ii) How much money did the council save from year 1 to year 2 by reducing the amount of metal they sent to landfill?

b) Suggest one way the council could have reduced the amount of waste metal that was sent to landfill.

5. Properties and Uses of Metals

Learning Objectives:

- Know the location of the transition metals in the periodic table.
- Know that the transition metals have the same basic properties as other metals and know what these properties are.
- Understand that the properties of metals make them useful for many different uses.
- Know that the properties of copper make it ideal for use as electrical wiring and in plumbing.
- Know that aluminium and titanium are useful metals because of their low density and resistance to corrosion.
- Know that metals are useful structural materials but there are disadvantages to using them.

Specification Reference C1.3, C1.3.3

Once you've got hold of metals you can use them for all sorts of different things. What you use them for is determined by their individual properties, but all metals have some basic properties in common.

Basic properties of metals

Most of the elements are metals — so they cover most of the periodic table. In fact, only the elements on the far right are non-metals (see Figure 1).

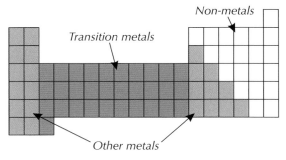

Figure 1: *A diagram of the periodic table showing the location of metals.*

All metals, including transition metals, have some fairly similar basic properties:

- They are strong (hard to break).
- They can be bent or hammered into different shapes.
- They're great at conducting heat.
- They conduct electricity.

Metals (and especially **transition metals**) have loads of everyday uses because of these properties...

- Their strength and 'bendability' makes them handy for making into things like bridges and car bodies.
- Their ability to conduct heat makes them ideal if you want to make something that heat needs to travel through, like a saucepan base.
- Their electrical conductivity makes them great for making things like electrical wires.

Figure 2: *Metals have to be bent into shape to make car bodies.*

Copper, aluminium and titanium

The properties mentioned above are typical properties of metals. Not all metals are the same though — you need to learn the specific properties of copper, aluminium and titanium (see next page).

1. Copper

Copper is a good conductor of electricity. It's hard and strong but can be bent. It also doesn't react with water.

2. Aluminium

Aluminium is corrosion-resistant and has a low density — this low density means that it's lightweight. Pure aluminium isn't particularly strong, but it forms hard, strong alloys.

3. Titanium

Titanium is another low density metal. Unlike aluminium it's very strong. It is also corrosion-resistant.

Tip: Metal corrosion is where metals gradually break down as they react with their environment. Rusting is an example of corrosion — it's the corrosion of iron.

Tip: An alloy is a mixture of a metal with either another metal or a non-metal. There's more about them on pages page 53 and 54.

Uses of metals

Different metals are chosen for different uses because of their specific properties.

> **Examples**
>
> - If you were doing some plumbing, you'd pick a metal that could be bent to make pipes and tanks, and is below hydrogen in the reactivity series so it doesn't react with water. Copper is great for this.
>
> - If you wanted to make electrical wires, you'd pick a metal that is a good conductor of electricity and can be drawn out into wires. Copper is an ideal choice for this.
>
> - If you wanted to make an aeroplane, you'd probably use metal as it's strong and can be bent into shape. But you'd also need it to be lightweight, so an aluminium alloy would be a good choice.
>
> - If you were making replacement hips, you'd use a metal that won't corrode when it comes in contact with water. It'd have to be light and not too bendy. Titanium has all of these properties so is used for this.

Figure 3: A replacement hip joint made from titanium.

Metals are very useful structural materials, but some corrode when exposed to air and water, so they need to be protected — for example, by using paint. If metals corrode, they lose their strength and hardness.

Metals can also get 'tired' when stresses and strains are repeatedly put on them over time. This is known as **metal fatigue** and leads to metals breaking, which can be very dangerous. For example, in planes it's really important that metal components aren't fatigued so they are safe during flights. To help prevent fatigue, metal parts are specially designed and regularly checked.

HOW SCIENCE WORKS

Exam Tip
You might be asked to weigh up the advantages and disadvantages of using a metal for a particular purpose. You'll need to use your own knowledge and the information given in the question to answer it.

Q1 Give the letter that corresponds to the transition metals on this periodic table.

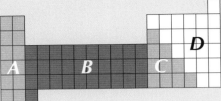

Q2 Metals are good at conducting electricity.

a) Suggest one metal product in which this property is important.

b) Give two other basic properties of metals.

Q3 Aluminium alloys are used to make lots of aeroplane parts. Why are they suitable for this use?

Q4 Give two reasons why copper is ideal for use in plumbing.

Q5 Which properties of titanium make it a suitable metal for replacement hips?

Q6 Give two disadvantages of using metals as structural materials.

Practice Question — Application

Q1 Rachel is buying a new bicycle. She can buy either a steel, aluminium or titanium frame. This table shows some properties of these metals.

	Steel	Aluminium	Titanium
Price	Low	Quite high	Very expensive
Strength	Very strong	Quite strong	Strong
Resistance to corrosion	Good	Excellent	Excellent
Relative density	High	Very low	Low

She would like a bike that's not too heavy or expensive. Use the table to suggest a type of frame for Rachel and give reasons for your choice.

6. Alloys

Metals are often made into alloys. And that's what the next few pages are about — alloys. What they are, why they're made and some different types.

What is an alloy?

Alloys are mixtures of two or more metals, or a mixture of a metal and a non-metal. Iron is often used to make alloys. Before it's made into an alloy it needs to be extracted from its ore in a blast furnace and then purified.

Purification of iron

'Iron' straight from the blast furnace is only about 96% iron. The other 4% is impurities such as carbon. This impure iron is used as cast iron. It can be poured into shapes, so it's handy for making ornamental railings. It can also be used for structures that need to withstand being compressed, for example in columns. But cast iron has limited other uses because the impurities that it contains make it brittle.

To make the iron less brittle, the impurities are removed from most of the blast furnace iron to create pure iron. This pure iron has a regular arrangement of identical atoms. The layers of atoms can slide over each other (see Figure 1), which makes the iron soft and easily shaped. This iron is far too bendy for most uses, so most of it is converted into alloys.

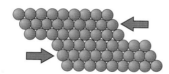

Figure 1: *The arrangement of atoms in pure iron.*

Learning Objectives:

- Know that iron straight out of the blast furnace is 96% iron and is used as cast iron.
- Know that cast iron is brittle due to the impurities it contains and this means its uses are limited.
- Know that most iron is made into steels (alloys containing iron and carbon).
- Know the properties of low-carbon, high-carbon and stainless steels.
- Know that most of the metals we use are alloys.
- Know that copper, gold, aluminium and iron are made into alloys to make them harder.
- Understand that alloys can be designed to have certain properties and for a specific purpose.

Specification Reference C1.3.2

Conversion of iron to steel

Most of the pure iron is changed into alloys called steels. Steels are formed by adding small amounts of carbon and sometimes other metals to the iron. There are several different types of steel. They have different uses because of their different properties — see Figure 3.

Type of Steel	Properties	Uses
Low-carbon steel (0.1% carbon)	Easily shaped	Car bodies
High-carbon steel (1.5% carbon)	Very hard, inflexible	Blades for cutting tools, bridges
Stainless steel (chromium added, and sometimes nickel)	Corrosion-resistant	Cutlery, containers for corrosive substances

Figure 3: *Table showing the properties and uses of three different types of steel.*

Figure 2: *A blast furnace in a steel foundry which is used to make iron.*

Properties of alloys

Most metals in use today are actually alloys. Pure copper, gold, aluminium and iron are too soft for many uses so are made into alloys to make them more usable.

Alloys are harder than pure metals because they are made from atoms of different elements. Different elements have different sized atoms. So when an element such as carbon is added to pure iron, the smaller carbon atoms will upset the layers of pure iron atoms, making it more difficult for them to slide over each other.

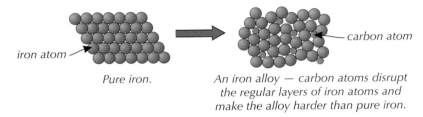

iron atom

carbon atom

Pure iron.

An iron alloy — carbon atoms disrupt the regular layers of iron atoms and make the alloy harder than pure iron.

Figure 4: *The arrangement of atoms in an iron alloy.*

In the past, the development of alloys was by trial and error. But nowadays we understand much more about the properties of metals, so alloys can be designed to have particular properties that make them suitable for a specific purpose.

Common alloys

Here are some examples of common alloys:

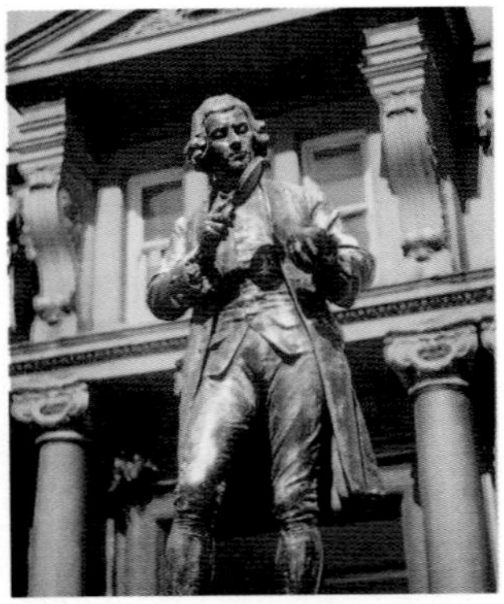

Bronze

Bronze is an alloy of copper and tin. It's harder than copper and it's good for making medals and statues from.

Cupronickel

Cupronickel is an alloy of copper and nickel. It's hard and corrosion-resistant. It's used to make "silver" coins.

Gold alloys

Gold alloys are used to make jewellery as pure gold is too soft. Metals such as zinc, copper, silver, palladium and nickel are used to harden the "gold".

Aluminium alloys

Aluminium alloys are used to make aircraft. Aluminium has a low density, but it's alloyed with small amounts of other metals to make it stronger.

Figure 5: *A bronze statue.*

Practice Questions — Fact Recall

Q1   What percentage of iron does iron from a blast furnace contain?

Q2   Why does cast iron have few uses?

Q3   Why is pure iron easily bent?

Q4   What element is added to iron to make steels?

Q5   Name a type of steel that is resistant to corrosion.

Q6   Why is pure aluminium made into an alloy?

Q7   Name the metals that form these alloys:

a) Bronze

b) Cupronickel

Q8   Why isn't pure gold used to make jewellery?

Practice Questions — Application

Q1   Many car parts, such as axles, need to be hard and rigid.
Suggest a type of steel that could be used for this purpose.

Q2   Steel containers are used in kitchens and laboratories. They need to
be resistant to corrosion. Suggest a type of steel that could be used
for these containers.

Section Checklist — Make sure you know...

Metal Ores

☐ That some metals are found as the metal itself but most exist as compounds and need to be extracted from ores.

☐ That a rock with enough metal in to make it economic to extract the metal is called an ore.

☐ Why the economics of metal extraction can change over time.

☐ That most metals need to be extracted from their ores using a chemical reaction such as reduction, electrolysis or displacement.

Extracting Metals from Rocks

☐ That if a metal is below carbon in the reactivity series, it is extracted by reduction with carbon.

☐ That if a metal is above carbon in the reactivity series, it is extracted by electrolysis.

☐ That in a reduction reaction, oxygen is removed.

☐ That aluminium and titanium can't be extracted from their ores by reduction with carbon.

☐ That the extraction of aluminium and titanium from their ores is expensive because the processes used have lots of stages and need lots of energy.

cont...

Extracting Copper

☐ That copper can be extracted from its ore by smelting (heating it in a furnace).

☐ How electrolysis can be used to purify copper.

☐ That the supply of copper-rich ores is limited so it's important to recycle as much copper as possible.

☐ The two new methods that have been developed for extracting copper from low-grade ores — bioleaching (using bacteria) and phytomining (using plants that absorb copper from soil).

☐ The advantages and disadvantages of using bioleaching and phytomining instead of traditional extraction methods to extract copper from low-grade ores.

☐ How copper can be extracted from solution using a displacement reaction with scrap iron.

Impacts of Extracting Metals

☐ The social, economic and environmental impacts of mining for metal ores.

☐ That recycling metal, rather than extracting more metal, saves limited metal resources, requires less energy, saves fossil fuels and reduces the amount of waste going to landfill.

Properties and Uses of Metals

☐ Where the transition metals are in the periodic table.

☐ That metals have similar basic properties — they are strong, can be bent into shape, and conduct heat and electricity.

☐ What the specific properties of copper, aluminium and titanium are, and that these mean they are suitable for certain uses.

☐ That the downsides to using metals as structural materials are that they may corrode or break due to metal fatigue.

Alloys

☐ That an alloy is a mixture of two metals, or a mixture of a metal and a non-metal.

☐ That iron from a blast furnace needs to be purified as it contains impurities that make it brittle. It's then made into alloys because its softness means it has limited uses as a pure metal.

☐ That steel is an alloy of iron and carbon and that most iron is made into steel.

☐ The properties of low-carbon steel, high-carbon steel and stainless steel.

☐ That copper, gold and aluminium are made into alloys to make them harder and so more usable.

☐ That alloys can be designed for specific purposes.

Exam-style Questions

1   Car bodies can be made out of steel or aluminium alloys.

1 (a) (i)   Steel is an alloy. Define the term 'alloy'.

(2 marks)

1 (a) (ii)   Carbon is one element in steel. Name the other main element in steel.

(1 mark)

1 (a) (iii)   Circle the correct word to complete the sentence.

Metals are often made into alloys to make them   softer.

harder.   *(1 mark)*

1 (b)   Low-carbon steel can be used to make car bodies.
Give **one** property that makes low-carbon steel suitable for this purpose.

(1 mark)

1 (c)   A disadvantage of using steel to make car bodies is that it can corrode. To help prevent this a layer of zinc is often applied to the steel. This process is called galvanisation.

1 (c) (i)   Galvanisation isn't necessary for aluminium car bodies.
Explain why this is the case.

(1 mark)

1 (c) (ii)   Give **one** other property of aluminium that makes it a better material for making car bodies from than steel.

(1 mark)

1 (c) (iii)   Why would pure aluminium not be a suitable material for building car bodies?

(1 mark)

1 (c) (iv)   Car bodies containing aluminium are more expensive than those made from steel as the extraction of aluminium from its ore is expensive. Explain why it is expensive to extract aluminium from its ore.

(2 marks)

2   Calcium hydroxide is an alkali that has many uses in industry and in agriculture.

2 (a) (i)   Name the **two** reactants involved in the formation of calcium hydroxide.

(1 mark)

2 (a) (ii) Write the symbol equation for this reaction.

(2 marks)

2 (b) (i)   Calcium hydroxide can be dissolved in water to form a solution.
What is the common name for this solution?

(1 mark)

2 (b) (ii) A solution of calcium hydroxide can be used to test for the presence of carbon dioxide.
If carbon dioxide was bubbled through the solution, what would you expect to see?

(1 mark)

2 (b) (iii) Fill in the blanks in this equation for the reaction of calcium hydroxide
with carbon dioxide.

$$Ca(OH)_2 \ + \ CO_2 \ \rightarrow \ \rule{2cm}{0.4pt} \ + \ \rule{2cm}{0.4pt}$$

(2 marks)

2 (c)   The pH of soil can affect plant growth. Calcium hydroxide can be applied to fields
(a process called liming) to alter the pH of the soil. This graph shows soil pH in a field
during one year. During this time the farmer applied calcium hydroxide once.

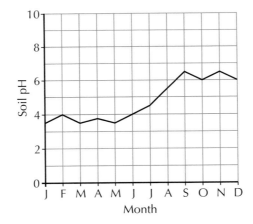

2 (c) (i)   What effect does calcium hydroxide have on soil pH?

(1 mark)

2 (c) (ii) What type of reaction causes this effect?

(1 mark)

2 (c) (iii) Using the graph, suggest the month when liming took place. Explain your answer.

(2 marks)

3   Malachite is a copper ore that contains 57% copper.
Copper can be extracted from malachite by the process shown in this diagram.

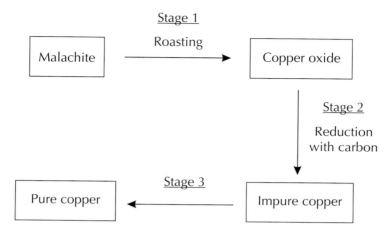

3 (a)   Malachite is mostly copper carbonate.
Give the chemical formula of copper carbonate.

(1 mark)

3 (b)   Stage 1 (roasting) takes place at a very high temperature. The copper carbonate breaks down to form copper oxide and one other product.

3 (b) (i)   What type of reaction occurs during roasting?

(1 mark)

3 (b) (ii)   Copper oxide is one product of roasting, what is the other?

(1 mark)

3 (c)   Name the process used to obtain pure copper in Stage 3.

(1 mark)

3 (d)   Chalcopyrite is another type of copper ore. It's a copper sulfide that is 10% copper.

3 (d) (i)   Explain why copper isn't extracted from chalcopyrite using the method outlined in the diagram.

(2 marks)

3 (d) (ii)   Suggest a method that could be used to extract copper from chalcopyrite and give **two** advantages of this method over the one outlined in the diagram.

(3 marks)

3 (e)   Copper is used to make electrical wiring.

3 (e) (i)   Give **two** reasons why copper is suitable for this use.

(2 marks)

3 (e) (ii)   Give **one** other application of copper.

(1 mark)

4 Buildings and other structures can be made from a range of materials, including metals and products made from limestone.

4 (a) Limestone can be made into a number of useful building materials.
Use the correct words from the box to complete the paragraph.

bauxite	sand	concrete	limestone	aggregate	clay

Limestone is heated with .... to make cement.

.... and water are added to cement to make mortar.

Sand and .... are added to cement to make ....

(4 marks)

4 (b) Limestone based building materials can be used in combination with metals.
Iron is an example of a metal that is commonly used with limestone products.

4 (b) (i) Iron is usually found as iron oxide. Describe how iron is extracted from iron oxide.

(3 marks)

4 (b) (ii) Iron extracted from iron oxide with no further processing is usually brittle.
Explain why.

(1 mark)

4 (b) (iii) Some metals do not need to be extracted from ores — they are found in the earth as the pure metal. Give one example of a metal found in its elemental form, and explain why it is not found as an ore.

(2 marks)

4 (c) Mining for metal ores and quarrying for limestone have impacts on the environment.

4 (c) (i) Tick **two** statements that are environmental impacts of extracting metal ores and limestone.

Statement	Environmental Impact Tick (✔)
Jobs are created in the local area.	
Traffic to and from the mine/quarry causes pollution.	
Habitats are destroyed.	
Dust from the site can cause health problems for local people.	

(2 marks)

4 (c) (ii) Describe one way that mining and quarrying can contribute to global warming.

(2 marks)

1. Fractional Distillation of Crude Oil

Crude oil is a fossil fuel that is formed deep underground from the remains of plants and animals. Loads of useful products can be made from crude oil using a technique called fractional distillation.

What is crude oil?

Crude oil is a **mixture** of many different compounds. A mixture consists of two (or more) elements or compounds that aren't chemically bonded to each other. Most of the compounds in crude oil are **hydrocarbon** molecules. Hydrocarbons are basically fuels such as petrol and diesel. They're made of only carbon and hydrogen.

Properties of mixtures

There are no chemical bonds between the different parts of a mixture, so the different hydrocarbon molecules in crude oil aren't chemically bonded to one another. This means that they all keep their original properties, such as their boiling points (the temperature at which they turn from a liquid into a gas). The properties of a mixture are just a mixture of the properties of the separate parts.

Separating mixtures

Because the substances in a mixture all keep their original properties, the parts of a mixture can be separated out by physical methods.

Example

Crude oil can be split up into its separate fractions by fractional distillation. Each fraction contains molecules with a similar number of carbon atoms to each other.

Fractional distillation

Crude oil can be split into separate groups of hydrocarbons using a technique called fractional distillation. The crude oil is pumped into piece of equipment known as a fractionating column, which works continuously (it doesn't get switched off). This fractionating column has a temperature gradient running through it — it's hottest at the bottom and coldest at the top.

Learning Objectives:

- Know that crude oil is a mixture of lots of different compounds.
- Know that the substances in a mixture are not chemically bonded to each other.
- Know that most of the compounds in crude oil are hydrocarbons.
- Know that the properties of substances are not changed when the substance is in a mixture.
- Know that mixtures can be separated using physical methods such as distillation.
- Understand how fractional distillation is used to separate crude oil into fractions.

Specification Reference C1.4.1, C1.4.2

Figure 1: *A fractionating column.*

The crude oil is first heated so that it vaporises (turns into a gas) and is then piped in at the bottom of the column. The gas rises up the column and gradually cools. Different compounds in the mixture have different boiling points, so they condense (turn back into a liquid) at different temperatures. This means they condense at different levels in the fractionating column.

Hydrocarbons that have a similar number of carbon atoms in have similar boiling points, so they condense at similar levels in the column.

Tip: There's more about how the number of carbon atoms affects the properties of a hydrocarbon coming up on page 65.

Tip: The temperature at which a compound condenses is the same as its boiling point. E.g. If a compound had a boiling point of 120 °C, it would condense at 120 °C.

Example

- Hydrocarbons with lots of carbon atoms in have high boiling points, so they condense near the bottom of the column.

- Hydrocarbons with a small number of carbon atoms in have low boiling points, so they condense near the top of the column.

The groups of hydrocarbons that condense together are called **fractions**. The various fractions are constantly tapped off from the column at the different levels where they condense.

The process of fractional distillation is illustrated in Figure 2.

Exam Tip
Don't worry — you don't need to know the names, lengths or condensing temperatures of specific fractions. Just make sure you understand the general principles of fractional distillation for the exam.

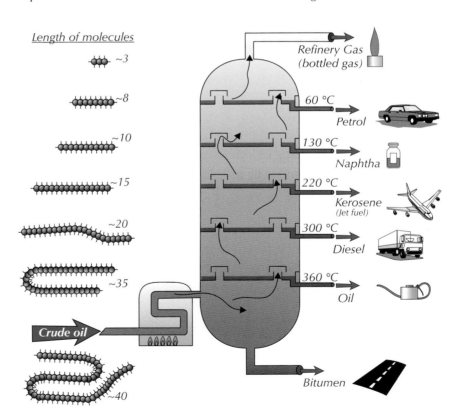

Length of molecules

~3
~8
~10
~15
~20
~35

Crude oil

~40

Refinery Gas (bottled gas)

60 °C — Petrol

130 °C — Naphtha

220 °C — Kerosene (Jet fuel)

300 °C — Diesel

360 °C — Oil

Bitumen

Figure 2: *The process of fractional distillation.*

Practice Questions — Fact Recall

Q1 What is a mixture?

Q2 What is a hydrocarbon?

Q3 Name the process that is used to separate crude oil into fractions.

Q4 Where do compounds with a small number of carbon atoms leave the fractionating column — near the bottom or near the top?

Practice Questions — Application

Q1 This table shows the number of carbon atoms in some of the hydrocarbons found in crude oil.

Hydrocarbon	Number of carbon atoms
Butane	4
Decane	10
Icosane	20
Tetracontane	40

a) Which of the hydrocarbons in the table will condense at the lowest temperature?

b) Which of the hydrocarbons in the table will condense nearest the bottom of a fractionating column?

Q2 This table contains data on some of the fractions of crude oil that are separated out during fractional distillation.

Fraction	Approximate boiling temperature range (°C)
Petrol	30 – 80
Naphtha	80 – 190
Kerosene	190 – 250
Diesel	250 – 350

a) Which of the fractions in the table will be removed closest to the top of the fractionating column?

b) Octane has a boiling point of 125 °C.

i) At what temperature will octane condense?

ii) In which of the fractions in the table will octane be found?

> **Tip:** Don't forget — the fractionating column is hottest at the bottom and coolest at the top.

- Know that most of the hydrocarbons in crude oil are alkanes.
- Be able to recognise alkanes from their chemical and displayed formulae.
- Know that alkanes are saturated hydrocarbons.
- Know that alkanes have the general formula C_nH_{2n+2}.
- Know how the boiling point, viscosity and flammability of alkanes change depending on the size of the molecules.
- Understand how the properties of an alkane influence how it is used as a fuel.

Specification Reference
C1.4.1, C1.4.2

Exam Tip
You need to be able to recognise methane, ethane, propane and butane in the exam, so make sure you learn these structures and formulas.

Tip: Saturated means a compound only has single carbon-carbon bonds.

Tip: You can work out the chemical formula of any alkane using the general formula, as long as you know how many carbon atoms it has.

2. Properties and Uses of Crude Oil

The different fractions that you get when you separate crude oil have very different properties. This means they can be used for different things.

Alkanes

Most of the fractions of crude oil consist of hydrocarbons called alkanes. Alkanes are made up of chains of carbon atoms surrounded by hydrogen atoms. Different alkanes have chains of different lengths.

Example

The first four alkanes are methane (natural gas), ethane, propane and butane.

Methane has just one carbon atom and four hydrogen atoms, so its chemical formula is CH_4. The displayed structure of methane is shown in Figure 1. The green lines in this structure represent covalent bonds.

Figure 1: Methane.

Ethane (C_2H_6) has a chain of two carbon atoms, propane (C_3H_8) has three carbon atoms and butane (C_4H_{10}) has four carbon atoms. Their displayed structures are shown in Figure 2.

Ethane

Propane

Butane

Figure 2: The structures of ethane, propane and butane.

Carbon atoms form four bonds and hydrogen atoms only form one bond. In alkanes, there are no carbon-carbon double bonds so all the atoms have formed bonds with as many other atoms as they can — this means they're saturated.

General formula of alkanes

Alkanes all have the general formula C_nH_{2n+2}. In this formula, n is the number of carbon atoms. If an alkane has n carbon atoms, it will always have 2n + 2 hydrogen atoms.

Example

If an alkane has 5 carbons, it's got to have (2 × 5) + 2 = 12 hydrogens. So the chemical formula of an alkane with 5 carbon atoms is C_5H_{12}.

Properties of alkanes

The properties of alkanes change depending on how long the carbon chain is. There are three trends in the properties of alkanes that you need to know.

- The shorter the molecules, the more runny the hydrocarbon is — that is, the less **viscous** it is.

- The shorter the molecules, the more **volatile** they are. "More volatile" means they turn into a gas at a lower temperature. So, the shorter the molecules, the lower the temperature at which that fraction vaporises or condenses — and the lower its boiling point.

- The shorter the molecules, the more **flammable** the hydrocarbon is.

So, alkanes with very long carbon chains are viscous, have very high boiling points and are not very flammable.

Tip: How <u>flammable</u> something is is how easy it is to ignite.

Uses of hydrocarbons

The uses of hydrocarbons depend on their properties.

Examples

The volatility helps decide what the fraction is used for.

- The refinery gas fraction has the lowest boiling point — in fact it's a gas at room temperature. This makes it ideal for using as bottled gas. It's stored under pressure as liquid in 'bottles'. When the tap on the bottle is opened, the fuel vaporises and flows to the burner where it's ignited.

- The petrol fraction has a higher boiling point. Petrol is a liquid which is ideal for storing in the fuel tank of a car. It can flow to the engine where it's easily vaporised to mix with the air before it is ignited.

The viscosity also helps decide how the hydrocarbons are used.

- The really gloopy, viscous hydrocarbons are used for lubricating engine parts or for covering roads.

Figure 3: *Bottled gas.*

Practice Questions — Fact Recall

Q1 Draw the displayed structure of methane.

Q2 Name the alkane that has the chemical formula C_3H_8.

Q3 Why are alkanes described as being "saturated"?

Q4 Describe the trend in flammability of the alkanes.

Practice Questions — Application

Q1 Octane has eight carbon atoms in it. What is its chemical formula?

Q2 Hexadecane is an alkane with long carbon chains. Explain why hexadecane is a suitable alkane to use in lubricating oil.

- Know that most fuels contain carbon and/or hydrogen.
- Know that when fuels are burnt, the carbon and hydrogen in the fuels are oxidised and energy is released.
- Know that the substances released when fuels are burnt can include carbon dioxide, water, carbon monoxide, sulfur dioxide, oxides of nitrogen and solid carbon particulates.
- Know that sulfur dioxide and nitrogen oxides can cause acid rain.
- Know that it's possible to remove the sulfur from fuels before they are burned.
- Know that sulfur dioxide can be removed from waste gases after a fuel has been burned.
- Know that carbon dioxide contributes to global warming and solid carbon particulates contribute to global dimming.
- Understand the social, economic and environmental impacts of using fuels.

Specification Reference
C1.4.3

Tip: **H** See page 30 for more on balancing chemical equations.

3. Environmental Problems

HOW SCIENCE WORKS

Crude oil, coal and natural gas are all fossil fuels. Fossil fuels make great fuels, but burning them to release energy can be bad for the environment.

Burning fuels (combustion)

We burn **fossil fuels** (coal, oil and natural gas) to get energy for lots of different processes. Power stations burn huge amounts of fossil fuels to make electricity. Cars are also a major culprit in burning fossil fuels.

Fossil fuels contain carbon and hydrogen. During **combustion** (when the fuel is burnt), the carbon and hydrogen react with oxygen from the air so that carbon dioxide and water vapour are released into the atmosphere. The carbon and hydrogen are said to be oxidised. Energy (heat) is also released.

Complete and partial combustion

When there's plenty of oxygen, all the fuel burns — this is called complete combustion. When a fuel is completely combusted only carbon dioxide and water are produced. This is the equation for the complete combustion of a hydrocarbon:

hydrocarbon + oxygen → carbon dioxide + water vapour

If there's not enough oxygen, some of the fuel doesn't burn completely — this is called partial combustion. Under these conditions, solid particles (called particulates) of soot (carbon) and unburnt fuel may be released, as well as carbon dioxide and water. Carbon monoxide (a poisonous gas) is also released.

Writing equations for combustion Higher

In the exam, you could be asked to write a balanced symbol equation for the complete combustion of a particular fuel. All you have to do is put the chemical formula of your fuel and O_2 for oxygen on one side, CO_2 for carbon dioxide and H_2O for water on the other side and then make sure the equation balances.

Example — Higher

Write an equation for the complete combustion of propane.

Propane has the chemical formula C_3H_8 (you saw this on page 64.)

If you put C_3H_8 and O_2 on one side of the equation and CO_2 and H_2O on the other side of the equation you get:

$$C_3H_8 + O_2 \rightarrow CO_2 + H_2O$$

Balancing the equation gives you:

$$C_3H_8 + 5O_2 \rightarrow 3CO_2 + 4H_2O$$

This is the equation for the complete combustion of propane.

You could also be asked to write an equation for the partial combustion of a fuel. If so, you'll be told in the question what the products of the reaction are and you'll just need to balance the equation.

Other products of combustion

If the fuel contains sulfur impurities, the sulfur will be released as sulfur dioxide when the fuel is burnt. Oxides of nitrogen will also form if the fuel burns at a high temperature. This is because at very high temperatures, nitrogen and oxygen in the air react with one another.

Tip: The chemical formula for carbon monoxide is CO and the chemical formula for particulate carbon is just C.

Tip: Partial combustion is also known as incomplete combustion.

Acid rain

Sulfur dioxide is one of the gases that causes acid rain. When the sulfur dioxide mixes with the water in the clouds it forms dilute sulfuric acid. This then falls as acid rain (see Figure 1).

Figure 1: *The formation of acid rain.*

Oxides of nitrogen cause acid rain by forming dilute nitric acid in clouds.

Consequences of acid rain

Acid rain causes lakes to become acidic and many plants and animals die as a result. Acid rain also kills trees (see Figure 2), damages limestone buildings and ruins stone statues (see Figure 3). Links between acid rain and human health problems have also been suggested.

Reducing acid rain

The benefits of electricity and travel have to be balanced against the environmental impacts. Governments have recognised the importance of this and international agreements have been put in place to reduce emissions of air pollutants such as sulfur dioxide.

One way to reduce sulfur dioxide emissions is to remove the sulfur from fuels before they're burnt. The problem is, this costs money. Also, removing sulfur from fuels takes more energy. This usually comes from burning more fuel, which releases more of the greenhouse gas carbon dioxide. Nevertheless, petrol and diesel are starting to be replaced by low-sulfur versions.

Another way to reduce sulfur dioxide emissions is to remove the sulfur dioxide from waste gases before they are released. Power stations now have Acid Gas Scrubbers to take the harmful gases out before they release their fumes into the atmosphere. The other way of reducing acid rain is simply to reduce our usage of fossil fuels.

Figure 2: *Trees that have been killed by acid rain.*

Figure 3: *A statue that has been damaged by acid rain.*

Global warming and climate change

The level of carbon dioxide in the atmosphere is increasing — because of the large amounts of fossil fuels humans burn. There's a scientific consensus that this extra carbon dioxide has caused the average temperature of the Earth to increase — global warming (see Figure 4).

Tip: Atmospheric CO_2 concentration is measured in ppm — this stands for parts per million. 1 ppm is equivalent to 0.0001%

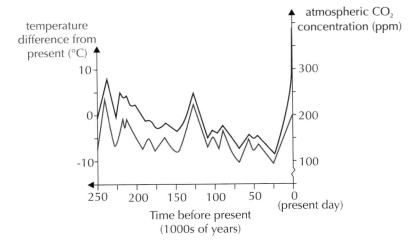

Figure 4: *Graph showing how the atmospheric concentration of CO_2 and the temperature have changed over the last 250 000 years.*

Tip: Don't get confused. Global warming and climate change are not the same things — global warming is a type of climate change.

Global warming is a type of climate change and causes other types of climate change, e.g. changing rainfall patterns. It could also cause severe flooding due to the polar ice caps melting.

Global dimming

In the last few years, some scientists have been measuring how much sunlight is reaching the surface of the Earth and comparing it to records from the last 50 years. They have been amazed to find that in some areas nearly 25% less sunlight has been reaching the surface compared to 50 years ago. They have called this global dimming.

They think that it is caused by particles of soot and ash that are produced when fossil fuels are burnt. These particles reflect sunlight back into space, or they can help to produce more clouds that reflect the sunlight back into space. However, there are many scientists who don't believe the change is real and blame it on inaccurate recording equipment.

Figure 5: *Thick black smoke being released into the air. The particulate carbon in this smoke could contribute to global dimming.*

Practice Questions — Fact Recall

Q1 a) What two products are formed when a hydrocarbon fuel is completely combusted?

b) What other products may be released if a hydrocarbon fuel undergoes partial combustion?

Q2 What gas other than carbon dioxide and water vapour will be formed if a fuel containing sulfur impurities is burnt in air?

Q3 Under what conditions will nitrogen oxides form when a hydrocarbon fuel is burned?

Q4 a) Name two gases that can cause acid rain.

b) Give two ways in which acid rain can damage the environment.

c) Suggest one way of reducing acid rain.

Q5 a) What is global warming?

b) Suggest one consequence of global warming.

Practice Questions — Application

Q1 Hexadecane ($C_{16}H_{34}$) can be used as a fuel. When it undergoes complete combustion carbon dioxide and water vapour are released.

a) Will using hexadecane as a fuel contribute to climate change? Explain your answer.

b) Could burning hexadecane result in acid rain? Explain your answer.

Q2 A study by scientists at a local weather station has shown that over the last 50 years, the amount of sunlight reaching the weather station has decreased. Suggest a possible explanation for this finding.

Q3 Write a balanced symbol equation for the complete combustion of pentane (C_5H_{12}).

Q4 Some hexane (C_6H_{14}) burns incompletely producing carbon monoxide and water as the only products. Write a balanced symbol equation for this combustion.

Exam Tip
You could get a question like this in the exam where you're asked to consider the environmental impacts of a fuel you've never heard of before. Just read the question carefully — all the information you need is there.

4. Alternative Fuels

There are lots of problems with using fossil fuels, so scientists are developing some alternative fuel sources. The trouble is, there are advantages and disadvantages to using all of these alternative fuels too.

Learning Objectives:

- Know that ethanol and biodiesel are biofuels, and that biofuels are produced from plants.

- Know that hydrogen gas can also be used as an alternative fuel.

- Understand the advantages and disadvantages of using alternative fuels.

Specification Reference C1.4.3

Developing alternative fuels

Some alternative fuels have already been developed, and there are others in the pipeline (so to speak). Many of them are renewable fuels so, unlike fossil fuels, they won't run out. However, none of them are perfect — they all have pros and cons.

Biofuels

Biofuels are fuels that are made from plant material. There are two types of biofuel you need to know about — ethanol and biodiesel.

Ethanol

Ethanol's made by fermentation of plants and is used to power cars in some places. It's often mixed with petrol to make a better fuel. Here are some of the advantages of using ethanol as a fuel.

- The CO_2 released when ethanol is burnt was taken in by the plant as it grew, so it's 'carbon neutral'. The only other product when ethanol burns is water and the process of making ethanol doesn't require much energy, so ethanol is better for the environment than fossil fuels.

- Ethanol is a renewable resource because it's made from plants.

- Growing the crops to make ethanol is labour intensive so provides employment for local people.

Disadvantages of using ethanol include:

- Engines need to be converted before they'll work with ethanol fuels.

- Ethanol fuel isn't widely available.

- There are worries that as demand for it increases farmers will switch from growing food crops to growing crops to make ethanol — this will increase food prices.

Tip: Fuels are described as carbon neutral if there is no net release of carbon dioxide when the fuel is burnt — any carbon dioxide released into the atmosphere when the fuel burns was taken out of the atmosphere when the fuel was made.

Biodiesel

Biodiesel can be produced from vegetable oils such as rapeseed oil and soybean oil. It can be mixed with ordinary diesel fuel and used to run a diesel engine. Here are some of the advantages of using biodiesel.

- Like ethanol, biodiesel is 'carbon neutral', renewable and provides jobs for local people.

- Engines don't need to be converted before they can run on biodiesel.

- Biodiesel produces much less sulfur dioxide and 'particulates' than ordinary diesel or petrol.

Figure 1: *A biodiesel fuel pump.*

Disadvantages of using biodiesel include:

- We can't make enough to completely replace diesel.
- Biodiesel is expensive to make.
- It could increase food prices like using more ethanol could.

Hydrogen gas

Hydrogen gas can also be used to power vehicles. You get the hydrogen from the electrolysis of water — but it takes electrical energy to split it up. This energy can come from a renewable source, e.g. solar. Some of the advantages of using hydrogen gas include:

- Hydrogen combines with oxygen in the air to form just water — so it's very clean.
- The hydrogen gas comes from water and there's lots of water about.

Here are some of the disadvantages of using hydrogen gas:

- You need a special, expensive engine to use hydrogen as a fuel.
- Hydrogen isn't widely available as a fuel.
- You still need to use energy from another source to make it.
- Hydrogen's hard to store because it is extremely flammable.

> **Tip:** Electrolysis of water means using electricity to split water up into hydrogen and oxygen.

Figure 2: Hydrogen powered vehicles.

Practice Questions — Fact Recall

Q1 What is a biofuel? Give two examples of biofuels.

Q2 Give one advantage and one disadvantage of using ethanol as a fuel.

Q3 What is biodiesel made from?

Practice Questions — Application

Q1 A distribution company wants to reduce its impact on the environment. Its fleet of distribution vans currently runs on diesel fuel. Suggest a way that this company could become more environmentally friendly without having to replace all of the vans it already has.

Q2 A company makes hydrogen gas from the electrolysis of water. The electricity needed for this process comes from a fossil fuel power station. The company claims that their hydrogen is a completely clean fuel because the only product formed when hydrogen burns is water.

a) Explain why this claim is incorrect.

b) What could the company do to make its hydrogen a completely clean fuel?

Section Checklist — Make sure you know...

Fractional Distillation of Crude Oil

☐ That crude oil is a mixture of many different compounds, most of which are hydrocarbons (compounds made from only hydrogen and carbon).

☐ That the substances in a mixture are not chemically bonded to each other.

☐ That the substances in a mixture keep all of their original properties (e.g. boiling point) and so can be separated from each other using physical methods (e.g. distillation).

☐ How crude oil can be separated into fractions using fractional distillation.

Properties and Uses of Crude Oil

☐ That most of the compounds in crude oil are a type of hydrocarbon known as alkanes and how to recognise alkanes from either their chemical formula or their displayed structure.

☐ The chemical formulae and displayed structures of methane, ethane, propane and butane.

☐ That alkanes have the general formula C_nH_{2n+2} and are described as saturated hydrocarbons because all of the atoms in an alkane have formed bonds with as many other atoms as they possibly can.

☐ That the shorter the molecules the less viscous a hydrocarbon is, the more volatile a hydrocarbon is and the more flammable a hydrocarbon is.

☐ Why alkanes with different properties are used in different ways.

Environmental Problems

☐ That most fuels (including the fossil fuels coal, oil and natural gas) contain carbon and hydrogen.

☐ That when fuels are burnt, the carbon is oxidised to carbon dioxide, the hydrogen is oxidised to water and energy is released.

☐ That carbon monoxide, carbon particulates and unburnt fuel can be released if there is not enough oxygen available when a fuel burns (this is called partial combustion).

☐ **H** How to write balanced symbol equations for the complete and partial combustion of fuels.

☐ That sulfur dioxide can be released when a fuel burns if the fuel contains sulfur impurities and oxides of nitrogen can be released if the fuel burns at a high temperature.

☐ That sulfur dioxide and nitrogen oxides can cause acid rain if they mix with the water in clouds.

☐ That acid rain can be reduced by removing sulfur from fuels before they are burnt, or by removing sulfur dioxide from waste gases before they are released.

☐ That carbon dioxide contributes to global warming (a type of climate change) and that carbon particulates in the atmosphere may have caused global dimming.

Alternative Fuels

☐ That ethanol and biodiesel are examples of biofuels (fuels that are produced from plant material).

☐ That hydrogen gas (produced by electrolysis of water) can be used as a fuel source.

☐ The advantages and disadvantages of using each of these alternative fuels.

Exam-style Questions

1   Many modern cars use petrol as their fuel source.
Petrol is produced from crude oil via a process known as fractional distillation.

1 (a) (i)   Describe the process of fractional distillation.

(4 marks)

1 (a) (ii) Petrol is removed from near the top of the fractionating column.
What does this tell you about the hydrocarbons that make up petrol?

(1 mark)

1 (b)   *In this question you will be assessed on the quality of your English,
the organisation of your ideas and your use of appropriate specialist vocabulary.*

Outline the environmental impacts of using petrol as a fuel.

(6 marks)

2   Many scientists are developing alternatives to fossil fuels, such as biofuels.

2 (a)   Give **two** reasons why an alternative to fossil fuels is needed.

(2 marks)

2 (b)   Ethanol is an example of a biofuel. Ethanol is described as being 'carbon neutral'.

2 (b) (i)   Explain why ethanol is a 'carbon neutral' fuel.

(1 mark)

2 (b) (ii) Suggest **two** reasons why most people have not switched to using
ethanol powered cars.

(2 marks)

2 (c)   Biodiesel is another example of a biofuel.

2 (c) (i)   Biodiesel produces much less sulfur dioxide when it is burned
than normal diesel does. Explain why this is an advantage.

(2 marks)

2 (c) (ii) Discuss **one** positive and **one** negative social impact of producing
and using biodiesel.

(4 marks)

3   Alkanes are a type of saturated hydrocarbon.

3 (a)   What is the general formula of the alkanes?

(1 mark)

3 (b)   This table contains information about some common alkanes.

Alkane	Formula	Length of carbon chain
Propane	C_3H_8	3
Heptane	C_7H_{16}	7
Decane	$C_{10}H_{22}$	10

3 (b) (i) Which of the alkanes in the table is likely to be the least flammable?
Explain your answer.

(1 mark)

3 (b) (ii) Which of the alkanes in the table would be most suitable to use in bottled gas?
Explain your answer.

(2 marks)

3 (c)   Heptane is often found in fuels such as petrol.

3 (c) (i) Write a balanced symbol equation for the complete combustion of heptane.

(3 marks)

3 (c) (ii) Under what conditions would carbon monoxide form when heptane is burned?

(1 mark)

3 (c) (iii) Describe how oxides of nitrogen could be formed when heptane is burned.

(2 marks)

4   A town council wants to be more environmentally friendly and is planning to swap
its diesel powered buses for a fleet of buses that are powered by hydrogen gas.

4 (a)   Why is using hydrogen more environmentally friendly than using diesel?

(1 mark)

4 (b)   At a meeting, a number of the town's residents voiced concerns about the plan.
One of the main concerns raised was the cost of replacing all the town's buses.

4 (b) (i) Suggest **two** other concerns (besides cost) that the town's residents might have.

(2 marks)

4 (b) (ii) Suggest a cheaper option the town council could use for making its buses more
environmentally friendly. Explain your answer.

(3 marks)

1. Cracking Crude Oil

Some fractions of crude oil are more useful than others — for example, short-chain hydrocarbons are often more useful than long-chain hydrocarbons. Cracking is used to break long-chain hydrocarbons down into shorter ones.

What is cracking?

Long-chain hydrocarbons form thick gloopy liquids like tar which aren't all that useful, so a lot of the longer molecules produced from fractional distillation are turned into smaller ones by a process called **cracking**.

Some of the products of cracking are useful as fuels, like petrol for cars and paraffin for jet fuel. Cracking also produces substances like ethene, which are needed for making plastics (see page 81). The process of cracking is illustrated in Figure 1.

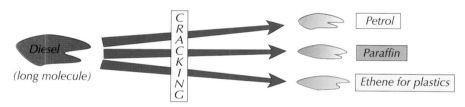

Figure 1: *Cracking. In this example, diesel (a long-chain hydrocarbon) is being broken down into the shorter-chain hydrocarbons petrol, paraffin and ethene.*

Learning Objectives:

- Know that cracking is a process used to convert large hydrocarbon molecules into smaller, more useful hydrocarbons.
- Know that cracking produces some products that can be used as fuels.
- Know that cracking is a thermal decomposition reaction.
- Know that cracking involves heating the hydrocarbon and passing it over a catalyst or mixing it with steam at very high temperatures.
- Know that cracking produces alkanes and alkenes.

Specification Reference C1.5.1

How cracking works

Cracking is a **thermal decomposition** reaction — breaking molecules down by heating them. The first step is to heat the long-chain hydrocarbon to vaporise it (turn it into a gas). The vapour can then be passed over a powdered catalyst at a temperature of about 400 °C – 700 °C. Aluminium oxide is one of the catalysts used. The long-chain molecules split apart or "crack" on the surface of the specks of catalyst — see Figure 3.

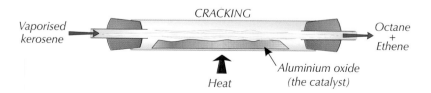

Figure 3: *The cracking of kerosene into octane and ethene using an aluminium oxide catalyst.*

Figure 2: *A catalytic cracker at an oil refinery.*

Tip: Broken pottery can be used as a catalyst for cracking because the pottery contains aluminium oxide.

Alternatively, the vapour can be mixed with steam and heated to a very high temperature. This will also lead to thermal decomposition of long-chain hydrocarbon molecules to form smaller ones.

Products of cracking

Most of the products of cracking are **alkanes** and unsaturated hydrocarbons called **alkenes**.

Tip: See page 64 for more about alkanes and page 79 for more about alkenes.

Figure 4: *Kerosene — one of the less useful products from crude oil.*

Tip: Kerosene is also known as decane.

Example

Kerosene is a long-chain hydrocarbon molecule (it has 10 carbon atoms). There's lots of kerosene in crude oil, but kerosene itself isn't that useful. Cracking is used to break kerosene down into octane and ethene (see Figure 5). Octane is a shorter-chain alkane which is useful for making petrol. Ethene is an alkene which is useful for making plastics.

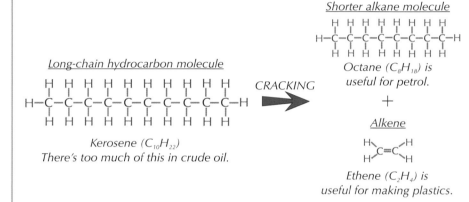

Figure 5: *The cracking of kerosene into an alkane (octane) and an alkene (ethene).*

Practice Questions — Fact Recall

Q1 a) What is cracking and why is it useful?

   b) Give two things that the products of cracking can be used for.

Q2 What type of reaction is cracking?

Q3 a) Describe how an aluminium oxide catalyst can be used to crack a long-chain hydrocarbon.

   b) How can cracking be performed without using a catalyst?

Q4 Name two types of hydrocarbon that are produced in cracking.

2. Using Crude Oil

We use fractions of crude oil for loads of different things,
but we need to watch out — there are problems with using it.

Learning Objective:

- Understand the advantages and disadvantages of using crude oil products as fuels and as raw materials for making plastics and other chemicals.

Specification Reference C1.5

Why do we use crude oil?

There are lots of advantages to using crude oil. Crude oil fractions release lots of energy when they burn and they burn cleanly, so they make good fuels. Most modern transport is fuelled by a crude oil fraction, e.g. cars, boats, trains and planes. Parts of crude oil are also burned in central heating systems in homes and in power stations to generate electricity.

There's a massive industry with scientists working to find oil reserves, take it out of the ground, and turn it into useful products. As well as fuels, crude oil also provides the raw materials for making various chemicals, including plastics.

Often, alternatives to using crude oil fractions as fuel are possible. For example, electricity can be generated by nuclear power or wind power, there are ethanol-powered cars, and solar energy can be used to heat water. But things tend to be set up for using oil fractions so crude oil fractions are often the easiest and cheapest thing to use.

Figure 1: *An offshore oil rig.*

Example

Cars are designed for petrol or diesel and it's readily available. There are filling stations all over the country, with storage facilities and pumps specifically designed for these crude oil fractions.

Crude oil fractions are often more reliable than other energy sources too. For example, solar and wind power won't work without the right weather conditions, whereas crude oil can be used any time. Nuclear energy is reliable, but there are lots of concerns about its safety and the storage of radioactive waste.

Disadvantages of using crude oil

There are two major disadvantages to using crude oil.

1. It's bad for the environment

Oil spills can happen as the oil is being transported by tanker — this spells disaster for the local environment. Birds get covered in the stuff and are poisoned as they try to clean themselves. Other creatures, like sea otters and whales, are poisoned too.

You also have to burn oil to release the energy from it. But burning oil is thought to be a major cause of global warming, acid rain and global dimming.

Figure 2: *Volunteers cleaning up an oil spill.*

Tip: See pages 67 and 68 for more on acid rain, global warming and global dimming.

2. Crude oil is non-renewable

Most scientists think that oil will run out — it's a non-renewable fuel. No one knows exactly when it'll run out but there have been heaps of different predictions — for example, about 40 years ago, scientists predicted that it'd all be gone by the year 2000. New oil reserves are discovered from time to time and technology is constantly improving, so it's now possible to extract oil that was once too difficult or expensive to extract.

In the worst-case scenario, oil may be pretty much gone in about 25 years — and that's not far off. Some people think we should immediately stop using oil for things like transport, for which there are alternatives, and keep it for things that it's absolutely essential for, like some chemicals and medicines.

It will take time to develop alternative fuels that will satisfy all our energy needs (see page 70 for more info). It'll also take time to adapt things so that the fuels can be used on a wide scale. For example, we might need different kinds of car engines, or special storage tanks built.

One alternative is to generate energy from renewable sources — these are sources that won't run out. Examples of renewable energy sources are wind power, solar power, tidal power and biofuels. So however long oil does last for, it's a good idea to start conserving it and finding alternatives now.

Tip: Deciding whether or not to continue using non-renewable resources like crude oil is an important decision that society has to make.

HOW SCIENCE WORKS

Practice Questions — Fact Recall

Q1 Why do crude oil fractions make good fuels?

Q2 a) Suggest an alternative energy source that can be used instead of crude oil.

b) Give two reasons why crude oil fractions are still used for fuels even though alternatives are available.

Q3 Give two reasons why using crude oil can be bad for the environment.

Q4 40 years ago, scientists predicted that all the crude oil would be gone by the year 2000. Explain why this prediction did not come true.

Q5 Some people think that we should stop using oil as a fuel for transport immediately. Explain why people might think this.

3. Alkenes and Ethanol

Alkenes are really useful. You can make alkenes by cracking long-chain hydrocarbon molecules that come from crude oil. Once you have an alkene, you can use it to make loads of cool stuff, including ethanol.

Learning Objectives:
- Know that alkenes are a type of unsaturated hydrocarbon with the general formula C_nH_{2n}.
- Be able to recognise alkenes from their chemical and displayed formulae.
- Know how to test for alkenes using bromine water.
- Know how ethene can be used to produce ethanol.
- Know how ethanol can be produced from sugars by fermentation.
- Understand the advantages and disadvantages of making ethanol from both ethene and sugar.

Specification Reference
C1.5, C1.5.1, C1.5.3

What are alkenes?

Alkenes are hydrocarbons which have a double covalent bond between two of the carbon atoms in their chain — see Figure 1.

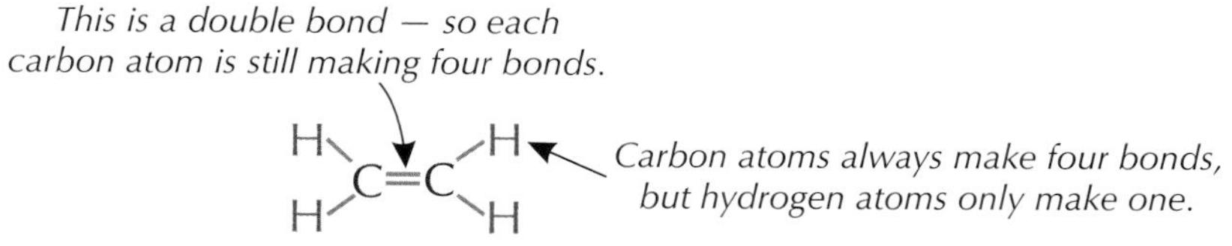

This is a double bond — so each carbon atom is still making four bonds.

Carbon atoms always make four bonds, but hydrogen atoms only make one.

Figure 1: *An alkene — all alkenes have a double bond in them.*

Alkenes are known as **unsaturated** because you can add more atoms to them — the double bond can open up, allowing the two carbon atoms to bond with other atoms. The first two alkenes are ethene (with two carbon atoms) and propene (three carbon atoms) — see Figure 2.

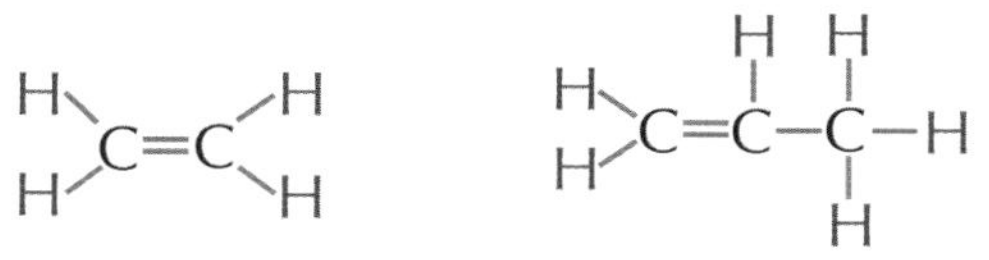

Ethene (C_2H_4)   *Propene (C_3H_6)*

Figure 2: *The structures of ethene and propene.*

All alkenes have the general formula C_nH_{2n} — they have twice as many hydrogens as carbons. You can use this general formula to recognise alkenes in your exam. If a molecule only has hydrogen and carbon atoms in it, and there are twice as many hydrogens as carbons, then it must be an alkene. You can also recognise alkenes from a displayed formula by looking out for the carbon-carbon double bond.

Exam Tip
If you're asked to give the general formula of the alkenes, make sure you give the C and the H as capital letters and the n and the 2n as subscript. If you just write cnh2n, you won't get the mark.

Testing for alkenes

You can test for an alkene by adding the substance to bromine water. An alkene will decolourise the bromine water, turning it from orange to colourless — see Figures 3 and 4. This is because the double bond has opened up and formed bonds with the bromine.

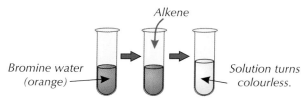

Alkene

Bromine water (orange)

Solution turns colourless.

Figure 4: *Using bromine water to test for alkenes.*

Figure 3: *The orange to colourless colour change when an alkene is added to bromine water.*

Making ethanol from ethene

Tip: Ethanol is an alcohol. There's lots more on alcohols on page 267.

Ethene (C_2H_4) can be reacted with steam (H_2O) in the presence of a catalyst to make ethanol. This is called a hydration reaction. At the moment this is a cheap process, because ethene's fairly cheap and not much of it is wasted. The trouble is that ethene's produced from crude oil, which is a non-renewable resource that could start running out fairly soon. This means using ethene to make ethanol will become very expensive.

Making ethanol from sugars

The alcohol in beer and wine, etc. isn't made from ethene — it's made by **fermentation**. The raw material for fermentation is sugar. This is converted into ethanol using yeast. The word equation for this is:

$$\text{sugar} \;\rightarrow\; \text{carbon dioxide} \;+\; \text{ethanol}$$

Tip: Weighing up the relative advantages and disadvantages of two techniques (like these two techniques for making ethanol) is an important skill that all scientists need. *HOW SCIENCE WORKS*

This process needs a lower temperature and simpler equipment than when making ethanol using ethene. It also requires less energy and therefore results in less CO_2 production, so fermentation is better for the environment. Another advantage is that the raw material is a renewable resource. Sugar is grown as a major crop in several parts of the world, including many poorer countries.

The ethanol produced this way can also be used as quite a cheap fuel in countries which don't have oil reserves for making petrol. There are disadvantages though. The ethanol you get from this process needs to be purified and it isn't very concentrated, so if you want to increase its strength you have to distil it (as in whisky distilleries). There are also concerns that growing more sugar to make ethanol could lead to more deforestation.

Practice Questions — Fact Recall

Q1 Draw the chemical structure of propene.

Q2 Explain why alkenes are described as unsaturated.

Q3 a) Give two techniques that can be used to produce ethanol.

    b) Discuss the advantages and disadvantages of each of these techniques.

Practice Questions — Application

Q1 A chemist has mixed up his bottles of propane and propene. When he adds bromine water to bottle A the resulting solution is colourless. When he adds bromine water to bottle B the resulting solution is orange. Which bottle contains propene and which contains propane?

Q2 Which of these is an alkene?

    A: C_5H_{12} B: $C_3H_6Cl_2$ C: C_4H_8 D: C_2H_4O

4. Using Alkenes to Make Polymers

Ethanol isn't the only thing you can make from alkenes. Lots of alkenes are used to make polymers. Plastics are polymers... and we all know how useful plastics are.

Polymerisation

Probably the most useful thing you can do with alkenes is **polymerisation**. This means joining together lots of small alkene molecules (**monomers**) to form very large molecules — these long-chain molecules are called **polymers**.

Example

Many ethene molecules can be joined up to produce poly(ethene) or "polythene".

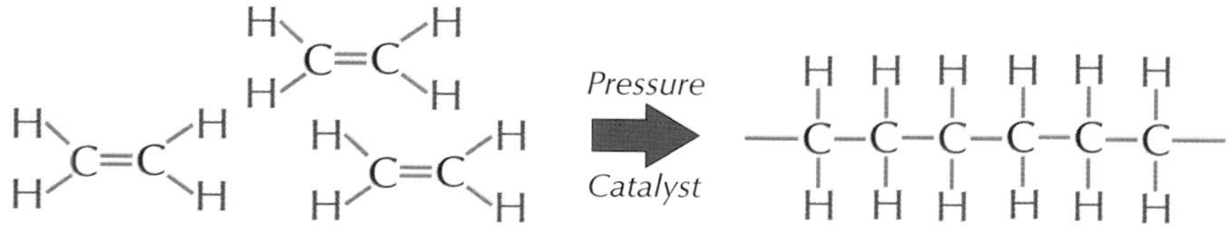

Many ethene monomers

Pressure / *Catalyst*

A section of poly(ethene)

This reaction can be shown like this...

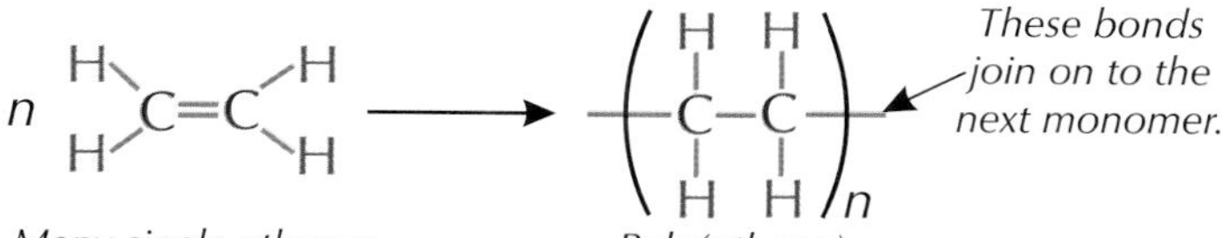

Many single ethenes

Poly(ethene)

These bonds join on to the next monomer.

... where *n* is a very large number of monomers.

For the exam you need to know the structures of poly(ethene) and one other polymer, called poly(propene). Poly(propene) is made when lots of propene monomers join together (see Figure 1).

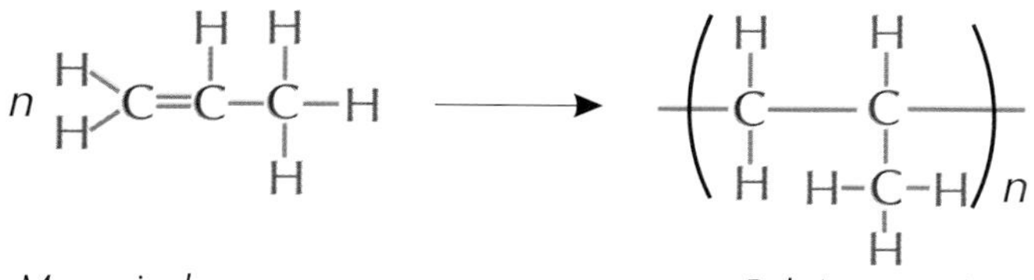

Many single propenes

Poly(propene)

Figure 1: *The polymerisation of propene monomers to form poly(propene).*

Learning Objectives:

- Know that alkenes can undergo polymerisation reactions to form polymers.
- Know how to show the formation of polymers from monomers.
- Know some of the main uses of polymers.
- Know that many polymers are difficult to dispose of because they aren't biodegradable.
- Know that biodegradable polymers are being developed and understand why this is important.

Specification Reference C1.5, C1.5.2

Tip: The polymers that are made from alkenes are called <u>addition polymers</u>, because they're formed by <u>adding</u> lots of alkenes together.

Tip: The names of polymers can be written with or without brackets. E.g. poly(ethene) or polyethene.

Finding monomers and naming polymers

In the exam, you might be given a polymer and asked to draw the monomer that makes it. All you have to do is take the bit of the polymer that repeats, remove the bonds from either side and add a double bond into it.

Example

The monomer that makes this polymer is...

Tip: To find the polymer that is made from a monomer you do the opposite — take out the double bond and add bonds to either side.

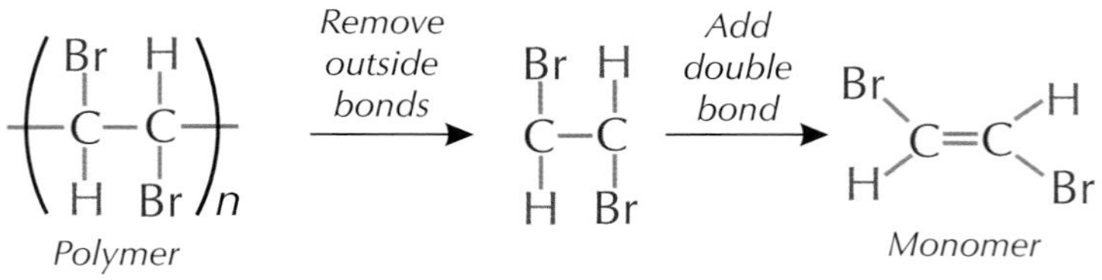

You could also be asked to name a polymer that you haven't come across before. Naming polymers is easy. All you have to do is put 'poly' in front of the name of the monomer.

Example

The polymer that is formed from but-2-ene is called poly(but-2-ene).

The polymer that is formed from bromoethene is called poly(bromoethene).

Exam Tip
You don't have to learn any of these names. You'll be given the name of the monomer if you need to name a polymer in the exam — you just need to remember to add 'poly' to it.

Properties and uses of polymers

The physical properties of a polymer depend on what it's made from. Polyamides are usually stronger than poly(ethene), for example.

A polymer's physical properties are also affected by the temperature and pressure of polymerisation. Poly(ethene) made at 2000 atmospheres pressure and 200 °C is flexible, and has low density. But poly(ethene) made at 60 °C and a few atmospheres pressure with a catalyst is rigid and dense.

The fact that different polymers have different properties means they are useful for different things.

Examples

- Light, stretchable polymers such as low density poly(ethene) are used to make plastic bags.
- Elastic polymer fibres are used to make super-stretchy LYCRA® fibre for tights.

New uses for polymers are developed all the time. Some waterproof coatings for fabrics are made of polymers, and so are many new packaging materials. Dental polymers are used in resin tooth fillings. Polymer hydrogel wound dressings keep wounds moist.

Memory foam is an example of a **smart material**. It's a polymer that gets softer as it gets warmer. Mattresses can be made of memory foam — they mould to your body shape when you lie on them.

Tip: The properties of smart materials can change in response to external stimuli, like heat or pressure.

Problems with using polymers

Most polymers aren't "**biodegradable**" — they're not broken down by microorganisms, so they don't rot. This means it's difficult to get rid of them — if you bury them in a landfill site, they'll still be there years later. The best thing is to reuse them as many times as possible and then recycle them if you can. However, new biodegradable packaging materials are being developed. Plastic bags and other biodegradable plastics made from polymers and cornstarch are being produced.

Things made from polymers are usually cheaper than things made from metal. However, as crude oil resources get used up, the price of crude oil will rise. Crude oil products like polymers will get dearer. It may be that one day there won't be enough oil for fuel and plastics and all the other uses. Choosing how to use the oil that's left means weighing up advantages and disadvantages on all sides.

Figure 2: *Plastic waste in a landfill site.*

Practice Questions — Fact Recall

Q1 Describe what happens during a polymerisation reaction.

Q2 Give two factors that affect the physical properties of a polymer.

Q3 What property of memory foam makes it a good material to make mattresses out of?

Q4 a) What does the term biodegradable mean?

b) Are most polymers biodegradable or non-biodegradable?

Q5 Explain why the cost of making things from polymers is likely to rise in the future.

Practice Questions — Application

Q1 What is the name of the polymer that is formed from chloroethene?

Q2 Draw the monomers that each of these polymers are made from:

a)
$$\left(\begin{array}{cc} \overset{\displaystyle F}{\underset{\displaystyle H}{C}} & \overset{\displaystyle H}{\underset{\displaystyle H}{C}} \end{array}\right)_n$$

b)
$$\left(\begin{array}{cc} \overset{\displaystyle F}{\underset{\displaystyle F}{C}} & \overset{\displaystyle F}{\underset{\displaystyle F}{C}} \end{array}\right)_n$$

Q3 Draw the polymer that would be formed from each of these monomers:

a)
$$\overset{H}{\underset{H}{}}C=C\overset{H}{\underset{Br}{}}$$

b)
$$\overset{H}{\underset{H}{}}C=C\overset{H}{\underset{OH}{}}$$

Section Checklist — Make sure you know...

Cracking Crude Oil

☐ That long-chain hydrocarbons can be broken down into shorter, more useful hydrocarbons using a process known as cracking.

☐ That some of the products that are made when long-chain molecules are cracked are useful as fuels, while others are useful as raw materials for making other substances, such as plastics.

☐ That cracking is a type of thermal decomposition reaction (a reaction where molecules are broken down by heating them).

☐ That the first step in the cracking process is to vaporise the long-chain hydrocarbon (turn it into a gas). The vapour is then passed over an aluminium catalyst at high temperatures (around 400 - 700 °C) or mixed with steam and heated to a very high temperature.

☐ That cracking can be used to produce alkanes and alkenes.

Using Crude Oil

☐ That using crude oil is bad for the environment because oil spills can occur when the oil is transported and burning crude oil contributes to global warming, global dimming and acid rain.

☐ That crude oil is a non-renewable resource and will eventually run out.

☐ Some of the advantages and disadvantages of using products from crude oil.

Alkenes and Ethanol

☐ That alkenes are unsaturated hydrocarbons that contain a carbon-carbon double bond and have the general formula C_nH_{2n}.

☐ That alkenes are described as unsaturated because the double bond can open up, allowing the two carbon atoms to bond with other atoms.

☐ How to recognise alkenes like ethene and propene from their chemical and displayed formulae.

☐ How bromine water can be used to test for the presence of alkenes in a solution.

☐ That ethanol can be made by hydrating ethene with steam in the presence of a catalyst.

☐ That ethanol can also be produced by fermenting sugars.

☐ The relative advantages and disadvantages of using ethene and fermentation to produce ethanol.

Using Alkenes to Make Polymers

☐ That many small alkene molecules (monomers) can be joined together to form long polymers.

☐ How to represent polymerisation reactions using diagrams and how to find the monomer that is used to make a particular polymer (and vice versa).

☐ How the properties of a polymer influence what the polymer is used for.

☐ That most polymers are non-biodegradable and this makes them difficult to dispose of.

☐ That new biodegradable polymers are being developed that contain cornstarch.

Exam-style Questions

1   Polyvinyl chloride (PVC) is a very commonly used type of plastic.
This diagram shows the structure of PVC.

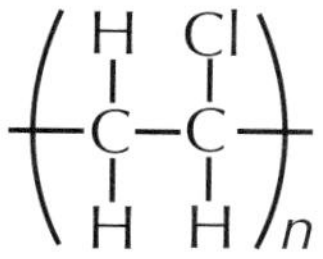

$$\left(\begin{array}{cc} H & Cl \\ | & | \\ -C-C- \\ | & | \\ H & H \end{array}\right)_n$$

1 (a)   Draw the monomer that can be used to make PVC.

(2 marks)

1 (b)   The monomer used to make PVC can be made from ethene (C_2H_4).
Ethene is produced from fractions of crude oil by a process called cracking.

1 (b) (i)   What type of hydrocarbon is ethene?

(1 mark)

1 (b) (ii)   Describe how a fraction of crude oil could be cracked.

(4 marks)

1 (b) (iii)   Ethene can be used to make many things other than polymers.
Name the product that is made when ethene is reacted with steam
in the presence of a catalyst.

(1 mark)

2   Propene is an alkene. Like other alkenes, propene can undergo polymerisation.

2 (a) (i)   What is the general formula of an alkene?

(1 mark)

2 (a) (ii)   Are alkenes saturated or unsaturated? Explain your answer.

(2 marks)

2 (a) (iii)   Describe a chemical test that can be used to show that alkenes
are present in a solution

(2 marks)

2 (b) (i)   Give the name of the polymer that will be formed form propene.

(1 mark)

2 (b) (ii)   Describe what happens when propene undergoes polymerisation.

(2 marks)

2 (c)   Lots of people recycle polymers. Explain why it is important to
reduce the amount of polymer waste going into landfill sites.

(2 marks)

Learning Objectives:

- Know that you can extract oil from some plant material.
- Understand how oils can be extracted from oily fruits, seeds and nuts by crushing and pressing them.
- Understand how plant oils can be extracted using distillation.
- Know that vegetable oils are good foods because they contain energy and important nutrients.
- Be able to explain why vegetable oils are used to cook food.
- Know that vegetable oils can be turned into fuels.

Specification Reference C1.6.1

1. Plant Oils

You can get oils from lots of different plants. They're pretty useful too — they go into all sorts of food products and you can even turn them into fuels.

Extracting oils from plants

Some fruits, nuts and seeds contain a lot of oil.

> **Examples**
>
> - Avocados and olives are oily fruits.
> - Sesame oil, rapeseed oil and sunflower oil are all made from seeds.
> - Peanuts, almonds and walnuts are used to make nut oils.

Oil can be extracted from plant material by crushing and pressing it, or using distillation.

Crushing and pressing

One way to get the oil out is to crush the plant material. The crushed plant material is then pressed between metal plates to squash the oil out — see Figure 1. This is the traditional method of producing olive oil.

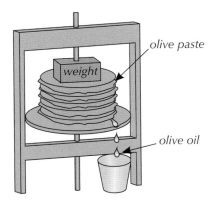

Figure 1: Extracting olive oil.

***Figure 2:** A working olive oil press.*

The oil needs to be separated from any water and crushed plant material that has been collected with it. This is often done using a centrifuge — the oily paste is spun round at very high speeds and this causes the oil and the water to separate out.

Distillation

Another way to extract oils from plant material is **distillation**. This is when you heat the plant material until the oils that are in it **evaporate**. Then you collect the vapour and cool it down so that it **condenses** back into pure liquid oil.

The plant material is usually heated using steam. Water is boiled to make the steam, which is then passed down a pipe and over the plant material. This method is usually used to extract oils from delicate plant material, like lavender flowers. The apparatus that you need for steam distillation is shown in Figure 3.

Tip: Distillation is also used to purify oils that have been extracted by pressing fruits, seeds or nuts. It's another way of getting rid of any water and impurities that have been collected along with the oil.

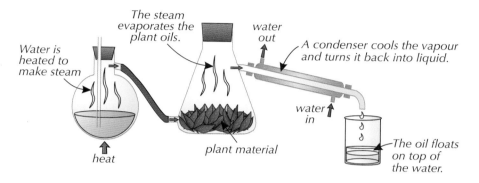

The steam evaporates the plant oils.

water out

A condenser cools the vapour and turns it back into liquid.

Water is heated to make steam

water in

heat

plant material

The oil floats on top of the water.

Figure 3: *Extracting plant oil using steam distillation.*

Tip: You can do a simpler version of this experiment by crushing up the plant material with some water and heating it directly. You'll still need a condenser to cool the vapour though.

Often the oil and water is collected in a funnel with a tap on the bottom, called a separating funnel. This means that you can just open the tap and run the water off, leaving the layer of pure oil behind.

Uses of plant oils

Plant oils are used for lots of things. They are used to flavour or cook food, and they can even be turned into fuels.

Using plant oils in food

Vegetable oils make good foods because they provide us with a lot of energy — they have a high energy content. There are lots of useful nutrients in vegetable oils too.

> **Examples**
>
> - Oils from seeds contain vitamin E.
> - Vegetable oils contain essential fatty acids, which the body needs for many metabolic processes.

Using plant oils to cook

There are a number of advantages of using oils to cook food. Vegetable oils have higher boiling points than water, so they can be used to cook foods at higher temperatures. This means that the food cooks faster.

Figure 4: *Cooking a stir fry. Because of the high temperature of the vegetable oil, the food cooks very quickly.*

Cooking with vegetable oil also gives food a different flavour. This is because of the oil's own flavour, but it's also down to the fact that many flavours come from chemicals that are soluble in oil. This means the oil 'carries' the flavour, making it seem more intense.

Using oil to cook food increases the energy we get from eating it. This makes it fattening — eating lots of food cooked in oil makes us put on weight.

Using plant oils as fuels

Vegetable oils such as rapeseed oil and soybean oil can be processed and turned into fuels. Because vegetable oils can provide a lot of energy they're really suitable for use as fuels.

Example

A particularly useful fuel made from vegetable oils is called **biodiesel**. Biodiesel has similar properties to ordinary diesel fuel — it burns in the same way, so you can use it to fuel a diesel engine.

Tip: There's more about biodiesel on page 70.

Practice Questions — Fact Recall

Q1 Plant oils can be extracted from fruits like olives by pressing them.

a) Outline the basic method that is used to extract oil from olives.

b) Give one way that the oil could be separated from any water and plant material that has been collected with it.

Q2 Some plant oils can't be extracted just by crushing the plant. Name one other way of extracting oils from plants.

Q3 Vegetable oils in food provide us with a lot of energy. Give one other reason why vegetable oils make good foods.

Q4 Cooking food in vegetable oil is quicker than cooking it in boiling water.

a) Explain why food cooks quicker in vegetable oil than in water.

b) Give one other advantage of cooking food in vegetable oil.

c) Give one disadvantage of cooking food in vegetable oil.

Q5 Vegetable oils can be turned into fuels.

a) Why are vegetable oils suitable for use as fuels?

b) Name one example of a fuel that is made from vegetable oils.

Tip: There's more about the advantages and disadvantages of using oils and fats in food coming up in the next topic.

2. Unsaturated Oils

Learning Objectives:
- Know that unsaturated oils contain carbon-carbon double bonds.
- Be able to describe a simple test for unsaturation in oils using bromine water.
- **H** Understand how unsaturated oils react with hydrogen in the presence of a nickel catalyst at 60 °C.
- **H** Know that the reaction with hydrogen is used to harden vegetable oils.
- **H** Be able to explain why hardened vegetable oils are useful.
- Know some of the health effects of using different oils and fats in foods.

Specification Reference
C1.6, C1.6.3

Vegetable oils, like olive oil, are liquids at room temperature, whereas animal fats, like lard, tend to be solid instead. This is down to whether they're saturated or unsaturated, and it affects what they can be used for.

What is an unsaturated oil?

Oils and fats contain long-chain molecules with lots of carbon atoms. They can be either **saturated** or **unsaturated**. Unsaturated oils contain double bonds between some of the carbon atoms in their carbon chains. Saturated fats don't contain any carbon-carbon double bonds.

There are two types of unsaturated fat. **Monounsaturated fats** contain one C=C double bond somewhere in their carbon chains. **Polyunsaturated fats** contain more than one C=C double bond.

Testing for unsaturation

You can test for unsaturation using bromine water. Bromine water is orange, but it will decolourise when you add an unsaturated oil to it (see Figure 1).

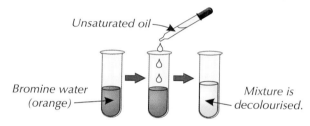

Unsaturated oil

Bromine water (orange) *Mixture is decolourised.*

Figure 1: *An unsaturated oil decolourises bromine water.*

Exam Tip
If an exam question asks you to give the result of the bromine water test, make sure you only use the words decolourised or colourless. Don't say 'clear' or 'transparent' — you won't get the mark.

Hydrogenation of unsaturated oils `Higher`

Unsaturated vegetable oils are liquid at room temperature. They can be hardened by reacting them with hydrogen in the presence of a nickel catalyst at about 60 °C. This is called **hydrogenation**. The hydrogen adds to the double-bonded carbons, opening out the double bonds.

`Example` — `Higher`

Hydrogenating the unsaturated hydrocarbon ethene makes the saturated hydrocarbon ethane.

$$H_2C=CH_2 + H_2 \xrightarrow[\text{nickel catalyst}]{60\ °C} H_3C-CH_3$$

ethene *ethane*

Hydrogenated oils have higher melting points than unsaturated oils, so they're more solid at room temperature. This means that they can be used as spreads — many margarines are made from hydrogenated vegetable oils.

Hydrogenated oils are used in the food industry for baking cakes and pastries. The oils are a lot cheaper than butter and they keep longer — this makes the products cheaper and gives them a long shelf life.

The more you hydrogenate an oil, the more saturated fat it will contain and the harder it will become. Fats are often only partially hydrogenated so that they don't become too solid.

Example — **Higher**

Margarine is usually made from partially hydrogenated vegetable oil — turning all the double bonds in vegetable oil to single bonds would make margarine too hard and difficult to spread. Hydrogenating most of them gives margarine a nice, buttery, spreadable consistency.

Figure 2: *A food information label. The markings show that this pie contains high levels of fat and saturated fat.*

Vegetable oils and health

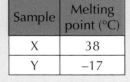

Vegetable oils tend to be unsaturated, while animal fats tend to be saturated. In general, saturated fats are less healthy than unsaturated fats, as saturated fats increase the amount of cholesterol in the blood, which can block up the arteries and increase the risk of heart disease. Unsaturated fats like olive oil reduce the amount of blood cholesterol.

Cooking food in oil, whether saturated, unsaturated or partially hydrogenated, makes it more fattening. That's why it's healthier to use cooking methods that don't involve oil.

Practice Questions — Fact Recall

Q1 What is the difference between a saturated oil and an unsaturated oil?

Q2 Describe a test that you could do to find out if an oil is unsaturated.

Q3 Unsaturated vegetable oils can by hydrogenated to harden them.

   a) Give the catalyst and the temperature used for this reaction.

   b) Give one use of hydrogenated vegetable oils.

Q4 Explain why unsaturated fats are healthier than saturated fats.

Practice Question — Application

Tip: [H] Remember, hydrogenating oils gets rid of double bonds.

Q1 The melting points of two samples of sunflower oil are shown in the table. One has been hydrogenated and the other has not.

Sample	Melting point (°C)
X	38
Y	−17

   a) Which sample is the hydrogenated oil? Explain your answer.

   b) Which sample will contain a higher proportion of unsaturated fat?

   c) What would you expect to see if bromine water was added to sample Y? Explain your answer.

3. Emulsions

When you mix a watery liquid and an oily fat together and shake you end up with an emulsion. Emulsions have loads of uses, especially in foods.

Making emulsions

Oils don't dissolve in water. However, you can mix an oil with water to make an **emulsion**. Emulsions are made up of lots of droplets of one liquid suspended in another liquid. You can make an emulsion by putting two liquids that don't mix (like oil and water) into a sealed container and giving it a really good shake.

There are two main types of emulsion — an oil-in-water emulsion (oil droplets suspended in water) or a water-in-oil emulsion (water droplets suspended in oil) — see Figure 1.

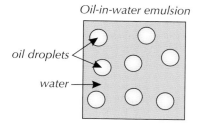
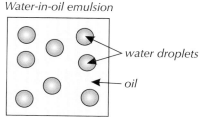

Figure 1: An oil-in-water emulsion and a water-in-oil emulsion.

Learning Objectives:

- Know that oils will not dissolve in water.
- Understand what an emulsion is.
- Know how to make an emulsion.
- Understand that an emulsion will have different properties from the liquids used to make it.
- Know some examples of emulsions.
- Know that an emulsifier will stop an emulsion from separating out.
- H Understand how emulsifier molecules can stop an emulsion separating out.
- Know the advantages and disadvantages of using emulsifiers in foods.

Specification Reference C1.6, C1.6.2

Uses of emulsions

Emulsions are thicker than either oil or water. Generally, the more oil you've got in an oil-in-water emulsion, the thicker it is. The physical properties of emulsions make them suited to lots of uses in food.

Examples

- Some salad dressings and sauces are emulsions. A salad dressing made by shaking olive oil and vinegar together forms an emulsion that coats salad better than plain oil or plain vinegar. An emulsified salad dressing has a smooth and glossy appearance too.

- Mayonnaise is an emulsion of sunflower oil (or olive oil) and vinegar — it's thicker than either.

- Milk is an oil-in-water emulsion with not much oil and a lot of water. There's about 3% oil in full-fat milk. Single cream has a bit more oil (about 18%). Double cream has lots of oil (nearly 50%) — that's why it's so much thicker than single cream.

- Whipped cream and ice cream are oil-in-water emulsions with an extra ingredient — air. Air is whipped into cream to give it a fluffy, frothy consistency for use as a topping. Whipping air into ice cream gives it a softer texture, which makes it easier to scoop out of the tub.

Figure 2: Some vinegar and oil in a bottle (left) and the emulsion that is formed when the bottle is shaken (right).

Emulsions also have non-food uses. Most moisturising lotions are oil-in-water emulsions. The smooth texture of an emulsion makes it easy to rub into the skin. Some paints are emulsions too — their creamy texture makes them easy to apply to the wall and gives them a smooth, even appearance when they dry.

Emulsifiers

Oil and water mixtures naturally separate out. **Emulsifiers** can be added to emulsions to make them more stable and stop them from separating.

> **Examples**
>
> - Lots of salad dressings contain emulsifiers, like egg yolk or lecithin. They help to keep the emulsion stable, so the dressing can sit on the shelf of a shop (or your cupboard) for a long time without separating out.
>
> - Ice creams often contain emulsifiers too — they help keep the texture of the product nice and smooth.

How emulsifiers work `Higher`

Emulsifiers are molecules with one part that's attracted to water and another part that's attracted to oil or fat (see Figure 3). The bit that's attracted to water is called **hydrophilic**, and the bit that's attracted to oil is called **hydrophobic**.

Hydrophilic head
(likes water, hates oil).
Hydrophobic tail
(likes oil, hates water).

Figure 3: *An emulsifier molecule.*

The hydrophilic end of each emulsifier molecule latches onto water molecules. The hydrophobic end of each emulsifier molecule attaches to oil molecules.

When you shake oil and water together with a bit of emulsifier, the oil forms droplets, surrounded by a coating of emulsifier with the hydrophilic bit facing outwards. Other oil droplets are repelled by the hydrophilic bit of the emulsifier, while water molecules latch on. So the emulsion won't separate out (see Figure 5).

Figure 4: *Emulsifiers in action. The salad dressing without an emulsifier (left) has separated out. The salad dressing with an emulsifier (right) has not separated.*

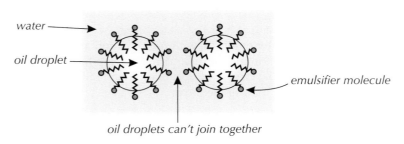

water

oil droplet

emulsifier molecule

oil droplets can't join together

Figure 5: *How emulsifier molecules prevent an emulsion separating out.*

Advantages and disadvantages of emulsifiers

You need to know the advantages and disadvantages of using emulsifiers.

Advantages

- Emulsifiers stop emulsions from separating out and this gives them a longer shelf-life.

- Emulsifiers allow food companies to produce food that's lower in fat but that still has a good texture.

Disadvantages

- Some people are allergic to certain emulsifiers. For example, egg yolk is often used as an emulsifier — so people who are allergic to eggs need to check the ingredients very carefully.

Tip: Low fat margarines contain less fat and more water than normal margarines. Emulsifiers help them to keep a nice spreadable texture. Otherwise you'd end up with a gunky mess of separated water, oils and hard fats.

Practice Questions — Fact Recall

Q1 Do oils dissolve in water?

Q2 a) Draw a simple diagram showing an oil-in-water emulsion.

b) Give one way that the physical properties of an oil-in-water emulsion will be different to the properties of either oil or water.

Q3 a) Name two food products that are emulsions.

b) Name one non-food product that is an emulsion.

Q4 a) What job does an emulsifier do?

b) Give one advantage and one disadvantage of using emulsifiers in food products.

Q5 a) Draw and label an emulsifier molecule.

b) Explain how emulsifier molecules stop an emulsion separating.

Practice Questions — Application

Q1 Kevin has 30 ml of olive oil and 10 ml of vinegar.
He wants to make them into an emulsion to use as a salad dressing.

a) Describe how Kevin could prepare the emulsion.

Anna is also making a salad dressing. She has the same amount of oil and vinegar as Kevin, but she decides not to mix them.

b) Which method will make a better salad dressing?
Explain your answer.

Q2 Polysorbate 80 is a commonly used emulsifier. What does this tell you about the structure of a molecule of Polysorbate 80?

Exam Tip
Make sure you can remember how to make an emulsion — it's a simple little detail, but it might just come up.

Section Checklist — Make sure you know...

Plant Oils

☐ That some plants contain oils which you can extract.

☐ How to get oils out of nuts, seeds and fruits by crushing and pressing them.

☐ How to get oils out of other plant material using distillation.

☐ That vegetable oils in food provide you with energy and useful nutrients.

☐ Why you might choose to cook food in vegetable oil rather than boiling water.

☐ That you can make fuels (like biodiesel) from vegetable oils because they contain lots of energy.

Unsaturated Oils

☐ That unsaturated oils have double bonds in their carbon chains.

☐ That an unsaturated oil will decolourise bromine water.

☐ H That an unsaturated oil will react with hydrogen in the presence of a nickel catalyst at 60 °C, opening out its double bonds. This is called hydrogenation.

☐ H That hydrogenation makes oils harder.

☐ H Some of the uses of hydrogenated vegetable oils.

☐ Why unsaturated oils are better for you than saturated fats.

☐ That all oils are fattening because they contain lots of energy.

Emulsions

☐ That oil does not dissolve in water.

☐ That an emulsion is a mixture where lots of tiny droplets of one liquid are suspended in another liquid.

☐ That you can make an emulsion by shaking water and oil in a sealed container.

☐ That an emulsion will be thicker than either the oil or water it was made from.

☐ That salad dressings, mayonnaise, ice creams, moisturisers and paints are examples of emulsions.

☐ That emulsifiers make emulsions more stable and stop them from separating out.

☐ H That an emulsifier molecule has a hydrophilic end and a hydrophobic end.

☐ H How emulsifier molecules stops emulsions from separating out.

☐ Some of the advantages and disadvantages of using emulsifiers in food products.

Exam-style Questions

1   A student tested whether some common kitchen substances could act as emulsifiers.

1 (a)   Explain why you might add an emulsifier to an emulsion.

(1 mark)

The student measured out oil and water into six test tubes. He added his test substances and shook each tube well. Then he timed how long it took for each emulsion to separate out. This table shows his results.

Tube	A	B	C	D	E	F
Substance added to oil and water	Nothing	Washing-up liquid	Salt	Sugar	Mustard	Vinegar
Time taken to separate (mins)	5	40	4.5	5	42	4.5

1 (b) (i)   Name the substance(s) in the table that can act as emulsifiers.

(1 mark)

1 (b) (ii)   Explain your answer to part **(i)**.

(2 marks)

2   Cottonseed oil is used in the food industry to make biscuits and as a cooking oil.

2 (a)   Suggest how oil could be extracted from cottonseeds.

(1 mark)

2 (b)   Cottonseed oil contains 25% saturated fat. Olive oil contains 15% saturated fat.
Explain why cottonseed oil might be considered less healthy than olive oil.

(2 marks)

2 (c)   Give **one** reason you might choose to cook a food in cottonseed oil rather than water.

(1 mark)

2 (d)   Before cottonseed oil can be used in baking it needs to be hardened.
Describe how this could be done.

(3 marks)

1. Plate Tectonics

When a scientist puts forward a theory it can be ages before that theory is generally accepted by the scientific community. A perfect example of this is Alfred Wegener and his theory of continental drift. Read on to find out more.

Wegener's theory of continental drift

The Earth's surface isn't smooth — it's covered in mountains and valleys. In the olden days, scientists thought that these structures were formed due to the surface of the Earth shrinking as the Earth cooled down after it was formed. But scientists now think that the Earth's surface is split up into big chunks called **tectonic plates** and that mountains are formed when these tectonic plates collide.

The idea that the Earth's surface is not stable and is made up of parts that move was first put forward by Alfred Wegener. He proposed a theory known as the theory of **continental drift**.

Wegener said that about 300 million years ago, there had been just one 'supercontinent'. This landmass, called Pangaea (see Figure 1), broke into smaller chunks which moved apart. He claimed that these chunks (our modern-day continents) were still slowly 'drifting' apart.

Figure 1: *Pangaea — what the Earth looked like 300 million years ago according to Wegener's theory.*

Evidence for continental drift

Alfred Wegener came across some work listing the fossils of very similar plants and animals which had been found on opposite sides of the Atlantic Ocean (see Figure 2).

Tip: This discovery suggested to Wegener that South America and Africa were once close together.

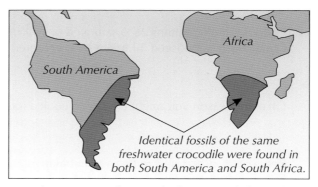

Identical fossils of the same freshwater crocodile were found in both South America and South Africa.

Figure 2: *Map showing the locations of identical fossils found in Africa and South America.*

He investigated further, and found other cases of very similar fossils on opposite sides of oceans.

Wegener had also noticed that the coastlines of Africa and South America seemed to 'match' like the pieces of a jigsaw. He wondered if these two continents had previously been one continent which then split. He started to look for more evidence, and found it.

Figure 3: *A Mesosaurus fossil. Fossils like this were used as evidence for continental drift.*

> **Example**
>
> There were matching layers in the rocks in different continents and fossils had been found in the 'wrong' places. Fossils of tropical plants had been discovered on Arctic islands, where the present climate would clearly have killed them off.

In 1915, Wegener felt he had enough evidence and he published his theory of "continental drift".

The reaction to Wegener's theory

The reaction from other scientists to Wegener's theory was mostly very hostile. A few scientists supported Wegener, but most of them didn't see any reason to believe such a strange theory. There were two main reasons why other scientists thought that Wegener's theory was wrong.

1. Wegener couldn't explain how the continents moved

The main problem was that Wegener's explanation of how the 'drifting' happened wasn't very convincing. At the time, other scientists thought that the continents were fixed and couldn't move and Wegener didn't have any evidence that the continents were moving.

Wegener thought that the continents were 'ploughing through' the sea bed, and that their movement was caused by tidal forces and the earth's rotation. Other geologists said this was impossible. One scientist calculated that the forces needed to move the continents like this would also have stopped the Earth rotating. (Which it hadn't.) Wegener had used inaccurate data in his calculations, so he'd made some rather wild predictions about how fast the continents ought to be moving apart.

Tip: Wegener's story is a classic example of how science works — someone puts forwards a theory, other scientists test the theory and when there's enough evidence to support it, the theory is accepted.

HOW SCIENCE WORKS

2. Land bridges could explain a lot of Wegener's evidence

Lots of Wegener's evidence for continental drift was based on things like similar fossils being found on the opposite sides of oceans and matching layers of rock on different continents.

Other people had noticed this too and in 1920, scientists came up with an alternative theory to explain Wegener's evidence. They thought that there had once been land bridges linking the continents — so animals had been able to cross (see Figure 4). The bridges had 'sunk' or been covered over since then.

Tip: Scientists accepted the land bridge theory because at the time it was the only explanation that made sense. We now know that the continents aren't fixed and it seems unlikely that land bridges would have existed... how times change.

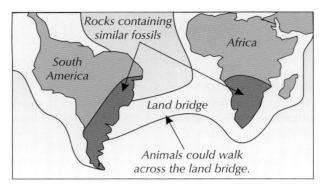

Figure 4: *Map showing how a land bridge could have once existed between South America and Africa.*

If Wegener's evidence could be explained by a different, more believable theory, why should they believe Wegener's theory of continental drift? It probably didn't help that Wegener wasn't a 'proper' geologist — he'd studied astronomy.

Acceptance of Wegener's theory

In the 1950s, scientists were able to investigate the ocean floor and found new evidence to support Wegener's theory. He wasn't right about everything, but his main idea was correct. By the 1960s, geologists were convinced. We now think the Earth's crust is made of several chunks called tectonic plates which move about, and that colliding chunks push the land up to create mountains.

Practice Questions — Fact Recall

Q1 a) How did scientists think that mountains were formed before Wegener's theory of continental drift?

b) How do scientists think that mountains are formed now?

Q2 Outline Wegener's theory of continental drift.

Q3 Wegener said that finding similar fossils on opposite sides of oceans was evidence that the continents were once close together. Suggest an alternative explanation.

2. The Earth's Structure

Wegener's theory of continental drift really made people think about what the structure of the Earth might be like. Now we know loads about the structure of the Earth... here's a summary.

The layers of the Earth

The Earth is almost spherical and it has a layered structure. The bit we live on, the **crust**, is very thin (it varies between 5 km and 50 km) and is surrounded by the **atmosphere**.

At the centre of the Earth is the **core**, which we think is made of iron and nickel. The core is the thickest layer of the Earth.

Surrounding that is the **mantle**. The mantle is about 2900 km thick and has all the properties of a solid, except that it can flow very slowly in convection currents. These convection currents are caused by the large amounts of heat produced by radioactive decay in the core below. The structure of the Earth is shown in Figure 1.

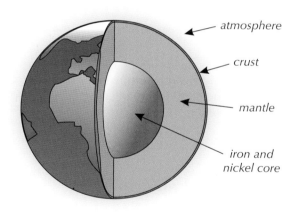

atmosphere

crust

mantle

iron and nickel core

Figure 1: *Structure of the Earth.*

Learning Objectives:

- Be able to describe the structure of the Earth with reference to the crust, mantle and core.
- Know that the Earth is surrounded by the atmosphere.
- Know that the heat generated by radioactive decay in the mantle causes convection currents.
- Know that the Earth's crust, atmosphere and oceans are the source of all our resources, including minerals.
- Understand that the Earth's crust is split up into tectonic plates.
- Know that movement of the tectonic plates is driven by convection currents.
- Understand that the tectonic plates mostly move very slowly, just a few cm per year, but that movements can be sudden.
- Know that earthquakes and volcanic eruptions occur at plate boundaries and understand why they are unpredictable.

Specification Reference C1.7, C1.7.1

The Earth's resources

The Earth's crust, oceans and atmosphere are the ultimate source of minerals and resources — we can get everything we need from them.

Examples

- Metals like gold and silver can be mined from the Earth's crust.
- We can get salt from the Earth's oceans.
- Gases like oxygen and nitrogen can be extracted from the atmosphere.

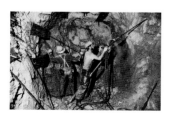

Figure 2: *Silver being mined from the Earth's crust.*

Tectonic plates

The crust and the upper part of the mantle are cracked into a number of large pieces called **tectonic plates**. These plates are a bit like big rafts that 'float' on the mantle.

Tip: The term 'mantle dynamics' can be used to describe the convection currents within the mantle.

The plates don't stay in one place though. That's because the convection currents in the mantle cause the plates to drift. The map in Figure 3 shows the edges of the plates as they are now, and the directions they're moving in (blue arrows).

Exam Tip
Don't panic! You don't need to know the names and locations of the plates for your exam. As long as you get the general concept you'll be fine.

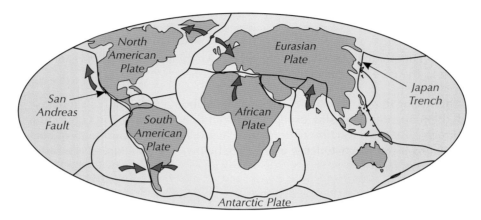

Figure 3: The tectonic plates that make up the surface of the Earth.

Tip: Alfred Wegener was the first person to suggest that the continents may drift. See page 96 for more on Wegener's theory of continental drift.

Most of the plates are moving at speeds of a few centimetres per year relative to each other. Occasionally, the plates move very suddenly, causing an earthquake. Volcanoes and earthquakes often occur at the boundaries between two tectonic plates.

Predicting earthquakes

Tectonic plates can stay more or less put for a while and then suddenly lurch forwards. Earthquakes are impossible to predict accurately because we can't see what's happening deep underground, but scientists are trying to find out if there are any clues that an earthquake might happen soon — things like strain in underground rocks.

Scientists can use these clues to predict that an earthquake will happen, but these predictions are sometimes ignored by local people and governments. Here are the reasons why.

- Even with all their clues scientists can only say that an earthquake's likely to happen, not that it definitely will happen. Scientists make many earthquake predictions every year and not all of them are right.

- If the earthquake does happen, it's impossible to predict exactly when. The earthquake could happen months after the initial prediction.

Figure 4: Damage to buildings following an earthquake.

- There's no way to accurately predict the strength of the earthquake. Many earthquakes cause little or no damage.

- Scientists can't accurately predict exactly where the earthquake will happen — it could be miles away from where it was initially predicted to happen.

- There's no way to stop an earthquake, so the only way that people can respond to a predicted earthquake is to evacuate. This is expensive and very inconvenient, so people don't want to evacuate unless they are sure that the earthquake will happen imminently, will happen where they live and will be strong enough to cause some serious damage and put their lives at risk.

Tip: The strength of an earthquake can be measured on the Richter scale.

Predicting volcanic eruptions

There are some clues that say a volcanic eruption might happen soon. Before an eruption, molten rock rises up into chambers near the surface, causing the ground surface to bulge slightly. This causes mini-earthquakes near the volcano. But sometimes molten rock cools down instead of erupting, so mini-earthquakes can be a false alarm.

Figure 5: A volcano erupting.

Practice Questions — Fact Recall

Q1 What is the outer layer of the Earth (the bit we live on) called?

Q2 Describe the properties of the mantle in terms of whether it is a solid or a liquid.

Q3 What do we think the Earth's core is made from?

Q4 What drives the movement of tectonic plates?

Q5 How quickly are most tectonic plates moving?

Q6 Where do earthquakes and volcanoes usually occur?

Q7 Give three things that scientists cannot accurately predict about an earthquake.

Practice Questions — Application

Q1 Catania is a city in Italy that is located near to an active volcano. In the last few days there have been some mini-earthquakes in the city and some of the residents are starting to evacuate.

a) Why are some of the residents evacuating?

b) Suggest why not all of the residents are evacuating.

Q2 Palmdale is a city in the USA. It lies on the San Andreas Fault, the location of which is shown in Figure 3 on page 100. Lots of earthquakes happen in Palmdale. Explain why.

Learning Objectives:
- Know that the composition of the atmosphere hasn't changed much in the last 200 million years.
- Know the relative abundances of nitrogen, oxygen and other gases in the atmosphere.
- Know that the early atmosphere and the oceans were formed due to volcanic activity.
- Know that one theory suggests that the early atmosphere was mainly made up of carbon dioxide.
- Know how carbon dioxide was removed from the atmosphere and that much of the carbon is now locked up in sedimentary rocks and fossil fuels.
- Know that the oxygen in the atmosphere was produced by plants and algae.
- Know that burning fossil fuels releases carbon dioxide back into the atmosphere and the environmental impacts this can have.
- **H** Understand how the gases in air can be separated using fractional distillation.

Specification Reference
C1.7.2

3. The Evolution of the Atmosphere

The Earth's atmosphere is really important — without it, life would never have evolved. This is the story of how the atmosphere came into being.

The atmosphere today

The Earth's **atmosphere** has been roughly as it is now for the last 200 million years or so. The main gases in the atmosphere are nitrogen and oxygen. Nitrogen is by far the most abundant gas — about four-fifths (80%) of the atmosphere is nitrogen. About one-fifth (20%) of the atmosphere is oxygen. There are small amounts of other gases in the atmosphere too. These include carbon dioxide, water vapour and noble gases (see page 22).

Formation of the early atmosphere and oceans

The Earth's surface was originally molten for many millions of years. It was so hot that any atmosphere just 'boiled away' into space. Eventually things cooled down a bit and a thin crust formed, but volcanoes kept erupting.

There was intense volcanic activity for the first billion years after the Earth was formed, and the volcanoes gave out lots of gas. Scientists think this was how the oceans and atmosphere were formed. There are lots of different theories, but the most popular theory suggests that the early atmosphere was probably mostly carbon dioxide (CO_2), with virtually no oxygen (O_2). There was probably water vapour too, and small amounts of methane (CH_4) and ammonia (NH_3). This is quite like the atmospheres of Mars and Venus today.

As the Earth cooled, the water vapour in the atmosphere condensed, forming the oceans.

Changes to the atmosphere

Although the early atmosphere was mostly carbon dioxide, it didn't stay that way for long. Most of the carbon dioxide was gradually removed from the atmosphere. This happened in a number of ways.

Absorption by the oceans

The oceans are a natural store of carbon dioxide. When the oceans formed, a lot of the carbon dioxide from the atmosphere dissolved into them.

Absorption by plants and algae

Green plants and algae evolved over most of the Earth. They absorbed some of the carbon dioxide in the atmosphere and used it for a process called **photosynthesis**. Photosynthesis produces oxygen as a by-product, so when the green plants and algae evolved, carbon dioxide was gradually removed from the atmosphere and oxygen was added.

Locking away the carbon

When the plants and algae that had absorbed the carbon dioxide died, they were buried under layers of sediment, along with the skeletons and shells of marine organisms that had slowly evolved. Some of the carbon inside these marine organisms was locked away as insoluble carbonates in sedimentary rocks.

Figure 1: *Limestone containing the fossilised remains of early marine organisms.*

> **Example**
>
> Limestone is a sedimentary rock that is formed from the shells and skeletons of marine organisms. A lot of the carbon from the carbon dioxide in the early atmosphere is now locked away in limestones.

Some of the carbon was locked away in fossil fuels such as coal and oil. These fossil fuels contain carbon and hydrocarbons that are the remains of plants and animals.

Problems of increasing carbon dioxide emissions

There is virtually no carbon dioxide left in the atmosphere now, but when we burn fossil fuels today, this 'locked-up' carbon is released and the concentration of carbon dioxide in the atmosphere rises. As the world has become more industrialised, more fossil fuels have been burnt in power stations and in car engines. This carbon dioxide is thought to be altering our planet in a couple of ways.

Global warming

An increase in carbon dioxide is causing **global warming** — an increase in the average temperature of the Earth. Global warming is a type of **climate change** and it could lead to dramatic changes in our weather.

Tip: See page 68 for more on global warming and climate change.

Acidic oceans

The oceans are a natural store of carbon dioxide — they absorb it from the atmosphere. However the extra carbon dioxide we're releasing is making them too acidic. This could lead to the death of many marine organisms including corals and shellfish. It also means that in the future the oceans won't be able to absorb any more carbon dioxide and this could accelerate global warming.

Fractional distillation of air   Higher

You can fractionally distil air to get a variety of products (e.g. nitrogen and oxygen) that can be used as raw materials in industry. The air is first filtered to remove dust. It's then cooled to around −200 °C and becomes a liquid. During cooling water vapour condenses and is removed. Carbon dioxide freezes, so that can be removed too.

Tip: Carbon dioxide that is extracted from the air in this way is used in some fire extinguishers.

The remaining gases are separated by **fractional distillation**. The fractional distillation of air is possible because the gases in air have different boiling points. This means that they will condense at different temperatures.

The liquefied air (with the water vapour and CO_2 removed) enters the fractionating column and is heated slowly so that it vaporises again. The gas then travels up the column and gradually cools. The different gases are extracted at the different levels in the column where they condense. Oxygen and argon come out together so another column is used to separate them.

The process of separating air is shown in Figure 2.

Tip: The fractional distillation of air is very similar to the fractional distillation of crude oil (see pages 61-62).

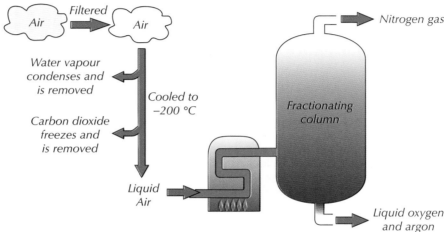

Figure 2: Separating air using fractional distillation.

Practice Questions — Fact Recall

Q1 What are the two most abundant gases found in the Earth's atmosphere today?

Q2 Describe the likely composition of the Earth's early atmosphere.

Q3 How did the Earth's oceans form?

Q4 Why did the evolution of green plants and algae lead to a decrease in the concentration of carbon dioxide in the atmosphere?

Q5 What happened to most of the carbon from the carbon dioxide in the early atmosphere?

Q6 a) Name the gas released when fossil fuels are burnt that is thought to be contributing to global warming.

b) How is the increase in the concentration of this gas in the atmosphere affecting the Earth's oceans?

Q7 Name the process that can be used to separate air into its component gases.

Figure 3: A fossil fuel power station.

Practice Questions — Application

Q1 This graph shows how the composition of gases in the atmosphere has changed over the last 4.5 billion years.

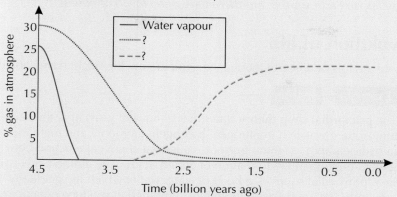

Tip: This graph is an estimate of how the composition of the atmosphere has changed over time. No one knows for sure how the atmosphere has changed so scientists have to use the evidence they have to make the best guess they can.

HOW SCIENCE WORKS

a) Describe and explain the change in the concentration of water vapour in the atmosphere between 4.5 and 4 billion years ago.

b) The other two lines on the graph are not labelled. Suggest which gases these lines represent, giving reasons for your answers.

Q2 This graph shows how the acidity of the oceans has changed over the last 150 years.

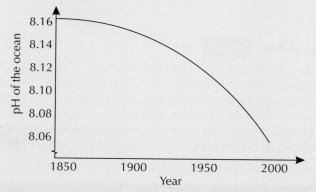

Tip: pH is a measure of how acidic something is — the lower the pH, the more acidic it is.

a) Describe how the pH of the oceans has changed over the last 150 years.

b) Suggest a possible explanation for this change.

c) What consequences could these changes have in the long term?

- Know that there are many theories to explain how life on Earth might have started.
- **H** Know that one of these theories is the primordial soup theory.
- **H** Understand why we don't know for certain how life began.

Specification Reference
C1.7, C1.7.2

4. Life on Earth

Living organisms have been around for billions of years. No one really knows how life on Earth started, but there have been lots of theories.

Evolution of life

There are lots of different theories to explain how life might have evolved.

Example **Higher**

The **primordial soup theory** states that billions of years ago, the Earth's atmosphere was rich in nitrogen, hydrogen, ammonia and methane (a hydrocarbon). Lightning struck, causing a chemical reaction between the gases, resulting in the formation of amino acids. The amino acids collected in a 'primordial soup' — a body of water out of which life gradually crawled. The amino acids gradually combined to produce organic matter which eventually evolved into simple living organisms.

In the 1950s, Miller and Urey carried out an experiment to prove this theory. They sealed a mixture of the relevant gases in their apparatus, heated them and applied an electrical charge for a week. They found that amino acids were made, but not as many as there are on Earth. This suggests the theory could be along the right lines, but isn't quite right.

The mystery of life   **Higher**

All the theories to explain how life began are just that — theories. We may never know for certain how or why life began. The problem is, life started about 3 billion years ago, so it's unlikely that any evidence of the earliest life forms will still be around today. We can guess, but we can't really know for sure what the conditions were like when life started and we don't yet have the capability to test a lot of the theories.

Practice Questions — Fact Recall

Q1 How did life begin according to the 'primordial soup' theory?

Q2 Explain why we can't be certain how life began.

Section Checklist — Make sure you know...

Plate Tectonics

☐ How scientists used to think mountains were formed and how they think mountains are formed now.

☐ That Alfred Wegener's theory of continental drift suggested that our modern day continents were originally one land mass (called Pangaea) which broke into chunks that gradually drifted apart.

☐ Why it took a long time for Wegener's theory of continental drift to be accepted.

cont...

The Earth's Structure

- [ ] That the Earth has a layered structure consisting of a core, a mantle and a crust and that the Earth is surrounded by an atmosphere.
- [ ] That the mantle is mostly solid but can flow very slowly and that radioactive decay in the core generates heat which drives convection currents in the mantle.
- [ ] That we can get all the minerals and other resources that we need from the Earth's crust, the atmosphere and the Earth's oceans.
- [ ] That the Earth's crust is divided into chunks called tectonic plates and that the movement of these tectonic plates is driven by the convection currents in the mantle.
- [ ] That movement of most tectonic plates is very slow (a few cm per year) but that earthquakes and volcanic eruptions can occur at the boundaries between tectonic plates if the plates move suddenly.
- [ ] Why earthquakes and volcanoes are difficult to predict and why scientists' predictions of earthquakes and volcanic eruptions are often ignored.

The Evolution of the Atmosphere

- [ ] That the composition of the atmosphere has been roughly the same for the last 200 million years — 80% nitrogen, 20% oxygen, with small amounts of carbon dioxide, water vapour and noble gases.
- [ ] That the early atmosphere was formed from gases that were released by volcanoes and that the oceans were formed when the Earth cooled, allowing the water vapour in the air to condense.
- [ ] That according to one theory, the early atmosphere was mostly carbon dioxide with small amounts of water vapour, methane (a hydrocarbon) and ammonia, but very little oxygen.
- [ ] That a lot of the CO_2 in the early atmosphere either dissolved into the oceans or was absorbed by green plants and algae when they evolved — there is now very little CO_2 left in the atmosphere.
- [ ] That green plants and algae used the CO_2 in photosynthesis — a process that produces oxygen.
- [ ] That when ancient plants, algae and marine organisms died, the carbon from the CO_2 they had absorbed was locked away in fossil fuels and as carbonates in sedimentary rocks.
- [ ] That burning fossil fuels today releases carbon dioxide back into the atmosphere.
- [ ] That the concentration of carbon dioxide in the atmosphere is increasing and that this is causing global warming and the oceans (which absorb CO_2) to become more acidic.
- [ ] [H] That fractional distillation can be used to separate air into it's component gases, according to their boiling point — these gases can then be used as raw materials in industry.
- [ ] [H] That prior to fractional distillation, air is filtered to remove dust and cooled to −200 °C so the water vapour and carbon dioxide can be removed from it.

Life on Earth

- [ ] That there are many theories as to how life on Earth might have begun.
- [ ] [H] That one theory is the primordial soup theory. This states that lightning struck causing a chemical reaction between nitrogen, hydrogen, hydrocarbons (like methane) and ammonia in the air, which led to the formation of amino acids.
- [ ] [H] Why it is impossible to know exactly how life started billions of years of ago.

Exam-style Questions

1   This diagram shows the structure of the Earth.

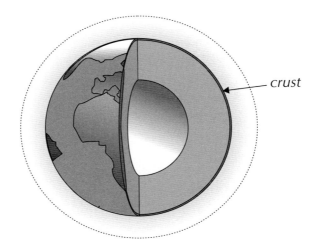

crust

1 (a)   Complete the diagram by labelling the atmosphere, the core and the mantle.

(3 marks)

1 (b)   The Earth's crust is divided into tectonic plates that move relative to one another.

1 (b) (i)   The idea that the continents move was first proposed by Alfred Wegener in 1915. Give **two** pieces of evidence that supported Wegener's theory of continental drift.

(2 marks)

1 (b) (ii)   Suggest why Wegener's theory was not initially accepted by other scientists.

(1 mark)

1 (c)   Scientists now know that the movement of tectonic plates is driven by convection currents in the mantle.

1 (c) (i)   What process produces the heat that drives the convection currents in the mantle?

(1 mark)

1 (c) (ii)   Complete this sentence describing the movement of tectonic plates.

Most tectonic plates move very ...., at a rate of a

few .... per year.

(2 marks)

1 (d) The movement of tectonic plates can be sudden. In 2011, sudden movements of tectonic plates caused an earthquake that resulted in a tsunami hitting Japan.

Put an X on the map to mark a possible location of the earthquake.

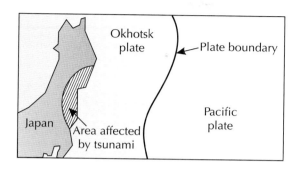

(2 marks)

2 The composition of the Earth's atmosphere has changed a lot over the last 4.5 billion years.

2 (a) Name the gas that is most abundant in our atmosphere today.

(1 mark)

2 (b) Scientists think that the most abundant gas in the atmosphere 4.5 billion years ago was carbon dioxide. Now, there is almost no carbon dioxide in our atmosphere.

2 (b) (i) Where did the gases that formed the early atmosphere come from?

(1 mark)

2 (b) (ii) Give **two** reasons why the concentration of carbon dioxide in the atmosphere decreased to the level that it is at today.

(2 marks)

2 (c) The burning of fossil fuels is now causing the concentration of carbon dioxide in the atmosphere to rise again. Give **two** environmental impacts that increased levels of carbon dioxide in the atmosphere may cause.

(2 marks)

2 (d) Some scientists believe that life may have evolved from the gases in the early atmosphere. Describe **one** theory to explain how life may have begun.

(3 marks)

Learning Objectives:
- Know that when atoms of more than one element are chemically joined together a compound is formed.
- Understand that bonding occurs when electrons are transferred or shared between atoms.
- Know that bonding occurs so that the outer shells of atoms are filled.

Specification Reference C2.1.1

1. Bonding in Compounds

You learnt a bit about compounds and bonding in Section 1.1, all the way back on pages 25-28. And here it is again, in a bit more detail this time...

What is a compound?

A **compound** is a substance that's formed when atoms of two or more elements are chemically combined. For example, carbon dioxide is a compound formed from a chemical reaction between carbon and oxygen. It's difficult to separate the two original elements out again.

Types of bonding

The two main types of bonding that you need to know about are **ionic bonding** (see pages 111-115) and **covalent bonding** (see pages 116-119). Both types of bonding occur because atoms prefer to have full outer shells of electrons, rather than part-filled shells.

A full outer shell gives an atom a stable electronic structure, just like a noble gas. Most atoms don't have a full outer shell though, so they either need to lose, gain or share electrons to achieve it.

Atoms can gain electrons from other atoms (this is part of ionic bonding), or by sharing electrons (covalent bonding). Atoms can lose electrons by giving them up to other atoms (also part of ionic bonding). Ionic and covalent bonding are covered in more detail over the next few pages. For now, the important things to remember are:

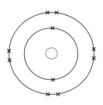

Figure 1: *The electronic structure of neon. Neon is a noble gas so has a full outer shell of electrons.*

- Atoms can form bonds by transferring electrons or sharing electrons.
- They do this so that they can achieve a stable electronic structure — a full outer shell of electrons.

Tip: Have a look back at pages 23-24 for how to work out electronic structures. They show how many electrons an atom needs to gain or lose to achieve a full outer shell.

Practice Questions — Fact Recall

Q1 What is a compound?

Q2 Name two types of bonding.

Q3 Why do atoms form chemical bonds?

Q4 Chemical bonds are formed when electrons are transferred between atoms. Give one other way that a chemical bond can be formed.

2. Ionic Bonding

There's loads to know about ionic bonding — what it is, how it works, the charges on ions, representing ions, working out formulae... So best crack on...

What is ionic bonding?

Ionic bonding is a strong electrostatic attraction between oppositely charged ions that holds ions in an ionic compound together. Electrostatic attraction is the force of attraction between negatively charged ions and positively charged ions. Here's how ionic bonding works...

All the metal atoms over at the left-hand side of the periodic table, for example, sodium, potassium and calcium, have just one or two electrons in their outer shell (highest energy level). They're keen to get rid of them, because then they'll have full shells, which is how they like it.

On the other side of the periodic table, the non-metal elements in Group 6 and Group 7, such as oxygen and chlorine, have outer shells which are nearly full. They're keen to gain that extra one or two electrons to fill the shell up.

When metals react with non-metals, electrons are transferred from the metal atoms to the non-metal atoms. The metal atoms lose electrons to become positively charged ions with a full outer shell of electrons. The non-metal atoms gain electrons and become negatively charged ions with a full outer shell of electrons. The oppositely charged ions are strongly attracted to each other, and this strong electrostatic attraction holds the ions together. This is known as ionic bonding.

Example

- A potassium atom has one electron in its outer shell.
- A chlorine atom has seven electrons in its outer shell.
- Potassium and chlorine react to form the compound potassium chloride, which is held together by ionic bonding.
- The potassium ion and the chloride ion both have full outer shells.

The potassium atom gives up its outer electron to the chlorine atom.

A positively charged potassium ion is formed.

A negatively charged chloride ion is formed.

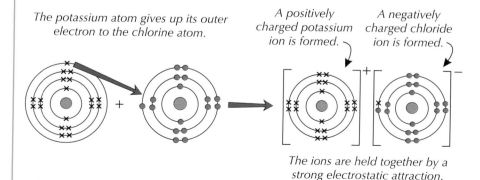

The ions are held together by a strong electrostatic attraction.

Figure 1: *The formation of potassium chloride.*

Charges on ions

The elements that most readily form ions are those in Groups 1, 2, 6 and 7. The charge on an ion depends on the number of electrons that have been lost or gained — and that depends on the number of electrons in their outer shell.

Tip: The charge on an ion depends on the number of protons and the number of electrons the ion contains. Have a look back at page 26 if you can't remember how to work out the charges on ions.

Examples

- Group 1 elements (the alkali metals) have one electron in their outer shell. So when they form an ion they lose one electron, which gives them a charge of 1^+. For example, K^+, Na^+, Li^+.

- Group 2 elements have two electrons in their outer shell. So they need to lose two electrons to achieve a stable electronic structure. This means they form ions with a charge of 2^+. For example, Be^{2+}, Ca^{2+}, Mg^{2+}.

- Group 7 elements (the halogens) have seven electrons in their outer shell. So when they form an ion they gain one electron, which gives them a charge of 1^-. For example, Cl^-, F^-.

- Group 6 elements have six electrons in their outer shell. So they need to gain two electrons to achieve a stable electronic structure. This means they form ions with a charge of 2^-. For example, O^{2-}.

The positive and negative charges we talk about, (for example Na^+ for sodium), just tell you what type of ion the atom will form in a chemical reaction. In sodium metal there are only neutral sodium atoms, Na. The Na^+ ions will only appear if the sodium metal reacts with something.

Formulae of compounds

Any of the positive ions mentioned above can combine with any of the negative ions to form an ionic compound. Only elements at opposite sides of the periodic table will form ionic compounds.

Tip: The reaction of an alkali metal with a halogen is the classic example of ionic bonding, so make sure you know how it works.

Example

- Group 1 elements will react with Group 7 elements to form ionic compounds.
- The metal ion in these ionic compounds has a single positive charge.
- The non-metal ion in the compound has a single negative charge.

The overall charge of any compound is zero. So all the negative charges in the compound must balance all the positive charges. You can use the charges on the individual ions present to work out the formula of the ionic compound.

Example 1

Sodium chloride contains Na^+ and Cl^- ions.

Because a sodium ion has a 1^+ charge and a chloride ion has a 1^- charge only one of each ion is needed to balance out the charges.

$$(+1) + (-1) = 0$$

So the formula for sodium chloride is NaCl.

Example 2

Magnesium chloride contains Mg^{2+} (+2) and Cl^- (−1) ions.

Because a chloride ion only has a 1^- charge we will need two of them to balance out the 2^+ charge of a magnesium ion.

$$(+2) + (-1) + (-1) = 0$$

This gives us the formula $MgCl_2$.

Exam Tip
In the exam, you could be given the chemical symbols and ionic charges for certain elements and be asked to write the formulae of the compound they form, so make sure you know how to do it. The important thing to remember is that the charges must balance.

Representing ionic structures

A useful way of representing ions is by drawing out their electronic structure. Just use a big square bracket and a + or − to show the charge. You need to know how to draw the ions that form sodium chloride, magnesium oxide and calcium chloride. Here they are:

1. Sodium chloride

Sodium chloride consists of sodium ions and chloride ions.

Exam Tip
Don't forget to include the charge when you're drawing the electronic structures of ions — you won't get all the marks without it.

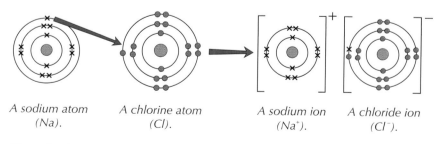

A sodium atom (Na). A chlorine atom (Cl). A sodium ion (Na⁺). A chloride ion (Cl⁻).

Figure 2: *A representation of the electronic structures of the ions in sodium chloride.*

2. Magnesium oxide

Magnesium oxide consists of magnesium ions and oxygen ions.

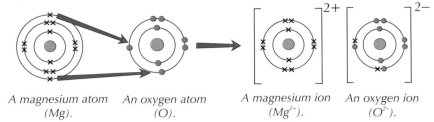

A magnesium atom (Mg).   *An oxygen atom (O).*   *A magnesium ion (Mg²⁺).*   *An oxygen ion (O²⁻).*

Figure 3: *A representation of the electronic structures of the ions in magnesium oxide.*

The formula of magnesium oxide is MgO — the charge on one magnesium ion (2⁺) balances out the charge on one oxygen ion (2⁻).

3. Calcium chloride

Calcium chloride consists of calcium ions and chloride ions.

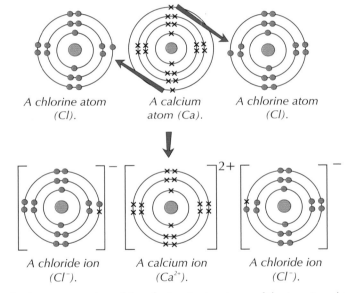

A chlorine atom (Cl).   *A calcium atom (Ca).*   *A chlorine atom (Cl).*

A chloride ion (Cl⁻).   *A calcium ion (Ca²⁺).*   *A chloride ion (Cl⁻).*

Figure 4: *A representation of the electronic structures of the ions in calcium chloride.*

Tip: The electrons in the oxygen ion are represented by dots AND crosses, so that you can see which electrons have been transferred from the magnesium atom. You don't have to draw ions like this though — once the electrons have been transferred it doesn't matter where they came from, so you could draw all the electrons in an ion as dots or all as crosses if you wanted to.

Tip: A chlorine atom is just called 'chlorine'. But when chlorine is part of an ionic compound, we say that there are 'chloride ions' present. It's quite common for the names of ions to be slightly different from the elements.

The structure of ionic compounds

Ionic compounds are giant structures made of ions. The ions are held together in a lattice (a closely-packed regular arrangement). The strong electrostatic forces of attraction between the ions act in all directions.

> **Example**
>
> A single crystal of sodium chloride (salt) is one giant ionic lattice, which is why salt crystals tend to be cuboid in shape. The Na⁺ and Cl⁻ ions are held together in a regular lattice.
>
>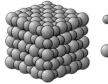
> ● sodium ion
> ● chloride ion

Figure 5: *Crystals of salt.*

Practice Questions — Fact Recall

Q1 What is ionic bonding?

Q2 Which groups in the periodic table contain elements that have outer shells of electrons that are almost full?

Q3 Do metals form positively charged ions or negatively charged ions?

Q4 Do non-metal atoms gain or lose electrons to become ions?

Q5 What is the charge on an ion of a Group 1 element?

Q6 What is the charge on an ion of a Group 7 element?

Q7 Draw the electronic structure of:

a) a chloride ion.

b) a magnesium ion.

c) an oxygen ion.

d) a calcium ion.

Q8 Describe the structure of an ionic compound.

Tip: You can use the periodic table on the inside of the back cover to help you answer these questions.

Practice Questions — Application

Q1 What ions would the following elements form?
Give the chemical symbol and the charge on the ion.

a) Rubidium   b) Bromine

c) Barium   d) Sulfur

Q2 Write the formulae of the ionic compounds listed below.

a) Sodium bromide

b) Calcium fluoride

c) Sodium oxide

d) Calcium oxide

Tip: Before working out the formula of a compound, you need to work out the charge on each of the ions in the compound.

Q3 Potassium reacts with iodine to form potassium iodide.

a) What ions are formed during this reaction? (Give the chemical symbols and the charges).

b) What is the formula of potassium iodide?

c) Describe, in terms of electron transfer, the reaction between potassium and iodine.

Q4 Describe, in terms of electrons and bonding, the formation of magnesium chloride from magnesium and chlorine. Include details of electronic structures, electron transfer and electrostatic attraction in your answer.

- Know that a covalent bond is a shared pair of electrons and that covalent bonds are very strong.
- Be able to represent the bonding in the simple molecules H_2, Cl_2, HCl, CH_4, NH_3, H_2O and O_2.
- Know that macromolecules such as silicon dioxide and diamond are giant covalent structures.

Specification Reference C2.1, C2.1.1

Shell	Max. number of electrons
1st	2
2nd	8
3rd	8

Figure 1: *Table showing the number of electrons each shell (energy level) can hold.*

Tip: In a molecule of hydrogen there are two hydrogen atoms joined by one pair of electrons. This single shared pair of electrons is a <u>single covalent bond</u>.

3. Covalent Bonding

Ionic bonding — done. Next up is covalent bonding, which is all about atoms sharing their electrons. There are a fair few diagrams coming your way over the next few pages and yes — you do need to know them all.

What is covalent bonding?

Some elements bond ionically (see page 111) but others form **covalent bonds**. A covalent bond is a shared pair of electrons. Covalent bonds are very strong bonds and are formed when atoms share electrons with each other so that they've got full outer shells (highest energy levels). They only share electrons in their outer shells and both atoms involved in the bond end up with the electronic structure of a noble gas.

Each covalent bond provides one extra shared electron for each atom. Each atom involved has to make enough covalent bonds to fill up its outer shell. See Figure 1 for a reminder of how many electrons each shell can hold.

Simple molecules

Simple molecules are molecules made up of just a few atoms. You need to know the bonding in seven different simple molecules. Here they are:

1. Hydrogen (H_2)

Hydrogen atoms have just one electron. They only need one more to complete the first shell, so they often form **single covalent bonds** to achieve this (see Figure 2).

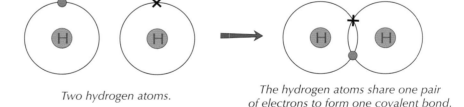

Two hydrogen atoms.

The hydrogen atoms share one pair of electrons to form one covalent bond. Both atoms now have full outer shells.

Figure 2: *The formation of a covalent bond between hydrogen atoms.*

You can show the covalent bond by drawing out the electronic structure of the hydrogen atoms (as in Figure 2), but there are also other ways that the covalent bond can be represented — see Figure 3.

In this representation, only the electrons are shown.

Here, the line represents the covalent bond.

Figure 3: *Representations of covalent bonding in hydrogen.*

2. Chlorine (Cl$_2$)

Chlorine atoms need one more electron to gain a stable electronic structure. So, two chlorine atoms each share one of their electrons to form a chlorine molecule containing one shared pair of electrons — a single covalent bond.

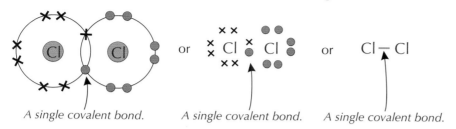

A single covalent bond.   *A single covalent bond.*   *A single covalent bond.*

Figure 4: *Representations of covalent bonding in chlorine.*

Tip: You don't need to show all the electrons in the atoms when drawing covalent bonding — just the ones in the outer shell.

3. Hydrogen chloride (HCl)

The bonding in hydrogen chloride is very similar to the bonding in H$_2$ and Cl$_2$. Again, both atoms only need one more electron to complete their outer shells, so they share one pair of electrons and one single covalent bond is formed.

Figure 5: *Representations of covalent bonding in hydrogen chloride.*

Tip: Hydrogen chloride dissolves in water to form hydrochloric acid.

4. Methane (CH$_4$)

Carbon has four outer electrons, which is half a full shell. So it forms four covalent bonds to make up its outer shell. Hydrogen atoms only need to form one covalent bond to achieve a full outer shell. So a carbon atom will form covalent bonds with four hydrogen atoms to form a CH$_4$ molecule (methane).

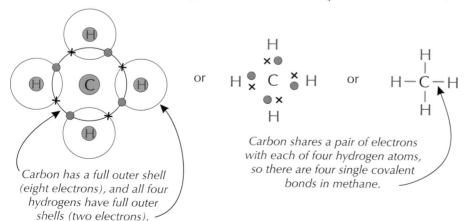

Carbon has a full outer shell (eight electrons), and all four hydrogens have full outer shells (two electrons).

Carbon shares a pair of electrons with each of four hydrogen atoms, so there are four single covalent bonds in methane.

Tip: The diagrams where covalent bonds are shown using dots and crosses are imaginatively called 'dot and cross diagrams'. The diagrams where lines are used to show covalent bonds are called displayed formulae.

Figure 6: *Representations of covalent bonding in methane.*

5. Ammonia (NH₃)

Nitrogen has five outer electrons so it needs to form three covalent bonds to make up the extra three electrons needed. Hydrogen needs one extra electron, so a single covalent bond is formed between nitrogen and each of three hydrogen atoms.

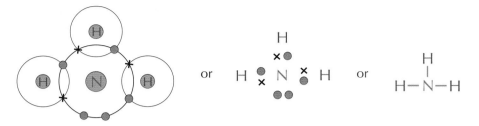

Figure 7: Representations of covalent bonding in ammonia.

6. Water (H₂O)

Exam Tip
Always check you've got the bonding right by counting the number of electrons each atom has in its outer shell. If it's not got a full outer shell you've gone wrong somewhere.

Oxygen atoms have six outer electrons. They sometimes form ionic bonds by taking two electrons from other atoms to complete their outer shell. However they'll also form covalent bonds and share two electrons instead. In water molecules, the oxygen shares electrons with two hydrogen atoms to form two single covalent bonds.

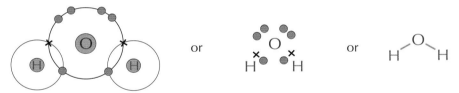

Figure 8: Representations of covalent bonding in water.

7. Oxygen (O₂)

In oxygen gas, an oxygen atom shares two electrons with another oxygen atom to get a full outer shell. So there are two pairs of electrons shared between two oxygen atoms. This is called a **double covalent bond**.

Tip: If an atom shares one pair of electrons with one atom and another pair of electrons with another atom then there are two single bonds. You get <u>double bonds</u> when two atoms share two pairs of electrons with each other.

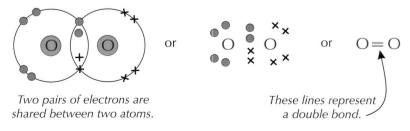

Two pairs of electrons are shared between two atoms.

These lines represent a double bond.

Figure 9: Representations of covalent bonding in oxygen.

Chemistry 2.1 **Structure and Bonding**

Macromolecules

All the molecules on the previous couple of pages are simple molecules, as they're only made up of a few atoms. But covalent bonding can also lead to giant structures called **macromolecules**.

Tip: There's much more on macromolecules such as silicon dioxide and diamond on pages 124-125.

Examples

- Silicon dioxide (SiO_2) is a macromolecule formed when many silicon and oxygen atoms are covalently bonded to form a giant covalent structure.

- Diamond is a macromolecule formed from many covalently bonded carbon atoms.

Figure 10: A molecular model showing the giant covalent structure of diamond.

Practice Questions — Fact Recall

Q1 What is a covalent bond?

Q2 Name the molecules shown by the dot and cross diagrams below.

a)   b)

Q3 Draw dot and cross diagrams to represent the following molecules.

    a) hydrogen   b) chlorine   c) methane

Q4 Using displayed formulae, draw the bonding in the molecules below.

    a) chlorine   b) ammonia   c) oxygen

Q5 What is a double covalent bond?

Q6 Name two macromolecules.

Practice Questions — Application

Q1 An element, 'A', has 3 shells of electrons. Its 3rd shell contains seven electrons. 'A' covalently bonds to hydrogen. Describe and explain the bonding in the molecule that is formed.

Q2 a) Which of the molecules below contains a double covalent bond? Explain your answer.

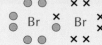
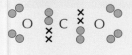

      Molecule A   Molecule B   Molecule C

    b) Draw the displayed formula of the molecule that contains the double bond.

Learning Objectives:
- Know that metals are giant structures.
- Know how the atoms in a metal are arranged.
- **H** Know that electrons from the outer shells of metal atoms are delocalised.
- **H** Understand how these delocalised electrons hold the metal atoms together.
- **H** Be able to draw diagrams to represent the bonding in metals.

Specification Reference
C2.1, C2.1.1

4. Metallic Bonding

Metallic bonding is the final type of bonding in this section and, luckily for you, there's not a huge amount that you need to know. For now that is...

The structure of metals

Metals consist of a giant structure. The atoms in a metal are arranged in a regular pattern (see Figure 1). Metals are said to have giant structures because they have lots of atoms. Exactly how many depends on how big the piece of metal is.

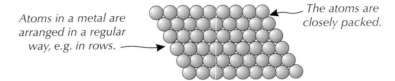

Atoms in a metal are arranged in a regular way, e.g. in rows.

The atoms are closely packed.

Figure 1: The structure of a metal.

Bonding in metals `Higher`

In metals, the electrons in the outer shells of the atoms are **delocalised**. This means that they aren't associated with a particular atom or bond — they're free to move through the whole structure (see Figure 2). There are strong forces of electrostatic attraction between the positive metal ions and the negative electrons, and these forces hold the metal structure together.

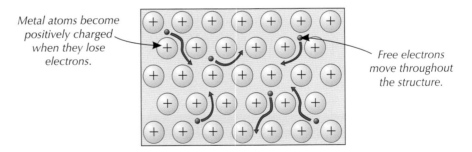

Metal atoms become positively charged when they lose electrons.

Free electrons move throughout the structure.

Figure 2: Delocalised electrons within a giant metallic structure.

Practice Questions — Fact Recall

Q1   Describe the structure of a metal.

Q2   What are delocalised electrons?

Q3   a) What type of forces hold the particles in a metal together?

b) Why do these forces exist in a metal?

Section Checklist — Make sure you know...

Bonding in Compounds

- [ ] That a compound is a substance that's formed from atoms of two or more elements, chemically bonded together.
- [ ] That atoms bond together in order to achieve a full outer shell of electrons (like noble gases).
- [ ] That atoms can achieve a full outer shell of electrons through ionic bonding or covalent bonding.

Ionic Bonding

- [ ] That ionic bonding is a strong electrostatic attraction between oppositely charged ions.
- [ ] That metal atoms can lose electrons to form positively charged ions with stable electronic structures and non-metal atoms can gain electrons to form negatively charged ions with stable electronic structures.
- [ ] How to work out the charge on an ion from the position of the element in the periodic table.
- [ ] That alkali metals and halogens react to form ionic compounds containing one metal ion with a single positive charge and one non-metal ion with a single negative charge.
- [ ] How to work out the formulae of ionic compounds from the chemical symbols and charges on ions.
- [ ] How to represent the electronic structures of sodium ions, chloride ions, magnesium ions, oxygen ions and calcium ions.
- [ ] That ionic compounds are giant structures and that the ions are held together in a regular arrangement (a lattice) by electrostatic forces that act in all directions.

Covalent Bonding

- [ ] That a covalent bond is a shared pair of electrons, and that covalent bonds are very strong.
- [ ] That atoms form covalent bonds by sharing one or more of their electrons with another atom.
- [ ] That atoms need to make enough covalent bonds to fill their outer electron shell.
- [ ] That a single covalent bond is formed when two atoms share one pair of electrons and a double covalent bond is formed when two atoms share two pairs of electrons.
- [ ] How to represent the covalent bonds in hydrogen, water, chlorine, hydrogen chloride, methane, ammonia, water and oxygen using dot and cross diagrams and displayed formulae.
- [ ] That macromolecules like silicon dioxide and diamond are giant covalent structures.

Metallic Bonding

- [ ] That metals are giant structures, with atoms arranged in a regular pattern.
- [ ] **H** That metallic structures have delocalised electrons that are free to move through the structure.
- [ ] **H** That the delocalisation of electrons gives rise to positive metal ions and that the strong electrostatic attraction between the delocalised electrons and the positive ions holds the structure together.

1. Ionic Compounds

The last section was about the different types of bonding that hold substances together. This section is all about how the bonding affects the properties of a substance, and therefore the uses. First up — ionic compounds.

Melting point and boiling point

Ionic compounds have a regular arrangement of ions called a giant ionic lattice. Ionic compounds all have high melting points and high boiling points due to the strong electrostatic attraction between the ions. It takes a large amount of energy to overcome this attraction. When ionic compounds melt, the ions are free to move and they'll carry electric current — see Figure 1.

Tip: Remember, an electrostatic attraction is the force of attraction between oppositely charged ions.

positive ions   negative ions   free ions

Melting — electrostatic forces are overcome.

Strong forces acting in all directions hold the ions in a lattice.

The ions are free to move. They can carry an electrical current through the substance.

Figure 1: *A particle diagram of an ionic compound when solid and melted.*

Solubility

Ionic compounds dissolve easily in water. The ions separate and are all free to move in the solution, so they'll carry electric current — see Figure 2.

Tip: Have a look back at pages 111-114 for more on ionic compounds and the bonding that holds the ions together.

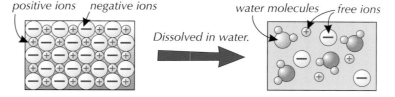

positive ions   negative ions   water molecules   free ions

Dissolved in water.

Strong forces acting in all directions hold the ions in a lattice.

The ions are free to move. They can carry an electrical current through the substance.

Figure 2: *A particle diagram of an ionic compound when solid and in solution.*

Practice Questions — Fact Recall

Q1   Do ionic compounds have high melting points or low melting points? Explain your answer.

Q2   Ionic compounds conduct electricity when they are dissolved in water. Explain why.

2. Covalent Substances

There are two very different types of covalent substances — simple molecules and macromolecules. The properties of these types of substances are different, because the bonding in them is different. All will be explained...

Simple molecules

Substances with covalent bonds can be **simple molecules** — molecules made up of only a few atoms. Hydrogen, chlorine, hydrogen chloride, methane, ammonia, water and oxygen are all examples of simple molecules.

Properties of simple molecules

All simple molecular substances have similar properties.

> **Examples**
>
> ■ They have low melting and boiling points.
>
> ■ They are mostly gases or liquids at room temperature (because they have relatively low melting and boiling points). But they can be solids.
>
> ■ They don't conduct electricity — there are no ions or free electrons so there's nothing to carry an electrical charge.

Bonding in simple molecular substances   Higher

In molecular substances, atoms form very strong covalent bonds to make small molecules of several atoms. By contrast, the forces of attraction between these molecules (**intermolecular forces**) are very weak (see Figure 1).

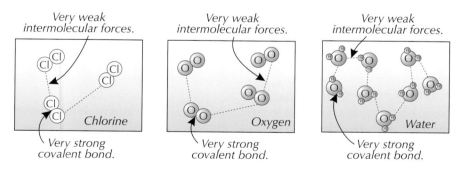

Figure 1: *The bonding within and between simple molecules.*

It's the intermolecular forces that get broken when simple molecular substances melt or boil — not the much stronger covalent bonds. Because the intermolecular forces are weak, not much energy is needed to overcome them, and the molecules are easily parted from each other. That's why simple molecular substances have low melting and boiling points.

Learning Objectives:

■ Know the general properties of simple molecular substances.

■ H Be able to explain, in terms of intermolecular forces, why simple molecular substances have low melting and boiling points.

■ Know that diamond, graphite and silicon dioxide are giant covalent structures (macromolecules).

■ Understand why macromolecules have high melting points.

■ Be able to explain, in terms of its bonding, why diamond is hard.

■ Know that graphite is slippery because it consists of layers of covalently bonded atoms that are free to slide over each other.

■ H Be able to explain why graphite is slippery in terms of intermolecular forces.

■ H Be able to explain why graphite is a good conductor.

Specification Reference C2.2.1, C2.2.3

Tip: Covalent substances contain covalent bonds. A covalent bond is a shared pair of electrons. See pages 116-119 for more on covalent bonding.

Giant covalent structures (macromolecules)

Giant covalent structures are similar to giant ionic structures (lattices) except that there are no charged ions. All the atoms are bonded to each other by strong covalent bonds. A lot of energy is needed to overcome these bonds and this means that giant molecules have very high melting and boiling points. Most don't conduct electricity — not even when molten. The main examples of macromolecules are diamond and graphite, which are both made only from carbon atoms, and silicon dioxide (silica — see Figure 2).

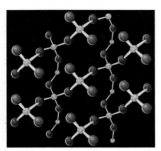

Figure 2: The structure of silicon dioxide. Silicon dioxide, sometimes called silica, is what sand is made of. Each grain of sand is one giant structure of silicon and oxygen.

Diamond

In diamond, each carbon atom forms four covalent bonds in a very rigid giant covalent structure (see Figure 3). This structure makes diamond the hardest natural substance, so it's used for drill tips.

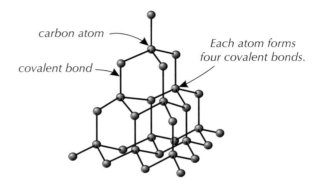

carbon atom

covalent bond

Each atom forms four covalent bonds.

Figure 3: The structure of diamond.

Figure 4: A cut, polished and sparkly diamond.

Exam Tip
If you're doing the Foundation exam you just need to know the basics about graphite. If you're taking Higher you'll need to learn the basics and the more in-depth stuff too. Sorry!

Graphite

Graphite — the basics

In graphite, each carbon atom only forms three covalent bonds. This creates layers of carbon atoms (see Figure 6 on the next page). The layers are free to slide over each other because there are no covalent bonds between them. The layers can even be rubbed off onto paper (that's how a pencil works). Because the layers aren't covalently bonded to each other, graphite is soft and slippery.

Graphite — in-depth `Higher`

The layers in graphite are held loosely together by weak **intermolecular forces**. These are easily overcome, which is why the layers can slide over each other, making graphite soft and slippery.

Carbon atoms have four electrons in their outer electron shells, so they need four more to achieve a full outer shell. Usually, carbon forms four covalent bonds, but in graphite each carbon atom only forms three covalent bonds. The outer shell electrons that don't form covalent bonds are **delocalised.** This means they are free to move throughout the structure (just like the delocalised electrons in metals — see page 120). Because one electron from each carbon atom is delocalised, graphite is a good conductor of heat and electricity.

Figure 5: Graphite. Not as nice as diamond :(

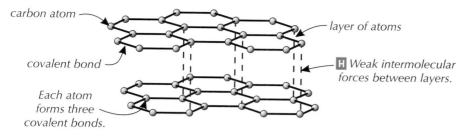

carbon atom

layer of atoms

covalent bond

H Weak intermolecular forces between layers.

Each atom forms three covalent bonds.

Figure 6: The structure of graphite.

Tip: Figure 6 only shows a tiny section of the structure of graphite. In reality, the outer carbon atoms are bonded to more carbon atoms and the overall structure is much bigger.

Practice Questions — Fact Recall

Q1 What is a simple molecule?

Q2 What type of bonding holds atoms in a simple molecule together?

Q3 Give three examples of simple molecular substances.

Q4 Simple molecular substances have low melting points. Explain why.

Q5 Diamond has a high melting point. Explain why.

Q6 Which statement(s) below describe(s) the structure of graphite?

　　a) Each carbon atom is covalently bonded to four other atoms.

　　b) The layers are held together by weak intermolecular forces.

　　c) Electrons not involved in covalent bonding are delocalised.

　　d) The structure is very hard.

Q7 What properties does graphite have that are unusual for a non-metal?

Practice Questions — Application

Q1 Diamonds can be used as cutting tools. What property of diamond makes it suitable for use as a cutting tool?

Q2 Graphite can be used as a lubricant. What property of graphite makes it suitable for use as a lubricant?

Tip: A lubricant is a substance that reduces friction, allowing things to move more smoothly.

Q3 The table below shows the melting points of graphite, oxygen and diamond (under certain conditions), and whether they conduct electricity or not.

Substance	Melting Point	Conducts Electricity?
A	3500 °C	No
B	3500 °C	Yes
C	−218 °C	No

　　a) Which substance (A, B or C) is graphite?

　　b) Which substance (A, B or C) is oxygen?

　　c) Which substance (A, B or C) is diamond?

Learning Objectives:

- Know that the atoms in a metal are arranged in layers.
- Know that these layers can slide over each other, which allows metals to be bent and made into different shapes.
- **H** Know that metals have delocalised electrons that are free to move throughout the metal.
- **H** Know that the delocalised electrons make metals good conductors of heat and electricity.
- Know what an alloy is and why alloys are harder than pure metals.

Specification Reference
C2.2.4

3. Metallic Structures

Metals are up next, and once again you need to know about how the bonding in metals (see page 120) affects their properties.

Properties of metals

Malleability

Metals consist of atoms held together in a regular structure. The atoms form layers that are able to slide over each other — see Figure 1. This allows metals to be bent and shaped (they are malleable).

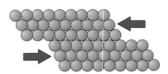

Figure 1: *Layers of atoms in a metal sliding over each other.*

Conductivity Higher

Metals have delocalised electrons that are free to move through the whole structure (see page 120 for more). Because of this, they are good conductors of heat and electricity. The electrons carry the current and the heat energy through the structure.

Alloys

Tip: You've already covered alloys in Chemistry 1.3 (see pages 53-54), but you need to know about them for this unit too.

Pure metals often aren't quite right for certain jobs. So scientists mix two or more metals together — creating an **alloy** with the properties they want.
Different elements have different sized atoms. So when another metal is mixed with a pure metal, the new metal atoms will distort the layers of metal atoms, making it more difficult for them to slide over each other (see Figure 2). This makes alloys harder than pure metals.

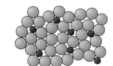

Figure 2: *Distorted layers of atoms in an alloy.*

Practice Questions — Fact Recall

Q1 Explain why metals can be easily bent.

Q2 Metals are good conductors of heat. Explain why.

Q3 Why are alloys harder than pure metals?

4. New Materials

*Nowadays, we don't have to rely only on materials that occur naturally —
we can make new materials. The great thing about this is that we can design
them to have exactly the properties we want.*

Smart materials

Smart materials behave differently depending on the conditions, for example,
the temperature. **Shape memory alloys** are a type of smart material — their
shape can be changed, but they'll return to their original shape when heated
(see Figure 1).

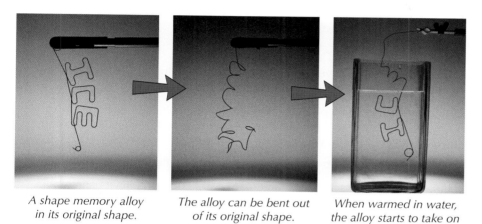

A shape memory alloy   The alloy can be bent out   When warmed in water,
in its original shape.   of its original shape.   the alloy starts to take on
                                                         its original shape again.

Figure 1: *A shape memory alloy.*

Learning Objectives:

- Know that a shape
  memory alloy is a
  material whose shape
  can be changed, but
  that will return back
  to its original shape
  when heated.

- Know some uses of
  shape memory alloys.

- Know what
  nanoparticles are and
  that they can have
  different properties to
  the bulk material.

- Know that
  nanoparticles have a
  high surface area to
  volume ratio.

- Know some of the
  uses of nanoparticles.

- **H** Know that
  fullerenes are
  nanoparticles made
  up of hexagonal rings
  of carbon atoms.

- **H** Know some of the
  uses of fullerenes.

**Specification Reference
C2.2.3, C2.2.4, C2.2.6**

Example

Nitinol is a shape memory alloy. It's a metal alloy (about half nickel, half
titanium) but when it's cool you can bend it and twist it like rubber. Bend
it too far, though, and it stays bent. If you then heat it above a certain
temperature, it goes back to its "remembered" shape.

It's really handy for glasses frames (see Figure 2). If you accidentally bend
them, you can just pop them into a bowl of hot water and they'll jump back
into shape.

Figure 2:
Nitinol glasses.

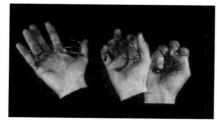

Nitinol is also used for dental braces. In the mouth it warms and tries to
return to a 'remembered' shape, and so it gently pulls the teeth with it.

Nanoparticles

Tip: 1 nm is really, really small. It's the same as 0.000 000 001 m.

Really tiny particles, 1–100 nanometres across, are called '**nanoparticles**'. Nanoparticles contain roughly a few hundred atoms. A nanoparticle has very different properties from the 'bulk' chemical that it's made from.

> **Example**
>
> Silver nanoparticles can kill bacteria, so they're added to the polymer fibres used to make surgical masks. Normal silver particles are much bigger and can't kill bacteria.

Using nanoparticles is known as nanoscience. Many new uses of nanoparticles are being developed.

> **Examples**
>
> - Nanoparticles have a huge surface area to volume ratio, so they could help make new industrial catalysts.
>
> - You can use nanoparticles to make sensors to detect one type of molecule and nothing else. These highly specific sensors are already being used to test water purity.
>
> - Nanotubes can be used to make stronger, lighter building materials.
>
> - New cosmetics, e.g. sun tan cream and deodorant, have been made using nanoparticles. The small particles do their job but don't leave white marks on the skin.
>
> - New lubricant coatings are being developed using nanoparticles. These coatings reduce friction a bit like ball bearings and could be used in all sorts of places from artificial joints to gears.
>
> - Nanotubes conduct electricity, so they can be used in tiny electric circuits for computer chips.

Tip: Nanotubes are tiny tube shaped nanoparticles.

Fullerenes Higher

Fullerenes are a type of nanoparticle — they're molecules of carbon, shaped like hollow balls or closed tubes. The carbon atoms are arranged in hexagonal rings (see Figure 3). Different fullerenes contain different numbers of carbon atoms.

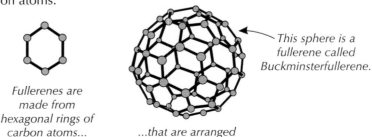

Fullerenes are made from hexagonal rings of carbon atoms...

...that are arranged into larger shapes.

This sphere is a fullerene called Buckminsterfullerene.

Figure 3: *The structure of fullerenes.*

Uses of fullerenes Higher

- Fullerenes can be used in lubricants and as catalysts (see previous page).

- Fullerenes could one day be used in medicine. They're absorbed more easily by the body than most particles. This means they could deliver drugs right into the cells where they're needed.

- Fullerenes can be joined together to form carbon nanotubes — teeny tiny hollow carbon tubes, a few nanometres across (see Figures 4 and 5). All those covalent bonds make carbon nanotubes very strong. They can be used to reinforce materials, such as graphite in tennis rackets.

Figure 4: *A model of a carbon nanotube.*

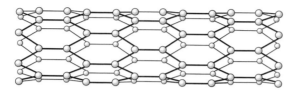

Figure 5: *A nanotube.*

Practice Questions — Fact Recall

Q1 Which sentence below is true?

a) Shape memory alloys return to their original shape when cooled.

b) Shape memory alloys can 'remember' and return to a variety of different shapes, depending on their temperature.

c) When heated, shape memory alloys return to their original shape.

Q2 Name one shape memory alloy.

Q3 How big (in nanometres) are nanoparticles?

Q4 Give three uses of nanoparticles.

Q5 Fullerenes are made from carbon atoms arranged into a particular shape. Which of the diagrams below shows the arrangement of carbon atoms found in all fullerenes?

A   B   C

Q6 Give two uses of fullerenes.

- Know that there are no cross-links between polymer chains in thermosoftening polymers.
- Know that thermosetting polymers are made up of polymer chains with cross-links between them. .
- Know that thermosetting polymers don't melt when they are heated.
- **H** Know that the intermolecular forces between polymer chains in thermosoftening polymers are weak and that this allows the polymer to be softened and remoulded repeatedly.
- Know that the reactants and the reaction conditions when a polymer is formed affect the properties of the polymer.
- Be able to link the properties of polymers to their uses.

Specification Reference
C2.2, C2.2.5

5. Polymers

You've come across polymers before — way back in Section 1.5. But polymers are mighty useful things, and there's loads to know about them, so here they are again, in a bit more detail this time...

Types of polymers

Polymers are very large molecules formed when many small molecules, called monomers, join together. Strong covalent bonds hold the atoms together in long chains. You need to know about two different types of polymers — **thermosoftening polymers** and **thermosetting polymers**.

1. Thermosoftening polymers

Thermosoftening polymers are made of individual tangled chains of polymers (see Figure 1).

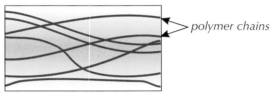

polymer chains

Figure 1: *Polymer chains in a thermosoftening polymer.*

2. Thermosetting polymers

Thermosetting polymers have cross-links between their polymer chains (see Figure 2). These mean that the polymer doesn't melt when it's heated. When the polymer reaches a certain temperature it just burns instead.

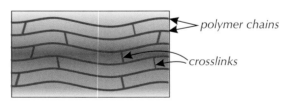

polymer chains

crosslinks

Figure 2: *Polymer chains in a thermosetting polymer.*

Figure 3: *A telephone made of Bakelite — the first thermosetting polymer in widespread use.*

Intermolecular forces in polymers `Higher`

It's the bonds or the intermolecular forces between different polymer chains that determine the properties of a polymer.

The cross-links between the polymer chains in thermosetting polymers are very strong. They hold the chains firmly together in a solid structure. They make thermosetting polymers tough — they're strong, hard and rigid.

Thermosoftening polymers don't have cross-linking between chains. The chains are held together by weak intermolecular forces, and are free to slide over each other. The forces between the chains are really easy to overcome, so it's dead easy to melt the plastic. When it cools, the polymer hardens into a new shape. You can melt these polymers and remould them as many times as you like. This makes it relatively easy to recycle thermosoftening polymers.

Exam Tip
Thermo<u>setting</u> polymers are <u>set</u> in one shape and won't melt. Thermo<u>softening</u> polymers can be <u>softened</u> and re-shaped.

Properties of polymers

The starting materials and reaction conditions will both affect the properties of a polymer.

Example

Two types of polythene can be made using different conditions:

Low density (LD) polythene is made by heating ethene to about 200 °C under high pressure. It's flexible and is used for bags and bottles.

High density (HD) polythene is made at a lower temperature and pressure (with a catalyst). It's more rigid and is used for water tanks and drainpipes.

Tip: Polythene is also known as poly(ethene). See page 81 for more on polythene.

Uses of polymers

The use of a polymer depends on its properties. You might get exam questions where you have to relate the properties of polymers to their uses.

Example

Choose from the table the polymer that would be best suited for making:

1. a disposable cup for hot drinks,
2. clothing,
3. a measuring cylinder.

Give reasons for each choice.

Tip: Plastics are polymers. That's why plastics can be used for so many different things — there are lots of different types, all with different properties.

Polymer	Cost	Resistance to chemicals	Melting point	Transparency	Rigidity	Can be made into fibres
W	High	High	High	Low	High	No
X	Low	Low	Low	Low	Low	Yes
Y	High	High	High	High	High	No
Z	Low	Low	High	High	High	No

Answers: 1. Z — low cost (disposable) and high melting point (for hot drinks).

2. X — flexible (essential for clothing) and able to be made into fibres (clothing is usually woven).

3. Y — transparent and resistant to chemicals (you need to be able to see the liquid inside and the liquid and measuring cylinder mustn't react with each other).

Practice Questions — Fact Recall

Q1   Give the name of the type of polymer that's made up of polymer chains with cross-links between the chains.

Q2   Which type of polymer will melt when it is heated — a thermosetting polymer or a thermosoftening polymer?

Q3   Explain the difference in the properties of thermosetting polymers and thermosoftening polymers in terms of the forces between the polymer chains.

Q4   The reactants used to make a polymer affect the properties of the polymer. Give one other factor that affects the properties of a polymer.

Q5   Give the names of two types of polythene.

Practice Questions — Application

Q1   Melamine resin is a polymer used to make kitchenware such as plates, ladles and spatulas. Suggest whether melamine resin is a thermosetting or thermosoftening polymer. Give a reason for your answer.

Q2   Polystyrene softens when it's heated above 100 °C. It can then be moulded to make lots of different products, including test-tubes and petri dishes. Suggest what type of polymer polystyrene is. Give a reason for your answer.

Q3   The table shows some of the properties of four different polymers.

Tip: You can use each polymer in Q3 once, more than once, or not at all in your answers.

Polymer	Properties
LD polythene	Soft, flexible, waxy.
Polyvinyl chloride	Strong, hard, rigid.
Expanded polystyrene	Poor conductor of heat, good shock absorber, lightweight.
Poly(methyl methacrylate)	Hard, transparent, shatter-resistant.

Using the information in the table, suggest a polymer that would be suitable for each of the uses listed below. Give reasons for your choices.

a) A packaging material for glassware.

b) A protective barrier for spectators at an ice-hockey game.

c) Insulation material in a house.

d) Pipes for sewage.

Section Checklist — Make sure you know...

Ionic Compounds

☐ That ionic compounds are giant lattices of ions held together by strong electrostatic forces.

☐ That a lot of energy is needed to overcome these electrostatic forces and melt or boil the compound, so ionic compounds have high melting points and boiling points.

☐ That melted or dissolved ionic compounds can conduct electricity because the ions are free to move.

Covalent Substances

☐ That simple molecules have low melting points, low boiling points and don't conduct electricity.

☐ **H** That the intermolecular forces in simple covalent substances are very weak and not much energy is needed to overcome them, so simple covalent substances have low melting and boiling points.

☐ That all the atoms in macromolecules are joined by strong covalent bonds and large amounts of energy are needed to break these bonds, so macromolecules have very high melting points.

☐ Why diamond is very hard and why graphite is soft and slippery.

☐ **H** That each carbon atom in graphite provides one delocalised electron, and that these delocalised electrons allow graphite to conduct heat and electricity.

Metallic Structures

☐ That metals can be bent and shaped because the layers of metal atoms can slide over each other.

☐ **H** That metals have delocalised electrons, which allows them to conduct electricity.

☐ That alloys are harder than pure metals because atoms of another element are added, disrupting the layers and stopping them from sliding over each other.

New Materials

☐ That shape memory alloys can be bent out of shape but will return to their original shape on heating.

☐ That nanoparticles are tiny particles with a high surface area to volume ratio and that they have different properties to the bulk material.

☐ Some of the uses of nanoparticles, e.g. as catalysts, in computers, as lubricants and in cosmetics.

☐ **H** What fullerenes are and some uses of fullerenes, e.g. in drug delivery and strengthening materials.

Polymers

☐ That thermosoftening polymers are made of individual chains of polymers tangled together and that thermosetting polymers have cross-links between their polymer chains.

☐ That thermosetting polymers don't melt when heated.

☐ **H** That thermosoftening polymers soften when heated because they only have weak intermolecular forces between their polymer chains, which are easily overcome.

☐ That the reactants and reaction conditions used when a polymer is made determine its properties.

Exam-style Questions

1   Different substances have different structures.

1 (a)   Draw a straight line from each structure listed below to the name of the substance that has that structure.

<u>Structure</u>   <u>Substance</u>

Structure	Substance
Giant ionic	Silicon dioxide
Simple molecular	Sodium chloride
Giant covalent	Ammonia
Giant metallic	Aluminium

(4 marks)

1 (b)   The structure of a substance affects its properties. The melting point, boiling point and electrical conductivity of four substances were tested. The results are shown in the table below.

Substance	Melting point (°C)	Boiling point (°C)	Good electrical conductor?
A	–218.4	–182.96	No
B	1535	2750	Yes
C	1410	2355	No
D	801	1413	When molten

Use the words in the box to complete the sentences below.
You can use each structure once, more than once or not at all.

giant ionic   simple molecular   giant covalent   giant metallic

1 (b) (i)   Substance A has a .... structure.

1 (b) (ii)   Substance B has a .... structure.

1 (b) (iii)   Substance C has a .... structure.

1 (b) (iv)   Substance D has a .... structure.

(4 marks)

2 Lithium chloride is formed from the reaction between potassium and chlorine.
   The diagrams below show the electronic structures of lithium and chlorine atoms.

       Lithium atom   Chlorine atom

2 (a) Chlorine (Cl_2) is a gas at room temperature.

2 (a) (i) Name the type of bonding found in chlorine gas.

(1 mark)

2 (a) (ii) Explain, as fully as you can, why chlorine is a gas at room temperature.

(3 marks)

2 (b) The electronic structures of lithium and chlorine change when they react together.

2 (b) (i) Describe and explain the changes in the electronic structures of lithium
     and chlorine when they react.

(3 marks)

2 (b) (ii) Draw a diagram to show the electronic structures of the particles formed during the
     reaction of lithium and chlorine.

(2 marks)

2 (b) (iii) Give the chemical formula of lithium chloride.

(1 mark)

2 (c) Lithium chloride has a high melting point. Explain why.

(2 marks)

3 Polycaprolactone is a biodegradable polymer with a melting point of 60 °C.

3 (a) Circle the correct term in the box below.

            ┌──────────────────────────┐
            │ thermosetting polymer. │
   Polycaprolactone is a │   │
            │ thermosoftening polymer. │
            └──────────────────────────┘

3 (b) The atoms in a polymer chain are held together by covalent bonds.

3 (b) (i) Explain, as fully as you can, what happens when a covalent bond is formed.

(2 marks)

3 (b) (ii) Covalent bonds are very strong but polycaprolactone has a relatively
     low melting point. Explain why.

(2 marks)

3 (c) Urea formaldehyde is a thermosetting polymer.
     Explain why this makes it difficult to recycle.

(3 marks)

3 (d) Polymers are macromolecules. Give the name of **one** other macromolecule.

(1 mark)

4   Carbon can exist in different forms. How the atoms are arranged and the bonding between the atoms determines which form of carbon is made.

4 (a)   *In this question you will be assessed on the quality of your English, the organisation of your ideas and your use of appropriate specialist vocabulary.*

The photos below show diamond and graphite.
Diamond is very hard, but graphite is soft and slippery.

Explain why diamond is hard and graphite is soft and slippery.
Your answer should include details of:

- how the atoms are arranged in diamond and graphite
- the bonding in the structures.

(6 marks)

4 (b)   Carbon can also form nanoparticles called carbon nanotubes. Carbon nanotubes are a type of fullerene. Tick the two statements below that are true.

Carbon nanotubes have different properties to bulk carbon.	
A nanoparticle is made up of thousands of atoms.	
Carbon nanotubes have a low surface area to volume ratio.	
Carbon nanotubes contain carbon atoms arranged in hexagons.	

(2 marks)

5   Sterling silver is a silver alloy.

5 (a)   Sterling silver and silver are both good conductors of electricity. Explain why.

(2 marks)

5 (b)   The diagrams below show the arrangement of atoms in a sample of pure silver and in a sample of sterling silver.

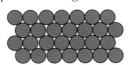
Diagram A

Diagram B

5 (b) (i)   Which diagram shows the atoms in sterling silver? Explain your answer.

(1 mark)

5 (b) (ii)   Which substance is harder, pure silver or sterling silver? Explain your answer.

(2 marks)

1. Atoms and Isotopes

Learning Objectives:

- Know that atoms can be represented as chemical symbols with a mass number and an atomic number.
- Know that the mass number is the total number of protons and neutrons in an atom.
- Know the relative masses of protons, neutrons and electrons.
- Know that isotopes are atoms that have the same number of protons but different numbers of neutrons.

Specification Reference C2.3.1

By now, you should know that everything is made up of atoms and that atoms are made up of protons, neutrons and electrons. Time to find out a bit more...

Atomic number and mass number

In the periodic table, atoms are represented by chemical symbols with two numbers next to them. The bottom number is the **atomic number** — this tells you how many protons there are in the atom. The top number is the **mass number** — this is the total number of protons and neutrons in the atom (see Figure 1).

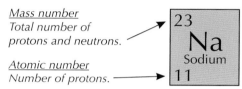

Figure 1: *The mass and atomic numbers of the element sodium.*

Atoms of the same element all have the same number of protons — so atoms of different elements will have different numbers of protons.

Finding the number of neutrons

To find the number of neutrons in an atom, you just subtract the atomic number from the mass number.

> **Tip:** You've come across atomic number and mass number before — see page 21 for a recap.

Example

Sodium (above) has an atomic number of 11 (it contains 11 protons). It has a mass number of 23 (there are 23 protons and neutrons altogether). So an atom of sodium contains 23 – 11 = 12 neutrons.

Relative masses of protons, neutrons and electrons

Electrons aren't counted in the mass number because their relative mass is very small — see Figure 2.

Particle	Relative mass
Proton	1
Neutron	1
Electron	very small

Figure 2: *Table showing the relative masses of protons, neutrons and electrons.*

> **Tip:** The actual masses of protons and neutrons are tiny, so chemists use relative mass instead to make life simpler. The masses of protons and neutrons are very similar, so they are each given a relative mass of 1.

Isotopes

Exam Tip
Examiners love to ask you about isotopes, so make sure you know what isotopes are and how to spot them.

Isotopes are different atomic forms of the same element, which have the same number of protons but a different number of neutrons. Isotopes must have the same atomic number but different mass numbers. If they had different atomic numbers, they'd be different elements altogether.

Example

Carbon-12 and carbon-14 are an important pair of isotopes. They each have 6 protons (and so an atomic number of 6). But carbon-12 has 6 neutrons (giving it a mass number of 12), while carbon-14 has 8 neutrons (giving it a mass number of 14) — see Figure 3.

Carbon-12

$^{12}_{6}C$

6 protons
6 electrons
6 neutrons

Carbon-14

$^{14}_{6}C$

6 protons
6 electrons
8 neutrons

Figure 3: *The atomic structures of carbon-12 and carbon-14.*

Practice Questions — Fact Recall

Q1 a) What does the atomic number tell you about an atom?

b) What does the mass number tell you about an atom?

Q2 How would you find the number of neutrons in an atom from the mass number and the atomic number?

Q3 What is the relative mass of:

a) a proton.   b) an electron.   c) a neutron.

Q4 What is an isotope?

Exam Tip
If you're ever asked what an isotope is, it's fine to start your answer "Isotopes are...". It's really hard to explain it if you don't start with a plural.

Practice Questions — Application

Q1 Write down how many protons and neutrons each of the following atoms have:

a) $^{16}_{8}O$ b) $^{27}_{13}Al$ c) $^{51}_{23}V$ d) $^{108}_{47}Ag$

Q2 Which of these is the chemical symbol of an isotope of $^{35}_{17}Cl$?

A: $^{37}_{17}Cl$ B: $^{35}_{16}Cl$ C: $^{36}_{16}Cl$ D: $^{17}_{35}Cl$

2. Relative Formula Mass

Relative atomic masses and relative formula masses sound a lot scarier than they actually are. Give these pages a read and you should have got to grips with them in no time...

Relative atomic mass

Relative atomic mass (A_r) is a way of comparing the masses of atoms of different elements. The relative atomic mass is usually just the same as the **mass number** of the element in the periodic table.

Examples

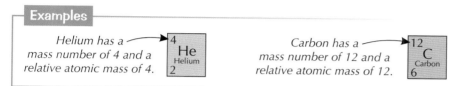

Helium has a mass number of 4 and a relative atomic mass of 4.

$$\begin{array}{c} 4 \\ \text{He} \\ \text{Helium} \\ 2 \end{array}$$

Carbon has a mass number of 12 and a relative atomic mass of 12.

$$\begin{array}{c} 12 \\ \text{C} \\ \text{Carbon} \\ 6 \end{array}$$

More on relative atomic mass `Higher`

The relative atomic mass of an element is just how heavy atoms of that element are compared with the mass of an atom of carbon-12. Carbon-12 has an A_r of exactly 12 by definition (scientists decided it would be that) — the relative atomic masses of all the other elements were set relative to it.

When an element has more than one stable **isotope**, the relative atomic mass is an average value of all the different isotopes (taking into account how much there is of each isotope).

Example `Higher`

Chlorine has two stable isotopes — chlorine-35 and chlorine-37. There's lots more chlorine-35 around than chlorine-37, so the average relative atomic mass of chlorine turns out to be about 35.5.

Calculating relative formula mass

The **relative formula mass** (M_r) of a compound is just all the relative atomic masses of the atoms in that compound added together.

Examples

- Magnesium chloride ($MgCl_2$) contains one atom of magnesium and two atoms of chlorine. Magnesium has a relative atomic mass of 24 and chlorine has a relative atomic mass of 35.5, so the relative formula mass of magnesium chloride is $24 + (2 \times 35.5) = 95$.

- Iron oxide (Fe_2O_3) contains two atoms of iron and three atoms of oxygen. Iron has an A_r of 56 and oxygen has an A_r of 16, so the relative formula mass of iron oxide is $(2 \times 56) + (3 \times 16) = 160$

Learning Objectives:

- Know the term 'relative atomic mass'.
- **H** Know that relative atomic mass tells you how heavy the atoms of an element are compared to atoms of carbon-12.
- Know what is meant by the term 'relative formula mass'.
- Be able to calculate the relative formula mass for a compound.
- Know how relative formula mass is linked to moles.

Specification Reference C2.3.1

Tip: See page 138 for a recap of isotopes.

Exam Tip
You can get the A_r of any element from the periodic table, though if you need to use them in an exam question they'll usually be given to you.

Tip: The relative atomic mass of chlorine is multiplied by 2 here because there are two chlorine atoms in $MgCl_2$.

Figure 1: Carbon has an A_r of 12, so one mole of carbon weighs exactly 12 g.

The mole

The relative mass (A_r or M_r) of a substance in grams is known as one **mole** of that substance.

Examples

- Iron (Fe) has an A_r of 56. So one mole of iron weighs exactly 56 g.
- Nitrogen gas (N_2) has an M_r of $2 \times 14 = 28$. So one mole of N_2 weighs exactly 28 g.

You can convert between moles and grams using this formula:

$$\text{Number of moles} = \frac{\text{Mass in g (of element or compound)}}{M_r \text{ (of element or compound)}}$$

Tip: If you're finding the number of moles of an element, you can always use A_r instead of M_r in the equation.

Example 1

How many moles are there in 42 g of carbon?

The A_r of carbon is 12, so the number of moles in 42 g of carbon is:

$$\text{Moles} = \frac{\text{mass}}{A_r} = \frac{42}{12} = 3.5 \text{ moles}$$

Example 2

How much would 0.8 moles of sulfuric acid (H_2SO_4) weigh in grams?

The M_r of sulfuric acid is $(2 \times 1) + 32 + (4 \times 16) = 98$.

Rearrange the formula to find mass (multiply both sides by M_r):

$$\text{mass} = \text{moles} \times M_r = 0.8 \times 98 = 78.4 \text{ g}$$

So 0.8 moles of sulfuric acid would weigh 78.4 g

Exam Tip
You could be expected to rearrange equations like this in the exam. There's more on how to rearrange equations on page 294.

Practice Questions — Fact Recall

Q1 What is the relative atomic mass (A_r) of an element?

Q2 Explain why relative atomic masses aren't always whole numbers.

Q3 Describe how you would work out the relative formula mass (M_r) of a compound.

Q4 What equation can you use to convert between moles and grams?

Practice Questions — Application

Use the periodic table on the back cover to answer the questions below.

Q1 Find the relative atomic masses of the following elements:

a) Beryllium (Be)

b) Phosphorus (P)

c) Zinc (Zn)

d) Copper (Cu)

Q2 What is the relative formula mass of:

a) Oxygen (O_2)

b) Potassium hydroxide (KOH)

c) Nitric acid (HNO_3)

d) Calcium carbonate ($CaCO_3$)

Q3 How many moles are there in each of the following?

a) 19.5 g of potassium (K)

b) 23.4 g of sodium chloride (NaCl)

c) 76.8 g of sulfur dioxide (SO_2)

d) 31.9 g of copper sulfate ($CuSO_4$)

Q4 How much would the following weigh in grams?

a) 0.8 moles of nickel (Ni)

b) 0.5 moles of magnesium oxide (MgO)

c) 1.6 moles of ammonia (NH_3)

d) 1.4 moles of calcium hydroxide ($Ca(OH)_2$)

Figure 2: *One mole of a variety of compounds.*

- Know how to
  calculate the
  percentage of
  an element in a
  compound.
- **H** Know how
  to work out the
  empirical formula of a
  compound.

**Specification Reference
C2.3.3**

Tip: Methane only
contains carbon and
hydrogen. So once
you know that 75% of
its mass is made up of
carbon atoms, you can
also say that 25% of its
mass must be made up
of hydrogen atoms.

3. Formula Mass Calculations

*If you're not all that fond of maths, then brace yourself. This topic is all about
the calculations you can do using the relative formula mass of a compound.*

Calculating percentage mass

The percentage mass is a way of saying what proportion of the mass of a
compound is due to atoms of a particular element.

Example

The percentage mass of carbon (C) in methane (CH_4) is 75%. This means
that 75% of the mass of methane is made up of carbon atoms — so if you
have 100 g of methane, it will contain 75 g of carbon.

If you know the molecular formula of a compound, you can work out the
percentage mass of a particular element within that compound using this
formula:

$$\text{Percentage mass of an element in a compound} = \frac{A_r \times \text{No. of atoms (of that element)}}{M_r \text{ (of the whole compound)}} \times 100$$

Example 1

Find the percentage mass of magnesium in magnesium oxide, MgO.

The A_r of magnesium = 24 and the A_r of oxygen = 16.

So the M_r of MgO = 24 + 16 = 40

% Mass of Mg = $\dfrac{A_r \text{ of Mg} \times \text{No. of Mg atoms}}{M_r \text{ of MgO}} \times 100 = \dfrac{24}{40} \times 100 = 60\ \%$

This means that magnesium makes up 60% of the mass of magnesium oxide.

Example 2

Find the percentage mass of sodium in sodium carbonate, Na_2CO_3.

The A_r of sodium = 23, the A_r of carbon = 12 and the A_r of oxygen = 16.

So the M_r of Na_2CO_3 = (2 × 23) + 12 + (3 × 16) = 106

% Mass of Na = $\dfrac{A_r \text{ of Na} \times \text{No. of Na atoms}}{M_r \text{ of } Na_2CO_3} \times 100 = \dfrac{23 \times 2}{106} \times 100 = 43.4\ \%$

This means that sodium makes up 43.4% of the mass of sodium carbonate.

Finding the empirical formula `Higher`

The **empirical formula** of a compound gives the simplest possible whole number ratio of atoms of each element within that compound. It's slightly different to the **molecular formula** of a compound, which gives you the actual number of atoms of each element within the compound. Often, the empirical and molecular formulae of a compound will be the same.

> **Example — Higher**
>
> The molecular formula of sodium hydroxide is NaOH.
>
> This can't be simplified so NaOH is also the empirical formula.

But occasionally they're different.

> **Example — Higher**
>
> The molecular formula of glucose is $C_6H_{12}O_6$.
>
> This can be simplified to CH_2O, which is the empirical formula of glucose.

Tip: The molecular formula is always a multiple of the empirical formula. In the case of glucose, you multiply the empirical formula by six to get the molecular formula.

If you know the actual mass or the percentage mass of each element that's in a compound, you can find its empirical formula. Here's what you do:

1. List all the elements in the compound (there's usually only two or three).

2. Underneath them, write their masses or percentages.

3. Divide each mass or percentage by the A_r of that particular element.

4. Take each of these numbers and divide them by the smallest answer from step 3. This will give you the ratio of the elements in the compound.

5. If any of your answers are not whole numbers, you'll need to multiply everything up to get the lowest possible whole number ratio.

Tip: Step 5 may look a bit tricky, but it's simple really. For example, if one of your Step 4 answers ends in a half, it just means multiplying them all by 2.

> **Example 1 — Higher**
>
> **A compound contains 26.1% carbon, 4.3% hydrogen and 69.6% oxygen by mass. Find the empirical formula of this compound.**
> **(A_r for carbon = 12, A_r for hydrogen = 1, A_r for oxygen = 16)**
>
> 1. List the three elements in the compound:
>
> | C | H | O |
> |---|---|---|
>
> 2. Write out the experimental percentages given in the question:
>
> | 26.1 | 4.3 | 69.6 |
> |---|---|---|
>
> 3. Divide each percentage by the A_r of that element:
>
> | $\frac{26.1}{12} = 2.2$ | $\frac{4.3}{1} = 4.3$ | $\frac{69.6}{16} = 4.4$ |
> |---|---|---|
>
> 4. Divide by the smallest answer (2.2 in this case):
>
> | $\frac{2.2}{2.2} = 1$ | $\frac{4.3}{2.2} = 2$ | $\frac{4.4}{2.2} = 2$ |
> |---|---|---|
>
> 5. This is a whole number ratio.
>
> So the empirical formula must be CH_2O_2.

Tip: You might need to round your answers in step 4 to the nearest whole number of atoms. For example, 4.3 ÷ 2.2 is actually 1.9545... but that's close enough that you can round it to 2.

Example 2 — Higher

Find the empirical formula of the iron oxide produced when 44.8 g of iron reacts with 19.2 g of oxygen. (A$_r$ for iron = 56, A$_r$ for oxygen = 16)

Tip: You need to know that doing an experiment like this is the only way of getting the data you need to find the formula of a compound. You might know that rust is iron oxide, but is it FeO, or Fe$_2$O$_3$? An experiment to determine the empirical formula will tell you for certain.

		Fe	O
1.	List the two elements in iron oxide:		
2.	Write out the experimental masses given in the question:	44.8	19.2
3.	Divide each mass by the A$_r$ of that element:	$\frac{44.8}{56} = 0.8$	$\frac{19.2}{16} = 1.2$
4.	Divide by the smallest number (0.8 in this case):	$\frac{0.8}{0.8} = 1$	$\frac{1.2}{0.8} = 1.5$
5.	Multiply to get the lowest whole number ratio (in this case multiply by 2).	2	3

So the empirical formula must be Fe$_2$O$_3$.

Practice Questions — Fact Recall

Q1 Which formula would you use to calculate the percentage mass of an element in a compound?

Q2 What is the empirical formula of a compound?

Q3 Describe how you would find the empirical formula of a compound from experimental masses.

Practice Questions — Application

Use the periodic table on the back cover to answer these questions.

Q1 Find the percentage mass of:

a) hydrogen (H) in hydrochloric acid (HCl).

b) sodium (Na) in sodium hydroxide (NaOH).

c) aluminium (Al) in aluminium oxide (Al$_2$O$_3$).

d) oxygen (O) in copper hydroxide (Cu(OH)$_2$).

Tip: Make sure you've got a calculator handy to help you with these calculations.

Q2 Find the empirical formula of the nitrogen oxide produced when 5.6 g of nitrogen reacts with 12.8 g of oxygen.

Q3 A hydrocarbon contains 80% carbon and 20% hydrogen by mass. Find the empirical formula of this hydrocarbon.

Q4 Find the empirical formula of the compound that contains 10.8 g of carbon, 2.4 g of hydrogen and 9.6 g of oxygen.

Q5 Find the empirical formula of the compound that contains 52.3% iron, 44.9% oxygen and 2.8% hydrogen by mass.

4. Calculating Masses in Reactions

Learning Objective:
- **H** Know how to calculate masses of reactants and products from balanced symbol equations.

Specification Reference
C2.3.3

If you know the mass of one reactant in a reaction, you can use the symbol equation for that reaction and a nifty bit of maths to work out the mass of product you should get. Here's what you do...

How to calculate the mass of a product Higher

If you want to work out the mass of product you would expect to make from a certain mass of reactant, you need to follow these steps:

1. Write out the balanced equation for the reaction.

2. Find the M_r of the reactant and the product that you're interested in.

3. Apply the rule: Divide to get one, then multiply to get all:
   - Divide both relative formula masses by the M_r of the reactant — this tells you how much product would be formed from 1 g of the reactant.
   - Multiply this by the amount of reactant given in the question to find out how much product would be formed from that much reactant.

Example 1 **Higher**

What mass of magnesium oxide is produced when 60 g of magnesium is burned in air?

1. The balanced symbol equation for this reaction is:
$$2Mg + O_2 \rightarrow 2MgO$$

2. The reactant you've got is 2Mg. The product you want is 2MgO.
   The M_r of 2Mg = 2 × 24 = 48
   The M_r of 2MgO = 2 × (24 + 16) = 80

Tip: Make sure you include the numbers in front of the symbols when you're working out the relative masses of the products and reactants.

3. Apply the rule: divide to get one, then multiply to get all.

   - First, you need to know how much magnesium oxide can be made from 1 g of magnesium. So start by dividing both relative formula masses by the M_r of the reactant (that's the magnesium).

   ÷ 48 ⟮ 48 g of magnesium reacts to give 80 g of magnesium oxide. ⟯ ÷ 48
   1 g of magnesium reacts to give 1.67 g of magnesium oxide.

   - The question asks you to find the mass of magnesium oxide produced when 60 g of magnesium is burned in air. So now you need to multiply both sides by 60.

   × 60 ⟮ 1 g of magnesium reacts to give 1.67 g of magnesium oxide. ⟯ × 60
   60 g of magnesium reacts to give 100 g of magnesium oxide.

   So there you have it — 60 g of Mg will produce 100 g of MgO.

Figure 1: *Magnesium burning in air.*

Example 2 | Higher

What mass of calcium chloride (CaCl$_2$) is produced when 24 g of calcium hydroxide (Ca(OH)$_2$) reacts with an excess of hydrochloric acid (HCl)?

1. The balanced symbol equation for this reaction is:

$$Ca(OH)_2 + 2HCl \rightarrow CaCl_2 + 2H_2O$$

2. The reactant you've got is Ca(OH)$_2$. The product you want is CaCl$_2$.

    The M$_r$ of Ca(OH)$_2$ = 40 + (2 × (16 + 1)) = 74
    The M$_r$ of CaCl$_2$ = 40 + (2 × 35.5) = 111

3. Apply the rule, divide to get one, then multiply to get all.

    ▪ First divide both relative formula masses by the M$_r$ of Ca(OH)$_2$:

    ÷ 74 ⟨ 74 g of Ca(OH)$_2$ reacts to give 111 g of CaCl$_2$.
    1 g of Ca(OH)$_2$ reacts to give 1.5 g of CaCl$_2$. ⟩ ÷ 74

    ▪ Then multiply both sides by 24:

    × 24 ⟨ 1 g of Ca(OH)$_2$ reacts to give 1.5 g of CaCl$_2$.
    24 g of Ca(OH)$_2$ reacts to give 36 g of CaCl$_2$. ⟩ × 24

    So 24 g of Ca(OH)$_2$ will produce 36 g of CaCl$_2$.

Tip: The mass of product is called the yield of a reaction — see page 148 for more.

How to calculate the mass of a reactant Higher

You can use the same basic method to find how much reactant you'd need to use to make a certain mass of product. The only difference is in Step 3 — this time you divide both relative formula masses by the M$_r$ of the product. This tells you how much reactant you would need to form 1 g of product. Then you just multiply everything by the mass of product given in the question.

How much zinc carbonate (ZnCO$_3$) would need to decompose to form 24.2 g of zinc oxide (ZnO)?

1. The balanced symbol equation for this reaction is:

$$ZnCO_3 \rightarrow ZnO + CO_2$$

2. The reactant you want is ZnCO$_3$. The product you've got is ZnO.

    The M$_r$ of ZnCO$_3$ = 65 + 12 + (3 × 16) = 125
    The M$_r$ of ZnO = 65 + 16 = 81

3. Apply the rule, divide to get one, then multiply to get all.

    ▪ This time, you want to know how much zinc carbonate you would need to produce 1 g of zinc oxide. So start by dividing both relative formula masses by the M$_r$ of the product (zinc oxide).

Exam Tip
In the exam, you might be expected to know the equation for a reaction (if it's one you've studied), or you might be given the balanced symbol equation in the question.

$$\div 81 \Bigg(\begin{array}{l} 125 \text{ g of } ZnCO_3 \text{ reacts to give } 81 \text{ g of } ZnO. \\ 1.54 \text{ g of } ZnCO_3 \text{ reacts to give } 1 \text{ g of } ZnO. \end{array}\Bigg) \div 81$$

- Now all you have to do is multiply both sides by 24.2 to find how much zinc carbonate you would need to make 24.2 g of zinc oxide.

$$\times 24.2 \Bigg(\begin{array}{l} 1.54 \text{ g of } ZnCO_3 \text{ reacts to give } 1 \text{ g of } ZnO. \\ 37.3 \text{ g of } ZnCO_3 \text{ reacts to give } 24.2 \text{ g of } ZnO. \end{array}\Bigg) \times 24.2$$

So, 37.3 g of $ZnCO_3$ would need to decompose to form 24.2 g of ZnO.

Practice Questions — Application

Use the periodic table on the back cover to answer these questions.

Q1 Calculate the mass of potassium chloride (KCl) that will be formed if 36.2 g of potassium bromide (KBr) reacts with an excess of chlorine. The balanced symbol equation for this reaction is:

$$2KBr + Cl_2 \rightarrow 2KCl + Br_2$$

Q2 Calculate the mass of aluminium chloride ($AlCl_3$) that will be made if 15.4 g of hydrochloric acid (HCl) reacts with an excess of aluminium. The balanced symbol equation for this reaction is:

$$6HCl + 2Al \rightarrow 2AlCl_3 + 3H_2$$

Q3 28.5 g of calcium carbonate ($CaCO_3$) reacts with an excess of sulfuric acid (H_2SO_4) to form calcium sulfate ($CaSO_4$), carbon dioxide (CO_2) and water (H_2O). Calculate the mass of calcium sulfate that will be formed in this reaction.

> **Tip:** For Q3 you need to write and balance the symbol equation yourself — but all the information you need is given in the question.

Q4 Calculate the mass of potassium hydroxide (KOH) that would be needed to form 25.0 g of potassium nitrate (KNO_3) in this reaction:

$$HNO_3 + KOH \rightarrow KNO_3 + H_2O$$

Q5 Ethanol (C_2H_6O) can be made from ethene (C_2H_4) using this reaction:

$$C_2H_4 + H_2O \rightarrow C_2H_6O$$

Calculate the amount of ethene that would be needed to make 60.0 g of ethanol using this reaction.

Q6 Iron oxide (Fe_2O_3) can be reduced with carbon to form iron (Fe) and carbon dioxide, as shown by the equation below.

$$2Fe_2O_3 + 3C \rightarrow 4Fe + 3CO_2$$

Calculate the amount of iron oxide needed to form 32.0 g of iron.

> **Tip:** You should be familiar with a lot of these reactions — they're all covered elsewhere in this book.

Learning Objectives:
- Know that the yield is the amount of product formed in a reaction.
- Know that the percentage yield is the yield of the reaction compared to the maximum theoretical yield, given as a percentage.
- **H** Know how to calculate percentage yields.
- Know that some reactions are reversible and can go in either direction.
- Know why the percentage yield is never 100%.
- Understand why high yields are important for sustainable development.

**Specification Reference
C2.3, C2.3.3**

5. Percentage Yield

Percentage yield is a good way of measuring how much of a chemical has been wasted during a reaction. Read on to find out how to calculate percentage yield and why it's important in the chemical industry.

What is percentage yield?

The amount of product you get in a reaction is known as the **yield**. The more reactant you start with, the higher the yield will be. But the **percentage yield** doesn't depend on the amount of reactant you started with — it's a percentage.

The percentage yield is a comparison between the amount of product you expect to get and the amount of product you actually get. It is always somewhere between 0 and 100%. A 100% yield means that you got all the product you expected to get. A 0% yield means that no reactants were converted into product, i.e. no product at all was made.

Calculating the percentage yield Higher

The predicted yield of a reaction can be calculated from the balanced reaction equation (see page 145). If you know the predicted yield of a reaction and the actual yield of a reaction, you can calculate the percentage yield using the following formula:

$$\text{percentage yield} = \frac{\text{actual yield (grams)}}{\text{predicted yield (grams)}} \times 100$$

> **Example Higher**
>
> If you reacted 24 g of calcium hydroxide with an excess of hydrochloric acid, you would expect to make 36 g of calcium chloride. If you actually only made 28.2 g of calcium chloride, then the percentage yield would be:
>
> $$\% \text{ yield} = \frac{\text{actual yield}}{\text{predicted yield}} \times 100 = \frac{28.2}{36} \times 100 = 78.3\%$$

Why percentage yields are never 100%

Even though no atoms are gained or lost in reactions, in real life, you never get a 100% yield. Some product or reactant always gets lost along the way — and that goes for big industrial processes as well as school lab experiments. There are several reasons for this.

1. The reaction is reversible

A **reversible reaction** is one where the products of the reaction can themselves react to produce the original reactants. Reversible reactions can be represented like this:

$$A + B \rightleftharpoons C + D$$

Example

The breakdown of ammonium chloride into ammonia and hydrogen chloride is a good example of a reversible reaction. Here's the equation:

ammonium chloride $\rightleftharpoons$ ammonia + hydrogen chloride

The ammonia and hydrogen chloride that form when ammonium chloride breaks down can react with each other to reform the ammonium chloride.

If a reaction is reversible, it means that the reactants will never be completely converted to products because the reaction goes both ways. Some of the products are always reacting together to change back to the original reactants. This will mean a lower yield.

2. Product is lost when it's separated from the reactants

When you filter a liquid to remove solid particles, you nearly always lose a bit of liquid or a bit of solid. So, some of the product may be lost when it's separated from the reaction mixture. This will also result in a lower yield.

3. Unexpected reactions may be happening

Things don't always go exactly to plan. Sometimes there can be other unexpected reactions happening which use up the reactants. This means there's not as much reactant to make the product you want.

Figure 1: Copper sulfate crystals being filtered from copper sulfate solution — some liquid and some solid will be lost in this process.

Sustainable development

HOW SCIENCE WORKS

Thinking about product yield is important for sustainable development. Sustainable development is about making sure that we don't use resources faster than they can be replaced — there needs to be enough for future generations too.

There are a few things that can be done to help make industrial processes sustainable:

- Use reactions with high percentage yields. Using a reaction with a low percentage yield uses up resources and wastes a lot of chemicals.

- Use reactions that don't require much energy. When you save energy you don't need to burn as much fuel — this means that you use up less fossil fuels and create less pollution.

- Use raw materials that come from renewable sources. The more that we use reactants and fuels from non-renewable sources (like fossil fuels), the faster we'll run out of them.

Tip: Sustainable development is all about making sure we can continue to use important resources in the distant future.

Tip: A low percentage yield isn't so much of a problem if you can recycle any unreacted chemicals. The Haber process is a good example of this (see page 262).

Tip: There's more about these two reactions on page 80.

| Example |

Ethanol can be made either by hydrating ethene or by fermenting sugar.

- Hydrating ethene isn't very sustainable because the ethene comes from non-renewable crude oil. The reaction is done at a high temperature, so it uses lots of energy. The overall percentage yield is high though.

- Fermenting sugar is more sustainable because sugar comes from plants, so it's a renewable resource. The reaction works at a much lower temperature too, so it uses less energy. But the percentage yield is low.

Practice Questions — Fact Recall

Q1 What is the yield of a reaction?

Q2 What is the percentage yield of a reaction?

Q3 Give the formula that you would use to calculate the percentage yield of a reaction.

Q4 Give three reasons why percentage yields are never 100%.

Q5 Explain why high percentage yields are important for sustainable development.

Practice Questions — Application

Q1 Look at the reaction below:

$$N_2 + 3H_2 \rightleftharpoons 2NH_3$$

Use information from the equation to explain why the percentage yield of this reaction will not be 100%.

Q2 A scientist has developed a new way of making a certain chemical. His new method has a higher percentage yield than the old method and works at a lower temperature. Explain why the new method will be better for the environment than the old method.

Q3 The predicted yield of a reaction was 34.6 g of iron. The actual yield was 28.6 g of iron. Calculate the percentage yield of this reaction.

Q4 A scientist performed an experiment that involved reacting sodium hydroxide with sulfuric acid. She expected to get 41.9 g of sodium sulfate, but actually only got 33.4 g of sodium sulfate. Calculate the percentage yield of this reaction.

Q5 A reaction produced 10.3 g of copper sulfate. The predicted yield of the reaction was 15.2 g of copper sulfate. Calculate the percentage yield of this reaction.

Q6 A student worked out that his experiment should make 8.45 g of sodium chloride. He actually only ended up with 4.27 g of sodium chloride. Calculate the percentage yield of his experiment.

6. Chemical Analysis

This topic is all about how substances can be analysed to find out what they're made up of. Often, the best way to analyse substances is to use instrumental methods — this basically means getting a machine to do it for you.

Paper Chromatography

Chemical analysis is used to identify the different additives that are present in foods. For example, if you know that a food colouring is made up of a mixture of dyes, you can use a technique called **paper chromatography** (see Figure 1) to find out which dyes are in it. Here's what you do:

- Extract the colour from the food sample by placing it in a small cup with a few drops of solvent (can be water, ethanol, salt water, etc.).

- Put a spot of the coloured solution on a pencil baseline on some filter paper. (Don't use pen because it might dissolve and confuse everything.)

- Put the sheet in a beaker with some solvent — but keep the baseline above the level of the solvent.

- The solvent seeps up the paper, taking the dyes with it. Different dyes form spots in different places.

Learning Objectives:

- Know that food additives can be identified using chemical analysis.

- Know how paper chromatography is used to identify dyes in artificial colourings.

- Know that instrumental methods (using machines) can be used to analyse substances.

- Know why instrumental methods are usually better than manual methods.

- Know how gas chromatography-mass spectrometry (GC-MS) works.

- **H** Know that a mass spectrometer can be used to find out the relative molecular mass of a substance.

Specification Reference C2.3.2

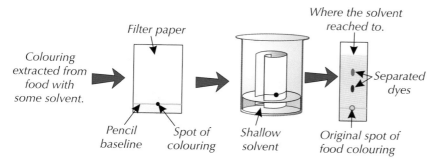

Colouring extracted from food with some solvent.

Filter paper

Pencil baseline

Spot of colouring

Shallow solvent

Where the solvent reached to.

Separated dyes

Original spot of food colouring

Figure 1: The process of paper chromatography.

Analysing the results

The piece of filter paper you get at the end, with the separated spots on, is called a chromatogram. A chromatogram gives you information about:

- What dyes different colourings contain. Each dye will move up the paper at a different rate and form a spot at a different distance from the baseline. So if you test two different colourings and they both contain a spot that's moved the same distance, it's likely to be the same dye.

- How many dyes a colouring contains. Be careful though — four spots means at least four dyes, not exactly four. It could be five, if two of the dyes have travelled such similar distances that their spots have joined up.

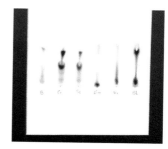

Figure 2: Paper chromatography being used to analyse dyes.

Tip: You couldn't get four spots from three dyes though — one dye can't split into two spots.

Example

On the chromatogram in Figure 1, the original spot of colouring has separated into two spots (a blue one and a pink one). This shows that the food colouring contains at least two different dyes (but it may be more).

Instrumental methods

You can identify elements and compounds using **instrumental methods** — this just means using machines. There are a number of advantages to using instrumental methods, instead of analysing substances manually:

- They are very sensitive — they can detect even the tiniest amounts of substances, which is really handy if your sample is small.

- They are very fast and tests can be automated, so using instrumental methods saves a lot of time.

- They are very accurate — machines don't make mistakes like people do.

Gas chromatography

A good example of an instrumental method that is commonly used in chemistry labs is **gas chromatography** (see Figure 3). Gas chromatography can separate out a mixture of compounds and help you identify the substances present. Here's how it works:

- A gas is used to carry a mixture of substances through a column (tube) packed with a solid material.

- The substances travel through the column at different speeds, so they're separated.

- The time each substance takes to reach the detector is called its retention time. It can be used to help identify the substance.

- The recorder draws a gas chromatogram (see Figure 3).

Tip: Each substance has its own retention time. You can identify substances by looking up their retention times in a database. Or you could run samples of pure substances through your machine to find their retention times.

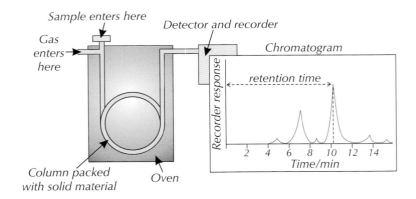

Figure 3: The process of gas chromatography.

The number of peaks on the chromatogram shows the number of different substances in the sample.

> **Example**
>
> On the chromatogram in Figure 3, there are six peaks, so the mixture being analysed must contain six different substances.

Figure 4: A gas chromatography machine.

The gas chromatography column can also be linked to a mass spectrometer. This process is known as GC-MS (Gas Chromatography-Mass Spectrometry). The mass spectrometer can be used to identify the substances leaving the column and can accurately detect very small quantities.

Analysing mass spectrometry results `Higher`

A mass spectrometer can be used to accurately identify the separated substances leaving a gas chromatography column, because it tells you the relative molecular mass of each one. You can work out the relative molecular mass of the substances from the graphs that the mass spectrometer draws. You just read off the value of the molecular ion peak (see Example below).

`Example` — `Higher`

Here's one graph from a mass spectrometer. The substance being analysed here has a relative molecular mass of 25.

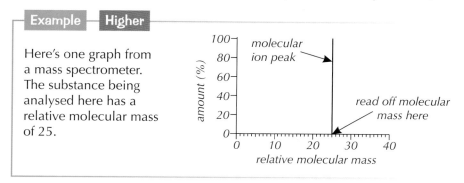

Practice Questions — Fact Recall

Q1 Describe how you could use paper chromatography to separate the dyes in some food colouring.

Q2 Give three advantages of using instrumental methods to analyse substances.

Q3 Describe how gas chromatography can be used to separate mixtures.

Q4 When a gas chromatography column is linked to a mass spectrometer, what information is obtained from the mass spectrometer?

Practice Questions — Application

Q1 Paper chromatography was used to analyse the dyes in some food colouring. The result is shown on the right. How many dyes does this colouring contain? Explain your answer

A: Three or less.   B: Exactly three.   C: Three or more

Q2 A mixture was analysed using gas chromatography. The results are shown on the right.

a) How many substances does this mixture contain?

b) What is the retention time of the tallest peak to the nearest minute?

Section Checklist — Make sure you know...

Atoms and Isotopes

☐ That atoms have a mass number (which tells you the total number of protons and neutrons in the atom) and an atomic number (which tells you the number of protons in the atom).

☐ That protons and neutrons have a relative mass of 1, while the relative mass of an electron is tiny.

☐ That isotopes have the same number of protons but different numbers of neutrons.

Relative Formula Mass

☐ ▣ That the relative atomic mass (A_r) of an element is the average mass of atoms of that element measured relative to the mass of one atom of carbon-12.

☐ What relative formula mass (M_r) is and how to calculate it using relative atomic masses.

☐ That the relative formula mass (A_r for elements or M_r for compounds) of a substance in grams is known as one mole of that substance.

☐ How to convert mass to moles and vice versa using the equation moles = mass (in g) $\div M_r$.

Formula Mass Calculations

☐ How to calculate the percentage mass of an element in a compound.

☐ ▣ How to work out the empirical formula of a compound from masses or percentage masses.

Calculating Masses in Reactions

☐ ▣ How to calculate the masses of reactants used or products made in a reaction.

Percentage Yield

☐ That yield is the amount of product formed in a reaction and percentage yield is a comparison between the amount of product expected and the amount of product actually obtained.

☐ ▣ How to calculate percentage yields.

☐ That in reversible reactions the products can react with each other to form the reactants.

☐ The reasons why percentage yields are never 100%.

☐ That high percentage yields, low energy needs and renewable reactants make reactions sustainable.

Chemical Analysis

☐ How paper chromatography can be used to separate and identify dyes in artificial colourings.

☐ What instrumental methods are and some advantages of using instrumental methods.

☐ How GC-MS can be used to separate and identify the compounds in a substance.

☐ ▣ That the mass spectrometer in GC-MS tells you the relative molecular mass of the compounds.

Exam-style Questions

1   A scientist is making some sodium hydroxide (NaOH) from calcium hydroxide (Ca(OH)$_2$) and sodium carbonate (Na$_2$CO$_3$).

When calcium hydroxide and sodium carbonate are mixed, the following reaction occurs.

$$Ca(OH)_{2(aq)} + Na_2CO_{3(s)} \rightarrow CaCO_{3(s)} + 2NaOH_{(aq)}$$

1 (a)   The scientist starts with 25.0 g of sodium carbonate.

1 (a) (i)   How many moles are there in 25.0 g of sodium carbonate?

(2 marks)

1 **(a) (ii)**   Calculate the mass of sodium hydroxide the scientist could expect to form if he reacts 25.0 g of sodium carbonate with an excess of calcium hydroxide.

(2 marks)

1 (b)   The scientist separated the sodium hydroxide solution from the solid calcium carbonate using filter paper.

Next he crystallised the solution and weighed the solid sodium hydroxide crystals. He found that he had only made 10.4 g of sodium hydroxide.

1 **(b) (i)**   Use the information above and your answer from (a) part (ii) to calculate the percentage yield of this reaction.

(If you were unable to answer (a) part (ii), use a value of 22.4 g for the expected yield of sodium hydroxide — this is not the correct answer.)

(2 marks)

1 (b) (ii)   Even if all of the sodium carbonate is converted to sodium hydroxide, the yield of this reaction will never be 100%. Suggest **one** reason why.

(1 mark)

1 (b) (iii) Suggest **one** reason why chemical companies try to avoid using reactions that have low percentage yields.

(1 mark)

2   A chemist is using gas chromatography linked to mass spectrometry (GC-MS) to analyse a mixture of substances. Her results are shown below.

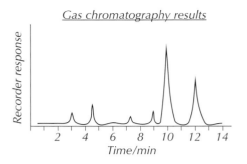

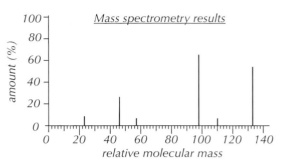

The table below contains information on some of the compounds that might be in this mixture.

Compound	Molecular Formula	Retention time (min)
Phosphoric acid	H_3PO_4	9.97
Fumaric acid	$C_4H_4O_4$	10.94
Aspartic acid	$C_4H_7NO_4$	12.00
Malic acid	$C_4H_6O_5$	12.79
Glutamic acid	$C_5H_9NO_4$	13.34

2 (a) (i)   What is the relative formula mass of phosphoric acid?
(Relative atomic masses: H = 1, O = 16, P = 31)

(1 mark)

2 (a) (ii)   Using the information above, give **two** pieces of evidence to suggest that phosphoric acid is in the mixture the chemist is analysing.

(2 marks)

2 (b)   Aspartic acid is also present in the mixture. The M_r of aspartic acid is 133.
Calculate the percentage mass of carbon in aspartic acid. Carbon has an A_r of 12.

(2 marks)

2 (c)   A sample of another compound in the mixture was found to contain 4.8 g of carbon, 1.2 g of hydrogen and 3.2 g of oxygen. Find the empirical formula of this compound.
(Relative atomic masses: H = 1, C = 12, O = 16)

(3 marks)

2 (d)   GC-MS is an instrumental method. Give **one** advantage that instrumental methods have over manual methods.

(1 mark)

1. Rate of Reaction

Chemical reactions don't all happen at the same rate — some reactions happen faster than others. There are a number of factors that affect how quickly a reaction goes. Read on to find out more...

Different reaction rates

Reactions can go at all sorts of different rates. Some reactions happen very quickly, while others happen really slowly.

> **Examples**
>
> - The rusting of iron is a pretty slow reaction — it can take years for a lump of iron to go rusty.
>
> - A moderate speed reaction is a metal (like magnesium) reacting with acid to produce a gentle stream of bubbles.
>
> - A really fast reaction is an explosion, where it's all over in a fraction of a second.

Factors that affect the rate of a reaction

There are four main factors that affect how quickly a reaction goes:

- Temperature — the higher the temperature, the faster the reaction goes.

- Concentration (or pressure for gases) — the more concentrated the reactants (or the higher the pressure), the faster the reaction goes.

- Surface area (size of solid pieces) — the larger the surface area (the smaller the pieces), the faster the reaction goes.

- Catalysts — reactions with a catalyst can go faster than reactions without.

Collision theory

Reaction rates are explained by **collision theory**. Collision theory just says that the rate of a reaction depends on how often and how hard the reacting particles collide with each other.

The basic idea is that particles have to collide in order to react, and they have to collide hard enough (with enough energy). This means there are two ways to increase the rate of reaction:

Learning Objectives:

- Know that particles have to collide with enough energy in order to react.

- Understand why increasing the temperature increases the rate of a reaction.

- Understand why increasing the concentration (or pressure) increases the rate of a reaction.

- Understand why increasing the surface area of solid reactants increases the rate of reaction.

- Know what is meant by the term activation energy.

- Know that a catalyst is a substance that can speed up a reaction without being changed or used up itself.

- Understand why catalysts are important in industry.

- Be able to weigh up the advantages and disadvantages of using catalysts in industry.

Specification Reference C2.4, C2.4.1

- Increase the number of collisions, so that the probability of a **successful collision** (a collision that results in a reaction) increases.
- Increase the energy of the collisions, so that more of the collisions are successful collisions.

Increasing the number of collisions

The effects of temperature, concentration (or pressure) and surface area on the rate of reaction can be explained in terms of how often the reacting particles collide.

Temperature

When the temperature is increased the particles all move quicker. If they're moving quicker, they're going to collide more often and more collisions means a faster rate of reaction — see Figure 1.

Tip: Increasing the temperature also increases the energy of the collisions — more on this on the next page.

Cold

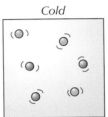

Hot

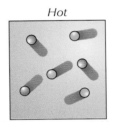

Particles move slowly. Not many collisions. *Particles move quickly. Lots of collisions.*

Figure 1: A diagram showing why increasing the temperature increases the rate of a reaction.

Concentration (or pressure)

If a solution is made more concentrated it means there are more particles of reactant knocking about between the water molecules, which makes collisions between the important particles more likely.

Similarly, in a gas, increasing the pressure means the particles are more squashed up together, so there will be more frequent collisions (see Figure 2). More frequent collisions means a faster rate of reaction.

Tip: This makes sense if you think about it — you're much more likely to bump into someone when you're in a crowd of people than when there aren't many people around.

Low concentration (or low pressure)

High concentration (or high pressure)

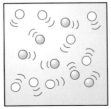

Particles far apart. Not many collisions. *Particles close together. Lots of collisions.*

Figure 2: A diagram showing why increasing the concentration (or pressure) increases the rate of a reaction.

Surface area

If one of the reactants is a solid then breaking it up into smaller pieces will increase the total surface area. This means the particles around it in the solution will have more area to work on, so there'll be more frequent collisions and the rate of reaction will be faster — see Figure 3.

Small surface area

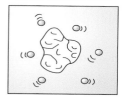

Large surface area

Less area for collisions.
Not many collisions.

More area for collisions.
Lots of collisions.

Figure 3: *A diagram showing why increasing the surface area increases the rate of a reaction.*

Tip: You get the fastest rates of reactions with powders because powders have a very large surface area.

Increasing the energy of collisions

The effect of temperature on reaction rate can also be explained in terms of how much energy the particles have when they collide. A higher temperature doesn't only increase the frequency of collisions — it also increases the energy of the collisions, because it makes all the particles move faster.

Reactions only happen if the particles collide with enough energy. The minimum amount of energy that particles must have in order to react is called the **activation energy**. At a higher temperature there will be more particles colliding with enough energy to make the reaction happen.

Tip: For a collision to be successful, the energy of the particles must be greater than or equal to the activation energy. If the particles don't have enough energy, they will just bounce off each other without reacting.

Catalysts

Many reactions can be speeded up by adding a **catalyst**.

> A catalyst is a substance which can speed up a reaction, without being changed or used up in the reaction.

A solid catalyst works by giving the reacting particles a surface to stick to. This increases the number of successful collisions, speeding the reaction up.

Catalysts in industry

Catalysts are very important for commercial reasons — most industrial reactions use them. Catalysts increase the rate of the reaction, which saves a lot of money simply because the plant doesn't need to operate for as long to produce the same amount of stuff.

Some catalysts also allow the reaction to work at a much lower temperature. That reduces the energy used up in the reaction (the energy cost), which is good for sustainable development (see page 149) and can save a lot of money.

Tip: You've come across a few catalysts already. For example, aluminium oxide is a catalyst used in cracking (p. 75) and nickel is a catalyst used in the hydrogenation of oils (p. 89).

Another advantage is that catalysts never get used up in the reaction, so once you've got them you can use them over and over again.

There are disadvantages to using catalysts, though.

- They can be very expensive to buy, and often need to be removed from the product and cleaned.

- Different reactions use different catalysts, so if you make more than one product at your plant, you'll probably need to buy different catalysts for them.

- Catalysts can be 'poisoned' by impurities, so they stop working.

Example

Sulfur impurities can poison the iron catalyst used in the Haber process (used to make ammonia for fertilisers). That means you have to keep your reaction mixture very clean.

Tip: See pages 262-264 for more on the Haber process.

Practice Questions — Fact Recall

Q1 What must happen for a reaction to occur between two particles?

Q2 Explain why increasing the concentration of the reactants increases the rate of a reaction.

Q3 Give two reasons why increasing the temperature increases the rate of a reaction.

Q4 What is the definition of a catalyst?

Q5 a) Give one advantage of using catalysts in industry.

b) Give one disadvantage of using catalysts in industry.

Practice Questions — Application

Q1 The table below contains some rate of reaction data for the reactions of hydrochloric acid with different forms of calcium carbonate:

Form of calcium carbonate	Marble chips	Crushed marble chips	Powdered chalk
Initial rate of reaction (cm³/min)	0.6	1.4	5.6

Describe and explain these results.

Q2 A factory produces ethene by cracking larger hydrocarbons. The owner wants to increase productivity and suggests performing the reaction at a higher temperature.

a) Explain why this would increase productivity.

b) Suggest one other way that the owner could increase productivity.

Tip: Don't worry too much about what the units mean in Q1 for now — how to calculate rates of reaction is coming up in the next topic.

2. Measuring Rates of Reaction

Learning Objective:
- Know that the rate of a reaction can be calculated by dividing either the amount of reactant used or the amount of product formed by time.

Specification Reference C2.4.1

If you want to measure the rate of a reaction, you're going to need a way to follow what's happening. Here's a guide to measuring rates of reaction...

Calculating rates of reaction

You can find the rate of a reaction either by measuring how quickly the reactants are used up or how quickly the products are formed (although it's usually a lot easier to measure the products forming). Once you've taken these measurements, you can work out the reaction rate using this formula:

$$\text{Rate of reaction} = \frac{\text{Amount of reactant used or product formed}}{\text{Time}}$$

> **Example**
>
> **In a reaction, 14.4 cm³ of oxygen gas was produced in the first 8 seconds. Calculate the rate of this reaction.**
>
> $$\text{Rate} = \frac{\text{Amount of product formed}}{\text{Time}} = \frac{14.4}{8} = 1.8 \text{ cm}^3/\text{s}$$

Tip: Rate of reaction can have lots of different units. The ones you're most likely to come across are cm³/s and g/s.

Measuring the formation of product

There are a few different ways that the formation of products during a reaction can be measured.

Precipitation

This is when the product of the reaction is a **precipitate** which clouds the solution. You can observe a mark through the solution and measure how long it takes for the mark to disappear (see Figure 1). The quicker the mark disappears, the quicker the reaction.

Tip: A precipitate is basically a solid that is formed in a solution during a chemical reaction.

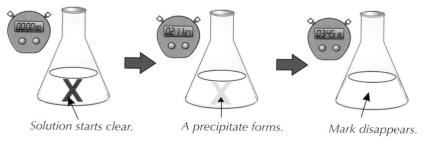

Solution starts clear.   A precipitate forms.   Mark disappears.

Figure 1: *Measuring the rate of a precipitation reaction.*

This method is simple and easy to do but it only works for reactions where the initial solution is see-through. Also, the result is very subjective — different people might not agree over the exact point when the mark 'disappears'.

Figure 2: *A reaction that produces a precipitate. When enough precipitate has formed, the cross disappears.*

Change in mass

You can measure the speed of a reaction that produces a gas using a mass balance. You just place the reaction vessel on the balance. As the gas is released the mass disappearing is easily measured — see Figure 3.
The quicker the reading on the balance drops, the faster the reaction.

Tip: Gases don't weigh very much so the change in mass can be quite small. The trick is to use a mass balance with a high <u>resolution</u>, so that very small changes in mass can be detected. See page 10 of the How Science Works section for more on resolution.

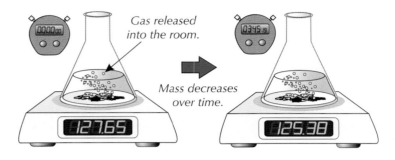

Gas released into the room.

Mass decreases over time.

Figure 3: *Measuring the rate of a reaction using a change in mass.*

This is the most accurate of the methods described in this topic because the mass balance is very accurate. But it has the disadvantage of releasing the gas straight into the room, which isn't very good if the gas is dangerous.

Volume of gas given off

You can also measure the rate of a reaction that produces a gas by using a gas syringe to measure the volume of gas given off — see Figure 4. The more gas given off during a given time interval, the faster the reaction.

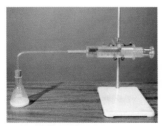

Figure 5: *The volume of gas produced in a reaction being measured.*

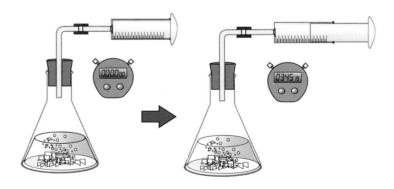

Figure 4: *Measuring the rate of a reaction using the volume of gas produced.*

Gas syringes usually give volumes to the nearest millilitre, so they're quite precise. Also, the gas isn't released into the room, which is useful if the gas produced is poisonous. You have to be quite careful though — if the reaction is too vigorous, you can easily blow the plunger out of the end of the syringe.

Practice Questions — Fact Recall

Q1 What is the formula for calculating the rate of a reaction?

Q2 Describe how you could measure the rate of a reaction where one of the products was a precipitate.

Q3 A student is measuring the rate of a reaction using a gas syringe.

a) Discuss the advantages and disadvantages of this technique.

b) Suggest another method that the student could use to measure the rate of this reaction.

Practice Questions — Application

Q1 The equation below shows the reaction between sulfuric acid and sodium hydrogen carbonate:

$$H_2SO_{4(aq)} + 2NaHCO_{3(s)} \rightarrow Na_2SO_{4(aq)} + 2H_2O_{(l)} + 2CO_{2(g)}$$

Suggest a method for measuring the rate of this reaction.

Q2 The equation below shows the reaction of sodium hydroxide with magnesium chloride:

$$2NaOH_{(aq)} + MgCl_{2(aq)} \rightarrow 2NaCl_{(aq)} + Mg(OH)_{2(s)}$$

Suggest a method for measuring the rate of this reaction. (If you need a clue, have a look at Figure 6.)

Q3 A reaction produced 4.3 cm³ of carbon dioxide gas in the first 5.0 seconds. Calculate the rate of this reaction in cm³/s.

Q4 Some potassium metal was added to water and the change in mass was measured on a mass balance. In the first 8.0 seconds, the mass of the reaction decreased from 34.31 g to 32.63 g. Calculate the rate of this reaction in g/s.

Tip: The tiny letters in brackets that you find in some equations are called state symbols. They tell you what state each chemical is in:
- (s) means solid,
- (l) means liquid,
- (g) means gas,
- (aq) means dissolved in water.

For more about state symbols, see page 178.

Figure 6: The reaction of sodium hydroxide with magnesium chloride.

Learning Objective:
- Be able to interpret graphs showing the rates of reactions.

Specification Reference C2.4

3. Rate of Reaction Graphs

Once you've measured the amount of product made or reactant used over time, you can plot your data on a graph.

Graphs showing the rate of a reaction

If you plot the amount of product formed (or the amount of reactant used) in a reaction against time you'll get a graph that looks something like the one in Figure 1. On a graph like this, the rate of the reaction is shown by the gradient (steepness) of the line. The steeper the line, the faster the rate (because it shows that products are being formed, or reactants used up, more quickly).

Graphs of product formed (or reactant used) against time are not straight lines — they're curves that start steep, get shallower and then level off. This is because reactions start quickly, then slow down and eventually stop.

Exam Tip
In the exam, you could be given a graph that shows the amount of reactant left over time. This will look like an upside down version of the graph in Figure 1:

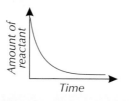

It's still a curve that starts steep and then levels off.

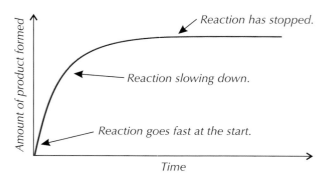

Figure 1: *A graph of amount of product formed against time for a reaction.*

Reactions start quickly because at the beginning of the reaction there are lots of reactant particles around, so collisions between them are very frequent. As the reaction progresses, the reactants get used up so the number of reactant particles decreases. This means collisions between reactant particles get less frequent and the reaction slows down. The reaction stops when all of the reactants are used up.

Tip: See page 158 for more on collision theory and why the concentration of the reactants affects the rate of reaction.

Comparing rates of reaction

You can compare the rate of a reaction performed under different conditions (for example at different temperatures) by plotting a series of lines on one graph. All of the lines will be curves, but the exact shape of each curve will depend on the rate of reaction and the amount of reactant that you started with.

- The fastest reaction will be the line with the steepest slope at the beginning. Also, the faster a reaction goes, the sooner it finishes, which means that the line will become flat earlier.

- Reactions that start off with the same amount of reactants will give lines that finish at the same level on the graph.

A student added some magnesium metal to an excess of hydrochloric acid that had been heated to 30 °C. He recorded the amount of gas formed at regular intervals.

The student repeated the experiment with the acid heated to 40 °C and then to 50 °C. Finally he tried heating the acid to 50 °C and adding double the mass of magnesium. This graph shows all of his results:

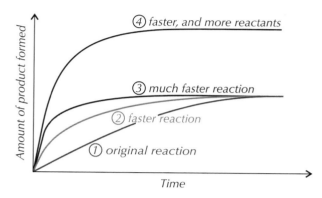

- Line 1 shows the original (fairly slow) reaction at 30 °C. The graph isn't very steep at the start and it takes a long time to level off.

- Lines 2 and 3 show the same reaction taking place at 40 °C and 50 °C. The initial rate of the reaction gets faster as the temperature increases, so the slope of the graphs gets steeper too.

- Lines 1, 2 and 3 all end up at the same level because they produce the same amount of product (though they take different times to get there).

- Line 4 shows the reaction taking place at 50 °C with double the mass of magnesium. It goes faster than the original reaction. It also finishes at a higher level because more reactants were added to begin with.

Exam Tip
You need to be able to interpret graphs like this in your exam so make sure you understand why the shapes of these curves are different.

Tip: There are more examples of rate of reaction graphs coming up on the next few pages.

Practice Questions — Application

Q1 The graph below shows the same reaction performed at three different temperatures. All other conditions were kept the same.

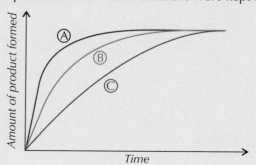

Which of these reactions (A, B or C) was performed at the highest temperature? Explain your answer.

Tip: Remember, you can increase the rate of a reaction by raising the temperature, increasing the reactant concentration (or pressure), adding a catalyst or crushing up a solid reactant (see pages 157-160).

The graph below shows the same reaction performed with three different concentrations of acid. All other conditions were kept the same.

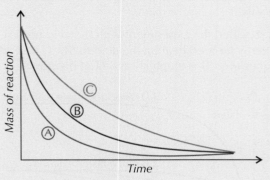

Tip: See page 158 for more on how and why concentration affects the rate of reaction.

Which of these reactions (A, B or C) was performed with the lowest concentration of acid? Explain your answer.

Q3 The graph below shows the amount of product formed over time in a reaction.

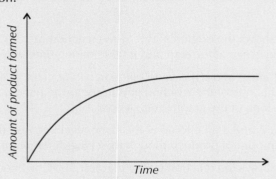

Copy this graph and sketch on the curves that would be produced if the reaction was performed:

a) with double the amount of reactant.

b) with the same amount of reactant but in the presence of a catalyst.

Tip: Don't forget — a catalyst is a substance that can speed up the rate of a reaction without being changed or used up in the reaction.

4. Rate of Reaction Experiments

To really understand how rates of reaction can be measured you need to know a few examples of rate of reaction experiments. Luckily there are some coming up right now...

Learning Objectives:
- Know some examples of rate of reaction experiments.
- Be able to interpret graphs showing the rates of reactions.

Specification Reference C2.4

Hydrochloric acid and marble chips

Marble is a form of calcium carbonate ($CaCO_3$). It will react with dilute hydrochloric acid (HCl). The equation for this reaction is shown below:

$$2HCl_{(aq)} + CaCO_{3(s)} \rightarrow CaCl_{2(aq)} + H_2O_{(l)} + CO_{2(g)}$$

Since this reaction produces carbon dioxide gas, you can find the rate by measuring the volume of gas produced — see Figure 1.

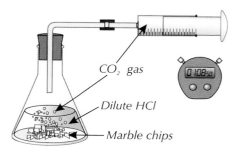

CO₂ gas

Dilute HCl

Marble chips

Figure 1: Measuring the rate of reaction of HCl with marble chips.

Tip: Remember, the little letters in brackets in equations like this one tell you what state the chemicals are in. See pages 163 and 178 for more on state symbols.

Tip: Have a look back at pages 161-162 for lots more on measuring rates of reaction.

This reaction is often used to show the effect of breaking a solid reactant up into smaller bits. Here's what you do:

- Measure the volume of gas evolved with a gas syringe and take readings at regular time intervals.

- Make a table of readings and plot them as a graph. Time goes on the x-axis and volume goes on the y-axis.

- Repeat the experiment with exactly the same volume of acid, and exactly the same mass of marble chips, but with the marble more crunched up.

- Then repeat with the same mass of powdered chalk instead of marble chips. (Chalk is just another form of calcium carbonate)

If you do that, you'll get a graph that looks something like Figure 2.

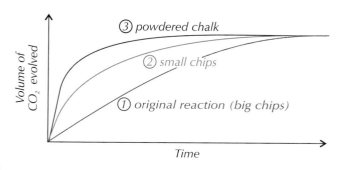

③ powdered chalk

② small chips

① original reaction (big chips)

Volume of CO₂ evolved

Time

Figure 2: Graph showing the reaction of HCl with different forms of $CaCO_3$.

Figure 3: A marble chip (left) and powdered chalk (right) reacting with HCl — the reaction with powdered chalk is much faster.

The graph in Figure 3 shows that using finer particles results in a faster rate of reaction. This is because using finer particles gives the reactant a larger surface area. And the larger the surface area, the faster the rate of reaction.

Figure 4 shows what happens if you use a greater mass of small marble chips. The extra surface area gives a faster reaction and more gas is evolved overall.

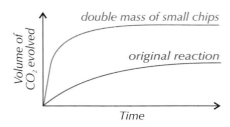

Figure 4: *Graph showing the reaction of HCl with different amounts and chip sizes of marble.*

Magnesium metal and hydrochloric acid

The reaction of magnesium metal with dilute hydrochloric acid can be used to show the effect of increased reactant concentration on the rate of a reaction. The equation for the reaction is:

$$2HCl_{(aq)} + Mg_{(s)} \rightarrow MgCl_{2(aq)} + H_{2(g)}$$

This reaction gives off hydrogen gas, so you can follow the rate of the reaction by measuring the loss in mass using a mass balance. Here's what you do:

- Take readings of mass at regular time intervals.

- Put the results in a table and work out the loss in mass for each reading. Plot a graph.

- Repeat with more concentrated acid solutions, but always with the same amount of magnesium. The volume of acid must always be kept the same too — only the concentration is increased.

Tip: You could also measure the amount of hydrogen produced using a gas syringe.

This should give you a result like the one shown in Figure 6.

Figure 5: *Magnesium ribbon reacting with hydrochloric acid — you can see the bubbles of hydrogen gas being produced.*

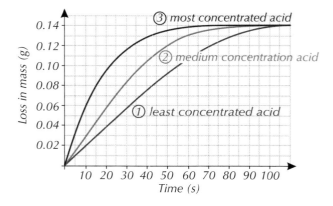

Figure 6: *Graph showing the reaction of Mg with different concentrations of HCl.*

The graph in Figure 6 shows the expected pattern — a higher concentration gives a steeper graph, with the reaction finishing much quicker.

Sodium thiosulfate and hydrochloric acid

Sodium thiosulfate and hydrochloric acid are both clear solutions. They react together to form a yellow precipitate of sulfur:

$$2HCl_{(aq)} + Na_2S_2O_{3(aq)} \rightarrow 2NaCl_{(aq)} + SO_{2(g)} + S_{(s)} + H_2O_{(l)}$$

The sodium thiosulfate and hydrochloric acid experiment involves watching a black mark disappear through the cloudy sulfur and timing how long it takes to go — see Figure 7.

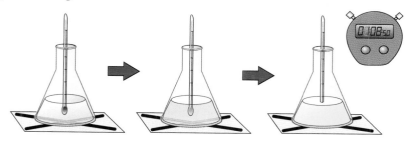

Figure 7: *Measuring the rate of the reaction between sodium thiosulfate and hydrochloric acid.*

This reaction can be repeated for solutions at different temperatures. In practice, it's a bit tricky to do accurately and safely (it's not a good idea to heat an acid directly). The best way to do it is to use a water bath to heat both solutions to the right temperature before you mix them. The volume of liquid and the container used must be kept the same each time, of course.

Tip: This reaction can also be used to test the effects of concentration.

The results will show that the higher the temperature the quicker the reaction and therefore the less time it takes for the mark to disappear. Some typical results are shown in Figure 8.

Temperature (°C)	20	25	30	35	40
Time taken for mark to disappear (s)	193	151	112	87	52

Figure 8: *Results of an experiment comparing the rate of reaction between sodium thiosulfate and hydrochloric acid at different temperatures.*

Tip: Unlike the other experiments in this topic, this one doesn't give you a set of graphs. You just get one lot of readings telling you how long it took for the mark to disappear at each temperature. You could still plot these on a graph though.

Decomposition of hydrogen peroxide

The decomposition of hydrogen peroxide is a good reaction for showing the effect of different catalysts on the rate of reaction. The equation for the decomposition of hydrogen peroxide is:

$$2H_2O_{2(aq)} \rightarrow 2H_2O_{(l)} + O_{2(g)}$$

This is normally quite slow but a sprinkle of manganese(IV) oxide catalyst speeds it up. Other catalysts that work are found in potato peel and blood.

One of the products of this reaction is oxygen gas, which provides an ideal way to measure the rate of reaction using the syringe method — see Figure 10.

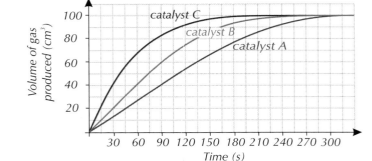

O₂ gas

Hydrogen peroxide

Catalyst

Figure 9: *Decomposition of hydrogen peroxide into water and oxygen gas.*

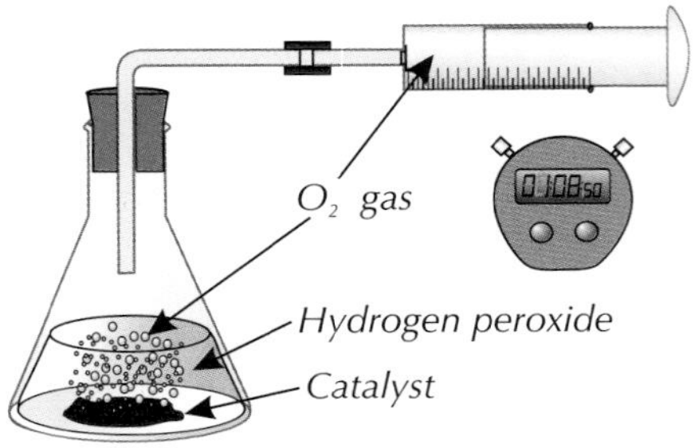

Figure 10: *Measuring the rate of the decomposition of hydrogen peroxide with a catalyst.*

By measuring the rate of gas production with different catalysts, you can work out which catalyst speeds up the reaction the most. The graph in Figure 11 shows the results that you would expect to get.

Tip: Without any catalyst added the curve would be very shallow.

Figure 11: *Graph showing the decomposition of hydrogen peroxide with different catalysts.*

Better catalysts give a quicker reaction, which is shown by a steeper graph that levels off quickly. This reaction can also be used to measure the effects of temperature, or of concentration of the H₂O₂ solution. The graphs will show the same pattern.

Practice Questions — Fact Recall

Q1 Describe an experiment using marble chips that could be used to demonstrate the effect of surface area on the rate of a reaction. What results would you expect?

Q2 Sketch a graph to show the results you would expect if a set mass of magnesium metal was reacted with two different concentrations of hydrochloric acid.

Tip: Sodium thiosulfate and hydrochloric acid react to form a yellow sulfur precipitate.

Q3 Describe one way that you could measure the rate of the reaction between sodium thiosulfate and hydrochloric acid.

Section Checklist — Make sure you know...

Rate of Reaction

☐ That in order for a reaction to take place, the reacting particles must collide with sufficient energy.

☐ That increasing the temperature, the concentration (or pressure), or the surface area of reactants will increase the rate of reaction, because they increase the number of collisions between particles.

☐ That increasing the temperature also increases the rate of reaction because it increases the energy of the reacting particles.

☐ That the minimum amount of energy required for a reaction to take place is known as the activation energy.

☐ That a catalyst is a substance that can increase the rate of a reaction without be changed or used up.

☐ That catalysts are important in industry because they decrease the time taken to produce the same amount of product and reduce the energy used in reactions.

☐ That disadvantages to using catalysts in industry include that they are expensive to buy, they only work with one reaction and they can be poisoned.

Measuring Rates of Reaction

☐ That a rate of reaction can be calculated by dividing either the amount of reactant used or the amount of product formed by time.

☐ That the rate of a reaction that produces a precipitate can be measured by observing a mark through the solution and timing how long it takes for the mark to disappear.

☐ That the rate of a reaction that produces a gas can be measured either by monitoring the decrease in mass of the reaction over time (using a mass balance) or by measuring the volume of gas produced (using a gas syringe).

Rate of Reaction Graphs

☐ That if you plot a graph showing the amount of product formed (or reactant used) against time, the steepness of the curve will represent the rate of the reaction — the steeper the curve, the faster the rate.

☐ That these types of graphs are usually curves because the reaction starts quickly, then slows down and eventually stops as the reactants get used up.

☐ That you can compare the rate of a reaction under different conditions by comparing the steepness of the curve at the start of the reaction and the time it takes for the curve to level off.

☐ That no matter how quickly the reaction goes, the curve will always finish at the same level, unless you add more reactant.

Rate of Reaction Experiments

☐ Some examples of rate of reaction experiments — for example, hydrochloric acid and marble chips, magnesium metal and hydrochloric acid, sodium thiosulfate and hydrochloric acid and the decomposition of hydrogen peroxide.

Learning Objectives:

- Know that energy is transferred to or from the surroundings during a chemical reaction.
- Know that if a reaction transfers energy to the surroundings it is exothermic.
- Know some examples of exothermic reactions and their uses.
- Know that if a reaction absorbs energy from the surroundings it is endothermic.
- Know some examples of endothermic reactions and their uses.
- Know that reversible reactions are endothermic in one direction and exothermic in the other direction.

Specification Reference C2.5.1

1. Energy Transfer in Reactions

When reactions take place, energy is transferred between the reaction and the surroundings. Some reactions give out heat, while others take energy in, making their surroundings colder. Read on to find out more...

Energy transfer

Whenever chemical reactions occur energy is transferred to or from the surroundings. This energy is usually transferred in the form of heat. If energy is transferred to the surroundings, the temperature of the surroundings will increase. If energy is transferred from the surroundings, the temperature of the surroundings will decrease.

Exothermic reactions

An **exothermic reaction** is one which transfers energy to the surroundings. This is shown by a rise in temperature. The best example of an exothermic reaction is burning fuels (combustion). This gives out a lot of heat — it's very exothermic. Neutralisation reactions (between an acid and an alkali) are also exothermic and many **oxidation** reactions are exothermic too.

Examples

- The reaction of potassium hydroxide with hydrochloric acid is a neutralisation reaction. This reaction produces heat — it's exothermic.

- Sodium is oxidised when it reacts with water — when sodium is added to water, it emits heat and moves about on the surface of the water as it is oxidised (see page 207). The fact that heat is released shows that this is an exothermic reaction.

Uses of exothermic reactions

Exothermic reactions have lots of everyday uses.

Examples

- Some hand warmers use the exothermic oxidation of iron in air (with a salt solution catalyst) to generate heat.

- Self-heating cans of hot chocolate and coffee also rely on exothermic reactions between chemicals in their bases.

Figure 1: *A chemical hand warmer. It uses an exothermic reaction.*

Endothermic reactions

An **endothermic reaction** is one which takes in energy from the surroundings. This is shown by a fall in temperature. Endothermic reactions are much less common than exothermic reactions, but thermal decomposition reactions are a good example.

Example

The thermal decomposition of calcium carbonate is endothermic. Heat must be supplied to make calcium carbonate decompose into calcium oxide and carbon dioxide. The equation for this reaction is:

$$CaCO_3 \rightarrow CaO + CO_2$$

Uses of endothermic reactions

Endothermic reactions also have everyday uses.

Example

A sports injury pack is a cold pack that can be placed on an injury like a sprain or strain to reduce swelling. Some sports injury packs use endothermic reactions — they take in heat and the pack becomes very cold. This is much more convenient than carrying ice around. Also, this type of cold pack is much more flexible than a block of ice, so it can be wrapped around an injury more easily.

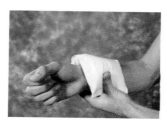

Figure 2: *A cold pack which uses an endothermic reaction being used to treat a sprained wrist.*

Energy transfer in reversible reactions

In reversible reactions, if the reaction is endothermic in one direction, it will be exothermic in the other direction. The energy absorbed by the endothermic reaction is equal to the energy released during the exothermic reaction.

Tip: See pages 258-260 for lots more on reversible reactions.

Example

A good example of a reversible reaction is the thermal decomposition of hydrated copper sulfate. The equation for this reaction is:

hydrated copper sulfate $\rightleftharpoons$ anhydrous copper sulfate + water

- If you heat blue hydrated copper sulfate crystals it drives the water off and leaves white anhydrous copper sulfate powder. This is endothermic.

- If you then add a couple of drops of water to the white powder you get the blue crystals back again and heat is given out. This is exothermic.

The amount of heat that you have to put in to drive all the water out of the anhydrous copper sulfate is the same as the amount of heat that is given out when you add all the water back in to form hydrated copper sulfate.

Tip: "Anhydrous" just means "without water", and "hydrated" means "with water".

Figure 3: Hydrated copper sulfate (blue) being heated to form anhydrous copper sulfate (white).

This reaction is shown in Figure 4.

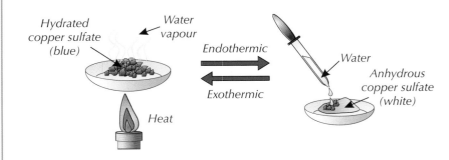

Figure 4: The reversible reaction between hydrated copper sulfate and anhydrous copper sulfate.

Practice Questions — Fact Recall

Q1 a) What is an exothermic reaction?

   b) Name one type of reaction that is exothermic.

Q2 a) When an endothermic reaction takes place, the temperature around the reaction decreases. Explain why.

   b) Give one example of an everyday use of an endothermic reaction.

Q3 If a reaction is exothermic in the forward direction will it give out heat or absorb heat in the reverse direction? Explain your answer.

Section Checklist — Make sure you know...

Energy Transfer in Reactions

☐ That during a chemical reaction, energy is either transferred from the reaction to the surroundings, or from the surroundings to the reaction.

☐ That exothermic reactions are reactions which transfer energy to the surroundings, resulting in an increase in temperature.

☐ That combustion, neutralisation reactions and some oxidation reactions are exothermic.

☐ That exothermic reactions are used in hand warmers and self-heating cans.

☐ That an endothermic reaction is a reaction which takes energy in from the surroundings, resulting in a decrease in temperature.

☐ That thermal decomposition reactions are examples of endothermic reactions.

☐ That endothermic reactions are used in sports injury packs.

☐ That reversible reactions that are exothermic in the forward direction will be endothermic in the backward direction (and vice versa) and the same amount of energy will be transferred each way.

☐ That the thermal decomposition of hydrated copper sulfate is an example of a reversible reaction. It is endothermic in one direction and exothermic in the other.

Exam-style Questions

1   A student is investigating the rate of the reaction between nitric acid and zinc carbonate. The equation for this reaction is shown below:

$$2HNO_{3(aq)} + ZnCO_{3(s)} \rightarrow Zn(NO_3)_{2(aq)} + CO_{2(g)} + H_2O_{(l)}$$

The student used a gas syringe to measure the volume of carbon dioxide produced by this reaction and recorded the volume every 2 minutes for 20 minutes.

1 (a)   Suggest another technique that the student could have used to measure the rate of this reaction.

(1 mark)

1 (b)   The student's results are shown on this graph.

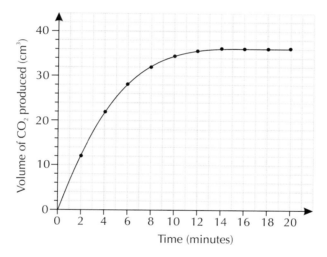

1 (b) (i)   Use the graph to estimate how long it took for all of the reactants to be used up in this reaction.

(1 mark)

1 (b) (ii)   Calculate the rate of reaction during the first 2 minutes of this reaction. Give your answer in cm³/min.

(2 marks)

1 (b) (iii)   Explain why the rate of this reaction decreased as the reaction progressed.

(2 marks)

1 (c)   The student repeated his experiment at a higher temperature. All other conditions were kept the same.

On the graph above, sketch a curve to show the results he might expect.

(2 marks)

2   In industry, vanadium(v) oxide is used as a catalyst in the following reaction:

$$2SO_{2(g)} + O_{2(g)} \rightleftharpoons 2SO_{3(g)}$$

Sulfur trioxide (SO_3) is used in the synthesis of sulfuric acid.

2 (a) (i)   What is a catalyst?

(1 mark)

2 (a) (ii)   Discuss the advantages and disadvantages of using catalysts in industrial reactions.

(4 marks)

2 (b)   Increasing the pressure changes the rate of this reaction.

2 (b) (i)   State the effect that using a higher pressure will have on the rate of this reaction.

(1 mark)

2 (b) (ii)   Explain why increasing the pressure has an effect on the rate of this reaction.

(2 marks)

3   A reusable hand warmer contains a solution of sodium acetate trihydrate. When the hand warmer is activated, the sodium acetate trihydrate crystallises and heat is released. The word equation for this reaction is shown below:

sodium acetate trihydrate solution $\rightleftharpoons$ solid sodium acetate trihydrate

3 (a)   What type of reaction is this? Circle the correct answer.

neutralisation   exothermic   combustion   endothermic

(1 mark)

3 (b) (i)   Using the information above, explain why hand warmers that contain sodium acetate trihydrate are reusable.

(2 marks)

3 (b) (ii)   Suggest how the hand warmer could be reset after use, so that it is ready to be used again. Explain your answer.

(2 marks)

1. pH and Neutralisation

The pH of a solution tells you whether it's acidic, alkaline or neutral. This topic is all about pH and how it's measured.

The pH scale

pH is a measure of how acidic or alkaline a solution is. The **pH scale** goes from 0 to 14 (see Figure 1).

- Anything with a pH of less than 7 is an **acid**. The lower the pH, the stronger the acid — the strongest acids have a pH of 0.

- Anything with a pH of greater than 7 is a **base** or an **alkali**. An alkali is a soluble base. The higher the pH, the more alkaline the substance is — the strongest bases and alkalis have a pH of 14.

- Neutral substances are neither acidic nor alkaline and have a pH of exactly 7. Pure water is an example of a neutral substance.

Testing pH

One way to test the pH of a solution is to use an **indicator**. An indicator is a dye that changes colour depending on whether it's above or below a certain pH. A commonly used indicator is **universal indicator**. This indicator is a combination of dyes which gives a different colour at different pH values (see Figure 1) — it's very useful for estimating the pH of a solution.

Tip: Water from the tap isn't pure so it won't have a pH of exactly 7.

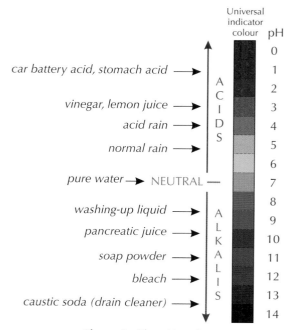

Figure 1:

		Universal indicator colour	pH
			0
car battery acid, stomach acid →	A		1
	C		2
vinegar, lemon juice →	I		3
acid rain →	D		4
normal rain →	S		5
			6
pure water → NEUTRAL —			7
			8
washing-up liquid →	A		9
pancreatic juice →	L		10
soap powder →	K		11
bleach →	A		12
	L		13
caustic soda (drain cleaner) →	I S		14

Figure 1: *The pH scale.*

Figure 2: *The colours of universal indicator in solutions with pHs from 0 to 14 (left to right).*

Acids and alkalis

Whether a substance is an acid or an alkali depends on the type of ions that are released when the substance is dissolved in water. Acids form hydrogen ions (H^+) when dissolved in water and alkalis form hydroxide ions (OH^-).

$H^+_{(aq)}$ ions make solutions acidic and $OH^-_{(aq)}$ ions make them alkaline.

State symbols

Tip: Although state symbols aren't only to do with acids and bases it's important you know about them now. It's <u>aqueous</u> H^+ or OH^- ions that make a solution acidic or alkaline, not solid or gaseous ions.

The (aq) after the H^+ and OH^- is an example of a **state symbol**. State symbols show the physical state that a substance is in — (aq) shows that the ions are dissolved in water (aqueous). There are a few other state symbols you need to know about in the box below.

(l) — liquid   (g) — gas   (s) — solid

Neutralisation reactions

An acid will react with a base to form a salt and water — this is called a **neutralisation** reaction. The general equation for a neutralisation reaction is shown below.

acid + base $\rightarrow$ salt + water

Neutralisation can also be shown in terms of H^+ and OH^- ions. During neutralisation reactions, hydrogen ions (H^+) from the acid react with hydroxide ions (OH^-) from the base to produce water. The equation for this reaction is:

$$H^+_{(aq)} + OH^-_{(aq)} \rightarrow H_2O_{(l)}$$

When an acid neutralises a base (or vice versa), the products are neutral — they have a pH of 7. An indicator can be used to show that a neutralisation reaction is over.

Example

Universal indicator turns green at the end of a neutralisation reaction — see Figure 3. This shows that the solution has become neutral (and therefore that the reaction has finished).

Figure 3: *Universal indicator turning green at the end of a neutralisation reaction.*

Practice Questions — Fact Recall

Q1   What is pH a measure of?

Q2   If a solution is neutral, what pH is it?

Q3   a) What range of pHs show that a substance is a base?

b) What is the difference between a base and an alkali?

c) Which type of ion makes solutions acidic and which makes solutions alkaline?

Q4   Which state symbol is used to show that a substance is dissolved in water?

Q5   a) What is the product of the reaction between hydrogen ions (H^+) and hydroxide ions (OH^-)?

b) Write the symbol equation for this reaction, including state symbols.

Practice Questions — Application

Q1   State whether the following solutions are acidic or alkaline.

a) A solution of hydrogen sulfide with a pH of 4.2.

b) A solution of calcium hydroxide with a pH of 12.4.

Q2   a) After adding universal indicator to a solution, the colour changes to yellow. Suggest the pH of this solution.

b) Another solution has a pH of 9. Suggest what colour this solution will go if universal indicator is added to it.

Q3   What states are the following compounds in?

a) $SO_{2(g)}$ b) $H_2O_{(l)}$

c) $NH_{4\ (aq)}^+$ d) $AgCl_{(s)}$

Q4   The base calcium carbonate reacts with hydrochloric acid.

a) What type of reaction is this?

b) A salt is formed. What is the other product of this reaction?

Tip: Have a look back at the pH scale on page 177 to help you work out the answer for Q2.

Learning Objectives:

- Know that you can make soluble salts by reacting acids with metals.

- Know that not all metals can be used to make salts — some are too reactive and others aren't reactive enough.

- Know that metal oxides and metal hydroxides are bases. Those that are soluble are alkalis.

- Know that you can make soluble salts by reacting acids with bases.

- Understand that the salt formed depends on the metal (or the metal within an oxide or hydroxide) and the acid that has been used to make it.

- Know that when ammonia dissolves in water an alkaline solution is made that can be used to make ammonium salts, which are important fertilisers.

Specification Reference C2.6.1, C2.6.2

2. Making Salts

Salts can be made from metals, metal oxides, metal hydroxides or ammonia. You need to know how this happens and be able to write equations for the reactions that are involved...

Making salts from metals

One way of making soluble salts is by reacting metals with acids. This reaction produces a salt and hydrogen, as shown in the equation below.

$$acid \; + \; metal \; \rightarrow \; salt \; + \; hydrogen$$

However, not all metals are suitable to use. Highly reactive metals like sodium are too reactive — many react explosively in the presence of strong acids so it isn't safe to make salts from these metals. Other metals, such as copper, aren't reactive enough — they don't react at all or the reaction is too slow for it to be worthwhile making salts from them.

Reactivity of metals with acids

You can see how reactive different metals are by monitoring the rate of hydrogen production when they react with an acid. The more reactive the metal, the faster the reaction will go. The speed of the reaction is indicated by the rate at which bubbles of hydrogen are given off — a speedy reaction is shown by bubbles being produced rapidly.

The production of hydrogen can be detected using the burning splint test. This involves putting a lit splint at the mouth of the tube containing the metal and the acid. If hydrogen is there you'll hear a 'squeaky pop'. The more reactive the metal, the more hydrogen is produced in a certain amount of time and the louder the 'squeaky pop'.

Figure 1: *Magnesium reacting with hydrochloric acid.*

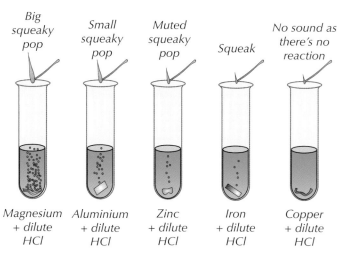

Figure 2: *The reactivity of different metals in the presence of hydrochloric acid.*

Which salt is formed?

The name of the salt produced depends on which metal and acid are used. The first part of the name of the salt come from the metal and the second part of the name comes from the acid that is used.

> **Example**
>
> When you react magnesium with hydrochloric acid you get magnesium chloride:
>
> hydrochloric acid + magnesium → magnesium chloride + hydrogen

Hydrochloric acid always produces chloride salts.

> **Examples**
>
> hydrochloric acid + aluminium → aluminum chloride + hydrogen
>
> $6HCl_{(aq)}$ + $2Al_{(s)}$ → $2AlCl_{3(aq)}$ + $3H_{2(g)}$
>
> hydrochloric acid + zinc → zinc chloride + hydrogen
>
> $2HCl_{(aq)}$ + $Zn_{(s)}$ → $ZnCl_{2(aq)}$ + $H_{2(g)}$

Tip: The way to remember which acid produces which salt is in the name. Hydro<u>chloric</u> acid produces <u>chloride</u> salts and <u>sulfuric</u> acid produces <u>sulfate</u> salts.

Sulfuric acid always produces sulfate salts.

> **Examples**
>
> sulfuric acid + magnesium → magnesium sulfate + hydrogen
>
> $H_2SO_{4(aq)}$ + $Mg_{(s)}$ → $MgSO_{4(aq)}$ + $H_{2(g)}$
>
> sulfuric acid + aluminium → aluminium sulfate + hydrogen
>
> $3H_2SO_{4(aq)}$ + $2Al_{(s)}$ → $Al_2(SO_4)_{3(aq)}$ + $3H_{2(g)}$

Nitric acid isn't quite so straightforward. It produces nitrate salts when neutralised (this is covered on page 182), but it can produce nitric oxides with metals (rather than nitrate salts) so we won't consider it here.

Exam Tip
In the exam you might be asked to work out the salt formed from two reactants or the reactants need to make a particular salt.
So it's important that you understand these examples.

Making salts from metal oxides and hydroxides

If for some reason you can't react a metal with an acid to make a soluble salt, another way of making the salt is to react a metal oxide or a metal hydroxide with an acid.

All metal oxides and hydroxides are **bases**. Some of them are **alkalis** because they are soluble in water. Because metal oxides and hydroxides are all bases, they react with acids in a neutralisation reaction. The products of neutralisation reactions are a salt and water. So the general equation for the reaction of metal oxides or metal hydroxides with acids is:

Tip: Remember, a base is a substance with a pH of more than 7. An alkali is a base that will dissolve in water.

> acid + metal oxide or metal hydroxide → salt + water

Tip: For more on neutralisation reactions see page 178.

Which salt is formed?

The name of the salt produced depends on the metal in the oxide or hydroxide and the acid that is used. The first part of the name of the salt is the metal in the oxide/hydroxide and the second part of the name comes from the acid that is used.

> **Example**
>
> Reacting hydrochloric acid with copper oxide will give you copper chloride:
>
> hydrochloric acid + copper oxide → copper chloride + water

Reaction with hydrochloric acid gives chlorides, with sulfuric acid gives sulfates and with nitric acid gives nitrates.

> **Examples**
>
>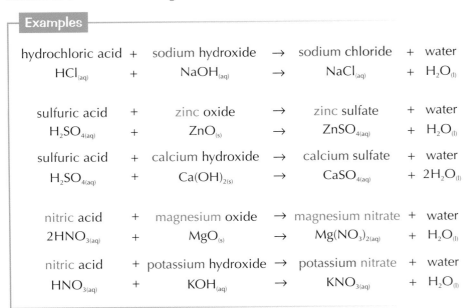
>
> hydrochloric acid + sodium hydroxide → sodium chloride + water
>
> $HCl_{(aq)}$ + $NaOH_{(aq)}$ → $NaCl_{(aq)}$ + $H_2O_{(l)}$
>
> sulfuric acid + zinc oxide → zinc sulfate + water
>
> $H_2SO_{4(aq)}$ + $ZnO_{(s)}$ → $ZnSO_{4(aq)}$ + $H_2O_{(l)}$
>
> sulfuric acid + calcium hydroxide → calcium sulfate + water
>
> $H_2SO_{4(aq)}$ + $Ca(OH)_{2(s)}$ → $CaSO_{4(aq)}$ + $2H_2O_{(l)}$
>
> nitric acid + magnesium oxide → magnesium nitrate + water
>
> $2HNO_{3(aq)}$ + $MgO_{(s)}$ → $Mg(NO_3)_{2(aq)}$ + $H_2O_{(l)}$
>
> nitric acid + potassium hydroxide → potassium nitrate + water
>
> $HNO_{3(aq)}$ + $KOH_{(aq)}$ → $KNO_{3(aq)}$ + $H_2O_{(l)}$

Tip: Whether you use an oxide or a hydroxide isn't important — it's the metal in the compound that determines which salt you'll get.

Making salts from ammonia

You can also make salts from ammonia. Ammonia dissolves in water to make an alkaline solution. When this aqueous ammonia reacts with nitric acid it is neutralised and you get a salt — ammonium nitrate:

Tip: This is a neutralisation reaction, but it's a bit different from other neutralisation reactions as there's no water produced — just the ammonium salt.

> ammonia + nitric acid → ammonium nitrate
>
> $NH_{3(aq)}$ + $HNO_{3(aq)}$ → $NH_4NO_{3(aq)}$

Ammonium salts, such as ammonium nitrate, are used as fertiliser. They supply nitrogen which is an essential nutrient that plants need to make proteins.

Practice Questions — Fact Recall

Q1 Salts can be made when a metal reacts with an acid.

    a) Give the general word equation for this reaction.

    b) Why are some metals not suitable for reacting with a strong acid to make salts? Give an example.

Q2 Salts can be made when metal hydroxides or metal oxides react with an acid.

    a) Are metal hydroxides and metal oxides acids or bases?

    b) Give the general word equation for the reaction of an acid with a metal hydroxide.

Q3 Ammonia dissolves in water to produce an alkaline solution.

    a) What would you react ammonia with to get ammonium nitrate?

    b) Give one use of ammonium nitrate.

Q4 Write a balanced symbol equation for the reaction used to produce ammonium nitrate (NH_4NO_3) from ammonia (NH_3).

Practice Questions — Application

Q1 a) If you react tin (Sn) with sulfuric acid (H_2SO_4), which of the following salts would be produced?

        $MgSO_{4(aq)}$ $SnCl_{2(aq)}$ $ZnSO_{4(aq)}$ $SnSO_{4(aq)}$

    b) What is the other product of this reaction?

Q2 Write a word equation for the reaction of hydrochloric acid with magnesium hydroxide.

Q3 Name the salt produced in each of the following reactions.

    a) Sulfuric acid reacting with iron.

    b) Hydrochloric acid reacting with calcium.

Q4 Name the salt produced in each of the following reactions.

    a) Nitric acid reacting with copper oxide.

    b) Sulfuric acid reacting with potassium hydroxide.

Q5 Write balanced symbol equations for the following reactions and name the salt produced.

    a) Hydrochloric acid reacting with magnesium.

    b) Nitric acid reacting with sodium hydroxide.

Exam Tip H
If you're a higher tier candidate you could be asked to write a balanced symbol equation for any of the reactions mentioned on the specification, including acid-metal reactions.

- Know that when you make a salt from a metal or insoluble base a filter is used to separate out the excess.

- Know that an indicator can be used to show when a reaction between an acid and an alkali to produce a salt solution is complete.

- Know that solid salts can be made by crystallisation of salt solutions.

- Know that precipitation reactions can be used to make insoluble salts and to remove certain ions from a solution.

Specification Reference
C2.6.1

Tip: Remember, some metals are unreactive and other metals are too reactive to use to make salts (see page 180).

3. Methods for Making Salts

There are three experimental techniques you can use to make salts in the lab. Have your conical flasks at the ready and read on to find out more...

Solubility of salts

If you're making a salt the first thing you need to know is whether it's soluble or not. This is important because it affects which method you need to use. Most chlorides, sulfates and nitrates are soluble — the main exceptions are lead chloride, lead sulfate and silver chloride.

Making soluble salts

When making a soluble salt, the first thing you need to do is choose appropriate reagents to produce that particular salt. This involves picking the right acid and the right metal, insoluble base (a metal oxide or metal hydroxide) or a soluble base (alkali) to react it with. You should be able to work out which are the right reagents to choose from the name of the salt you want to produce (see pages 181-182).

Examples

If you want to make potassium sulfate, you could react sulfuric acid (H_2SO_4) and potassium hydroxide (KOH). The KOH provides the potassium and the H_2SO_4 provides the sulfate, as shown below.

$$H_2SO_{4(aq)} + 2KOH_{(aq)} \rightarrow K_2SO_{4(aq)} + 2H_2O_{(l)}$$

If you want to make copper chloride, you could mix hydrochloric acid and copper oxide (you wouldn't use copper metal as it's not reactive enough to react with hydrochloric acid — see page 180).

$$2HCl_{(aq)} + CuO_{(s)} \rightarrow CuCl_{2(aq)} + H_2O_{(l)}$$

The exact method you use to make the salt depends on whether the reagents you choose are soluble or insoluble.

Making soluble salts from metals or insoluble bases

If you are making a soluble salt by adding an insoluble reagent to an acid, you can add it in excess and separate it out at the end of the reaction using filter paper. Metals are insoluble, as are many metal oxides and metal hydroxides, so this is the method you'd use if you're using any of those. Here's what you do:

1. Put the acid in a beaker. Add the insoluble reactant (the metal, metal oxide or metal hydroxide) and stir — it will dissolve in the acid as it reacts.

2. Keep adding the insoluble reactant until it is in excess. You'll know when this is because there will be some left over that won't react — this shows that all the acid has been neutralised and the reaction has finished.

3. Then you need to filter out the excess insoluble reactant to get the salt solution. This is done using filter paper and a filter funnel (see Figure 1).

filter paper

excess solid

filter funnel

salt solution

Figure 1: *Filtering out the excess insoluble reactant using filter paper and a filter funnel.*

Figure 2: *Filtering a copper sulfate ($CuSO_4$) solution to remove any excess insoluble reactant.*

Making soluble salts from alkalis

You can't use the method from the previous page with alkalis (soluble bases) like sodium hydroxide, potassium hydroxide or ammonium hydroxides, because you can't tell whether the reaction has finished (as the alkali is soluble in the acid). So you can't just add an excess to the acid and filter out what's left.

To get a pure salt solution you have to add exactly the right amount of alkali to just neutralise the acid — you need to use an **indicator** to show when the reaction has finished. Then you need to repeat it using exactly the same volumes of alkali and acid so the salt isn't contaminated with indicator.

Tip: For more about indicators have a look back at page 177.

Crystallising salts

Whether you're making a soluble salt from an insoluble reactant or an alkali, you'll be left with a salt solution at the end of the reaction. You can convert this into pure, solid crystals of salt using **crystallisation**.

To do this you first need to heat the salt solution to evaporate most of the water and make the solution more concentrated. Then leave the rest of the water to evaporate very slowly at room temperature — this allows the salt to crystallise.

Figure 3: *Copper sulfate ($CuSO_4$) crystals.*

Making insoluble salts

If the salt you want to make is insoluble you can use a **precipitation** reaction to make it. A precipitation reaction is a reaction where one of the products is insoluble and so forms as a solid precipitate in the solution. To make an insoluble salt you just need to pick two aqueous solutions that contain the ions you need and mix them together.

Tip: You couldn't use an insoluble reagent to make an insoluble salt because you wouldn't be able to separate them.

Example

To make lead chloride you need a solution which contains lead ions and one which contains chloride ions. You can mix lead nitrate solution (most nitrates are soluble) with sodium chloride solution (all Group 1 compounds are soluble) as shown below.

$$Pb(NO_3)_{2(aq)} \ + \ 2NaCl_{(aq)} \ \rightarrow \ PbCl_{2(s)} \ + \ 2NaNO_{3(aq)}$$

Once the salt has precipitated out (and is lying at the bottom of your flask), you can filter it from the solution, wash it and then dry it on filter paper.

Other uses of precipitation reactions

Precipitation reactions can also be used to remove particular ions from solutions, by making an insoluble salt precipitate that contains the ion. After you separate the precipitate from the solution, you can dispose of it leaving you with a solution that doesn't contain those ions. Precipitation reactions are used to remove ions from lots of things.

Examples

- To remove poisonous ions, such as lead, from drinking water.

- To remove calcium and magnesium ions from drinking water. These ions make water "hard", which stops soap lathering properly.

- To remove unwanted ions during the treatment of effluent (sewage).

Figure 4: *A water treatment works.*

Practice Questions — Fact Recall

Q1 Soluble salts can be made by reacting an alkali with an acid. What is used to determine when the reaction has finished?

Q2 Describe and name the process used to get solid salt crystals from a salt solution.

Q3 a) What type of reaction is used to make insoluble salts?

b) Name another use for this type of reaction.

Practice Questions — Application

Q1 A scientist is making the soluble salt tin chloride ($SnCl_2$) by reacting tin (Sn) with hydrochloric acid (HCl).

a) Write the word equation for this reaction.

b) Describe the experimental method used to make this salt.

Q2 Sam wants to make the insoluble salt magnesium carbonate ($MgCO_3$). To do this he plans to mix magnesium sulfate ($MgSO_4$) with sodium sulfate (Na_2SO_4). Explain why this reaction won't produce magnesium carbonate.

pH and Neutralisation

☐ That the pH scale measures how acidic or alkaline a solution is.

☐ That solutions with pH of less than 7 are acidic, solutions with a pH of more than 7 are basic or alkaline and solutions with a pH of exactly 7 are neutral.

☐ That an alkali is a base that is soluble in water.

☐ That aqueous hydrogen ions ($H^+_{(aq)}$) make a solution acidic and aqueous hydroxide ions ($OH^-_{(aq)}$) make a solution alkaline.

☐ That the state symbols in equations are: (s) for solid, (l) for liquid, (aq) for aqueous and (g) for gas.

☐ That in a neutralisation reaction, water is produced when hydrogen ions react with hydroxide ions.

Making Salts

☐ That soluble salts can be made by reacting hydrochloric acid or sulfuric acid with metals.

☐ That the general equation for the reaction of an acid with a metal is: acid + metal → salt + hydrogen.

☐ That some metals aren't suitable to use for making salts because they are too reactive (explode in acid) or aren't reactive enough.

☐ That metal oxides and metal hydroxides are bases. Those that are soluble in water are alkalis.

☐ That you can make soluble salts by reacting acids with metal oxides or metal hydroxides.

☐ That the general equation for the reaction of a metal oxide/hydroxide with an acid is: acid + metal oxide/metal hydroxide → salt + water.

☐ How the name of salts depends on the metal (or metal within an oxide or hydroxide) and the acid that is used to make it.

☐ That when ammonia dissolves in water it forms an alkaline solution. This can react with nitric acid to produce ammonium nitrate, which is commonly used as a fertiliser.

Methods for Making Salts

☐ That when making a salt by adding an excess of insoluble base or metal to an acid, the excess base or metal is filtered out at the end of the reaction.

☐ That when making a salt from an alkali, an indicator is used to show when the reaction has finished.

☐ That soluble salts are converted into solid salts by crystallisation of the salt solutions.

☐ That precipitation reactions are used to make insoluble salts.

☐ That precipitation reactions can also be used as a way of extracting undesired ions from solutions.

Exam-style Questions

1   The pH of a substance determines whether it is an acid, a base or neutral.

1 (a)   Complete the sentences using the words in the box below.

an acid   a base   neutral

1 (a) (i)   Toothpaste has a pH of 8.2 so it is _____ .

(1 mark)

1 (a) (ii)   Ethanol has a pH of 7.0 so it is _____ .

(1 mark)

1 (a) (iii)   Fresh milk has a pH of 6.5 so it is _____ .

(1 mark)

1 (b)   Niall has a substance with a pH of 4.

1 (b) (i)   What type of ions are released when this substance dissolves in water?

(1 mark)

1 (b) (ii)   Which of the following could Niall add to his solution to neutralise it?

Potassium hydroxide   Pure water   Sulfuric acid
(pH 13)   (pH 7)   (pH 1)

(1 mark)

1 (b) (iii)   Describe how Niall could determine when the neutralisation reaction has finished.

(2 marks)

1 (b) (iv)   Write an equation, including state symbols, to show what happens during a neutralisation reaction in terms of the ions involved.

(2 marks)

2   There are a number of different ways to make soluble salts.
2 (a)   One way of making soluble salts involves reacting acids with metal oxides.
2 (a) (i)   Copy and complete the general equation for this reaction shown below:

$$\text{acid } + \text{ metal oxide } \rightarrow \underline{\hspace{2cm}} + \underline{\hspace{2cm}}$$

(2 marks)

2 (a) (ii)   What type of reaction is the reaction between a metal oxide and an acid?

(1 mark)

2 (b)   Ryan is making a soluble salt by mixing magnesium oxide (MgO) with hydrochloric acid (HCl).

2 (b) (i)   Name the salt produced when magnesium oxide reacts with hydrochloric acid.

(1 mark)

2 (b) (ii)   Given that magnesium oxide is insoluble, explain how Ryan will know that the reaction between magnesium oxide and hydrochloric acid has finished.

(2 marks)

2 (b) (iii)   Describe how Ryan could get from the finished reaction mixture to pure solid salt crystals.

(3 marks)

3   Barium is a very reactive metal that can be used to make a variety of useful salts, including the soluble salt barium chloride ($BaCl_2$) and the insoluble salt barium sulfate ($BaSO_4$).

3 (a)   Barium chloride is made by reacting barium hydroxide ($Ba(OH)_2$) with hydrochloric acid (HCl).

3 (a) (i)   Write a balanced symbol equation for the reaction between barium hydroxide and hydrochloric acid.

(2 marks)

3 (a) (ii)   Barium hydroxide is an alkali. What is an alkali?

(2 marks)

3 (a) (iii)   Suggest why barium chloride isn't made by reacting barium directly with hydrochloric acid.

(1 mark)

3 (b)   Barium sulfate can be made from barium chloride using a precipitation reaction.

3 (b) (i)   Which acid would you react with barium chloride to make barium sulfate?

(1 mark)

3 (b) (ii)   In the context of making barium sulfate, why is it important that barium chloride is soluble?

(1 mark)

3 (b) (iii)   Precipitation reactions are used in industrial settings, as well as in the production of salts. Give **two** other uses for precipitation reactions.

(2 marks)

1. Electrolysis — The Basics

You've met electrolysis briefly before — it's used to extract metals from rocks. You need to know a bit more about it now though — how it works, how to predict the products of electrolysis, and (if you're doing higher tier) how to represent the different reactions that take place using equations. Here we go...

What is electrolysis?

If you pass an electric current through an ionic substance that's molten (has been melted) or in solution, it breaks down into the elements it's made of. This is called **electrolysis**. For example, the electrolysis of aluminium oxide breaks aluminium oxide down into aluminium and oxygen.

Electrolytes

Electrolysis requires a liquid to conduct the electricity, called the **electrolyte**. Electrolytes contain free ions — they're usually the molten or dissolved ionic substance (see Figure 1). In either case it's the free ions which conduct the electricity and allow the whole thing to work.

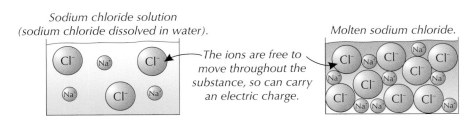

Sodium chloride solution (sodium chloride dissolved in water).

Molten sodium chloride.

The ions are free to move throughout the substance, so can carry an electric charge.

Figure 1: *Free ions in melted and dissolved sodium chloride.*

How electrolysis works

Electrolysis is based on an electrical circuit that includes an electrolyte and two electrodes. In electrolysis, the electrodes are placed into the electrolyte and ions move from one electrode to the other — this allows the conduction of electricity through the circuit. Electrons are taken away from ions at the positive electrode and given to other ions at the negative electrode. As ions gain or lose electrons they become atoms or molecules and are released. These atoms or molecules are the products of electrolysis.

Lead bromide ($PbBr_2$) is an ionic compound, so when it is molten it will conduct electricity. Electrolysis of lead bromide breaks it down into lead (Pb) and bromine (Br_2). So, the electrolyte is lead bromide and the products of electrolysis are lead and bromine. Here's how it works...

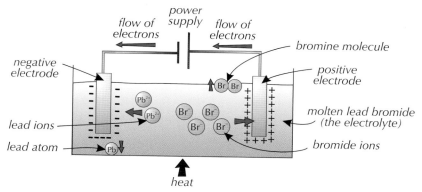

Figure 2: *The electrolysis of lead bromide.*

Molten lead bromide contains positively charged lead ions and negatively charged bromide ions.

- The positive ions are attracted towards the negative electrode. Here, each lead ion gains two electrons and becomes a lead atom.

- The negative ions are attracted towards the positive electrode. Here, bromide ions lose one electron each and form bromine molecules (Br_2).

Tip: How many electrons each ion needs to gain or lose to become an atom or molecule depends on the charge on the ion. Have a look back at pages 112-113 for more on this.

Oxidation and reduction

Electrolysis always involves an **oxidation** reaction and a **reduction** reaction.

- Oxidation is a loss of electrons.

- Reduction is a gain of electrons.

So, in electrolysis, reduction happens at the negative electrode (where ions gain electrons) and oxidation occurs at the positive electrode (where ions lose electrons).

Exam Tip
You can remember what oxidation and reduction are using the mnemonic OILRIG, which stands for: Oxidation Is Loss, Reduction Is Gain.

- In the electrolysis of lead bromide the lead ions gain electrons. This is a reduction reaction, and the lead ions are said to be reduced.

- The bromide ions lose electrons. This is an oxidation reaction and the bromide ions are said to be oxidised.

Tip: You can talk about reduction and oxidation in terms of the loss or gain of oxygen too (see page 44), but when you're dealing with electrolysis you need to describe them in terms of electrons.

Half equations Higher

Half equations show the reactions at the electrodes. Here's how to write a half equation for the reaction that takes place at the negative electrode:

Step 1: Write the symbol for the positive ion in the electrolyte on the left-hand side of the equation.

Step 2: Write the symbol for the neutral atoms or molecules produced on the right-hand side of the equation.

Step 3: Balance the number of atoms in the equation.

Step 4: Balance the charges by adding electrons (shown as e⁻).

You can do the same to get the half equation for the reaction at the positive electrode, starting with the negative ion on the left-hand side of the equation.

Tip: H For the half equation to show the reaction at the positive electrode you can balance the charges by adding or subtracting electrons. For the half equation for the negative electrode you can only add electrons.

Example ─ Higher

These are the half equations for the electrolysis of lead bromide:

Negative electrode:

Step 1: Pb^{2+}

Step 2: $Pb^{2+} \rightarrow Pb$

Step 3: There's one lead ion on the left and one lead atom on the right, so the number of atoms is balanced.

Step 4: A charge of 2+ on the left hand side needs to be balanced out by two electrons, so that the overall charge of both sides is the same (0). So the half equation for the reaction at the negative electrode is:

$Pb^{2+} + 2e^- \rightarrow Pb$

Tip: H These equations are called half equations because each one only shows half of the overall reaction that takes place during electrolysis.

Positive electrode:

Step 1: Br^-

Step 2: $Br^- \rightarrow Br_2$

Step 3: There are two bromine atoms on the right so there need to be two bromide ions on the left to balance the equation.

$2Br^- \rightarrow Br_2$

Step 4: A charge of 2– on the left hand side needs to be balanced out by two electrons on the right hand side, so that the overall charge on both sides is equal (2–). So the half equation for the reaction at the negative electrode is:

$2Br^- \rightarrow Br_2 + 2e^-$

Exam Tip H
You can check your half equations are correct by making sure that the charges balance and the atoms balance. If they don't, you've gone wrong somewhere.

Or, you could subtract two electrons from the left-hand side to give both sides a charge of zero. This would give you this half equation:

$2Br^- - 2e^- \rightarrow Br_2$

The charges in this half equation are still balanced because (–2) – (–2) = 0

Predicting the products of electrolysis

Sometimes there are more than two types of free ions in the electrolyte. For example, if a salt is dissolved in water there will be some H^+ and OH^- ions as well as the ions from the salt in the solution. In this situation, the products of electrolysis depend on how reactive the elements involved are.

At the negative electrode, if metal ions and H^+ ions are present, the metal ions will stay in solution if the metal is more reactive than hydrogen. This is because the more reactive an element, the keener it is to stay as ions. So, hydrogen will be produced unless the metal is less reactive than it.

At the positive electrode, if OH^- and halide ions (Cl^-, Br^-, I^-) are present then molecules of chlorine, bromine or iodine will be formed. If no halide is present, then oxygen will be formed.

> **Tip:** The electrolysis of sodium chloride solution is a classic example of electrolysis with more than two types of ions present. There's more on this on page 194.

> **Exam Tip**
> You'll be given a reactivity series in your exam, so you'll be able to look up whether a metal is more or less reactive than hydrogen. For now, you can use the one on page 43.

Practice Questions — Fact Recall

Q1 a) What happens to a molten ionic substance when an electric current is passed through it?

b) What is this process called?

Q2 Why are dissolved ionic substances able to conduct electricity?

Q3 Describe what happens at the positive electrode during electrolysis in terms of electrons.

Q4 What type of ions are attracted towards the negative electrode?

Q5 What is reduction?

Q6 At which electrode does reduction happen?

Q7 Bromide ions and hydroxide ions are in an electrolyte during electrolysis. What substance will form at the positive electrode?

Practice Questions — Application

Q1 Molten zinc chloride can undergo electrolysis. The ions in the electrolyte are Zn^{2+} and Cl^-. The electrodes are made of graphite.

a) Give the name of the electrolyte.

b) Which electrode do the chloride ions move towards?

c) Describe what happens to the chloride ions at this electrode.

d) Are the zinc ions oxidised or reduced during electrolysis?

Q2 The products of the electrolysis of potassium bromide solution are hydrogen and bromine. Explain why potassium is not produced.

Q3 Complete the half equations below to show the reactions that happen during the electrolysis of two different solutions:

a) $Br^- \rightarrow Br_2$ and $H^+ \rightarrow H_2$

b) $Cu^{2+} \rightarrow Cu$ and $O^{2-} \rightarrow O_2$

- Know that the products of the electrolysis of sodium chloride solution are hydrogen, chlorine and sodium hydroxide.
- Know the uses of chlorine and sodium hydroxide in industry.
- Be able to describe the electrolysis of sodium chloride solution in terms of ions, electrons, electrodes, oxidation and reduction.
- **H** Be able to write half equations for the electrolysis of sodium chloride solution.

Specification Reference C2.7.1

2. Electrolysis of Sodium Chloride

Now you've got the basics covered, it's time to have a look at an example of electrolysis in more detail — the electrolysis of sodium chloride solution...

The products of sodium chloride electrolysis

When common salt (sodium chloride, NaCl) is dissolved in water and electrolysed, it produces three useful products — hydrogen (H_2), chlorine (Cl_2) and sodium hydroxide (NaOH). These products are pretty useful in industry. Chlorine has many uses, for example, in the production of bleach and plastics. Sodium hydroxide is a very strong alkali and is used widely in the chemical industry, for example, to make soap.

The process of sodium chloride electrolysis

Sodium chloride solution contains sodium ions (Na^+), chloride ions (Cl^-), hydrogen ions (H^+) and hydroxide ions (OH^-). The hydrogen ions and hydroxide ions come from the water. The electrolysis of sodium chloride is shown in Figure 1.

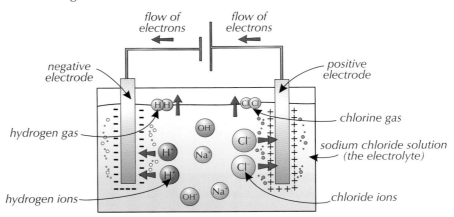

Figure 1: *The electrolysis of sodium chloride.*

At the negative electrode

The positive hydrogen ions are attracted to the negative electrode. Here, they gain one electron each and combine to form hydrogen molecules (H_2). This is a **reduction** reaction and causes hydrogen to be released at the negative electrode.

At the positive electrode

The negative chloride ions are attracted to the positive electrode. Here, they lose one electron each and combine to form chlorine molecules (Cl_2). This is an **oxidation** reaction, and causes chlorine to be released at the positive electrode.

Ions remaining in solution

The sodium ions stay in solution because they're more reactive than hydrogen. Hydroxide ions from water are also left behind. This means that sodium hydroxide (NaOH) is left in the solution.

Tip: See page 193 for more on how to work out whether the metal ions or hydrogen ions stay in solution.

Half equations Higher

To write the half equations for the electrolysis of sodium chloride, follow the steps on page 192.

Negative electrode:

Step 1: H^+

Step 2: $H^+ \rightarrow H_2$

Step 3:   There are two hydrogen atoms on the right, so there need to be two ions on the left to balance the equation.

$$2H^+ \rightarrow H_2$$

Step 4:   Balance out the charge of 2+ on the left hand side by adding two electrons, so that the overall charge of both sides is zero.

$$2H^+ + 2e^- \rightarrow H_2$$

Figure 2: *The electrolysis of sodium chloride. Hydrogen and chlorine gas are collected in the test tubes.*

Positive electrode:

Step 1: Cl^-

Step 2: $Cl^- \rightarrow Cl_2$

Step 3:   There are two chlorine atoms on the right, so there need to be two chloride ions on the left to balance the equation.

$$2Cl^- \rightarrow Cl_2$$

Step 4:   Balance out the charge of 2– on the left by adding two electrons on the right, so that the overall charge of both sides is 2–.

$$2Cl^- \rightarrow Cl_2 + 2e^-$$

Or, you could subtract two electrons from the left, to give both sides a charge of zero. This half equation would be:

$$2Cl^- - 2e^- \rightarrow Cl_2$$

Exam Tip H
For the half equation at the positive electrode it doesn't matter whether you add electrons to the right-hand side of the equation or take them away from the left-hand side. Just use the method that you're happiest with.

Practice Questions — Fact Recall

Q1   Sodium hydroxide is one product of the electrolysis of sodium chloride solution. What are the other two products?

Q2   Give one industrial use of sodium hydroxide.

Q3   Which product is formed at the negative electrode?

Q4   Which product is formed as the result of a reduction reaction?

Q5   Explain why sodium hydroxide is produced during the electrolysis of sodium chloride solution.

- Know that aluminium is extracted from aluminium oxide by electrolysis.
- Know why aluminium oxide is dissolved in molten cryolite before being electrolysed.
- Know that aluminium and oxygen are products of the electrolysis of aluminium oxide, and which electrodes they are formed at.
- Know why carbon dioxide is produced during electrolysis of aluminium oxide.
- H Be able to write half equations for the electrolysis of aluminium oxide.

Specification Reference C2.7.1

Tip: The normal rules of electrolysis apply here — the positive ions are attracted to the negative electrode where they're reduced, and the negative ions are attracted to the positive electrode where they're oxidised.

Exam Tip H
Make sure you're happy with how to work out these half equations. (Have a look at page 192 for the steps.) In the exam, you'll be given a data sheet with the formulae of some ions. So if you don't know the charges on the ions you can look them up.

3. Electrolysis of Aluminium Ore

Next up, the electrolysis of aluminium oxide to get pure aluminium. The basics of electrolysis are all the same here, but there are a few twists to learn...

Aluminium

Aluminium's a very abundant metal, but it is always found naturally in compounds. Its main ore is bauxite, and after mining and purifying, a white powder is left. This is pure aluminium oxide, Al_2O_3. The aluminium has to be extracted from this using electrolysis.

Extracting aluminium by electrolysis

Aluminium oxide (Al_2O_3) has a very high melting point of over 2000 °C — so melting it would be very expensive. Instead the aluminium oxide is dissolved in molten cryolite (a less common ore of aluminium). This brings the melting temperature down to about 900 °C, which saves energy, making the process cheaper and easier. The electrolysis of aluminium oxide is shown in Figure 1.

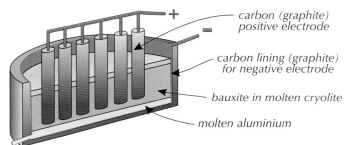

carbon (graphite) positive electrode
carbon lining (graphite) for negative electrode
bauxite in molten cryolite
molten aluminium

Figure 1: *The electrolysis of aluminium oxide.*

The electrodes are made of carbon (graphite), a good conductor of electricity. Aluminium forms at the negative electrode and oxygen forms at the positive electrode. The oxygen then reacts with the carbon in the electrode to produce carbon dioxide. This means that the positive electrodes gradually get 'eaten away' and have to be replaced every now and again.

Half equations   Higher

The half equations for these reactions are:

Negative electrode: $Al^{3+} + 3e^- \rightarrow Al$

Positive electrode: $2O^{2-} \rightarrow O_2 + 4e^-$

Practice Questions — Fact Recall

Q1 Why is aluminium oxide dissolved in molten cryolite before it undergoes electrolysis?

Q2 a) Give the name of the product formed at the positive electrode.

b) Give the name of the product formed at the negative electrode.

Q3 Why is carbon dioxide produced in this electrolysis reaction?

4. Electroplating

And finally, a clever use of electrolysis — electroplating.

What is electroplating?

Electroplating is a process that uses electrolysis to coat the surface of one metal with another metal. For example, you might want to electroplate silver onto a brass cup to make it look nice.

The negative electrode is the metal object you want to plate and the positive electrode is the pure metal you want it to be plated with. You also need the electrolyte to contain ions of the plating metal. The ions that plate the metal object come from the solution. These ions are replaced in the solution by more positive ions from the positive electrode.

Learning Objectives:

- Know that using electrolysis to coat an object in another material is called electroplating.
- Know that electroplating can be used to coat objects with silver or copper.

Specification Reference C2.7, C2.7.1

Example

To electroplate silver onto a brass cup, you make the brass cup the negative electrode (to attract the positive silver ions), and a lump of pure silver the positive electrode. Then you dip them both in a solution of silver ions (for example, silver nitrate). The silver ions in the solution are attracted towards the brass cup, where they gain electrons, turn into silver atoms and stick to it. The positive electrode releases more silver ions into the solution.

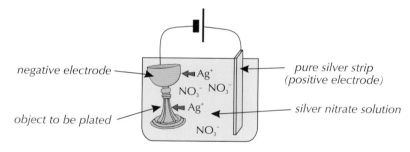

Figure 1: Electroplating silver onto a brass cup.

Figure 2: Objects above an electroplating tank. The objects are lowered into the tank to electroplate them.

Uses of electroplating

There are lots of different uses for electroplating. For example:

Decoration

Silver is attractive, but very expensive. It's much cheaper to plate a boring brass cup with silver, than it is to make the cup out of solid silver — but it looks just as pretty.

Conduction

Metals like copper conduct electricity well — because of this they're often used to plate metals for electronic circuits and computers.

Tip: Silver and copper are just two examples of metals that can be used for electroplating — lots of different metals can be used.

Practice Questions — Fact Recall

Q1   What is electroplating?

Q2   Name two metals that might be used to plate another material.

Q3   Give two uses of electroplating.

Section Checklist — Make sure you know...

Electrolysis — The Basics

☐ That dissolved and molten ionic substances contain free ions, so they can conduct electricity.

☐ That passing an electric current through a molten or dissolved ionic substance will break it down into its elements, and that this process is called electrolysis.

☐ That the liquid that conducts the electricity and is broken down is called the electrolyte.

☐ That positive ions are attracted to the negative electrode, where they gain electrons and form neutral atoms or molecules. This is called a reduction reaction.

☐ That negative ions are attracted to the positive electrode, where they lose electrons and form neutral atoms or molecules. This is called an oxidation reaction.

☐ **H** How to write half equations to show the reactions that take place at the electrodes.

☐ That if there are more than two types of free ions in solution during electrolysis, the products formed depend on how reactive the elements involved are.

Electrolysis of Sodium Chloride

☐ That the electrolysis of sodium chloride solution produces hydrogen, chlorine and sodium hydroxide.

☐ That chlorine is used to make bleach and plastics and sodium hydroxide is used to make soap.

☐ Why hydrogen is formed at the negative electrode and chlorine is formed at the positive electrode.

☐ That sodium ions and hydroxide ions (from water) are left in solution, forming sodium hydroxide.

Electrolysis of Aluminium Ore

☐ That electrolysis is used to extract aluminium from its ore (aluminium oxide).

☐ That aluminium oxide is dissolved in molten cryolite before electrolysis takes place, as this reduces the temperature at which it can be melted, and so reduces the cost.

☐ Why aluminium is formed at the negative electrode and oxygen is formed at the positive electrode.

☐ That the oxygen produced reacts with the carbon in the electrode to form carbon dioxide.

Electroplating

☐ That electroplating is when electrolysis is used to coat the surface of one metal with another.

☐ That objects can be electroplated with silver or copper, for decorative or practical purposes.

Exam-style Questions

You may use the reactivity series on page 43 to help you answer Q1.

1　　　Copper chloride is an ionic compound. When dissolved in water it forms copper chloride solution. Copper chloride solution can undergo electrolysis.

1 (a)　　Give the name of the electrolyte used in this electrolysis.

(1 mark)

1 (b)　　The ions present in the copper chloride solution are Cu^{2+}, Cl^-, H^+ and OH^-.

1 (b) (i)　Where do the H^+ and OH^- ions come from?

(1 mark)

1 (b) (ii)　Copper ions move towards the negative electrode.
　　　　　　Describe what happens to the copper ions at the negative electrode.

(2 marks)

1 (b) (iii)　Explain why copper metal is produced at the negative electrode, rather than hydrogen gas.

(2 marks)

1 (c)　　Chlorine gas is produced at the positive electrode.

1 (c) (i)　Give **one** industrial use of chlorine.

(1 mark)

1 (c) (ii)　Complete the half equation for the reaction that occurs at the positive electrode.

$$........Cl^- \quad \rightarrow \quad Cl_2 \quad + \quad ....$$

(2 marks)

2　　　Electrolysis can be used to coat a material with a layer of a metal. The equipment used to coat a ring with silver is shown below.

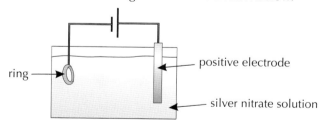

ring —— positive electrode

silver nitrate solution

2 (a)　　What name is given to the process of coating a material with metal using electrolysis?

(1 mark)

2 (b)　　What is the negative electrode in the process shown above?

(1 mark)

2 (c)　　What substance is broken down during the process shown above?

(1 mark)

2 (d)　　Oxidation occurs at the positive electrode. What is oxidation?

(1 mark)

- Know that early periodic tables arranged elements according to relative atomic mass.

- Know that in a periodic table elements with similar properties are arranged in columns.

- Know how the periodic table got its name.

- Know how Newlands arranged the elements in his version of the periodic table and why it was criticised.

- Know how Mendeleev arranged the elements in his periodic table and how he overcame some of the problems of earlier versions.

- Understand how elements are arranged in the modern periodic table.

- Understand why it took a long time for scientists to recognise the periodic table as a useful summary of atomic structure.

Specification Reference C3.1, C3.1.1, C3.1.2

1. History of the Periodic Table

By now you should be familiar with the periodic table and what it looks like — but the periodic table hasn't always looked like this. In fact, the modern periodic table was a long time in the making. Read on to find out more...

Early versions of the periodic table

In the early 1800s, scientists had no idea of atomic structure or of protons or electrons, so there was no such thing as atomic number to them. Back then, the only thing they could measure was **relative atomic mass**. As a result, the known elements were originally arranged in order of atomic mass.

Newlands' Law of Octaves

A scientist called Newlands had the first good stab at arranging the elements more usefully in 1864. After he arranged them in order of relative atomic mass, he noticed a pattern in the properties of the elements — every eighth element had similar properties. These sets of eight elements were called Newlands' Octaves.

Newlands listed his Octaves in rows of seven. This meant that the elements were in a table, arranged so that elements with similar properties were in columns, known as **groups**. Because similar properties occurred periodically (at regular intervals) the table was called the periodic table. This was one of the very earliest versions of the periodic table — see Figure 1.

H	Li	Be	B	C	N	O
F	Na	Mg	Al	Si	P	S
Cl	K	Ca	Cr	Ti	Mn	Fe

Figure 1: *An early version of the periodic table proposed by Newlands in 1864 — elements are listed in rows of seven.*

Newlands presented his ideas to the Chemical Society in 1865. But his work was criticised for a number of reasons:

- Some of his groups contained elements that didn't have similar properties, e.g. carbon and titanium were in the same group but they don't have similar properties.

- He mixed up metals and non-metals, e.g. oxygen (a non-metal) and iron (a metal) were in the same group.

- He didn't leave any gaps for elements that hadn't been discovered yet, so any new elements that were discovered would not fit into Newlands' system.

Figure 2: *John Newlands.*

Mendeleev's periodic table

In 1869 in Russia, Dmitri Mendeleev arranged about 60 known elements into his Table of Elements.

Mendeleev put the elements in order of atomic mass (like Newlands). But Mendeleev found he had to leave gaps in order to keep elements with similar properties in the same vertical columns (groups) — and he was prepared to leave some very big gaps in the first two rows before the transition metals come in on the third row (see Figure 3).

Mendeleev's Table of Elements

```
H

Li  Be                                          B   C   N   O   F

Na  Mg                                          Al  Si  P   S   Cl

K   Ca  *  Ti  V   Cr  Mn  Fe  Co  Ni  Cu  Zn  *   *   As  Se  Br

Rb  Sr  Y  Zr  Nb  Mo  *   Ru  Rh  Pd  Ag  Cd  In  Sn  Sb  Te  I

Cs  Ba  *  *   Ta  W   *   Os  Ir  Pt  Au  Hg  Tl  Pb  Bi
```

Figure 3: *The periodic table as proposed by Mendeleev.*

Figure 4: *Dmitri Mendeleev.*

The gaps were the really clever bit because they predicted the properties of so far undiscovered elements. When they were found and they fitted the pattern it proved that Mendeleev's system of classifying elements was a good one.

The modern periodic table

It was only in the 20th century after protons and electrons were discovered that it was realised the elements were best arranged in order of **atomic number**. Then, all the elements were put into groups to create the modern periodic table — see Figure 5.

Tip: For more about how the elements were arranged into groups see page 203.

Tip: There's a larger version of this periodic table on the inside of the back cover if you need to look anything up.

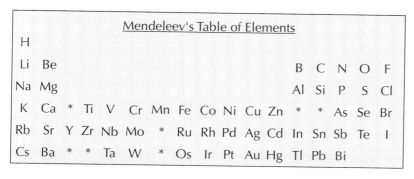

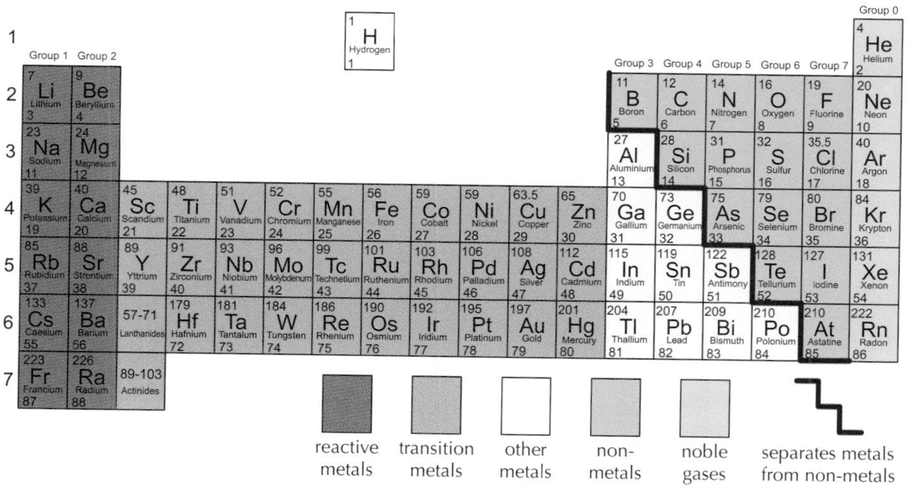

reactive metals | transition metals | other metals | non-metals | noble gases | separates metals from non-metals

Figure 5: *The modern periodic table.*

Importance of the periodic table

When the periodic table was first released, many scientists thought it was just a bit of fun. At that time, there wasn't all that much evidence to suggest that the elements really did fit together in that way — ideas don't get the scientific stamp of approval without evidence.

After Mendeleev released his work, newly discovered elements fitted into the gaps he left. This was convincing evidence in favour of the periodic table. Once there was more evidence, many more scientists realised that the periodic table could be a useful tool for predicting properties of elements. It really worked.

In the late 19th century, scientists discovered protons, neutrons and electrons. The periodic table matches up very well to what's been discovered about the structure of the atom. Scientists now accept that it's a very important and useful summary of the structure of atoms.

Tip: The ability to evaluate evidence is an important skill that scientists need to have.

HOW SCIENCE WORKS

Practice Questions — Fact Recall

Q1   What did Newlands and Mendeleev arrange the elements in order of?

Q2   a) How did Newlands arrange the elements into a table?

    b) Give two reasons why Newlands' version of the periodic table was heavily criticised.

Q3   a) Why did Mendeleev leave gaps in his periodic table?

    b) Give one piece of evidence that strongly suggested Mendeleev's system of classifying elements was correct.

Q4   How are elements arranged in the modern periodic table?

Q5   a) Suggest why many scientists didn't initially take the periodic table seriously.

    b) What happened to make scientists believe that the periodic table is a useful summary of atomic structure?

2. Trends in the Periodic Table

The modern periodic table is an extremely useful tool that can tell you a lot about the properties of an element. Here's a quick summary...

The periodic table and electron arrangement

The elements in the modern periodic table can be seen as being arranged by their electronic structure. Using the electron arrangement, you can predict the element's chemical properties.

Electrons in an atom are set out in shells which each correspond to an energy level. Apart from the transition metals, elements in the same group have the same number of electrons in their highest occupied energy level (outer shell). The group number is equal to the number of electrons in the highest occupied energy level.

Learning Objectives:

- Know that in the modern periodic table, the arrangement of the elements reflects their atomic structure.
- Know that the group number of an element tells you how many electrons atoms of that element have in their outer shell.
- **H** Know that there are trends in reactivity down groups.
- **H** Be able to explain the trends in reactivity down groups in terms of how easily electrons are lost or gained.

Specification Reference C3.1.2, C3.1.3

Examples

Calcium is in Group 2:

Group 2 elements have 2 electrons in their highest energy level (outer shell).

Chlorine is in Group 7:

Group 7 elements have 7 electrons in their highest energy level (outer shell).

Tip: See page 17 for more about the structure of an atom.

The rows in the periodic table are called **periods**. The period number of an element is equal to the number of energy levels (shells) it has.

Tip: Remember, <u>groups</u> are the <u>columns</u> of the periodic table and <u>periods</u> are the <u>rows</u>.

Examples

Magnesium is in period 3:

Elements in period 3 have 3 occupied energy levels (shells).

Potassium is in period 4:

Elements in period 4 have 4 occupied energy levels (shells).

Trends in reactivity `Higher`

The positive charge of the nucleus attracts electrons and holds them in place. The further from the nucleus the electron is, the less the attraction. The attraction of the nucleus is even less when there are a lot of inner electrons. Inner electrons "get in the way" of the nuclear charge, reducing the attraction. This effect is known as **shielding**.

As you move down a group, the atoms get larger and as a result, the distance from the nucleus to the outer electrons and the amount of shielding both increase. This means that it gets easier to lose electrons and harder to gain electrons. Atoms have to lose or gain electrons to react, so this means there are trends in the reactivity of elements as you move down a group.

Tip: Loss and gain of electrons can take place during bonding.
For more on bonding see pages 110-120.

Tip: Here are the Group 1 metals:

There's more about their properties on pages 206-208.

Example 1 — `Higher`

Reactivity of Group 1 metals

The reactivity of the Group 1 metals increases as you move down the group.

This is because Group 1 metals react by losing the single electron in their highest energy level. As you move down the group, the combination of increased distance and increased shielding means that this outer electron is more easily lost, because there's less attraction from the nucleus holding it in place. As a result, elements further down the group are more reactive. For example, potassium is more reactive than lithium (see Figure 1).

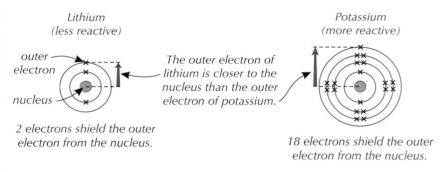

Figure 1: The electronic structures of lithium and potassium.

Example 2 — `Higher`

Reactivity of Group 7 elements

The reactivity of the Group 7 elements decreases as you go down the group.

This is because Group 7 elements react by gaining an electron in their highest energy level. As you move down the group, the increased distance and shielding means that the outer electron shell is less likely to gain an electron — there's less attraction from the nucleus pulling electrons into the atom. So elements further down the group are less reactive. For example, chlorine is less reactive than fluorine (see Figure 2).

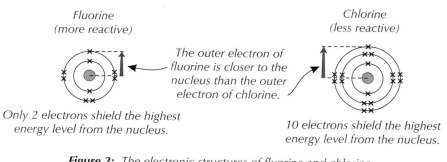

Fluorine
(more reactive)

Chlorine
(less reactive)

The outer electron of fluorine is closer to the nucleus than the outer electron of chlorine.

Only 2 electrons shield the highest energy level from the nucleus.

10 electrons shield the highest energy level from the nucleus.

Figure 2: _The electronic structures of fluorine and chlorine._

Tip: Here are the Group 7 elements.

There's more about their properties on pages 209-211.

Practice Questions — Fact Recall

Q1 What does the group number of an element tell you?

Q2 Give two reasons why the attraction between the nucleus and the outer electrons is weaker in larger atoms.

Q3 Caesium and lithium are both Group 1 metals. Caesium is more reactive than lithium. Explain why.

Q4 Fluorine and iodine are both in Group 7. Fluorine is more reactive than iodine. Explain why.

Practice Questions — Application

To answer these questions you will need to use the periodic table on the inside of the back cover.

Q1 How many electrons are in the outer shell of the following elements?

a) Phosphorus

b) Oxygen

c) Potassium

d) Silicon

e) Magnesium

f) Iodine

Q2 Metals in Group 2 of the periodic table react by losing two electrons from their outer shell. Use this information and your knowledge of reactivity trends to suggest which element is more reactive; magnesium or calcium. Explain your answer.

Q3 Elements in Group 6 of the periodic table react by gaining two electrons in their outer shell. Use this information and your knowledge of reactivity trends to suggest which element is more reactive; oxygen or sulfur. Explain your answer.

Tip: You can use the information you learnt about the reactivity of Groups 1 and 7 to help you answer questions 2 and 3. Even though these questions are asking about different groups, the reactivity of the elements depend on the same things.

- Know that the elements in Group 1 of the periodic table are called the alkali metals.
- Know that the alkali metals have a low density.
- Know that the reactivity of the alkali metals increases down the group.
- Know that the melting and boiling points of the alkali metals decrease down the group.
- Know how the alkali metals react with non-metals.
- Know that alkali metals react with water to form hydrogen and a metal hydroxide (which can dissolve in water to give alkaline solutions).

Specification Reference C3.1.3

3. Group 1 — The Alkali Metals

The elements in Group 1 are commonly known as the alkali metals. The next few pages are all about these metals and their properties.

Properties of the alkali metals

The **alkali metals** are the elements in Group 1 of the periodic table — they are lithium, sodium, potassium, rubidium, caesium and francium (see Figure 1).

They're all silvery solids that have to be stored in oil and handled with forceps (they burn the skin).

The alkali metals all have one outer electron. This makes them very reactive and gives them all similar properties. For example, the alkali metals all have low density. In fact, the first three in the group are less dense than water.

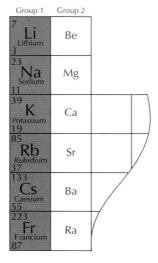

Figure 1: *Group 1 of the periodic table.*

Trends down Group 1

There are a couple of trends within the Group 1 elements that you need to know about.

Tip: H See page 204 for an explanation of why reactivity increases down Group 1.

Reactivity

Reactivity increases down the group, so elements at the bottom of the group are more reactive than elements at the top of the group — see Figure 3.

Melting and boiling points

The melting and boiling points of the Group 1 metals decrease down the group, so elements at the bottom of the group have lower melting points and lower boiling points than the elements at the top of the group — see Figure 3.

Figure 2: *The first three elements in Group 1 — lithium, sodium and potassium.*

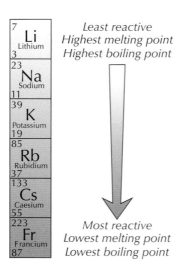

Figure 3: *Trends in Group 1.*

Reaction with non-metals

The alkali metals react with non-metals to form **ionic compounds**. This is because the alkali metals have only one electron in their outer shell, so they are keen to lose it to form a 1+ ion. They are so keen to lose the outer electron there's no way they'd consider sharing, so covalent bonding is out of the question — they always form ionic bonds.

Tip: See pages 111-114 for loads more about ionic bonding.

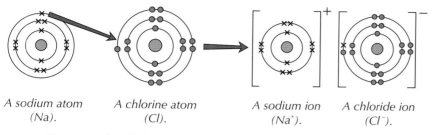

| A sodium atom (Na). | A chlorine atom (Cl). | A sodium ion (Na⁺). | A chloride ion (Cl⁻). |

Figure 4: *The alkali metal sodium (Na) reacts with the non-metal chlorine (Cl) to form the ionic compound sodium chloride (NaCl).*

The compounds that are produced when alkali metals react with non-metals are usually white solids that dissolve in water to form colourless solutions.

Figure 5: *Sodium chloride.*

Example

The alkali metal sodium (Na) reacts with chlorine (Cl) to form sodium chloride (NaCl) — see Figure 4. Sodium chloride is a white solid (see Figure 5) that will dissolve in water to form a colourless solution (see Figure 6).

Reaction with water

The alkali metals react with water to form a metal hydroxide and hydrogen gas. The general equation for this reaction is:

Figure 6: *Sodium chloride dissolved in water.*

alkali metal + water → metal hydroxide + hydrogen

Examples

- Sodium reacts with water to form sodium hydroxide and hydrogen:

$$2Na_{(s)} + 2H_2O_{(l)} \rightarrow 2NaOH_{(aq)} + H_{2(g)}$$

- Potassium reacts with water to form potassium hydroxide and hydrogen:

$$2K_{(s)} + 2H_2O_{(l)} \rightarrow 2KOH_{(aq)} + H_{2(g)}$$

Tip: You can test for the production of hydrogen in these reactions using the flaming splint test. A lighted splint will indicate hydrogen by producing the notorious "squeaky pop" as the H_2 ignites. See page 180 for more about this.

Because the alkali metals are so reactive, they react with water very vigorously. When lithium, sodium or potassium are put in water, they float and move around the surface, fizzing furiously as the hydrogen gas is produced — see Figure 8 on page 208. In some cases, the reaction can get hot enough to ignite the hydrogen. Elements below potassium in Group 1 react explosively with water.

Metal hydroxide solutions

The hydroxides that are formed when the alkali metals react with water will dissolve in water to give alkaline solutions. This is where the name 'alkali metals' comes from. The reaction of the alkali metals with water is illustrated in Figure 8.

Figure 7: *Sodium reacting with water.*

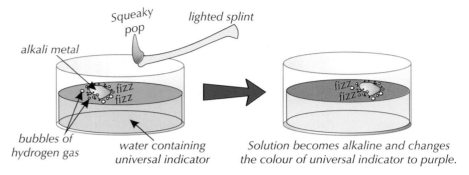

Figure 8: *The reaction of an alkali metal with water.*

Practice Questions — Fact Recall

Q1 Which group in the periodic table are the alkali metals?

Q2 Do the alkali metals have low density or high density?

Q3 State the trend in reactivity as you go down Group 1.

Q4 Which alkali metals have the lowest boiling points — those at the top of Group 1 or those at the bottom of Group 1?

Q5 Alkali metals can react with non-metals.

a) What type of bonds do alkali metals form during these reactions?

b) Give two properties of the compounds that are produced during these reactions.

Q6 a) Write down the general word equation for the reaction of an alkali metal with water.

b) Will the solution formed when a Group 1 metal reacts with water be acidic, neutral or alkaline?

Practice Questions — Application

Tip: You might need to have a peek back at the order of the elements in Group 1 at the top of page 206 to help you answer these questions.

Q1 Which is more reactive:

a) sodium or potassium?   b) lithium or rubidium?

Q2 Which has the higher melting point:

a) lithium or potassium?   b) caesium or potassium?

Q3 Is potassium oxide a covalent compound or an ionic compound?

Q4 Write a balanced symbol equation for the reaction of lithium with water. Include state symbols in your answer.

4. Group 7 — The Halogens

The elements in Group 7 are commonly known as the halogens.
The next few pages are about the halogens and their properties.

Learning Objectives:

- Know that the elements in Group 7 of the periodic table are called the halogens.
- Know that the reactivity of the halogens decreases down the group.
- Know that the melting and boiling points of the halogens increase down the group.
- Understand how the halogens react with metals.
- Understand that a more reactive halogen will displace a less reactive halogen from a solution of its salt.

Specification Reference C3.1.3

Properties of the halogens

The **halogens** are the elements in Group 7 of the periodic table — they include fluorine, chlorine, bromine and iodine (see Figure 1).

The halogens are all non-metals that have coloured vapours:

- Fluorine is a poisonous yellow gas.

- Chlorine is a poisonous dense green gas.

- Bromine is a dense, poisonous, red-brown volatile liquid.

- Iodine is a dark grey crystalline solid or a purple vapour.

All of the halogens exist as molecules which are pairs of atoms. For example, F_2, Cl_2, Br_2 or I_2.

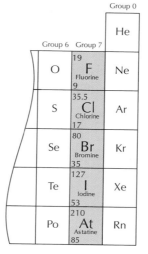

Figure 1: Group 7 of the periodic table.

Trends down Group 7

There are a couple of trends in the Group 7 elements that you need to know about.

Reactivity

Reactivity decreases down the group, so elements at the bottom of the group are less reactive than elements at the top of the group — see Figure 3.

Melting and boiling point

The melting and boiling points of the halogens increases down the group, so elements at the bottom of the group have higher melting points and higher boiling points than the elements at the top of the group — see Figure 3.

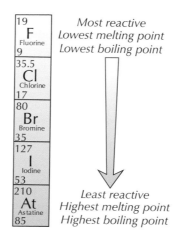

Figure 2: Some of the elements in Group 7 — chlorine, bromine and iodine.

Tip: H See pages 204-205 for an explanation of why reactivity decreases down Group 7.

Exam Tip
These trends are the opposite to the trends of the alkali metals on page 206 — make sure you don't get them mixed up in the exam.

Figure 3: Trends in Group 7.

Reaction with metals

The halogens have seven electrons in their outer shells, so they are keen to gain one extra electron and fill up that outer shell. When the halogens gain an electron they form 1⁻ ions, known as **halide ions**.

Examples

- When a chlorine atom gains an electron it forms a chloride ion (Cl^-).

- When a bromine atom gains an electron it forms a bromide ion (Br^-).

Tip: See pages 111-114 for lots more about ionic bonding.

The halogens can gain electrons by reacting with metals. When this happens, an **ionic compound** is formed, which is held together by ionic bonding.

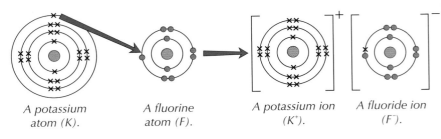

| A potassium atom (K). | A fluorine atom (F). | A potassium ion (K^+). | A fluoride ion (F^-). |

Figure 4: *The halogen fluorine (F) reacts with the metal potassium (K) to form the ionic compound potassium fluoride (KF).*

Displacement reactions

A more reactive halogen can displace (kick out) a less reactive halogen from an aqueous solution of its salt.

Examples

- Chlorine is more reactive than bromine, so chlorine will displace bromine from an aqueous solution of its salt (a bromide). For example:

  chlorine + potassium bromide → bromine + potassium chloride

  $$Cl_{2(g)} + 2KBr_{(aq)} \rightarrow Br_{2(aq)} + 2KCl_{(aq)}$$

- Chlorine is more reactive than iodine, so chlorine will displace iodine from an aqueous solution of its salt (an iodide). For example:

  chlorine + sodium iodide → iodine + sodium chloride

  $$Cl_{2(g)} + 2NaI_{(aq)} \rightarrow I_{2(aq)} + 2NaCl_{(aq)}$$

- Bromine is more reactive than iodine, so bromine will displace iodine from an aqueous solution of its salt (an iodide). For example:

  bromine + lithium iodide → iodine + lithium bromide

  $$Br_{2(g)} + 2LiI_{(aq)} \rightarrow I_{2(aq)} + 2LiBr_{(aq)}$$

Figure 5: *Chlorine water being added to potassium bromide. The chlorine displaces the bromide ions and bromine (orange) is formed.*

Fluorine is the most reactive halogen so it will displace any other halogen.

A less reactive halogen will not displace a more reactive halogen from the aqueous solution of its salt.

> **Example**
>
> If you mixed bromine with sodium chloride, nothing would happen — there wouldn't be any reaction. This is because chlorine is more reactive than bromine, so the bromine cannot displace the chlorine from the chloride salt.

Astatine is the least reactive halogen so it can't displace any other halogen.

Practice Questions — Fact Recall

Q1   Where are the most reactive halogens found — at the top of Group 7 or at the bottom of Group 7?

Q2   State the trend in melting points as you go down Group 7.

Q3   What is the charge on a halide ion?

Q4   Halogens can react with metals. What type of bonding exists in the compounds that are formed during these reactions?

Practice Questions — Application

Q1   Which is more reactive:

  a) chlorine or iodine?   b) bromine or fluorine?

Q2   Which has the higher boiling point:

  a) fluorine or iodine?   b) chlorine or bromine?

Q3   Would a displacement reaction occur between the following reactants?

  a) Chlorine and sodium bromide.

  b) Bromine and magnesium chloride.

  c) Iodine and lithium chloride.

  d) Fluorine and calcium iodide.

Q4   Write a balanced symbol equation for the reaction that would occur between:

  a) Chlorine (Cl_2) and potassium iodide (KI).

  b) Bromine (Br_2) and sodium iodide (NaI).

  c) Fluorine (F_2) and lithium chloride (LiCl)

> **Tip:** Have a look back at the order of Group 7 at the top of page 209 to help you answer these questions.

Learning Objectives:
- Know how some of the properties of the transition elements compare to the properties of elements in Group 1.
- Know that a transition element can often form more than one ion.
- Know that compounds containing transition elements are often colourful.
- Know that transition elements and their compounds make good catalysts.

Specification Reference
C3.1.3

5. Transition Elements

The elements in the middle block of the periodic table are known as the transition elements. The transition elements have lots of useful properties...

Properties of the transition elements

Transition elements make up the big clump of metals in the middle of the periodic table — see Figure 1.

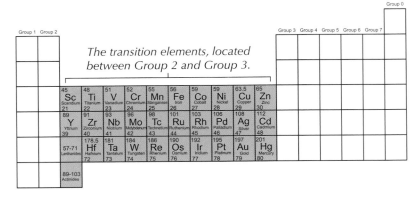

Figure 1: *The location of the transition elements in the periodic table.*

Figure 2: *An assortment of transition elements.*

Transition elements (or transition metals) are typical metals, and have the properties you would expect of a 'proper' metal, such as:

- They're good conductors of heat and electricity.

- They're very dense, strong and shiny.

Comparison with alkali metals

If you compare the transition metals to the **alkali metals** in Group 1 of the periodic table, you find that:

- The transition metals are much less reactive than Group 1 metals — they don't react as vigorously with water or oxygen, for example.

- They're much denser, stronger and harder than the Group 1 metals.

- They have much higher melting points than Group 1 metals (except for mercury, which is a liquid at room temperature). For example, iron melts at 1500 °C, copper at 1100 °C and zinc at 400 °C, whereas lithium melts at 181 °C and potassium melts at 63 °C.

Tip: See pages 206-208 for more about the properties of the alkali metals.

Transition metal ions

Most transition metals can form ions with different charges.

> **Examples**
>
> - Iron (Fe) can form Fe^{2+} or Fe^{3+} ions.
> - Copper (Cu) can form Cu^+ or Cu^{2+} ions.
> - Chromium (Cr) can form Cr^{2+} or Cr^{3+} ions.

The different ions usually form different-coloured compounds.

> **Example**
>
> Compounds containing Fe^{2+} ions are usually green in colour, while compounds containing Fe^{3+} ions are usually yellow.

Figure 3: Some colourful transition metal compounds.

Transition metal compounds

Transition metals compounds are very colourful. Their colours are due to the transition metal ion they contain.

> **Examples**
>
> - Potassium chromate(VI) is yellow.
> - Potassium manganate(VII) is purple.
> - Copper(II) sulfate is blue.

The colours in gemstones, like blue sapphires and green emeralds, and the colours in pottery glazes are all due to transition metals. And weathered copper is a lovely colourful green.

Tip: The number in brackets tells you what type of ion is present — e.g. copper(II) sulfate contains Cu^{2+} ions, while copper(I) sulfate would contain Cu^+ ions.

Transition metals as catalysts

Transition metals and their compounds all make good **catalysts**.

> **Examples**
>
> - Iron is the catalyst used in the Haber process for making ammonia.
> - Manganese(IV) oxide is a good catalyst for the decomposition of hydrogen peroxide.
> - Nickel is the catalyst used to hydrogenate oils.

Tip: Don't forget — catalysts speed up the rate of a reaction (see pages 159-160 for more about catalysts).

Tip: See pages 262-264 for more on the Haber process and page 89 for more on the hydrogenation of oils.

Practice Questions — Fact Recall

Q1 Where in the periodic table are the transition elements located?

Q2 Give two ways in which the transition metals are different to the alkali metals (the metals in Group 1).

Q3 Name one function of transition metals in industrial reactions.

Practice Questions — Application

Q1 This table contains information about two metals:

	Metal A	Metal B
Melting point (°C)	63	420
Density (g/cm³)	0.86	7.14

One of the metals is zinc, the other is potassium.
Suggest which metal is which, giving reasons for your answers.

Q2 Here is some information about three unidentified metals:

Metal X: Reacts vigorously with oxygen to form a white compound.
Metal Y: Reacts slowly with oxygen to form a red compound.
Metal Z: Reacts slowly with oxygen to form a black compound.

Which of these metals is most likely to be a transition metal?
Explain your answer.

Tip: If you look at the periodic table on the inside of the back cover you'll see that potassium is a Group 1 metal and zinc is a transition metal.

Section Checklist — Make sure you know...

History of the Periodic Table

☐ That Newlands' and Mendeleev's early versions of the periodic table had the elements arranged in order of relative atomic mass.

☐ That Newlands noticed that the properties of the elements were similar at regular intervals and arranged the elements in a table, so that elements with similar properties were in columns.

☐ That because similar properties occurred at regular intervals the table was called the periodic table.

☐ Why Newlands' work was criticised.

☐ That Mendeleev left gaps in his periodic table for elements that hadn't yet been discovered.

☐ That the discovery of elements that fitted into the gaps in Mendeleev's table provided good evidence that Mendeleev's system of classifying elements was a good one.

☐ That in the modern periodic table, elements are arranged by atomic (proton) number, and placed into suitable groups. This was possible due to the discovery of protons, neutrons and electrons.

cont...

Trends in the Periodic Table

- ☐ That in the modern periodic table, elements are arranged according to their electronic structure.
- ☐ That the group number of an element tells you have many electrons it has in its outer shell.
- ☐ **H** That there are trends in reactivity down groups within the periodic table and that these can be explained in terms of how easily elements gain or lose electrons.
- ☐ **H** How the distance between the nucleus and the outer shell affects how easily electrons are gained or lost.
- ☐ **H** How the shielding effect of inner electrons affects how easily electrons are gained or lost.

Group 1 — The Alkali Metals

- ☐ That the elements in Group 1 are known as the alkali metals.
- ☐ That the alkali metals all have low densities.
- ☐ That reactivity increases down Group 1 and both melting and boiling points decrease down Group 1.
- ☐ That the alkali metals lose electrons and form 1+ ions when they react with non-metals to form ionic compounds. These compounds are usually white solids that dissolve in water to form colourless solutions.
- ☐ That the alkali metals react with water to form hydrogen and metal hydroxides. These hydroxides form alkaline solutions when dissolved in water.

Group 7 — The Halogens

- ☐ That the elements in Group 7 are known as the halogens.
- ☐ That reactivity decreases down Group 7 and both melting and boiling points increase down Group 7.
- ☐ That the halogens gain electrons and form 1⁻ (halide) ions when they react with metals to form ionic compounds.
- ☐ That a more reactive halogen will displace a less reactive halogen from its salt when in solution.

Transition Elements

- ☐ That transition elements are less reactive than Group 1 metals so they don't react as vigorously with water or oxygen.
- ☐ That transition elements are stronger, denser, harder and have higher melting points than Group 1 metals.
- ☐ That many transition elements can form ions with different charges.
- ☐ That transition metal compounds are often colourful due to the transition metal ion they contain.
- ☐ That many transition elements and transition element compounds make good catalysts.

Exam-style Questions

Use the periodic table on the inside of the back cover to help you answer Q1 and Q2.

1   One of the earliest versions of the periodic table was proposed by Newlands in 1864.

1 (a) (i)   Describe how the elements were arranged in Newlands' version of the periodic table.

(3 marks)

1 (a) (ii)   Give **one** reason why Newlands' work was initially criticised.

(1 mark)

1 (b)   In 1869, Mendeleev devised an alternative version of the periodic table.

Give **one** similarity and **one** difference between the periodic tables of Newlands and Mendeleev.

(2 marks)

1 (c)   The modern periodic table was a development of Mendeleev's table and looks very similar to it. However, they are different in the way that the elements are arranged. What is this difference?

(1 mark)

1 (d)   The modern periodic table can tell you a lot about the properties of an element. Use the periodic table on the inside of the back cover to help you answer the following questions.

1 (d) (i)   How many electrons does an atom of selenium (Se) have in its highest occupied energy level?

(1 mark)

1 (d) (ii)   Selenium and sulfur both react by gaining electrons.
Explain why selenium is less reactive than sulfur.

(4 marks)

2   Copper(II) chloride ($CuCl_2$) is an ionic compound formed from the reaction of copper with chlorine.

2 (a) (i)   What type of metal is copper?

(1 mark)

2 (a) (ii)   Suggest **two** ways that the properties of copper are likely to be different to the properties of the alkali metal lithium.

(2 marks)

2 (b)   The reaction of copper with chlorine can also lead to the formation of copper(I) chloride (CuCl). Why can copper form two different chloride compounds?

(1 mark)

2 (c)   Chlorine is a gas in Group 7 of the periodic table.

2 (c) (i)   What name is commonly given to elements in Group 7 of the periodic table?

(1 mark)

2 (c) (ii) Name an element in Group 7 that will have a lower boiling point than chlorine.

(1 mark)

2 (d)   What would happen if bromine gas was bubbled through a solution of aqueous copper(II) chloride? Explain your answer.

(2 marks)

3   The elements in Group 1 of the periodic table are commonly known as the alkali metals. The alkali metals are generally very reactive.

3 (a) (i)   Describe the trend in reactivity down Group 1.

(1 mark)

3 (a) (ii) Explain the trend in reactivity down Group 1.

(3 marks)

3 (b)   The alkali metals react vigorously with water. When sodium (Na) is added to water, the metal fizzes and bubbles of gas can be seen.

3 (b) (i)   What gas is produced when sodium reacts with water?

(1 mark)

3 (b) (ii) If universal indicator was added to the solution at the end of the reaction, the solution would turn purple, showing that it was alkaline.
Explain why the solution is alkaline.

(2 marks)

3 (c)   Alkali metals can also react with non-metals.
When sodium reacts with bromine, sodium bromide is formed.

3 (c) (i)   Name the type of bonding present in sodium bromide.

(1 mark)

3 (c) (ii) What type of reaction would take place if chlorine gas was bubbled through a solution of the sodium bromide. Circle the correct answer.

Oxidation   Neutralisation   Displacement   Reduction

(1 mark)

1. Hard and Soft Water

Learning Objectives:

- Know that hard water usually contains calcium ions and magnesium ions, which dissolve into it from rocks.
- Know that soft water quickly forms a lather with soap.
- Understand why more soap is needed to form a lather with hard water than with soft water.
- Know the health benefits of hard water.
- Know that hard water can be permanent or temporary hard water, and the effect boiling has on each type of hard water.
- Understand why using hard water can be expensive.
- **H** Understand why heating temporary hard water can cause precipitates (scale) to form.
- Know how water hardness can be removed using sodium carbonate or ion exchange columns.

Specification References C3.2, C3.2.1

Water can be hard or soft — it varies from place to place. Water hardness depends on the rocks the water has passed over before it gets to you.

Water hardness

Water can be hard or soft depending on the minerals that it contains. Hard water usually contains lots of calcium ions (Ca^{2+}) and magnesium ions (Mg^{2+}), while soft water contains much lower concentrations of these ions. The ions get into water when it comes into contact with particular types of rocks (such as limestone, chalk and gypsum) and compounds like magnesium sulfate and calcium sulfate dissolve into the water.

Water hardness and soap

With soft water, you get a nice **lather** with soap. But with hard water you get a scum instead — unless you're using a soapless detergent. This happens because the dissolved calcium ions and magnesium ions in the water react with the soap to make scum, which is insoluble. So to get a decent lather with hard water you need to use more soap — and because soap isn't free, that means more money going down the drain.

Benefits of hard water

It's not all bad — there are some benefits of hard water.

> **Examples**
>
> - The calcium ions (Ca^{2+}) in hard water are good for the development and maintenance of healthy teeth and bones.
>
> - Studies have found that people who live in hard water areas are at less risk of developing heart disease than people who live in soft water areas. This could be to do with the minerals in hard water.

Types of water hardness

There are two types of water hardness — temporary and permanent. Temporary hard water can be softened by boiling, whereas permanent hard water remains hard after boiling.

When heated, temporary hard water forms furring or **scale** (mostly calcium carbonate) on the insides of pipes, boilers, washing machines and kettles (see Figure 1). Badly scaled-up pipes and boilers reduce the efficiency of heating systems, and may need to be replaced — all of which costs money.

Tip: Scale is sometimes called 'limescale'.

Scale can even eventually block pipes. Scale is also a bit of a thermal insulator. This means that a kettle with scale on the heating element takes longer to boil than a clean non-scaled-up kettle — so it becomes less efficient.

Softening temporary hard water Higher

Temporary hard water contains hydrogencarbonate ions (HCO_3^-). These ions are from dissolved calcium hydrogencarbonate ($Ca(HCO_3)_2$) and magnesium hydrogencarbonate ($Mg(HCO_3)_2$). When temporary hard water is heated the hydrogencarbonate ions decompose to produce carbonate ions (CO_3^{2-}). The carbonate ions then combine with calcium and magnesium ions to form insoluble precipitates of calcium carbonate and magnesium carbonate. These precipitates are the scale that can develop inside pipes and appliances. As the calcium and magnesium ions precipitate out to form scale, there are fewer calcium and magnesium ions dissolved in the water, so the water is softened.

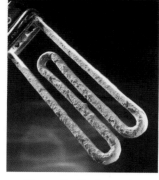

Figure 1: *Scale on the heating element of a washing machine.*

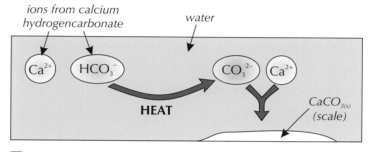

Figure 2: H *The formation of scale when temporary hard water is heated and softened.*

Permanent hard water contains other salts which don't decompose and form insoluble compounds when heated. This means the hardness isn't removed by heating — it is permanent (see Figure 3).

Softening temporary and permanent hard water

To convert permanent hard water into soft water you need to completely remove the dissolved calcium and magnesium ions which make it hard. There are two methods you can use to do this — adding sodium carbonate and using an ion exchange column.

1. Adding sodium carbonate

Both types of hardness can be softened by adding sodium carbonate (Na_2CO_3) to the water. The added carbonate ions react with the Ca^{2+} or Mg^{2+} ions to make an insoluble precipitate of calcium carbonate or magnesium carbonate — as shown in these equations:

$$CO_3^{2-}{}_{(aq)} + Ca^{2+}{}_{(aq)} \rightarrow CaCO_{3(s)}$$

$$CO_3^{2-}{}_{(aq)} + Mg^{2+}{}_{(aq)} \rightarrow MgCO_{3(s)}$$

The Ca^{2+} and Mg^{2+} ions are no longer dissolved in the water so they can't make it hard.

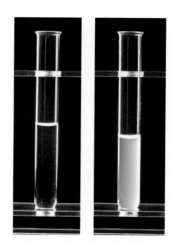

Figure 3: *These boiling tubes contain water which has been boiled. The left tube contains permanent hard water which does not change when boiled. The right tube contained temporary hard water — the cloudiness is caused by calcium and magnesium ions that have precipitated out, so it is no longer hard.*

2. Using ion exchange columns

Both types of hardness can also be removed by running the water through **ion exchange columns**, which are sold in shops. The columns have lots of sodium or hydrogen ions inside them which are trapped on insoluble resins. The sodium or hydrogen ions are 'exchanged' with calcium or magnesium ions in the water that runs through the column. For example, in the following equation a calcium ion becomes trapped on the resin and the sodium ion is released into the water.

$$Na_2Resin_{(s)} + Ca^{2+}_{(aq)} \rightarrow CaResin_{(s)} + 2Na^+_{(aq)}$$

Practice Questions — Fact Recall

Q1 Name the two main ions that cause water hardness.

Q2 a) Why does scum form when you mix hard water with soap?

b) How can you overcome scum formation to form a lather with soap and hard water?

Q3 State one health benefit of drinking hard water.

Q4 a) Name the two types of hard water.

b) Which type of hard water can be softened by boiling?

c) Which type of hard water forms scale when heated?

d) What impact does scale formation have on heating systems?

Q5 Temporary hard water can be caused by the hydrogencarbonate ion.

a) Give the chemical symbol of the hydrogencarbonate ion.

b) What happens when these hydrogencarbonate ions are heated?

Q6 Describe a way to soften permanent hard water.

Practice Questions — Application

Q1 Sharon lives in a hard water area. She is thinking of getting a water softener to convert the hard water into soft water.

a) Sharon has been told that having the water softener installed will save her money in the long run. Suggest why this is true.

b) Give one disadvantage to Sharon of installing a water softener.

Q2 Mike has several samples of hard water and wants to work out what type of hardness each one has. Describe a test Mike could use to identify the type of hardness of each sample.

2. Investigating Water Hardness

Learning Objective:
- Know how titration can be used to measure the hardness of water samples.

Specification Reference C3.2.1

Different water samples can be tested in the lab to work out the hardness. Thrilling I know, but at least there's some shaking involved...

Using titration to assess water hardness

You can use **titrations** to compare the hardness of different water samples. Here's what you do...

Method

1. Fill a burette with 50 cm³ of soap solution.

2. Add 50 cm³ of the first water sample into a flask.

3. Use the burette to add 1 cm³ of soap solution to the flask.

4. Put a bung in the flask and shake for 10 seconds.

5. Repeat steps 3 and 4 until a good lasting lather is formed — a lasting lather is one where the bubbles cover the surface for at least 30 seconds (see Figure 2).

6. Record how much soap was needed to create a lasting lather.

7. Repeat steps 1-6 with the other water samples.

8. Next, boil fresh samples of each type of water for ten minutes, and repeat the experiment.

Figure 1: *A burette.*

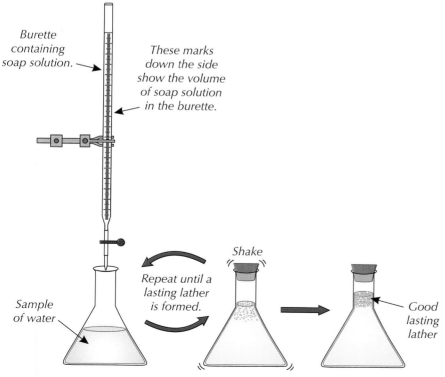

Burette containing soap solution.

These marks down the side show the volume of soap solution in the burette.

Sample of water

Shake

Repeat until a lasting lather is formed.

Good lasting lather

Figure 2: *Measuring the hardness of water samples.*

Tip: For more about titrations see pages 244-245.

Results

If you used this method with 3 different samples of water — distilled water, local tap water and imported tap water — you might get results that look something like these:

Sample	Volume of soap solution needed to give a good lather (cm³)	
	Using unboiled water	**Using boiled water**
Distilled water	1	1
Local water	7	1
Imported water	14	8

Figure 3: *The table of results from a titration using three water samples.*

The results tell you the following things about the water:

- Distilled water contains little or no hardness — only the minimum amount of soap was needed to give a good lather.

- The sample of imported water contains more hardness than local water — more soap was needed to produce a lather.

- The local water contains only temporary hardness — all the hardness is removed by boiling. You can tell because the same amount of soap was needed for boiled local water as for distilled water.

- The imported water contains both temporary and permanent hardness. The decrease in the amount of soap needed to produce a lather after boiling shows that some temporary hardness has been removed by boiling the water. But the fact that the amount of soap needed to produce a lather after boiling (8 cm³) is still much higher than the amount needed with the other two samples shows that some permanent hardness remains.

- If your brain's really switched on, you'll see that the local water and the imported water contain the same amount of temporary hardness. In both cases, the amount of soap needed in the boiled sample is 6 cm³ less than in the unboiled sample.

Practice Questions — Fact Recall

Q1 a) What type of experiment would you do to compare the hardness of two different water samples?

b) List the equipment you would need for the experiment.

Q2 Explain how you can tell if a lather is a 'lasting lather' or not.

Practice Questions — Application

Q1 This table shows the results of a titration using four different water samples.

Water sample	Volume of soap solution needed to give a good lather (cm³)	
	Using unboiled water	Using boiled water
A	6	1.5
B	21	9
C	1.5	1.5
D	15	6

a) One of the samples was distilled water.
   Suggest which one this was. Explain your answer.

b) Which sample(s) contained only temporary hard water?
   Explain your answer.

c) Which sample(s) contained permanent hard water?
   Explain your answer.

d) List the samples in order from the one with the most hardness to the one with the least hardness.

Q2 A group of students used titration with soap to test the hardness of distilled water, bottled water and tap water.

The distilled water was found to contain no water hardness.
The bottled water contained only temporary hardness. The tap water contained twice as much hardness overall as the bottled water, but it contained the same amount of temporary hardness.

Use this information to complete this results table.

Water sample	Volume of soap solution needed to give a good lather (cm³)	
	Using unboiled water	Using boiled water
	1	
	8	1

- Know that humans need water to survive and that drinking water should only contain small amounts of contaminants.
- Know that water is filtered then sterilised using chlorine to make it safe to drink.
- Know that filters containing carbon, silver and ion exchange resins can be used to further improve the quality of drinking water.
- Know the advantages and disadvantages of adding fluoride and chlorine to drinking water.
- Know that pure water can be produced by distillation.

Specification References
C3.2, C3.2.2

Tip: Treated drinking water isn't 100% pure. It's purified to a level that means it contains extremely low levels of contaminants.

3. Water Quality

The water that comes out of your taps has been treated to make it safe to drink. It's not exactly the most exciting process, but it's vitally important.

Producing drinking water

Water is essential for life, but to be suitable for drinking by humans it must be free from poisonous salts (e.g. phosphates and nitrates) and harmful **microbes** (e.g. bacteria, fungi or viruses). Microbes in water can cause diseases such as cholera and dysentery.

Sources of drinking water

The first step to safe drinking water is choosing an appropriate source. Most of our drinking water comes from **reservoirs**. Water flows into reservoirs from rivers and groundwater — water companies choose to build reservoirs where there's a good supply of clean water. Government agencies keep a close eye on pollution in reservoirs, rivers and groundwater.

Treatment of drinking water

Water from reservoirs goes to a water treatment works to make it safe to drink. There, it goes through the following stages to purify (clean) it:

1. The water passes though a mesh screen to remove big bits like twigs.

2. Chemicals are added to make solids and microbes stick together and fall to the bottom.

3. The water is filtered through gravel beds to remove all the solids.

4. Chlorine is added to the water to sterilise it (chlorination) — this kills off any harmful microbes that are left.

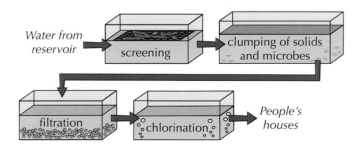

Figure 1: *The stages of water treatment.*

Some people choose to filter their water further to improve its taste and quality. They buy filters that contain carbon or silver to remove substances from their tap water. Carbon in the filters removes the chlorine taste and silver is supposed to kill bacteria and algae.

In hard water areas some people also buy water softeners, which contain ion exchange resins, to remove water hardness (see page 220).

Exam Tip
In the exam you might get a question where you are given detailed information about different water filters and asked to compare them.

Drinking water additives

Fluoride and chlorine can be added to drinking water. Both offer benefits, but there are also some drawbacks...

Benefits of adding fluoride and chlorine

Fluoride is added to drinking water in some parts of the country because it helps to reduce tooth decay. Chlorine is added to kill microbes and prevent disease (see previous page).

Problems associated with adding fluoride and chlorine

Some studies have linked adding chlorine to water with an increase in certain cancers. Chlorine can react with other natural substances in water to produce toxic by-products which some people think could cause cancer.

In high doses fluoride can cause cancer and bone problems in humans, so some people believe that fluoride shouldn't be added to drinking water. There is also concern about whether it's right to 'mass medicate' — people can choose whether to use a fluoride toothpaste, but they can't choose whether their tap water has added fluoride.

Levels of chemicals added to drinking water need to be carefully monitored. For example, in some areas the water may already contain a lot of fluoride, so adding more could be harmful.

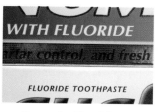

Figure 2: Fluoride is a popular ingredient in toothpaste to help prevent tooth decay.

Making water pure

Totally pure water with nothing dissolved in it can be produced by **distillation**. This involves boiling the water to make steam and then condensing the steam back into water. When the water evaporates to become steam, ions don't evaporate with it — this is why distilled water is pure.

Distillation uses large amounts of energy, which makes it expensive. It's too expensive to use to produce tap water — huge amounts of energy would be needed to boil all the water we use. But distilled water is used in chemistry labs.

Example

You'd use distilled water to make a salt solution, like potassium bromide (KBr), as you wouldn't want any other ions present in the water that might contaminate it.

Practice Questions — Fact Recall

Q1 Water treatment involves several stages.
Match the numbers in the diagram with these stages:
filtration, sterilisation, screening.

Water from reservoir → 1 → 2 → 3 → Clean, treated water

Q2 Drinking water can be filtered after it has been treated.
Name two substances that can be present in domestic water filters.

Q3 Chlorine can be added to drinking water to kill microbes.

a) i) Name another substance often added to drinking water.

ii) What is the benefit of adding this substance?

b) Name a health problem linked to adding these substances to drinking water.

Q4 a) Name the process used to produce pure water.

b) Why is this process expensive?

Practice Questions — Application

Q1 Water can be sterilised by exposing it to ultraviolet (UV) light.
In some areas this is used instead of chlorine.

Explain why using UV light to sterilise water instead of chlorine might be better for the health of people drinking the water.

Q2 Dave wants to filter tap water to improve its quality but doesn't need to improve the taste. What type of filter should he use?

Q3 Sally needs pure water for a lab experiment. She only has tap water.
Name the process she could carry out to get pure water.

Section Checklist — Make sure you know...

Hard and Soft Water

☐ That hard water contains dissolved compounds, usually with calcium and magnesium ions.

☐ That these calcium ions and magnesium ions dissolved into the water from rocks.

☐ That soft water quickly forms a lather with soap and hard water reacts with soap to form scum, so more soap is needed to form a lather with hard water than with soft water.

☐ That there are health benefits to drinking hard water.

☐ That hardness can be either temporary or permanent, and that temporary hard water can be softened by boiling.

☐ That scale can form when temporary hard water is heated. Scale can reduce the efficiency of heating systems and appliances (such as kettles).

☐ **H** That when heated, the hydrogencarbonate ions (HCO_3^-) in temporary hard water decompose to produce carbonate ions (CO_3^{2-}). These bond with calcium and magnesium ions and produce insoluble precipitates (scale).

☐ That sodium carbonate reacts with calcium and magnesium ions, causing them to precipitate out of solution and softening temporary and permanent hard water.

☐ That ion exchange columns can soften both types of hard water by replacing the calcium and magnesium ions with sodium or hydrogen ions.

Investigating Water Hardness

☐ How a titration involving soap solution can be used to work out the hardness of different water samples.

☐ How to use the results of titrations to draw conclusions about the hardness of different water samples.

Water Quality

☐ That humans need water to survive and that the water must only contain low levels of contaminants such as salts and microbes for it to be safe for humans to drink.

☐ That water is treated to make it safe to drink.

☐ That there are several stages to water treatment, including filtration and sterilisation using chlorine.

☐ That water filters containing carbon and silver can be used to filter drinking water further.

☐ That ion exchange resins can be used to soften water.

☐ That adding chlorine and fluoride to tap water can have health benefits, but that there are also disadvantages to using them.

☐ That pure water can be produced by the distillation of water.

☐ That distillation needs lots of energy, so it is very expensive.

Exam-style Questions

1   Water is treated to make it safe for humans to drink. It's treated so that harmful contaminants are either removed completely or reduced to very low levels. Some chemicals such as chlorine and fluoride may also be added to the water to improve its quality.

1 (a)   Name **two** types of contaminants that can only be present in water in low quantities if the water is safe for humans to drink.

(2 marks)

1 (b)   Some people use filters containing certain elements to improve the quality or taste of treated tap water even further. Give the name of one element that is used in water filters.

(1 mark)

1 (c)   *In this question you will be assessed on the quality of your English, the organisation of your ideas and your use of appropriate specialist vocabulary.*

Discuss the benefits and problems associated with adding fluoride and chlorine to drinking water.

(6 marks)

2   Soap can be added to water to make a lather. When soap is added to soft water it is easy to get a good lather. When soap is added to hard water an insoluble substance is formed.

2 (a)   Give the name of the insoluble substance formed when soap is added to hard water.

(1 mark)

2 (b)   The amount of soap flakes needed to hand-wash clothes varies depending on the hardness of the water used. In hard water areas more soap flakes are needed.

2 (b) (i)   Explain why more soap flakes are needed in hard water areas.

(1 mark)

2 (b) (ii) Using more soap flakes means that it costs more money to wash clothes. Give **one** other reason why hard water can lead to increased costs in the home.

(2 marks)

1. Energy in Reactions

Chemical reactions are all about breaking old bonds and making new ones. You need to put in energy to break bonds, but making bonds releases energy. That's why there's a change in energy when a chemical reaction happens.

Exothermic and endothermic reactions

Whenever a chemical reaction takes place, energy is transferred between the reaction and the surroundings. This energy can be transferred in either direction — chemical reactions can either absorb energy from the surroundings or release energy into the surroundings. This determines whether the reaction is **endothermic** or **exothermic**.

An exothermic reaction is one which gives out energy to the surroundings, usually in the form of heat and usually shown by a rise in temperature.

> **Example**
>
> When a fuel burns, lots of heat energy is transferred to the surroundings and the temperature increases — this is an exothermic reaction.

An endothermic reaction is one which takes in energy from the surroundings, usually in the form of heat and usually shown by a fall in temperature.

> **Example**
>
> When a substance thermally decomposes, it absorbs heat energy from the surroundings and the temperature drops — this is an endothermic reaction.

Energy and bonding

Energy is transferred in chemical reactions because old bonds are broken and new bonds are formed.

- Energy must be supplied to break existing bonds — so bond breaking is an endothermic process (see Figure 1).

- Energy is released when new bonds are formed — so bond formation is an exothermic process (see Figure 1).

Learning Objectives:

- Know that exothermic reactions release energy and that endothermic reactions absorb energy.

- Know that bond breaking is an endothermic process while bond making is exothermic.

- **H** Be able to explain why reactions are exothermic or endothermic in terms of bond breaking and bond making.

- **H** Be able to calculate energy changes in reactions using bond energies.

Specification Reference C3.3.1

Tip: Thermal decomposition is when one substance is heated and chemically changes into at least two new substances — see page 36 for more.

Tip: Energy transfer is usually measured in joules (J) — see page 236 for more.

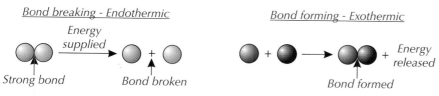

Bond breaking - Endothermic   *Bond forming - Exothermic*

Figure 1: *Energy changes during bond breaking and bond forming.*

Bond energy and overall energy change

Whether a reaction is exothermic or endothermic depends on what bond breaking and bond making is going on. It all comes down to whether the amount of energy absorbed when the bonds in the reactants are broken is more or less than the amount of energy released when the bonds in the products are made.

In an exothermic reaction, the energy released in bond formation is greater than the energy used in breaking old bonds. The leftover energy is released into the surroundings as heat and the temperature rises.

In an endothermic reaction, the energy required to break old bonds is greater than the energy released when new bonds are formed. The extra energy needed is absorbed from the surroundings and the temperature falls.

Figure 2: *Sodium reacting with water. This is a very exothermic reaction — it gives off lots of heat.*

Bond energy calculations   Higher

Not all bonds are the same strength — it requires more energy to break some bonds than others. Every chemical bond has a particular **bond energy** associated with it.

> ### Examples   Higher
>
> - A carbon-carbon (C–C) bond has a bond energy of 348 kJ/mol. This means that it takes 348 kJ of energy to break one mole of C–C bonds. It also means that 348 kJ of energy is released when one mole of C–C bonds is formed.
>
> - A carbon-hydrogen (C–H) bond has a bond energy of 413 kJ/mol. It takes 413 kJ of energy to break one mole of C–H bonds and 413 kJ of energy is released when one mole of C–H bonds are made.

Tip: There are 1000 J in a kJ, so 348 kJ is the same as 348 000 J — see page 236 for more.

Exam Tip
Bond energies vary slightly depending on what compound the bond is in. But don't worry about this — you'll be given any bond energies that you need in the exam.

You can use these bond energies to calculate the overall energy change for a reaction. Here's what you have to do:

- Draw out the displayed formulae of the molecules in the reaction so you can see all the bonds that are being broken and made.

- Work out the amount of energy used in bond breaking by adding up the bond energies of all the bonds in all the reactants.

- Work out the amount of energy given out from bond making by adding up the bond energies of all the bonds in all the products.

- Then, use this formula to work out the overall energy change:

Energy change = Energy of bond breaking – Energy of bond making

Example 1 — Higher

Calculate the overall energy change for this reaction: $H_2 + Cl_2 \rightarrow 2HCl$

The bond energies you need are:
H–H: 436 kJ/mol; Cl–Cl: 242 kJ/mol; H–Cl: 431 kJ/mol.

If you draw out the displayed formulae of the molecules in this reaction, it looks like this:

$$H-H \quad + \quad Cl-Cl \quad \rightarrow \quad \begin{array}{c} H-Cl \\ H-Cl \end{array}$$

As you can see, one mole of H–H bonds and one mole of Cl–Cl bonds are being broken and two moles of H–Cl bonds are being formed.

The amount of energy used in bond breaking is $436 + 242 = 678$ kJ/mol

The amount of energy released in bond making is $2 \times 431 = 862$ kJ/mol

So the overall energy change of the reaction is $678 - 862 = -184$ kJ/mol

Tip: You don't have to draw out the displayed formulae if you don't want to, but it makes it much easier to see all the bonds if you do.

Tip: An overall energy change that is negative means energy is released by the reaction.

Example 2 — Higher

Calculate the overall energy change for: $CH_4 + 2O_2 \rightarrow CO_2 + 2H_2O$

The bond energies you need are: C–H: 413 kJ/mol, O=O: 498 kJ/mol, C=O: 805 kJ/mol, O–H: 464 kJ/mol

Drawing out the displayed formulae of the molecules in this reaction gives you this:

$$H-\overset{\displaystyle H}{\underset{\displaystyle H}{C}}-H \quad + \quad \begin{array}{c} O=O \\ O=O \end{array} \quad \rightarrow \quad O=C=O \quad + \quad \begin{array}{c} H-O-H \\ H-O-H \end{array}$$

Four moles of C–H bonds and two moles of O=O bonds are being broken. Two moles of C=O bonds and four moles of O–H bonds are being formed.

The amount of energy used in bond breaking is
$(4 \times 413) + (2 \times 498) = 2648$ kJ/mol

The amount of energy released in bond making is
$(2 \times 805) + (4 \times 464) = 3466$ kJ/mol

So the overall energy change of the reaction is $2648 - 3466 = -818$ kJ/mol

Exam Tip
You can use the sign of the energy change to check your answer. If you know a reaction is exothermic and you end up with a positive energy change, you must have gone wrong somewhere.

The overall energy change for a reaction can be positive or negative. If the energy change is negative, it shows that more energy was released in bond making than was used in bond breaking — so the reaction is exothermic. If the energy change is positive, it shows that more energy was used in bond breaking than was released in bond making — so the reaction is endothermic.

Q1 What is the difference between an endothermic reaction and an exothermic reaction?

Q2 Are the following processes exothermic or endothermic?

a) Breaking chemical bonds.

b) Making chemical bonds.

Q3 Explain why energy is released to the surroundings during an exothermic reaction.

Q4 Give the formula that you could use to calculate the energy change of a reaction from the relevant bond energies.

Practice Questions — Application

Q1 Use the information in the table to calculate the overall energy change for the reaction, $2H_2 + O_2 \rightarrow 2H_2O$.

Bond	Bond energy (kJ/mol)
H–H	436
O=O	498
O–H	464

Figure 3: *Methanol burning in air.*

Q2 Methanol burns in air to form carbon dioxide and water, as shown by this equation:

$$2 \; H-\overset{\displaystyle H}{\underset{\displaystyle H}{\overset{|}{\underset{|}{C}}}}-O-H \; + \; 3O{=}O \; \rightarrow \; 2O{=}C{=}O \; + \; 4H-O-H$$

Calculate the overall energy change for this reaction.
Bond energies: C–H = 413 kJ/mol, C–O = 358 kJ/mol, O–H = 464 kJ/mol, O=O = 498 kJ/mol, C=O = 805 kJ/mol.

Q3 The following reaction occurs between methane and chlorine:

$$CH_4 + 4Cl_2 \rightarrow CCl_4 + 4HCl$$

a) Use these bond energies to calculate the overall energy change for this reaction.

Bond energies: C–H = 413 kJ/mol, Cl–Cl = 242 kJ/mol, C–Cl = 346 kJ/mol, H–Cl = 431 kJ/mol

b) Is this reaction exothermic or endothermic? Explain your answer.

2. Energy Level Diagrams

You can illustrate the energy changes that happen during a reaction using energy level diagrams. You need to be able to interpret energy level diagrams for the exam... so these pages are well worth a bit of concentration.

What are energy level diagrams?

An **energy level diagram** is a graph that shows how the energy in a reaction changes as the reaction progresses. The graph starts at the energy level of the reactants and finishes at the energy level of the products. These two points are usually joined by a smooth curve — see Figure 1.

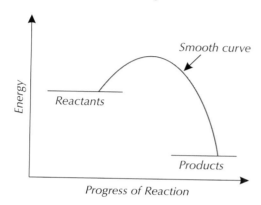

Figure 1: An energy level diagram showing how the energy in a reaction changes over time.

Learning Objectives:
- Know that energy level diagrams are used to show the energy changes in reactions.
- Know how to find the overall energy change and the activation energy for a reaction from an energy level diagram.
- Know how to determine if a reaction is exothermic or endothermic using an energy level diagram.
- Understand that a catalyst speeds up a reaction by lowering its activation energy.
- Be able to use an energy level diagram to show the effect that a catalyst has on the activation energy of a reaction.

Specification References
C3.1, C3.3.1

There are three useful pieces of information you can find from an energy level diagram:

1. The overall energy change

The overall energy change of a reaction is the difference between the energy of the reactants and the energy of the products. You can find the overall energy change of a reaction from an energy level diagram by looking at the difference in height from where the graph starts to where it finishes — see Figure 2.

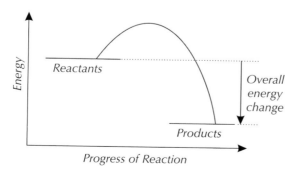

Tip: **H** You can also find the overall energy change of a reaction using bond energies — see page 230 for more.

Figure 2: Finding the overall energy change from an energy level diagram.

2. Whether the reaction is exothermic or endothermic

Energy level diagrams show the relative energies of the reactants and the products, so you can use them to work out whether a reaction is **exothermic** or **endothermic**.

In an exothermic reaction, the reactants have more energy than the products, because energy is released during the reaction. This means the energy level diagram will start high and finish lower than where it started.

In an endothermic reaction, the products have more energy than the reactants, because energy is taken in during the reaction. This means the energy level diagram will start low and finish higher than where it started — see Figure 3.

Tip: Don't forget — an <u>exothermic</u> reaction transfers energy <u>to</u> the surroundings and an <u>endothermic</u> reaction takes in energy <u>from</u> the surroundings (see pages 172-173 and page 229 for more).

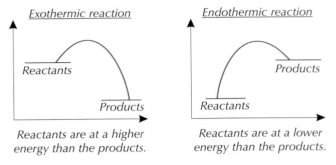

Figure 3: The energy level diagrams for an exothermic reaction and an endothermic reaction.

3. The activation energy

Energy level diagrams don't normally go straight from the reactants to the products — the graph will curve upwards before it starts to go down again. This is because some energy usually has to be put in to break the bonds in the reactants and get the reaction started.

The minimum amount of energy needed by reacting particles to break their bonds is called the **activation energy**. You can find the activation energy of a reaction from its energy level diagram by looking at the difference between where the curve starts and the highest point on the curve — see Figure 4.

Tip: Don't forget — breaking bonds absorbs energy (it's endothermic), but making bonds releases energy (it's exothermic).

Tip: See page 159 for more on activation energy.

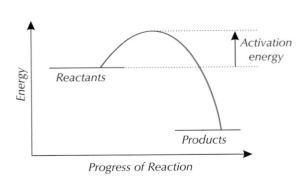

Figure 4: Finding the activation energy from an energy level diagram.

Energy level diagrams and catalysts

A **catalyst** is a substance that can speed up a chemical reaction without being changed or used up during the reaction. Catalysts work by providing a different pathway for a reaction that has a lower activation energy (so the reaction happens more easily and more quickly). You can see the effect that a catalyst has on the activation energy of a reaction by looking at an energy level diagram — see Figure 5.

Tip: See pages 159-160 for more about what catalysts do and what they are used for.

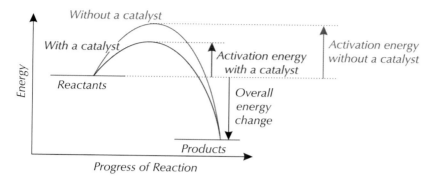

Figure 5: *An energy level diagram for a reaction with and without a catalyst.*

The activation energy is lower for the reaction with a catalyst than for the reaction without a catalyst. The overall energy change for the reaction remains the same though.

Practice Questions — Fact Recall

Q1 Sketch an energy level diagram and add the following labels to it.

a) The energy of the reactants. b) The energy of the products.

c) The activation energy. d) The overall energy change.

Q2 How are energy level diagrams different for endothermic reactions and exothermic reactions?

Q3 a) How do catalysts speed up reactions?

b) Describe how using a catalyst would change the shape of an energy level diagram.

Practice Question — Application

Q1 Are the following reactions exothermic or endothermic?

a)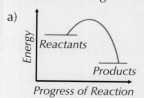

b)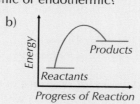

Learning Objectives:

- Know that energy is usually measured in joules.
- Know how to measure the energy transfer of a reaction in solution.
- Understand how calorimetry can be used to measure the energy released from fuels and foods.
- Be able to calculate the energy released in a reaction using the formula $Q = mc\Delta T$.

Specification Reference C3.3.1

Tip: There are 4.2 joules in 1 calorie — but you don't need to learn this.

Figure 1: *A reaction taking place in a polystyrene cup with no insulation and no lid — it will lose lots of heat energy to the surroundings.*

Tip: You can't burn things in a polystyrene cup, so you have to use another method called <u>calorimetry</u> to measure the energy transferred by combustion. It's coming up on the next page.

3. Measuring Energy Transfer

Scientists use experiments to measure the energy changes in reactions. There are a couple of types of experiment you need to know about that can be used for this. Read on to find out more...

Units of energy

Energy is usually measured in **joules** (J). Really big energy values are often given in kilojoules (kJ) — there are 1000 joules in a kilojoule.

When measuring energy transfer in reactions, the amount of energy released or absorbed will depend on how much reactant is used. As a result, energy transfer is sometimes measured in kilojoules per gram of reactant (kJ/g) or kilojoules per mole of reactant (kJ/mol), so that comparisons can be made between different reactions.

Although joules is the most commonly used unit of energy, it isn't the only unit of energy. For example, calories can also be used to measure energy (you'll probably recognise them as being used to measure the energy content of food). You could be asked to convert between joules and calories in the exam, but don't worry — you'll always be told how many joules are in one calorie (see page 293 for information on how to convert between different units).

Energy transfer of reactions in solution

You can find out how much energy is released or absorbed by a reaction in solution by taking the temperature of the liquid reagents, mixing everything together in a polystyrene cup and measuring the temperature of the solution at the end of the reaction (see Figure 2). You can use the change in the temperature to work out the energy change for the reaction.

The biggest problem with taking measurements like this is the amount of energy that's lost to the surroundings. You can reduce it a bit by putting the polystyrene cup into a beaker of cotton wool to give more insulation, and putting a lid on the cup to reduce energy lost by evaporation.

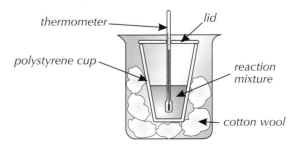

Figure 2: *Apparatus for measuring the energy change of a reaction in solution.*

This method works for reactions of solids with water (e.g. dissolving ammonium nitrate in water) as well as for reactions where you mix two solutions, like **neutralisation** reactions.

Here's what you'd do to measure the energy transfer when
sodium hydroxide neutralises hydrochloric acid:

- Place 25 cm³ of dilute hydrochloric acid in a polystyrene cup.

- Put 25 cm³ of dilute sodium hydroxide in a measuring cylinder.

- Record the temperature of both solutions. They need to be at the same
  temperature. (If they aren't, just stick them both in a water bath at
  about 30 °C for a little while.)

- Add the sodium hydroxide to the hydrochloric acid and stir.

- Take the temperature of the mixture every 30 seconds, and record the
  highest temperature that it reaches.

Tip: The acid and the
alkali have to start at
the same temperature,
otherwise it won't be a
fair test. See page 7 for
more on fair testing.

If the reaction is **exothermic**, energy will be released and the temperature
of the solution will increase. The more energy is released, the bigger the
increase in temperature will be. If the reaction is **endothermic**, energy will be
absorbed and the temperature of the solution will decrease. The more energy
that is absorbed, the bigger the decrease in temperature will be.

Tip: See pages 172
and 173 for more
on exothermic and
endothermic reactions.

Calorimetry

Different fuels release different amounts of energy. To measure the amount of
energy released when a fuel is burnt, you can simply burn the fuel and use the
flame to heat up some water. This is called **calorimetry**.

If you wanted to measure the amount of energy released when
methylated spirits burns, this is what you'd do:

- Put 50 g of water in a copper can and record its temperature
  (copper is used because it conducts heat so well).

- Weigh a spirit burner containing the
  methylated spirits, along with its lid.

- Put the spirit burner underneath the
  can, and light the wick. Heat the
  water, stirring constantly, until the
  temperature reaches about 50 °C.

- Use the lid of the spirit burner to put
  out the flame and measure the final
  temperature of the water.

- Weigh the spirit burner and lid again.

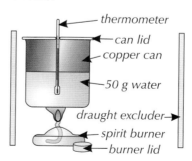

Figure 3: Calorimetry equipment.

Once you've done that, you can use the mass of fuel burned and the
temperature change of the water to calculate the energy released when the
fuel burns.

All you have to do is substitute your data into this formula:

Q	$=$	m	$\times$	c	$\times$	ΔT
(energy transferred, J)		(mass of water, g)		(specific heat capacity of water, 4.2)		(temperature change, °C)

Example

Here are the results from the calorimetry experiment on the previous page.

> Temperature of water in copper can before heating = 21.5 °C
> Temperature of water in copper can after heating = 52.5 °C
> Mass of spirit burner + lid before heating = 68.75 g
> Mass of spirit burner + lid after heating = 67.85 g

- The temperature change of the 50 g of water was 52.5 – 21.5 = 31.0 °C
  So the energy transferred in this experiment = 50 × 4.2 × 31 = 6510 J

- The mass of methylated spirits burned was 68.75 – 67.85 = 0.9 g
  So 0.9 g of methylated spirits releases 6510 joules of energy.

- Therefore, 1 g of meths releases $\frac{6510}{0.9} \times 1 = \textbf{7233 J}$ (or **7.233 kJ**).

You can use pretty much the same method to calculate the amount of energy contained in foods.

Practice Questions — Fact Recall

Q1 What unit is energy normally measured in?

Q2 a) Describe how you could measure the energy released by a chemical reaction between two solutions.

b) Suggest how you could reduce the amount of energy lost to the surroundings in an experiment like this.

Q3 State what Q, m, c and ΔT represent in the equation $Q = mc\Delta T$.

Practice Questions — Application

Q1 A student used a calorimeter to measure the energy released when ethanol burns. She burned 1 g of ethanol and used it to heat 200 g of water. The temperature of the water increased by 33 °C.

Calculate how much energy is released when 1 g of ethanol burns.

Q2 Malik burned 0.6 g of kerosene in a spirit burner and used it to heat 120 cm³ of water. He measured the starting temperature of the water as 12.5 °C and its final temperature as 55 °C. Use this information to calculate how much energy is released when 1 g of kerosene burns.

4. Energy from Hydrogen

Hydrogen can be used as a fuel. There are advantages and disadvantages to using hydrogen instead of other, more traditional fuels (like fossil fuels).

Problems with burning fuels

Fuels release energy which we use in loads of ways — for example, to generate electricity and to power cars. But we have to be careful, as there are problems associated with burning fuels.

> **Examples**
>
> - Burning fuels has various effects on the environment. Burning fossil fuels releases CO_2, a greenhouse gas. This causes **global warming** and other types of **climate change**. It'll be expensive to slow down these effects, and to put things right. Developing alternative energy sources (e.g. tidal power) costs money too.
>
> - Crude oil is running out. We use a lot of fuels made from crude oil (e.g. petrol and diesel) and as it runs out it will get more expensive. This means that everything that's transported by lorry, train or plane will get more expensive too. So the price of crude oil has a big economic effect.

Hydrogen as a fuel

The reaction between hydrogen and oxygen is **exothermic** — it releases energy. You can harness this energy by reacting hydrogen and oxygen in either a combustion engine or in a **fuel cell**. Some scientists believe that many of the problems associated with burning fuels could be overcome by using hydrogen as an alternative fuel.

Hydrogen in combustion engines

Hydrogen gas can be burnt in oxygen as a fuel in the combustion engines of vehicles. The advantage of using hydrogen in combustion engines is that hydrogen combines with oxygen in the air to form just water, as shown in the following equation — so it's very clean.

$$\text{hydrogen} + \text{oxygen} \rightarrow \text{water}$$
$$\boxed{\text{H}} \quad 2H_2 \quad + \quad O_2 \quad \rightarrow 2H_2O$$

One disadvantage is that you need a special, expensive engine to burn hydrogen. Another is that, although hydrogen can be made from water, which there's plenty of, you need to use energy from another source to make it. Also, hydrogen's hard to store safely — it's very explosive.

Learning Objectives:

- Understand that burning fuels has environmental and economic consequences.
- Know that hydrogen can be used as a fuel in combustion engines.
- Know that when hydrogen burns, the only product is water.
- Know that hydrogen can be used in fuel cells to generate electricity.
- Know that fuel cells that can be used to power vehicles are being developed.
- Understand the advantages and disadvantages of using hydrogen as a fuel.

**Specification References
C3.3, C3.3.1**

Tip: There's more on environmental problems caused by burning fossil fuels on pages 66-68.

Figure 1: *Hydrogen being pumped into the fuel tank of a car.*

Hydrogen fuel cells

A fuel cell is an electrical cell that's supplied with a fuel and oxygen and uses energy from the reaction between them to generate electricity. Hydrogen can be used as the fuel in a hydrogen-oxygen fuel cell.

Fuel cells were developed in the 1960s as part of the space programme, to provide electrical power on spacecraft — they were more practical than solar cells and safer than nuclear power.

Unlike a battery, a fuel cell doesn't run down or need recharging from the mains. It'll produce energy in the form of electricity and heat as long as fuel is supplied.

Figure 2: A simple hydrogen-oxygen fuel cell.

Hydrogen fuel cells and the car industry

The car industry is developing fuel cells to replace conventional petrol and diesel engines. Fuel cell vehicles don't produce any conventional pollutants — no greenhouse gases, no nitrogen oxides, no sulfur dioxide, no carbon monoxide. The only by-products are water and heat. This would be a major advantage in cities, where air pollution from traffic is a big problem.

Fuel cells could eventually help countries to become less dependent on crude oil. However, they're not likely to mean the end of either conventional power stations or our dependence on fossil fuels. There are a number of reasons for this:

Figure 3: A car that is powered by a hydrogen fuel cell.

- Hydrogen is a gas, so it takes up loads more space to store than liquid fuels like petrol.
- Hydrogen is very explosive so it's difficult to store safely
- The hydrogen fuel is often made either from **hydrocarbons** (from fossil fuels), or by **electrolysis** of water, which uses electricity (and that electricity has got to be generated somehow — usually this involves fossil fuels).

Practice Questions — Fact Recall

Q1   Give two disadvantages of burning fossil fuels.

Q2   Give the word equation for the combustion of hydrogen in air.

Q3   What is a fuel cell?

Q4   a) What is the main advantage of using hydrogen as a fuel in vehicles?

       b) Give two disadvantages of using hydrogen as a fuel in vehicles.

Section Checklist — Make sure you know...

Energy in Reactions

☐ That exothermic reactions release energy, while endothermic reactions absorb energy.

☐ That energy is released when bonds are made (bond making is exothermic) and energy must be absorbed to break bonds (bond breaking is endothermic).

☐ 🄷 That in an exothermic reaction, more energy is released forming the bonds in the products than is absorbed breaking the bonds in the reactants — so energy is given out to the surroundings.

☐ 🄷 That in an endothermic reaction, more energy is absorbed breaking the bonds in the reactants than is released forming the bonds in the products — so energy is absorbed from the surroundings.

☐ 🄷 How to calculate the overall energy change for a reaction from given bond energies.

Energy Level Diagrams

☐ That an energy level diagram starts at the energy level of the reactants, ends at the energy level of the products and shows how the energy in a reaction changes over time.

☐ That on an energy level diagram, the overall energy change of the reaction is the difference in height from where the graph starts to where it finishes.

☐ That on an energy level diagram, the activation energy is the difference in height from where the graph starts to the highest point on the curve.

☐ How to use an energy level diagram to determine if a reaction is exothermic or endothermic.

☐ That catalysts speed up reactions by offering alternative reaction pathways that have lower activation energies.

☐ How the addition of a catalyst affects the shape of an energy level diagram.

Measuring Energy Transfer

☐ That energy is usually measured in joules, but that other units (e.g. calories) can be used.

☐ That you can find the energy change of a reaction in solution by mixing the reactants in a well-insulated polystyrene cup and measuring the change in temperature of the reaction.

☐ How to measure the energy content of a food or fuel using calorimetry — this involves burning the substance, using the flame to heat some water and measuring the temperature change of the water.

☐ How to use the equation $Q = mc\Delta T$ to calculate the energy released when a food or fuel burns.

Energy from Hydrogen

☐ That there are consequences to using fuels — many damage the environment and aren't renewable.

☐ That when hydrogen is burned in air it combines with oxygen to make water.

☐ That hydrogen can be used as a vehicle fuel in combustion engines.

☐ That hydrogen can be used in fuel cells, which can be used to power vehicles.

☐ The advantages and disadvantages of using hydrogen as a fuel for vehicles.

Exam-style Questions

1 In industry, the Haber process is used to manufacture ammonia (NH_3) from nitrogen (N_2) and hydrogen (H_2) in the following reaction:

$$N_{2(g)} + 3H_{2(g)} \rightleftharpoons 2NH_{3(g)}$$

Here is the energy level diagram for this reaction:

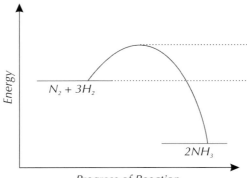

Progress of Reaction

1 (a) Use the energy level diagram to explain whether the formation of ammonia is endothermic or exothermic.

(1 mark)

1 (b) This table shows the bond energies of the bonds that are being broken and made during this reaction.

Bond	Bond energy (kJ/mol)
H–H	436
N≡N	945
N–H	391

1 (b) (i) Calculate the overall energy change for this reaction.

(3 marks)

1 (b) (ii) Draw and label an arrow on the energy level diagram that shows the overall energy change for this reaction.

(1 mark)

1 (c) The curve on the energy level diagram shows the reaction taking place with a catalyst.

On the graph, sketch and label another curve to show this reaction being performed without a catalyst.

(1 mark)

2   Hydrogen reacts with oxygen as shown in this equation:

$$2H_2 + O_2 \rightarrow 2H_2O$$

This reaction is exothermic.

2 (a) (i)   Sketch an energy level diagram to represent the energy changes that occur during this reaction.

(3 marks)

2 (a) (ii)   Explain in terms of bond making and bond breaking why this reaction gives out energy to the surroundings.

(2 marks)

2 (b)   Hydrogen can be burnt in combustion engines to power vehicles.

Give **one** advantage of using hydrogen as a fuel instead of traditional fuels like petrol or diesel.

(1 mark)

2 (c)   Hydrogen fuel can be produced by the electrolysis of water.
Explain why producing hydrogen fuel in this way might be bad for the environment.

(2 marks)

3   Some students are using calorimetry to measure the energy released when propane burns. This equation shows the combustion of propane:

$$C_3H_8 + 5O_2 \rightarrow 3CO_2 + 4H_2O$$

3 (a)   The students use a canister of propane gas to heat up 50 cm³ of water.

At the start of the experiment the temperature of the water was 21.4 °C and the gas canister weighed 34.56 g.

At the end of the experiment the temperature of the water was 90.3 °C and the gas canister weighed 34.04 g.

Calculate the amount of energy released when 1 g of propane burns.
(Use a value of 4.2 for the specific heat capacity of water.)

(4 marks)

3 (b)   One of the students used bond energies to calculate the amount of energy that should be released when 1 g of propane burns and found that this theoretical value was higher than the one they measured.

Explain why the energy change measured by calorimetry was lower than the energy change calculated from bond energies.

(2 marks)

Learning Objective:

- Know how to do a titration to find the volume of acid needed to neutralise a certain quantity of alkali (and vice versa).

Specification Reference C3.4.1

1. Titrations

You've met titrations before — back on page 221. But now you need to know about them in a bit more detail. Luckily, that's just what these pages are here to help you with.

What is a titration?

A **titration** is an experiment that lets you see what volume of a reactant is needed to react completely with a certain volume of another reactant. For example, you can use a titration to find out exactly how much acid is needed to neutralise a certain quantity of alkali (or vice versa). You can also use the results of a titration to find the concentration of one of the reactants — there's more on this on pages 247-249.

Figure 1: *36 cm³ of acid in a burette. The curve in the surface of the acid is called the meniscus.*

Carrying out a titration

The method below outlines how to carry out a titration to work out how much acid is needed to neutralise a measured amount of alkali. A diagram showing how the apparatus should be set up is shown in Figure 2 on the next page.

1. Use a pipette to measure out a volume of alkali (usually about 25 cm³).

2. Put the alkali in a flask along with some **indicator** (see next page).

3. Put the acid in a burette. Run a small amount through the tap, then turn the tap off. Set the burette up above the flask as shown in Figure 2.

4. Take a reading of the volume of acid in the burette. You should read off the value where the bottom of the meniscus (see Figure 1) touches the scale.

5. Add the acid to the alkali a bit at a time, giving the flask a regular swirl. Go especially slowly (a drop at a time) when you think the alkali's almost neutralised, so you don't add more acid than is needed to neutralise it.

6. The indicator changes colour when all the alkali has been neutralised. This is the end-point of the reaction.

7. Record the volume of acid left in the burette.

8. Calculate the amount of acid that was needed to neutralise the alkali by subtracting the final volume of acid in the burette from the initial volume of acid in the burette.

9. Repeat the whole process a few times.

10. Calculate the mean volume of acid that was needed to neutralise the alkali. See page 12 for more on calculating the mean.

Tip: It's helpful to do a trial run of your titration. This lets you see roughly how much acid you need to neutralise the alkali. Then you know when to slow down next time.

Tip: Doing the experiment more than once lets you see if your results are repeatable or not. Collecting lots of results and calculating a mean will improve the accuracy of your results as well. See the How Science Works section for more on this.

HOW SCIENCE WORKS

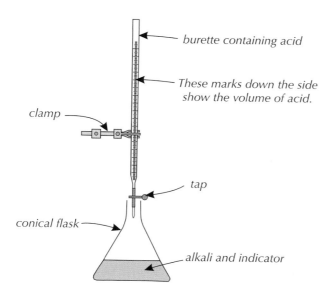

burette containing acid

These marks down the side show the volume of acid.

clamp

tap

conical flask

alkali and indicator

Figure 2: Equipment set up for a titration.

Figure 3: A burette being used to add acid to a conical flask containing alkali and indicator in a titration experiment.

Indicators

In the section on acids and alkalis you saw how universal indicator can be used to measure pH (see page 177). You can't use universal indicator in an acid-alkali titration though, because it changes colour gradually. You need an indicator that will give you a definite colour change so you can see the exact point where the alkali is neutralised by the acid (the end-point).

Phenolphthalein and methyl orange are good indicators to use for titrations. Phenolphthalein is pink in alkalis but colourless in acids, so if you're adding acid to alkali the end-point is when the solution changes from pink to colourless. Figure 4 shows the colour of phenolphthalein in acids and alkalis.

Methyl orange is yellow in alkalis but red in acids, so if there's methyl orange and alkali in the flask they'll be yellow at the beginning of the titration. When all the alkali has reacted with the acid that's added the indicator will turn from yellow to red, and you know you've reached the end-point. You can see the colour of methyl orange in acids and alkalis in Figure 4.

You can also do titrations by adding an alkali to an acid. For these titrations, the colour change would be colourless to pink when using phenolphthalein, and red to yellow when using methyl orange.

Figure 4: Phenolphthalein in acid (far left) and alkali (2nd from left). Methyl orange in acid (2nd from right) and alkali (far right).

Exam Tip
You don't need to know which indicators change to which colours for your exam.

Risk assessment

Before carrying out a titration you'll need to do a risk assessment to identify any hazards. You'll then need to take precautions to make sure that they don't cause any harm. The main hazards in titrations are the acid and the alkali.

Tip: See page 9 in the How Science Works section for more on hazards in experiments.

HOW SCIENCE WORKS

Example

Acids are often irritants or corrosive. Alkalis are often caustic. So you need to wear safety goggles to protect your eyes when using them. Sometimes concentrated acids or alkalis are diluted before they're used to stop them damaging the skin if they come into contact with it.

Q1 a) What is the end-point of a titration?

b) How can you tell when you have reached the end-point?

Q2 Describe how an acid should be added from a burette to an alkali in a flask when a titration is near its end-point.

Q3 Why is universal indicator not a suitable indicator to use in a titration?

Q4 Suggest one safety precaution that you should take when carrying out a titration using an acid and an alkali.

Q1 Sarah is carrying out a titration to work out how much acid is needed to neutralise 25.00 cm^3 of an alkali.

a) Suggest a piece of equipment that Sarah could use to measure out the alkali.

b) Sarah uses a burette to measure the volume of acid needed to neutralise the alkali. She repeats the titration three times. Her results are shown in this table:

	Titration 1	Titration 2	Titration 3
Initial volume of acid in burette	75.35 cm^3	70.20 cm^3	90.00 cm^3
Final volume of acid in burette	35.15 cm^3	30.05 cm^3	49.70 cm^3

i) Calculate the volume of acid needed to neutralise the alkali for each titration.

ii) Calculate the average volume of acid needed to neutralise 25.00 cm^3 of the alkali.

c) Sarah is using an indicator called methyl red. Methyl red is red in acids and yellow in alkalis. What colour would methyl red be at the end of the titration?

2. Titration Calculations

If you're feeling ambitious (and you're doing higher tier) you can use a titration to work out the concentration of one of your reactants.

Moles

Sometimes words are used to describe how many of something there are.

> **Example** ___ **Higher**
>
> - "A thousand" of something is 1000 of it.
> - "A million" of something is 1 000 000 of it.

"A mole" is also just a word used to describe a number.

> "One mole" is 6.023×10^{23}.

And that's all it is. Just a number. The reason it's important is because 6.023×10^{23} atoms of any element or compound weighs exactly the same number of grams as the relative formula mass (M_r or A_r) of that element or compound. For example, when you get precisely 6.023×10^{23} atoms of carbon-12 it weighs 12 g. So, you can use moles as a unit of measurement when you're talking about an amount of a substance.

Concentration and volume

Concentration is a measure of how crowded things are. The more solute you dissolve in a given volume, the more crowded the solute molecules are and the more concentrated the solution.

Units of volume

Whenever you're dealing with concentration you're also dealing with volume, because concentration is all about how much of something there is in a given volume. The units of volume you're most likely to come across are litres, cubic decimetres (dm^3) and cubic centimetres (cm^3). Here's how they're related to each other:

$$1 \text{ litre } = 1 \text{ dm}^3 = 1000 \text{ cm}^3$$

Units of concentration

The concentration of a solution can be measured in moles per dm^3. So, a solution with a concentration of 1 mole per dm^3 (or 1 mol/dm^3) has 1 mole of stuff in 1 dm^3.

Concentration can also be measured in grams per dm^3. For example, 56 grams of stuff dissolved in 1 dm^3 of solution has a concentration of 56 grams per dm^3 (or 56 g/dm^3).

Learning Objectives:

- **H** Know that you can use a titration to work out the concentration of a reactant when you know the concentration of the other reactant.
- **H** Be able to calculate the concentration of a reactant in a titration in moles per dm^3.
- **H** Be able to calculate the concentration of a reactant in a titration in grams per dm^3.

Specification Reference C3.4.1

Tip: You've come across moles before — back on page 140.

Tip: **H** A "solute" is a substance that is dissolved in a liquid (the "solvent"). When a solute is dissolved in a solvent they form a "solution".

Tip: **H** Sometimes 1 mol per dm^3 is written as 1 M (said as 1 molar).

Calculating concentrations

In the exam you might be given the results of a titration experiment and asked to calculate the concentration of the acid when you know the concentration of the alkali (or vice versa). You could be asked to work out the concentration in moles per dm³ or in grams per dm³. Here's what you need to do for each:

Tip: 🄷 For steps 1 and 3 you could use a formula triangle (see Figure 1) to work out the formulae you need to use (see page 294 for how to use formula triangles).

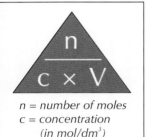

n = number of moles
c = concentration
    (in mol/dm³)
V = volume (in dm³)

Figure 1: *A formula triangle showing how number of moles, concentration and volume are related.*

Calculating concentrations in moles per dm³

Step 1: Work out how many moles of the "known" substance you have using this formula:

$$\text{Number of moles} = \text{concentration (mol/dm}^3) \times \text{volume (dm}^3)$$

Step 2: Write down the balanced equation of the reaction and work out how many moles of the "unknown" substance you must have had.

Step 3: Work out the concentration of the "unknown" stuff using this formula:

$$\text{Concentration (mol/dm}^3) = \text{number of moles} \div \text{volume (dm}^3)$$

This is the same formula as the one in step 1 — it's just been rearranged.

Example — Higher

Say you start off with 25.0 cm³ of sodium hydroxide (NaOH) solution in your flask, and you know that its concentration is 0.100 moles per dm³.

You then find from your titration that it takes 30.0 cm³ of sulfuric acid (H_2SO_4) to neutralise the sodium hydroxide.

You can work out the concentration of the acid in moles per dm³.

Step 1: Work out how many moles of sodium hydroxide you have:

$$\text{Number of moles} = \text{concentration (mol/dm}^3) \times \text{volume (dm}^3)$$

You need to know the volume in dm³, so start by converting 25.0 cm³ into dm³ by dividing by 1000:
25.0 cm³ ÷ 1000 = 0.0250 dm³

$$\begin{aligned}\text{Number of moles} &= \text{concentration} \times \text{volume}\\ &= 0.100 \text{ mol/dm}^3 \times 0.0250 \text{ dm}^3\\ &= 0.00250 \text{ moles of NaOH}\end{aligned}$$

Exam Tip 🄷
Always remember to check what units the data you're given is in. If you're given volume in cm³ you need to convert it into dm³ before putting the numbers into the equation.

Tip: 🄷 See page 30 for more on how to balance equations.

Step 2: Write down the balanced equation for the reaction.

$$2NaOH + H_2SO_4 \rightarrow Na_2SO_4 + 2H_2O$$

Using the equation, you can see that for every two moles of sodium hydroxide you had there was just one mole of sulfuric acid. So if you had 0.00250 moles of sodium hydroxide you must have had 0.00250 ÷ 2 = 0.00125 moles of sulfuric acid.

Step 3: Work out the concentration of the sulfuric acid.

Concentration (mol/dm³) = number of moles ÷ volume (dm³)

You need to know the volume of acid in dm³, so start by converting 30.0 cm³ into dm³ by dividing by 1000:
30.0 cm³ ÷ 1000 = 0.0300 dm³.

Tip: H See page 293 for more on converting between units.

Concentration (mol/dm³) = number of moles ÷ volume (dm³)
= 0.00125 mol ÷ 0.0300
= 0.04167 mol/dm³

Calculating concentrations in grams per dm³

For this method you need to know the concentration in mol/dm³ — so you might have to work that out first, using the previous method.

Tip: H Grams per dm³ is the same as grams per litre.

Step 1: Work out the relative formula mass for the acid. (See page 139 for how to work out relative formula masses.)

Step 2: Convert the number of moles from the concentration in mol/dm³ into grams. You can do this using the formula:

Mass in grams = moles × relative formula mass

You could use the formula triangle from Figure 2 to help you find this formula.

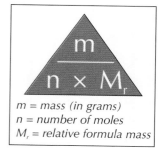

m = mass (in grams)
n = number of moles
M_r = relative formula mass

Figure 2: *A formula triangle showing how number of moles, mass and relative formula mass are related.*

| **Example** | **Higher** |

You can work out the concentration of the acid in the previous example in grams per dm³.

Step 1: Work out the relative formula mass of sulfuric acid from the relative atomic masses of the elements in the acid.

M_r of H_2SO_4 = (1 × 2) + 32 + (16 × 4)
= 98

Exam Tip H
You'll probably be given the relative atomic masses that you need, but if not, you can look them up in a periodic table.

Step 2: Convert the number of moles from the concentration in mol/dm³ (0.04167) into grams.

Mass in grams = moles × relative formula mass
= 0.04167 × 98
= 4.08 g

So the concentration is 4.08 g/dm³

Practice Questions — Fact Recall

Q1 a) How many dm^3 are in 1 litre?

b) How many cm^3 are in 1 dm^3?

Q2 Write the formula you would use to work out how many moles of a substance you have when you know its concentration in mol per dm^3 and its volume in dm^3.

Q3 Write the formula you would use to work out the concentration of a substance (in mol per dm^3) when you know how many moles of it you have and its volume in dm^3.

Q4 Write the formula you would use to work out the mass in grams of a substance when you know how many moles of the substance you have and its relative formula mass.

Practice Questions — Application

Q1 A solution of hydrochloric acid (HCl) has a concentration of 1.50 mol per dm^3. Calculate its concentration in grams per dm^3.

Q2 0.0350 dm^3 of sodium hydroxide (NaOH) solution was put in a flask. The concentration of the sodium hydroxide was 0.500 mol/dm^3. 0.0250 dm^3 of hydrochloric acid (HCl) was needed to neutralise it.

a) Calculate the number of moles of sodium hydroxide used.

b) How many moles of acid were needed to neutralise the NaOH?

c) Calculate the concentration of the hydrochloric acid in mol/dm^3.

Q3 25.0 cm^3 of sodium hydroxide (NaOH) solution was neutralised by 37.5 cm^3 of hydrochloric acid (HCl). The concentration of the sodium hydroxide was 0.750 mol/dm^3.

a) Calculate the number of moles of sodium hydroxide used.

b) How many moles of acid were needed to neutralise the NaOH?

c) Calculate the concentration of the hydrochloric acid in mol/dm^3.

Q4 27.5 cm^3 of sulfuric acid (H_2SO_4) was needed to neutralise 20.0 cm^3 of sodium hydroxide (NaOH) solution. The concentration of the sodium hydroxide was 1.00 mol/dm^3.
Calculate the concentration of the acid used in mol/dm^3.

Q5 25.0 cm^3 of nitric acid (HNO_3) was neutralised by 43.7 cm^3 of sodium hydroxide (NaOH) solution. The concentration of the nitric acid was 0.500 mol/dm^3.

a) Calculate the concentration of the sodium hydroxide in mol/dm^3.

b) Calculate the concentration of the sodium hydroxide in g/dm^3.

Tip: H You can use the periodic table on the inside of the back cover to find the relative atomic masses that you need for Q1 and Q5.

Tip: Don't forget to write <u>balanced</u> chemical equations for the acid-alkali reactions when you're working these answers out.

3. Tests for Ions

There are a whole load of chemical tests that you can carry out to work out what ions are in a substance. Here they are...

Testing ionic compounds

Ionic compounds are made up of positive and negative ions. You might be asked to find out exactly which ions a compound contains. To do this there are different tests that you can carry out which identify whether specific ions are present.

Tests for positive ions

Testing for metal ions — flame tests

Compounds of some metals burn with a characteristic colour. You can test for various metal ions by carrying out a **flame test**. This involves putting the substance in a flame and seeing what colour the flame goes (see Figure 1). You need to know the colours of the flames produced by the following metal ions:

- Lithium, Li^+, gives a crimson flame.

- Sodium, Na^+, gives a yellow flame.

- Potassium, K^+, gives a lilac flame.

- Calcium, Ca^{2+}, gives a red flame.

- Barium, Ba^{2+}, gives a green flame.

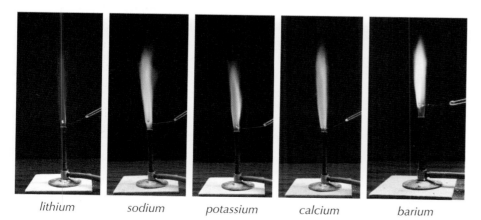

lithium	*sodium*	*potassium*	*calcium*	*barium*

Figure 1: *Flame tests for five different metal ions.*

To flame-test a compound in the lab, dip a clean wire loop into a sample of the compound, and put the wire loop in the clear blue part of the Bunsen flame (the hottest bit). Make sure the wire loop is really clean by dipping it into hydrochloric acid and then rinsing it with distilled water.

Learning Objectives:

- Know that flame tests can be used to identify certain metal ions.

- Know the colours of the flames produced when lithium, sodium, potassium, calcium and barium are flame-tested.

- Know the results of the reactions of calcium, copper(II), iron(II), iron(III), aluminium and magnesium ions with sodium hydroxide solution.

- Know how to test for carbonate ions using limewater.

- Know how to test for chloride, bromide and iodide ions using dilute nitric acid and silver nitrate solution.

- Know how to test for sulfate ions using dilute hydrochloric acid and barium chloride solution.

- Be able to use the results of chemical tests to identify compounds.

Specification Reference C3.4, C3.4.1

Tip: If there's more than one type of metal ion in a substance then you may not be able to identify them all using a flame test. The flame colour of one ion may mask the colours produced by other ions.

Testing for metal ions — precipitation reactions

Many metal hydroxides are insoluble and precipitate out of solution when formed. Some of these hydroxides have characteristic colours, so you can test for some metal ions by adding a few drops of sodium hydroxide solution to a solution of the substance you're testing. If you get a coloured insoluble hydroxide you can then tell which metal was in the compound. The colours of the precipitates formed by different metal ions are shown in Figure 2.

Metal ion	Colour of precipitate	Ionic reaction H
Calcium, Ca^{2+}	White	$Ca^{2+}_{(aq)} + 2OH^-_{(aq)} \rightarrow Ca(OH)_{2(s)}$
Copper(II), Cu^{2+}	Blue	$Cu^{2+}_{(aq)} + 2OH^-_{(aq)} \rightarrow Cu(OH)_{2(s)}$
Iron(II), Fe^{2+}	Green	$Fe^{2+}_{(aq)} + 2OH^-_{(aq)} \rightarrow Fe(OH)_{2(s)}$
Iron(III), Fe^{3+}	Brown	$Fe^{3+}_{(aq)} + 3OH^-_{(aq)} \rightarrow Fe(OH)_{3(s)}$
Aluminium, Al^{3+}	White at first, then redissolves in excess NaOH to form a colourless solution.	$Al^{3+}_{(aq)} + 3OH^-_{(aq)} \rightarrow Al(OH)_{3(s)}$ then $Al(OH)_{3(s)} + OH^- \rightarrow Al(OH)_4^-{}_{(aq)}$
Magnesium, Mg^{2+}	White	$Mg^{2+}_{(aq)} + 2OH^-_{(aq)} \rightarrow Mg(OH)_{2(s)}$

Figure 2: *The results of adding $NaOH_{(aq)}$ to solutions of different metal ions.*

Tests for negative ions

Testing for carbonate ions

You can test a gas to see if it's carbon dioxide by bubbling it through limewater. If carbon dioxide is present a white precipitate will form and the limewater will turn cloudy.

When a carbonate reacts with a dilute acid you get a salt, water and carbon dioxide. This means you can use the test for carbon dioxide to test for carbonate ions (CO_3^{2-}) — if you react a substance with an acid and it gives off a gas that turns limewater cloudy, then the gas is carbon dioxide and the substance must contain carbonate ions (see Figure 3).

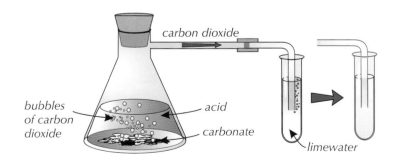

carbon dioxide

bubbles of carbon dioxide

acid

carbonate

limewater

Figure 3: *Using limewater to test for carbonate ions.*

Testing for halide ions

To test for chloride (Cl^-), bromide (Br^-) or iodide (I^-) ions, add dilute nitric acid (HNO_3), followed by silver nitrate solution ($AgNO_3$). A chloride gives a white precipitate of silver chloride. A bromide gives a cream precipitate of silver bromide. An iodide gives a yellow precipitate of silver iodide. The equations for these reactions are shown in Figure 4.

Halide ion	Colour of precipitate	Ionic reaction H
Chloride, Cl^-	White	$Ag^+_{(aq)} + Cl^-_{(aq)} \rightarrow AgCl_{(s)}$
Bromide, Br^-	Cream	$Ag^+_{(aq)} + Br^-_{(aq)} \rightarrow AgBr_{(s)}$
Iodide, I^-	Yellow	$Ag^+_{(aq)} + I^-_{(aq)} \rightarrow AgI_{(s)}$

Figure 4: *The results of adding dilute nitric acid and silver nitrate solution to solutions of different halide ions.*

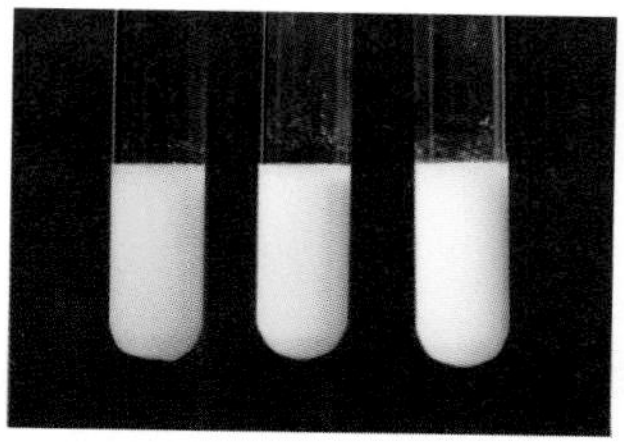

It's important to use dilute nitric acid for this test rather than hydrochloric acid. Hydrochloric acid would introduce chloride ions to the solution, so a white precipitate would be formed regardless of whether the solution originally contained chloride ions or not.

Figure 5: *The results of adding dilute nitric acid and silver nitrate solution to solutions of (from left to right) chlorine, bromine and iodine.*

Testing for sulfate ions

To test for a sulfate ion (SO_4^{2-}), add dilute hydrochloric acid (HCl), followed by barium chloride solution ($BaCl_2$). A white precipitate of barium sulfate means the original compound was a sulfate. The ionic equation for this reaction is:

$$\text{H} \quad Ba^{2+}_{(aq)} + SO_4^{2-}_{(aq)} \rightarrow BaSO_{4(s)}$$

Identifying compounds

You could be asked to identify a compound from the results of different tests. Just use the information that you're given to work out what you've got.

Figure 6: *A precipitate of barium sulfate*

Example

Substance A is a white powder that is soluble in water. When a sample of substance A is held in a Bunsen flame, the flame burns with a green colour. When dilute nitric acid is added to a solution of substance A there is no reaction and no gas is given off, but if silver nitrate solution is then added a white precipitate is formed. Identify substance A.

- The green flame in the flame test suggests that there are barium ions.

- There's no reaction with nitric acid, so there are no carbonate ions.

- The white precipitate formed when silver nitrate solution is then added tells us that there are chloride ions present.

So substance A is probably barium chloride.

Tip: Remember, an ionic compound is made up of positive and negative ions.

Practice Questions — Fact Recall

Q1 What colour flames are produced when compounds containing the metal ions below are held in a Bunsen flame?

a) Barium

b) Potassium

c) Lithium

Q2 a) Give the names of the three metals that will form a white precipitate when sodium hydroxide solution is added to a solution containing a compound of the metal.

b) Which one of these precipitates will redissolve when excess NaOH is added?

Q3 What gas is produced when a carbonate reacts with a dilute acid?

Q4 Describe how to test a solution to see if it contains bromide ions.

Q5 What ions can be detected by adding dilute hydrochloric acid followed by barium chloride solution?

Practice Questions — Application

Q1 Substance X is a white powder that is an ionic compound. When a flame test is done on the compound, a red flame is produced. When dilute sulfuric acid is added to substance X, the gas that is produced turns limewater cloudy. Give the name of compound X.

Q2 Substance Z is an ionic compound in solution. When sodium hydroxide solution is added to the solution containing substance Z, a blue precipitate is formed. When dilute hydrochloric acid is added followed by barium chloride solution, a white precipitate is formed. Name substance Z.

Q3 Tom thinks he has a sample of iron(II) chloride solution. Describe how he could test the sample to see if it is iron(II) chloride and state what results he would expect to see.

Section Checklist — Make sure you know...

Titrations

☐ That a titration can be used to work out what volume of an acid will react with a given volume of alkali (and vice versa).

☐ How to carry out a titration.

☐ How indicators are used in titration reactions.

☐ That before you carry out a titration you need to identify any potential hazards and take precautions to make sure the experiment is safe.

Titration Calculations

☐ H That moles are used as a measurement of the amount of a substance.

☐ H That 1000 cm³ = 1 dm³ = 1 litre.

☐ H That concentration can be measured in mol/dm³ and g/dm³.

☐ H How to use the formula 'number of moles = concentration (mol/dm³) × volume (dm³)'.

☐ H How to use the results of a titration to calculate the concentration of a reactant in mol/dm³.

☐ H How to use the formula 'mass in grams = moles × relative formula mass'.

☐ H How to use the results of a titration to calculate the concentration of a reactant in g/dm³.

Tests for Ions

☐ That flame tests are used to test for the presence of certain metal ions.

☐ The colours produced when lithium, sodium, potassium, calcium and barium are flame-tested.

☐ The colours of the precipitates formed when sodium hydroxide solution is added to solutions containing calcium, copper(II), iron(II), iron(III), aluminium or magnesium ions.

☐ That the white precipitate formed when aluminium ions react with sodium hydroxide solution dissolves when excess sodium hydroxide solution is added.

☐ That when an acid reacts with a carbonate a salt, water and carbon dioxide gas are produced.

☐ That carbon dioxide reacts with limewater to form a white precipitate (turning limewater cloudy).

☐ That you can test for the presence of carbonate ions by adding an acid and bubbling any gas produced through limewater. If the limewater turns cloudy then carbonate ions were present.

☐ That you can test for halide ions by adding dilute nitric acid followed by silver nitrate solution. A white precipitate shows that chloride ions are present, a cream precipitate shows that bromide ions are present, and a yellow precipitate shows that iodide ions are present.

☐ That you can test for sulfate ions by adding dilute hydrochloric acid followed by barium chloride solution. If a white precipitate is formed then sulfate ions are present.

☐ How to identify an ionic compound from the results of tests for positive and negative ions.

Exam-style Questions

1   A student carried out a titration to work out what volume of nitric acid reacted with 25.00 cm³ of sodium hydroxide solution. This is the equipment that she used:

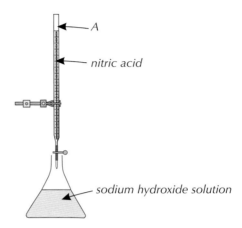

1 (a) (i)   Name the piece of equipment labelled A in the diagram.

(1 mark)

1 (a) (ii)   The student adds an indicator to the sodium hydroxide solution before starting the titration. Explain why.

(2 marks)

1 (a) (iii)   Towards the end of the titration the student adds the acid to the alkali a drop at a time. Explain why.

(1 mark)

1 (b)   The results of the student's titrations are shown in this table.

Titration	Initial volume of acid in burette	Final volume of acid in burette
1	78.65 cm³	46.20 cm³
2	87.00 cm³	54.45 cm³
3	71.00 cm³	38.70 cm³

1 (b) (i)   The student carried out the titration three times.
Give **one** reason why it is necessary to repeat the experiment.

(1 mark)

1 (b) (ii)   State **one** variable that must be kept constant each time the titration is carried out.

(1 mark)

1 (b) (iii)   Use the table of results to calculate the average volume of acid that reacted with 25.00 cm³ of sodium hydroxide solution.

(2 marks)

2   An acid-alkali titration was carried out using a solution of potassium hydroxide (KOH) and sulfuric acid. The concentration of the sulfuric acid used was 0.500 mol/dm³. 37.6 cm³ of acid was needed to neutralise 25.0 cm³ of the potassium hydroxide.

2 (a) (i)   How many moles of sulfuric acid were needed to neutralise the potassium hydroxide?

(2 marks)

2 (a) (ii)   Balance this equation to show the reaction that took place between the acid and alkali.

$$H_2SO_4 \quad + \quad \text{.......}KOH \quad \rightarrow \quad K_2SO_4 \quad + \quad \text{.......}H_2O$$

(1 mark)

2 (a) (iii)   Calculate the concentration of the potassium hydroxide solution used in the titration.

(3 marks)

2 (b)   Dilute hydrochloric acid was added to a sample of the sulfuric acid, followed by barium chloride solution. What would you expect to happen? Tick **one** box.

A yellow precipitate is formed	
A white precipitate is formed	
A white precipitate is formed, which will dissolve in excess barium chloride solution	
A gas is given off that turns limewater cloudy	

(1 mark)

3   A food scientist carried out a series of chemical tests on baking powder. The results of the tests are shown in this table.

Test	Test Description	Result
1	Flame test	Yellow flame.
2	Dilute hydrochloric acid is added and any gas produced is bubbled through limewater.	The powder fizzes and the limewater turns cloudy.
3	Dilute hydrochloric acid is added followed by barium chloride solution.	The powder fizzes. Nothing else happens.
4	Water is added followed by sodium hydroxide solution.	A white precipitate is formed which then dissolves as more sodium hydroxide solution is added.

3 (a)   Using the results table, identify the positive ion(s) that are in the baking powder.

(2 marks)

3 (b)   Using the results table, identify the negative ion(s) that are in the baking powder.

(1 mark)

3 (c)   Explain the results of Test 3.

(2 marks)

Learning Objectives:

- **H** Know that when a reversible reaction take places in a closed system it will reach a state of equilibrium.
- **H** Know that a reversible reaction reaches equilibrium when the forward and reverse reactions occur at exactly the same rate.
- **H** Know that the amounts of reactants and products present at equilibrium are affected by the temperature and pressure.
- **H** Know how changing the temperature alters the yield of a reversible reaction.
- **H** Know how changing the pressure can alter the yield of a reversible reaction involving gases.
- **H** Know that you need to think about temperature, pressure and rate of reaction when you're working out the optimum conditions for an industrial process.

Specification References C3.5, C3.5.1

1. Reversible Reactions Higher

If a reaction is reversible this means it can run in both directions. Sounds a bit complicated, but don't worry — all will be revealed in the next few pages.

What is a reversible reaction?

A **reversible reaction** is one where the products of the reaction can themselves react to produce the original reactants. Reversible reactions can be represented like this:

$$A + B \rightleftharpoons C + D$$

The double arrow means that the reaction can go in either direction.

Equilibrium

If a reversible reaction takes place in a closed system then a state of **equilibrium** will always be reached. Equilibrium is when the amounts of reactants and products reach a balance — their concentrations stop changing. A 'closed system' just means that none of the reactants or products can escape.

Equilibrium is reached when the reactions in both directions are taking place at exactly the same rate. Both reactions are still happening, but the overall effect is nil because the forward and reverse reactions cancel each other out.

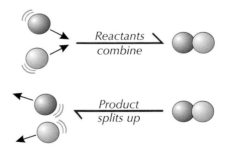

Figure 1: *At equilibrium the reactions in both directions are constantly occurring at exactly the same rate.*

Equilibrium and yield

In a reversible reaction the 'position of equilibrium' (the relative amounts of reactants and products) depends very strongly on the temperature and pressure of the reaction. This means that by altering the temperature and pressure you can alter the yield of your reaction — so you can make sure that you end up with more of the product you want (and less of the reactants).

Tip: For more about reversible reactions have a look back at pages 149 and 173.

Temperature

All reversible reactions are **exothermic** in one direction and **endothermic** in the other.

- If you raise the temperature, the yield of the endothermic reaction will increase and the yield of the exothermic reaction will decrease.

- If you reduce the temperature, the yield of the exothermic reaction will increase and the yield of the endothermic reaction will decrease.

Tip: Remember, an endothermic reaction takes in energy from the surroundings. An exothermic reaction transfers energy to the surroundings.

Example — **Higher**

The reaction below is used to make sulfur trioxide. It's exothermic in the forward direction and endothermic in the reverse direction.

$$Exothermic \rightarrow$$
$$2SO_{2(g)} + O_{2(g)} \rightleftharpoons 2SO_{3(g)}$$
$$\leftarrow Endothermic$$

- If you increase the temperature, the endothermic reverse reaction will increase to absorb the extra heat. This would result in a higher yield of SO_2 and O_2.

- If you decrease the temperature, the exothermic forward reaction will increase to produce more heat. This would result in a higher yield of SO_3 — the product that you want.

Tip: The yield is the amount of product you get from a reaction.

Pressure

Changing the pressure affects reactions where the reactants and products are gases. Many of these reactions have a greater volume on one side (either of products or reactants). Greater volume means there are more gas molecules on that side of the equation and less volume means there are fewer gas molecules.

- Raising the pressure favours the reaction which produces less volume (the least number of molecules).

- Lowering the pressure favours the reaction which produces more volume (the greatest number of molecules).

Tip: The general idea here is that when you make any change to the conditions, the reaction will try to counteract it. In other words, it will do whatever it can to get the temperature or pressure back to what it was before you started meddling with it.

Example — **Higher**

The reaction below is used to make hydrogen gas. It has 2 molecules on the left and 4 on the right.

$$CH_{4(g)} + H_2O_{(g)} \rightleftharpoons CO_{(g)} + 3H_{2(g)}$$

- If you increase the pressure, the reverse reaction will increase because the left side has fewer molecules than the right. This would result in a higher yield of CH_4 and H_2O.

- If you decrease the pressure, the forward reaction will increase because the right side has more molecules than the left. This would result in a higher yield of CO and H_2 — the product that you want.

Tip: Using a catalyst affects the rate of reaction but not the yield of products.

Using a catalyst

Adding a **catalyst** doesn't change the equilibrium position.

- Catalysts speed up both the forward and reverse reactions by the same amount.

- So, adding a catalyst means the reaction reaches equilibrium quicker, but you end up with the same amount of product as you would without the catalyst.

Optimum conditions

Tip: There's more about optimum conditions coming up in the next topic too — it's all about the conditions that are used for the Haber process (which is used to produce ammonia).

You need to consider temperature, pressure and rate of reaction when working out the **optimum conditions** for an industrial process.

The optimum conditions for a process are those that make the largest amount of the desired product for the smallest input of money, energy and time.

Figure 2: A bottle of methanol in a laboratory.

Example **Higher**

The reaction below is used to produce methanol.

$$Exothermic \rightarrow$$
$$CO_{(g)} + 2H_{2(g)} \rightleftharpoons CH_3OH_{(g)}$$
$$\leftarrow Endothermic$$

Conditions used: 300 °C and 50-100 atmospheres.

- The forward reaction is exothermic, so to get the best yield of methanol you'd need to use a low temperature.

- But using a low temperature would slow the reaction down too much (you'd get a high yield of methanol, but it would take ages). So a compromise temperature that's high enough to give a good rate is used.

- There are three molecules on the left-hand side and only one on the right. So a high pressure will give the best yields of methanol.

- A high pressure is used to give a good yield. But creating high pressure costs a lot and uses a lot of energy — so the pressure used is only as high as it needs to be to get a reasonable yield.

Using optimum conditions helps to keep reactions running as cost-effectively as possible, but it can also benefit the environment.

Examples **Higher**

- Lowering the temperature or pressure a reaction runs at saves energy. Using less energy means that less fossil fuels are burnt, so fewer pollutants and greenhouse gases are released into the atmosphere.

- Catalysts can be used to give a high reaction rate at a lower temperature. So using catalysts also saves energy and creates less pollution.

Practice Questions — Fact Recall

Q1 a) A reaction takes place in a 'closed system'. What does this mean?

b) If you run a reversible reaction in a closed system what will happen to the reaction?

Q2 What is happening to the rates of the forward and reverse reactions when equilibrium is reached?

Q3 If you decrease the temperature of a reversible reaction, is the endothermic or exothermic direction favoured?

Q4 If you increase the pressure in a gaseous reversible reaction, what determines which reaction is favoured?

Practice Questions — Application

Q1 Ammonium chloride decomposes on heating to form ammonia and hydrogen chloride. On cooling the reaction can be reversed. The equation for the reaction is shown below.

$$\text{NH}_4\text{Cl}_{(s)} \underset{\text{exothermic}}{\overset{\text{endothermic}}{\rightleftharpoons}} \text{NH}_{3(g)} + \text{HCl}_{(g)}$$

a) i) If you lower the temperature, which reaction will increase?

ii) Of which compound(s) will the yield increase?

b) i) If you raise the temperature, which reaction will increase?

ii) Of which compound(s) will the yield increase?

Q2 Sulfur dioxide reacts with oxygen to produce sulfur trioxide:

$$2\text{SO}_{2(g)} + \text{O}_{2(g)} \rightleftharpoons 2\text{SO}_{3(g)}$$

a) Which side of the equation has more volume?

b) Explain the effect of increasing the pressure on the yield of SO_3.

c) Explain the effect of decreasing the pressure on the yield of SO_3.

d) The forward reaction is exothermic. How would decreasing the temperature affect:

i) the yield of SO_3?

ii) the overall rate of the reaction?

Q3 Andrew is running a reversible reaction. He alters the temperature and this causes the yield of the endothermic reaction to decrease.

a) Did he increase or decrease the temperature?

b) How would he need to alter the temperature to cause the yield of the exothermic reaction to decrease?

> **Tip:** Think about all the things that you have to take into account when you're working out the optimum conditions for a reaction.

- Know that the Haber process is used to make ammonia.

- Know that nitrogen can be collected from the air and hydrogen is collected from natural gas (methane) or other sources.

- Know that purified nitrogen and hydrogen react with each other to produce ammonia and that this reaction is reversible.

- Know that the Haber process is carried out at a temperature of 450 °C, at a pressure of 200 atmospheres and in the presence of an iron catalyst.

- **H** Understand how changing temperature and pressure affects the yield of ammonia in the Haber process.

- Know that the ammonia gas produced in the Haber process liquefies on cooling and can be removed, while unused nitrogen and hydrogen are recycled.

- Understand that the Haber process uses a lot of energy and that producing this energy can be bad for the environment.

Specification Reference C3.5, C3.5.1

Tip: Remember, raising the temperature favours the endothermic reaction — see page 259.

2. The Haber Process

The Haber process is used to manufacture ammonia (NH$_3$), which has loads of important uses in industry, from fertilisers to cleaning products.

Raw materials

Nitrogen and hydrogen gas are used to make ammonia in the **Haber process**.

The nitrogen is obtained easily from the air, which is 78% nitrogen (and 21% oxygen). The hydrogen comes from natural gas (methane) or from other sources like crude oil.

The nitrogen and hydrogen are purified before being reacted with each other. The equation for this reaction is shown below.

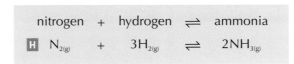

nitrogen + hydrogen ⇌ ammonia

H $N_{2(g)}$ + $3H_{2(g)}$ ⇌ $2NH_{3(g)}$

Some of the nitrogen and hydrogen reacts to form ammonia. Because the reaction is **reversible** (it occurs in both directions) some of the ammonia breaks down into nitrogen and hydrogen again.

Industrial conditions

The following conditions are used for the Haber process.

- Temperature: 450 °C
- Pressure: 200 atmospheres
- Catalyst: Iron

As the reaction is reversible, the temperature and pressure conditions used are a compromise.

Temperature Higher

The forward reaction is exothermic, which means that increasing the temperature will actually move the equilibrium the wrong way — away from ammonia and towards N$_2$ and H$_2$. So the yield of ammonia would be greater at lower temperatures.

The trouble is, lower temperatures mean a lower rate of reaction. So what they do is increase the temperature anyway, to get a much faster rate of reaction.

The 450 °C is a compromise between maximum yield and speed of reaction. It's better to wait just 20 seconds for a 10% yield than to have to wait 60 seconds for a 20% yield.

Pressure `Higher`

Higher pressures favour the forward reaction (since there are four molecules of gas on the left-hand side, for every two molecules on the right — see the equation on the previous page) and move the equilibrium towards ammonia and away from nitrogen and hydrogen. So higher pressures increase the yield of ammonia.

The pressure is set as high as possible to give the best percentage yield, without making the plant too expensive to build (it'd be too expensive to build a plant that would stand pressures of over 1000 atmospheres, for example). Hence the 200 atmospheres operating pressure.

Tip: **H** Remember, raising the pressure encourages the reaction (forwards or reverse) which produces less volume — see page 259.

Iron catalyst `Higher`

The iron catalyst makes the reaction go faster, which means that it reaches equilibrium faster. But remember, using a catalyst doesn't change the amount of products and reactants present at equilibrium (i.e. the percentage yield).

Without the catalyst the temperature would have to be raised even further to get a quick enough reaction — this would reduce the percentage yield even further and lead to higher energy costs. So the catalyst is very important.

Ammonia production

The Haber process is carried out in a reaction vessel like this:

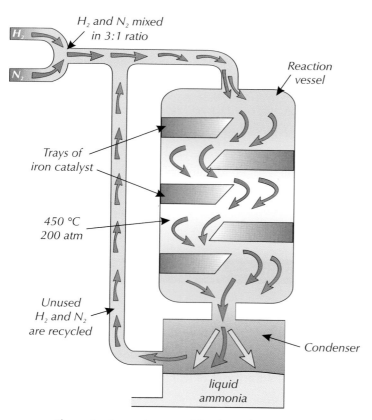

H₂ and N₂ mixed in 3:1 ratio

H_2

N_2

Reaction vessel

Trays of iron catalyst

450 °C 200 atm

Unused H₂ and N₂ are recycled

Condenser

liquid ammonia

Figure 1: *A reaction vessel for the Haber process.*

Tip: The symbol for atmospheres is atm. So 200 atm means 200 atmospheres.

Tip: In the condenser ammonia turns from a gas to a liquid.

The Haber process forms ammonia gas. This gas is then cooled in a condenser and liquefies (becomes a liquid). The liquid ammonia can then be removed from the reaction vessel.

The unused nitrogen (N_2) and hydrogen (H_2) are recycled. This reduces waste, saves resources and reduces costs.

Energy use and the environment

The conditions used for reactions in industry affect the amount of energy the process uses — and this has an impact on the environment.

A high pressure and a relatively high temperature are needed for the Haber process. Producing these conditions uses a lot of energy, which is often produced by burning fossil fuels. This leads to the release of pollutants and carbon dioxide (which contributes to global warming — see page 68). So manufacturers try to make sure that the pressure and temperature used are only as high as is needed to produce ammonia efficiently and no higher.

The iron catalyst also helps to reduce the energy used, as without it the temperature would have to be raised even higher to achieve a good rate of reaction. Also the recycling of hydrogen and nitrogen gases reduces the environmental impact of the process.

Figure 2: *A coal-fired power station. Burning coal produces energy, but it also gives out carbon dioxide.*

Tip: Saving energy also saves the manufacturer money — so it's a win-win situation.

Practice Questions — Fact Recall

Q1 a) Name the two raw materials used in the Haber process.

   b) Describe where each of these materials can be sourced from.

Q2 Give the word equation for the Haber process.

Q3 What is the catalyst used in the Haber process?

Q4 State the temperature and pressure conditions that are used in the Haber process.

Q5 a) What happens to the remaining (unused) nitrogen and hydrogen gas at the end of the Haber process?

   b) Describe how the ammonia is removed from the reaction vessel.

Practice Question — Application

 Kevin is an industrial chemist. He has been carrying out the Haber process using a higher pressure (350 atmospheres) and lower temperature (350 °C) than normal.

   a) What is the advantage of using a higher pressure than usual?

   b) What are the advantages of using a lower temperature than usual?

   c) What is the downside of using a lower temperature than usual?

Reversible Reactions

- ☐ H That a reversible reaction taking place in a closed system will reach a state of equilibrium.
- ☐ H That during equilibrium, the forward and reverse reactions are occurring at exactly the same rate.
- ☐ H That the temperature and pressure conditions affect the amounts of products and reactants present during equilibrium.
- ☐ H How changing the temperature alters the yield of the endothermic and exothermic reactions.
- ☐ H How raising the pressure favours the reaction that produces the least number of molecules.
- ☐ H That temperature, pressure and rate of reaction are important for working out the optimum conditions for industrial processes.

The Haber Process

- ☐ That the Haber process is used to produce ammonia by the reaction of nitrogen and hydrogen gas.
- ☐ That the nitrogen gas used in the Haber process is obtained from the air and the hydrogen gas comes from other sources including natural gas (methane).
- ☐ That purified nitrogen and hydrogen react to produce ammonia. As the reaction is reversible, some of the ammonia will break down to form nitrogen and hydrogen.
- ☐ That the word equation for the Haber process is: nitrogen + hydrogen ⇌ ammonia.
- ☐ H That the symbol equation for the Haber process is: $N_{2(g)} + 3H_{2(g)} \rightleftharpoons 2NH_{3(g)}$.
- ☐ That the Haber process is carried out in the presence of an iron catalyst at a temperature of about 450 °C and a pressure of about 200 atmospheres.
- ☐ H Why the temperature and pressure used in the Haber process were chosen.
- ☐ That the ammonia gas produced by the Haber process liquefies on cooling and is removed in this liquid form.
- ☐ That the unused nitrogen and hydrogen are recycled.
- ☐ That creating the temperature and pressure needed for the Haber process uses a lot of energy, which is often produced by burning fossil fuels.

Exam-style Questions

1   Ammonia is manufactured using the Haber process.

1 (a)   Fill in the gaps in the word equation below.

                  _____ + _____ $\rightleftharpoons$ ammonia

(2 marks)

1 (b)   Circle the pressure that the Haber process is carried out at.

             200 atm   400 atm   300 atm

(1 mark)

1 (c)   What material is used as a catalyst in the Haber process?

(1 mark)

1 (d) (i) What temperature is the Haber process carried out at?

(1 mark)

1 (d) (ii) Using a lower temperature would increase the yield of ammonia.
                  Explain why a relatively high temperature is used for the Haber process.

(2 marks)

2   Ethanol is produced using a reversible reaction between ethene and steam, as shown in the equation below.

$$C_2H_{4(g)} \quad + \quad H_2O_{(g)} \quad \overset{\text{exothermic}}{\underset{\text{endothermic}}{\rightleftharpoons}} \quad C_2H_5OH_{(g)}$$

        This reaction is carried out at 300 °C and 60-70 atmospheres.

2 (a)   The temperature that the reaction is carried out at is increased.
           What effect would this have on the yield of ethanol? Explain your answer.

(2 marks)

2 (b)   The pressure that the reaction is carried out at is increased.
           What effect would this have on the yield of ethanol? Explain your answer.

(2 marks)

1. Alcohols

In chemistry there are loads of different types of compound. You've come across a few already — alkanes, alkenes, carbonates, oxides and hydroxides. Now it's time to look at a few more. First up... it's alcohols.

What are alcohols?

The **alcohols** are a group of compounds that all contain an –OH group (an oxygen atom covalently bonded to a hydrogen atom). The –OH group is an example of a **functional group** — a group of atoms that are responsible for the chemical properties of a compound. The alcohols are an example of a **homologous series**. A homologous series is a group of chemicals that react in a similar way because they have the same functional group (in alcohols it's the –OH group).

The general formula of an alcohol is $C_nH_{2n+1}OH$. So an alcohol with two carbons has the formula C_2H_5OH. The basic naming system for alcohols is the same as for alkanes — but you replace the final '-e' with '-ol'. You need to know the first three alcohols in the homologous series. They are methanol, ethanol and propanol (see Figure 1).

	Methanol	*Ethanol*	*Propanol*
Chemical formulae:	CH_3OH	C_2H_5OH or CH_3CH_2OH	C_3H_7OH or $CH_3CH_2CH_2OH$
Displayed formulae:			

Figure 1: *Chemical and displayed formulae of the first three alcohols — methanol, ethanol and propanol.*

Representing and identifying alcohols

A compound isn't an alcohol unless it has an –OH group, so when you're giving the chemical formulae of alcohols it's important that you show the –OH group clearly.

Example

If you're giving the chemical formula of methanol, don't write CH_4O — it doesn't show the functional –OH group. Write CH_3OH instead.

Learning Objectives:
- Know that the alcohols are a group of compounds that all contain an –OH functional group.
- Know that the first three alcohols are methanol, ethanol and propanol.
- Be able to represent alcohols using chemical or displayed formulae.
- Be able to identify alcohols from their names or formulae.
- Know some of the main properties and uses of the first three alcohols.
- Be able to evaluate the positive and negative social and economic effects of using alcohols.

Specification Reference C3.6, C3.6.1

Exam Tip
There are lots of other alcohols, but methanol, ethanol and propanol are the only ones you need to learn for your exam.

For alcohols with more than one carbon in (like ethanol and propanol), there's more than one way to give the chemical formula:

1. You can just count up all the carbons and hydrogens and show them with the –OH group.

2. You can also write the formula out showing the groups attached to each carbon atom separately.

Examples

- The formula of ethanol can be written as C_2H_5OH. Or you can write it as CH_3CH_2OH.

- The formula of propanol can be written as C_3H_7OH. Or you can write it as $CH_3CH_2CH_2OH$.

Tip: It's not just alcohols that you can represent this way. For example, you could write propane (C_3H_8) as $CH_3CH_2CH_3$.

If you're asked to identify whether a compound is an alcohol or not in the exam it should be pretty easy — just look out for an –OH group in the formula. Alternatively, if you're given the name of the compound, look out for an '-ol' at the end of the name.

Example

The displayed formula shown here is butan-1-ol (C_4H_9OH).

You've probably never come across butan-1-ol before, but you can tell it's an alcohol because the name ends in '-ol'. You can also clearly see the –OH group.

Exam Tip
You could be asked about compounds you've never heard of before in the exam — don't let it put you off, any information you need will be given in the question.

Properties of alcohols

The first three alcohols have similar properties:

- Alcohols are flammable. They burn in air to produce carbon dioxide (CO_2) and water (H_2O).

Example

The equation for the combustion of methanol is:

$$2CH_3OH_{(l)} + 3O_{2(g)} \rightarrow 2CO_{2(g)} + 4H_2O_{(g)}$$

- The first three alcohols all dissolve completely in water to form neutral solutions (solutions with a pH of exactly 7) — they don't ionise like carboxylic acids do (see page 271).

- They also react with sodium to give hydrogen and alkoxides.

Example

Ethanol reacts with sodium to give sodium ethoxide and hydrogen. Here's the equation:

$$2C_2H_5OH_{(l)} + 2Na_{(s)} \rightarrow 2C_2H_5ONa_{(aq)} + H_{2(g)}$$

Figure 2: An alcohol burning in a beaker.

Uses of alcohols

Alcoholic drinks

Ethanol is the main alcohol in alcoholic drinks. It's not as toxic as methanol (which causes blindness if drunk) but it still damages the liver and brain.

Solvents

Alcohols such as methanol and ethanol can dissolve most compounds that water dissolves, but they can also dissolve substances that water can't dissolve.

> **Example**
>
> Things like hydrocarbons, oils and fats are insoluble in water, but they will dissolve in alcohols.

This makes ethanol, methanol and propanol very useful solvents in industry. Ethanol is the solvent for perfumes and aftershave lotions. It can mix with both the oils (which give the smell) and the water (that makes up the bulk).

'Methylated spirit' (or 'meths') is ethanol with chemicals (e.g. methanol) added to it. It's used to clean paint brushes and as a fuel (among other things). It's poisonous to drink, so a purply-blue dye is also added (to stop people drinking it by mistake).

Figure 3: A bottle of methylated spirit.

Fuels

Ethanol is used as a fuel in spirit burners — it burns fairly cleanly and it's non-smelly. Ethanol can also be mixed in with petrol and used as fuel for cars. Since pure ethanol is clean burning, the more ethanol in a petrol/ethanol mix, the less pollution is produced.

Some countries that have little or no oil deposits but plenty of land and sunshine (e.g. Brazil) grow loads of sugar cane, which they ferment to form ethanol. A big advantage of this is that sugar cane is a renewable resource (unlike petrol, which will run out).

Figure 4: A fuel pump dispensing a mixture of ethanol and petrol.

Tip: See page 80 for more on making ethanol from sugars.

Practice Questions — Fact Recall

Q1 What is the general formula for alcohols?

Q2 Give three properties that the first three alcohols have in common.

Q3 Give two uses of alcohols.

Practice Question — Application

Q1 Which of the following compounds are alcohols?

a) CH_3COCH_3

b) ethanone

c) $C_5H_{11}OH$

d)
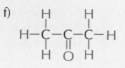

e) propan-2-ol

f)

2. Carboxylic Acids

The next type of compound you need to know about is carboxylic acids. Read on to find out what they are and what they're used for...

Learning Objectives:
- Know that the carboxylic acids are a group of compounds that all have a –COOH functional group.
- Know that the first three carboxylic acids are methanoic acid, ethanoic acid and propanoic acid.
- Be able to represent carboxylic acids using chemical or displayed formulae.
- Be able to identify carboxylic acids from their names or formulae.
- Know some of the main properties of carboxylic acids.
- H Understand why carboxylic acids are weak acids.
- H Know that weak acids have higher pHs than strong acids of the same concentration.
- Know how ethanol can be used to make ethanoic acid, which is used to make vinegar.
- Be able to evaluate the positive and negative social and economic effects of using carboxylic acids.

Specification Reference
C3.6, C3.6.1, C3.6.2

What are carboxylic acids?

The **carboxylic acids** are a group of compounds that all contain a –COOH functional group. The –COOH group consists of a carbon atom that has formed a double bond with a lone oxygen atom and a single bond with an oxygen atom in an –OH group — see Figure 1.

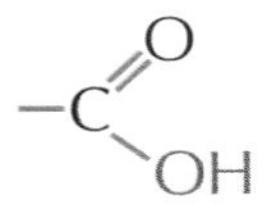

Figure 1: *The –COOH functional group.*

The names of carboxylic acids end in '-anoic acid' (and start with the normal 'meth-', 'eth-' or 'prop-'). You need to know the first three carboxylic acids. These are methanoic acid, ethanoic acid and propanoic acid (see Figure 2).

	Methanoic acid	*Ethanoic acid*	*Propanoic acid*
Chemical formulae:	$HCOOH$	CH_3COOH	C_2H_5COOH or CH_3CH_2COOH

Displayed formulae:

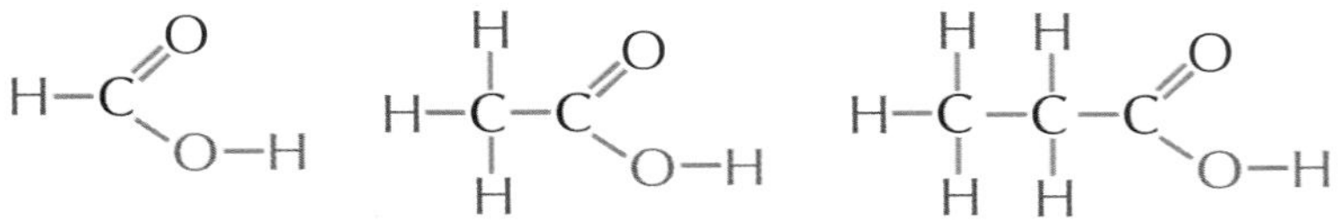

Figure 2: *Chemical and displayed formulae of the first three carboxylic acids — methanoic acid, ethanoic acid and propanoic acid.*

Representing and identifying carboxylic acids

When you're giving the chemical formula of a carboxylic acid it's crucial that you show the –COOH group clearly. As a result, the chemical formulae of carboxylic acids are usually written out in full.

Example

You would always give the formula of ethanoic acid as CH_3COOH. You wouldn't just give it as $C_2H_4O_2$, because then you wouldn't be able to see the –COOH functional group.

Exam Tip
Never give the formula of ethanoic acid as $C_2H_4O_2$ in the exam — you'll lose out on marks if you do.

To identify whether a compound is a carboxylic acid or not, just look out for a –COOH group or '-anoic acid' at the end of its name.

Example

This is 2-methylpropanoic acid. You know it's a carboxylic acid because it has a –COOH group and its name ends in '-anoic acid'.

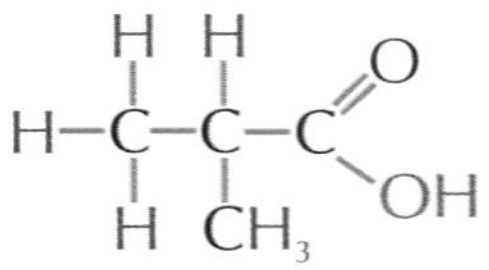

Properties of carboxylic acids

Carboxylic acids react like other acids. For example, they react just like any other acid with carbonates to produce carbon dioxide. The salts formed in these reactions end in '-anoate' — methanoic acid will form a methanoate, ethanoic acid an ethanoate, etc.

Tip: See pages 36-37 for more on the reactions of acids with carbonates.

> **Example**
>
> Ethanoic acid reacts with sodium carbonate to form carbon dioxide, water and a salt called sodium ethanoate. Here's the equation:
>
> ethanoic acid + sodium carbonate → carbon dioxide + sodium ethanoate + water

Carboxylic acids also dissolve in water to produce acidic solutions, just like other acids.

Strong acids and weak acids `Higher`

When acids dissolve in water, they ionise and release H^+ ions, which are responsible for making the solution acidic (see page 178). Acids can be described as either 'strong acids' or 'weak acids' depending on how well they ionise.

Strong acids (like sulfuric acid or hydrochloric acid) ionise completely in water. This means that if you put a sample of a strong acid in water, all of the acid molecules will ionise and release H^+ ions.

Weak acids only partially ionise in water — if you put a sample of a weak acid in water, only some of the acid molecules will ionise and release H^+ ions. As a result, weak acids have a higher pH (are less acidic) than aqueous solutions of strong acids with the same concentration. Carboxylic acids are weak acids (they don't ionise completely when dissolved in water).

Tip: H The strength of an acid isn't the same as its concentration. Concentration is how watered down your acid is and strength is how well it has ionised in water.

Tip: See pages 177-178 for lots more on acids and pH.

Uses of carboxylic acids

Carboxylic acids have lots of uses in industry:

> **Examples**
>
> - Carboxylic acids with longer chains of carbon atoms are used to make soaps and detergents.
>
> - Carboxylic acids are used in the preparation of esters (see page 273).
>
> - Ethanoic acid is a very good solvent for many organic molecules. (But ethanoic acid isn't usually chosen as a solvent because it makes the solution acidic.)
>
> - Ethanoic acid is the acid present in vinegar (see next page).
>
> - Citric acid (another carboxylic acid) is present in oranges and lemons, and is manufactured in large amounts to make fizzy drinks. You can use it to descale appliances like kettles too (see page 218 for more on scale).

Figure 3: *Litmus paper being used to show that this orange is acidic — it's the citric acid in oranges that makes them acidic.*

Making ethanoic acid

Ethanoic acid can be made by **oxidising** ethanol. There are two ways to oxidise ethanol — microbes (like yeast) can cause the ethanol to ferment and be oxidised or ethanol can be oxidised using oxidising agents.

The equation for the oxidation of ethanol to ethanoic acid is:

ethanol + oxygen → ethanoic acid + water

Ethanoic acid can be dissolved in water to make vinegar, which is used for flavouring and preserving foods.

Tip: If you leave wine open, the ethanol in it is oxidised — this is why wine smells vinegary when it goes off.

Practice Questions — Fact Recall

Q1 What functional group do all carboxylic acids have in common?

Q2 Name the first three carboxylic acids.

Q3 What gas is produced when a carboxylic acid reacts with a carbonate?

Q4 Why are carboxylic acids called 'weak acids'?

Q5 a) Give two ways that ethanol can be oxidised to ethanoic acid.

b) Write the word equation for the oxidation of ethanol to ethanoic acid.

c) Give one common use of ethanoic acid.

Practice Questions — Application

Q1 Which of the following compounds are carboxylic acids?

a) $CH_3CH_2CH_2COOH$ b) CH_3COOCH_3

c) Ethyl ethanoate   d) Butanoic acid

e)

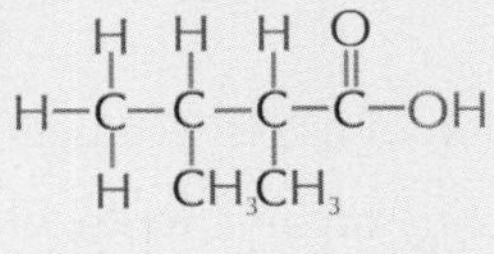

f)

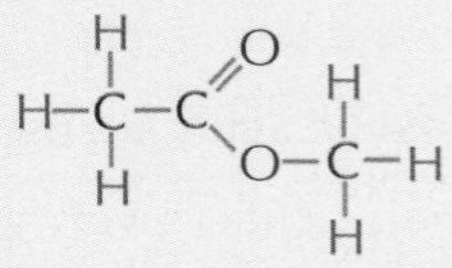

Q2 Pentanoic acid is a carboxylic acid with five carbon atoms. Draw the displayed formula of pentanoic acid.

Q3 Explain why a 1 mol/dm³ solution of ethanoic acid will have a higher pH than a 1 mol/dm³ solution of hydrochloric acid.

3. Esters

The last set of compounds you need to know about are the esters. The next two pages are crammed full of useful facts about esters so give 'em a read.

What are esters?

The **esters** are a group of compounds that all contain a –COO– functional group. This consists of a carbon atom that has formed a double bond with one oxygen atom and a single bond with another oxygen atom — see Figure 1.

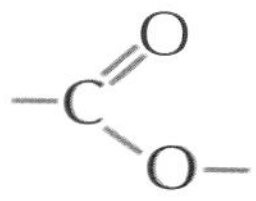

Figure 1: *The –COO– functional group.*

Making esters

Esters are formed from an alcohol and a carboxylic acid. An acid catalyst is usually used (e.g. concentrated sulfuric acid). The general equation for this reaction is:

alcohol + carboxylic acid → ester + water

Naming esters

The names of esters all end in '-oate' and are made up of two parts. The first part of the name comes from the alcohol that's used to make it. The second part of the name comes from the carboxylic acid.

Example

If you react ethanol with ethanoic acid, the ester you get is called ethyl ethanoate. This reaction is shown here.

Ethanoic acid   *Ethanol*   *Ethyl ethanoate*

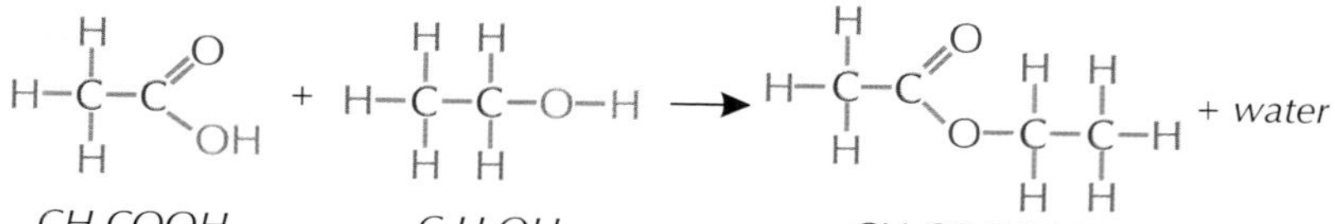

CH_3COOH C_2H_5OH $CH_3COOC_2H_5$ + water

Identifying esters

It's easy to identify if a compound is an ester — just look for the –COO– group in the chemical or displayed formula, or check to see if the name of the compound ends in '-oate'.

Example

This is methyl propanoate. You know it's an ester because it has a –COO– group and its name ends in '-oate'.

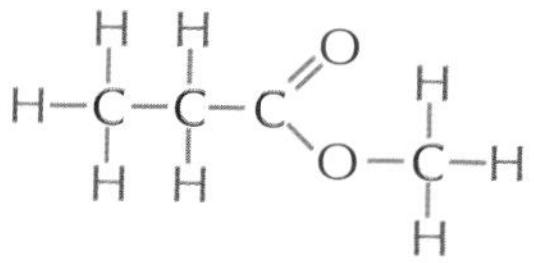

Learning Objectives:

- Know that the esters are a group of compounds that all contain a –COO– functional group.
- Know that esters can be made by reacting alcohols with carboxylic acids in the presence of an acid catalyst.
- Know that ethyl ethanoate is an ester that can be made by reacting ethanol with ethanoic acid.
- Be able to recognise esters from their names or formulae.
- Know some of the typical properties and uses of esters.
- Be able to evaluate the positive and negative social and economic effects of using esters.

Specification Reference C3.6, C3.6.2, C3.6.3

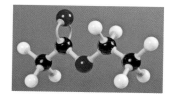

Figure 2: *Molecular model of ethyl ethanoate. Red balls are oxygen atoms, black balls are carbon atoms and white balls are hydrogen atoms.*

Tip: Methyl propanoate is made from methanol and propanoic acid.

Properties of esters

Tip: If a substance is volatile, that means it will easily turn into a gas.

Many esters have pleasant smells — often quite sweet and fruity. They're also **volatile**. This makes them ideal for perfumes (the evaporated molecules can be detected by smell receptors in your nose). However, many esters are flammable (or even highly flammable). So their volatility also makes them potentially dangerous.

Esters don't mix very well with water. (They're not nearly as soluble as alcohols or carboxylic acids.) But esters do mix well with alcohols and other organic solvents.

Uses of esters

Because many esters smell nice, they're used in perfumes. Esters are also used to make flavourings and aromas — e.g. there are esters that smell or taste of rum, apple, orange, banana, grape, pineapple, etc. Some esters are used in ointments (they give Deep Heat® its smell). Other esters are used as solvents for paint, ink, glue and in nail varnish remover. Esters are really useful, but there are some disadvantages to using esters.

Examples

- Inhaling the fumes from some esters irritates mucous membranes in the nose and mouth.

- Ester fumes are heavier than air and very flammable. If these fumes come into contact with a naked flame it could cause a flash fire.

- Some esters are toxic, especially in large doses. Some people worry about health problems associated with synthetic food additives such as esters.

Tip: Flash fires are intense and unexpected fires. They're often over quite quickly but they can be very dangerous.

However, esters aren't as volatile or as toxic as some other organic solvents — they don't release nearly as many toxic fumes as some of them. In fact esters have now replaced more toxic solvents that used to be used in many paints and varnishes.

Practice Questions — Fact Recall

Q1   Draw the functional group present in all esters.

Q2   a) What would you react with a carboxylic acid to make an ester?

b) What type of catalyst is used for this reaction?

Q3   What do the names of all esters end in?

Q4   Name the two compounds that would react to make ethyl ethanoate.

Q5   Give two properties that most esters have in common.

Q6   a) Give two common uses of esters.

b) Give one reason why caution must be taken when using esters.

Section Checklist — Make sure you know...

Alcohols

☐ That the alcohols are a homologous series of compounds that all contain the –OH functional group.

☐ That methanol (CH_3OH), ethanol (C_2H_5OH) and propanol (C_3H_7OH) are the first three alcohols in the homologous series.

☐ How to represent alcohols using chemical and displayed formulae.

☐ How to identify a compound as an alcohol from either the name of the compound or its formula.

☐ That alcohols are flammable, dissolve in water to give neutral solutions and react with sodium to give hydrogen and alkoxides.

☐ That the first 3 alcohols are used as solvents and fuels, and that ethanol is used in alcoholic drinks.

☐ How to evaluate the positive and negative social and economic effects of using alcohols.

Carboxylic Acids

☐ That the carboxylic acids are compounds that all contain the –COOH group.

☐ That methanoic acid (HCOOH), ethanoic acid (CH_3COOH) and propanoic acid (CH_3CH_2COOH) are examples of carboxylic acids.

☐ How to represent carboxylic acids using chemical and displayed formulae.

☐ How to identify a compound as a carboxylic acid from the name of the compound or its formula.

☐ That, like other acids, carboxylic acids react with carbonates to produce carbon dioxide and dissolve in water to produce acidic solutions.

☐ ⬛ That carboxylic acids are weak acids — they only partially ionise when they dissolve in water.

☐ ⬛ That aqueous solutions of weak acids (like carboxylic acids) will have a higher pH than aqueous solutions of the same concentration of strong acids (like HCl or H_2SO_4).

☐ That ethanoic acid can be made by oxidising ethanol, either by using microbes to ferment the ethanol or by using an oxidising agent.

☐ That ethanoic acid is the main ingredient in vinegar.

☐ How to evaluate the positive and negative social and economic effects of using carboxylic acids.

Esters

☐ That the esters are compounds that all contain the –COO– functional group.

☐ That if you react an alcohol with a carboxylic acid in the presence of an acid catalyst (such as concentrated H_2SO_4), esters are formed.

☐ That ethyl ethanoate is the ester made when ethanol reacts with ethanoic acid.

☐ How to recognise a compound as an ester from either the name of the compound or its formula.

☐ That esters are sweet-smelling, volatile, flammable and don't mix well with water.

☐ That esters are used to make perfumes and flavourings, amongst other things.

☐ How to evaluate the positive and negative social and economic effects of using esters.

Exam-style Questions

1   Ethanoic acid is a carboxylic acid that can be used to make ethyl ethanoate.

1 (a) (i) Name the compound that you would react with ethanoic acid to form ethyl ethanoate.

(1 mark)

1 (a) (ii) What type of compound is ethyl ethanoate? Circle the correct answer.

     an ester   an alcohol   an alkane   an alkoxide

(1 mark)

1 (b)   A 0.1 mol/dm^3 solution of ethanoic acid has a pH of 3. A 0.1 mol/dm^3 solution of hydrochloric acid has a pH of 1. Explain this difference.

(2 marks)

2   The diagram shows the structure of an organic compound.

$$H-\overset{\displaystyle H}{\underset{\displaystyle H}{C}}-\overset{\displaystyle H}{\underset{\displaystyle H}{C}}-\overset{\displaystyle H}{\underset{\displaystyle H}{C}}-\overset{\displaystyle OH}{\underset{\displaystyle H}{C}}-\overset{\displaystyle H}{\underset{\displaystyle H}{C}}-H$$

2 (a) (i) What information in the diagram tells you that this compound is an alcohol?

(1 mark)

2 (a) (ii) Suggest the pH of the solution that would be formed if this compound dissolved in water.

(1 mark)

2 (b)   This compound is flammable. Write a balanced symbol equation for the complete combustion of this compound in air.

(2 marks)

2 (c)   Name the gas that would be produced if this compound reacted with sodium.

(1 mark)

3   Niamh is comparing different alcohols for use as fuels. She has this information:

Alcohol	Number of C atoms	Energy produced by burning (kJ/l)	Price (£/l)	Health hazards
Methanol	1	18,000	£0.30	Toxic
Ethanol	2	23,000	£0.36	-
Propanol	3	27,000	£0.73	Irritant
Butanol	4	29,000	£0.80	Harmful

3 (a)   Draw the displayed formula of methanol.

(1 mark)

3 (b)   *In this question you will be assessed on the quality of your English, the organisation of your ideas and your use of appropriate specialist vocabulary.*

     Niamh decides ethanol is the best fuel to use. Use the information in the table to suggest and explain why she came to this decision.

(6 marks)

1. Controlled Assessment Structure

To get your Chemistry GCSE, you'll need to do a controlled assessment as well as all your exams. This section tells you all about the controlled assessment and what you'll have to do.

What is the controlled assessment?

The controlled assessment is a type of test that you'll sit during your Chemistry lessons at school. The assessment is known as an investigative skills assessment (ISA) and it'll involve doing some research and some practical work as well as answering some questions on an exam paper. The controlled assessment is designed to test your How Science Works skills, not your knowledge and understanding of specific topics. So it's a good chance for you to show that you're really good at science and not just good at memorising facts.

Tip: There's loads of information in the How Science Works section that'll help you with your controlled assessment so have a look at pages 2-16 before you get started.

What you'll have to do

There are five things that you'll need to do for the controlled assessment:

- First of all, you'll be given the outline of an investigation and you'll have to go away, come up with a hypothesis and plan an experiment.

- Next you'll have to sit an exam paper which will ask you questions about the research that you've done and the method you've chosen.

- Then you'll actually get to carry out the experiment that you've planned (or a similar one) and record some results.

- Once you've done the experiment you'll be given some time to process the data that you've got — you'll get to calculate some averages and draw some pretty graphs.

- Finally, you'll do another exam paper which will ask you questions about your experiment, your results and your conclusions.

Figure 1: *A student conducting an experiment.*

What is the controlled assessment worth?

The controlled assessment is worth 25% of the total marks for your GCSE. It's just as important as the other exams you'll do, even though you're doing some (or all) of it in class and not in an exam hall. Don't worry though, there's loads of stuff over the next few pages to help you prepare.

Tip: The controlled assessment might feel more informal, but you should take it just as seriously as all your other exams.

2. Planning and Research

The first step of the controlled assessment is to do some research and plan your experiment. Here's what you need to know...

What you'll be told

At the very beginning of your controlled assessment, your teacher will give you the context of an investigation. This context will usually be a problem that a scientist might come across out in the real world.

Example

The context for your investigation could be something like:

"A company is developing a new range of hand warmers that use exothermic reactions. The company wants to know how the concentrations of the reactants affect the amount of heat energy given out, so they know how to adjust the concentrations of reactants in their hand warmers to get the desired temperature."

What you need to do

Once you've been told the context of your investigation, you'll need to do some research then come up with a hypothesis and two possible methods for an experiment to solve the problem that's been outlined. You should also research the context of the experiment a bit, so you understand why your investigation will be useful.

Tip: You need to research two methods that you could use to investigate the problem, but you only need to look into one in detail.

Tip: Although your teacher will give you a context for the experiment, you'll have to do all the research on your own.

Tip: You might be given time to do your planning research in a lesson or you might be given it to do for homework.

Example

If you were given the context in the example above, you'd need to do a bit of research to find out the following:

- How you would expect the concentration of the reactants to affect the amount of heat energy given out — this'll let you come up with a suitable hypothesis.

- What experiments you could do to investigate the effect of reactant concentration on the heat energy given out by an exothermic reaction — this'll involve finding a suitable exothermic reaction to use and finding a way of measuring the heat energy given out by the reaction.

- Why it would be useful to know how the concentration of the reactants affects the heat energy given out by exothermic reactions.

When you're researching your method you need to think about what hazards might be associated with the experiment and what you need to do to make sure your experiment is a fair test (there's more on this on page 7). You should also think about what equipment you'll need and what recordings you'll need to make.

Where to find information

There are lots of places where you can find information. Textbooks are an excellent place to start. Your teacher might be able to provide these or you could get some from the library. The internet can also be an excellent source of information.

When you're doing your research, make sure you look at a variety of resources — not just one book or website. Also, make sure you jot down exactly where you've found your information. You will be asked about the research you've done in your first ISA test and just saying you used 'a textbook' or 'the internet' won't be good enough — you'll need to give the names of any textbooks and their authors, and the names of any websites that you used.

Exam Tip
As you're doing your research, think about why you've found a particular source useful. Was the explanation really clear? Or was there a helpful diagram? You could get asked about this in the exam.

How to write a good hypothesis

Writing a really good hypothesis is important at this stage in the controlled assessment. A hypothesis is a specific statement about the things that you'll be testing and the result you're expecting to get.

Tip: See page 2 for lots more on hypotheses.

Examples

These are all hypotheses:

- The higher the temperature, the faster the rate of a reaction.
- There is a link between the reactivity of a metal and the number of electrons it has in its outer shell.
- Increasing the temperature will increase the yield of a reversible reaction that is endothermic in the forward direction.

Tip: A hypothesis isn't a fact so it might not be true — it is just a statement that you are going to test.

To get good marks for your hypothesis you need to make sure it's clear and that it includes an independent and a dependent variable.

Example

If the context of your investigation is finding out how concentration affects the heat energy given out by an exothermic reaction (see previous page), your hypothesis could be:

"The greater the concentration of the reactants, the more heat energy will be given out in an exothermic reaction."

This hypothesis is clear and the key variables (reactant concentration and heat energy output) have been identified.

Tip: The independent variable is the factor you'll change, the dependent variable is the factor that you'll measure.

Your hypothesis should be based on the information that you researched.

> **Example**
>
> If you research exothermic reactions you should find that the energy
> changes of reactions are given in kJ/mol — so if more moles of reactant are
> present (as would be the case if you used more concentrated reactants),
> more energy would be given out. This is a good justification for the
> hypothesis that increasing the concentration of the reactants will increase
> the heat energy given out in the reaction.

Taking notes

As you're doing your research, you need to make some notes. You'll be
given a sheet of A4 paper on which to make your notes and you'll be able
to take these notes into your ISA tests with you — so it's in your interest to
make them top notch. This example shows you what your notes sheet might
look like and highlights the kind of notes you might make.

> **Example**
>
> **Hypothesis:**
> For an exothermic reaction, the greater the concentration of the reactants,
> the more heat energy will be given out in the reaction.
>
> **Research Sources:**
> CGP: GCSE Chemistry by A. N. Author (good diagram of equipment)
> www.chemencyclopaedia.com (no diagram, but control variables listed)
>
> **Method(s):**
> Use a neutralisation reaction as an example of an exothermic reaction.
> Mix acid of varying concentrations (e.g. 30 cm^3 of H_2SO_4 from
> 0.2 mol/dm^3 to 1 mol/dm^3) with alkali (e.g. 30 cm^3 of KOH) in a beaker.
> Record the change in temperature over time (e.g. every 20 seconds).
> Be sure to insulate the beaker as much as possible to minimise heat loss
> to the surroundings and make sure starting temperatures are the same.
>
> **Equipment:**
> Acid and alkali   Measuring cylinder   Stopwatch
> Glass beaker   Polystyrene cup
> Thermometer   Cotton wool
>
> **Risk Assessment Issues:**
> Acids and alkalis can burn if they touch the skin so wear gloves and
> goggles to protect your skin and eyes.
> Glass beakers and measuring cylinders can be dangerous if broken.
>
> **Relating the investigation to the context:**
> If increasing the reactant concentration does increase the heat energy
> given out by a reaction, then the temperature of the hand warmer could
> be adjusted by increasing/decreasing the concentration of the reactants.

Tip: You shouldn't write a really detailed method at this stage. In fact, your notes will be checked before you go into the ISA tests to make sure you've not gone into too much detail. Just jot down the main parts of the method(s) you could use, to help jog your memory.

Tip: You will need to explain how you are making your experiment a fair test in the ISA exam, so you should have researched the variables that will need to be controlled and the ways you will control them — making a brief note of them here.

3. Section 1 of the ISA test

After you've done your planning, you'll do Section 1 of the ISA test. This asks you questions about the research that you've done and the method you'll use.

Hypotheses and variables

In Section 1 of the ISA test you'll be asked to give your hypothesis, explain how you came up with it and how you'll test it. Your hypothesis should include an independent variable and a dependent variable. You could be asked to identify these.

Example

In this investigation, the independent variable is the concentration of the acid, the dependent variable is the temperature change of the reaction and the control variables are the volume of acid and alkali, the concentration of the alkali and the amount of insulation around the beaker.

Have a look at page 7 to help you work out what the different variables in your experiment are.

How to write a good method

In this part of the assessment you'll almost certainly be asked to write down a description of the method you're going to use. You need to give a clear and detailed description of how you would carry out your experiment. You must remember to include things like:

1. A list of all the equipment you're going to need.
2. A logical, step by step guide as to what you're going to do, including an explanation of what you're going to measure and how you're going to measure it.
3. What control variables you're going to regulate and how you're going to regulate them.
4. What hazards there are and how you're going to make sure the experiment is safe.

1. The equipment list

Your method should start with a list of the equipment that you'll need.

Example

To do the experiment planned in the previous topic, you'd need the following equipment:

- Some sulfuric acid of varying concentrations (0.2 mol/dm^3, 0.4 mol/dm^3, 0.6 mol/dm^3, 0.8 mol/dm^3 and 1.0 mol/dm^3) and some 0.5 mol/dm^3 potassium hydroxide.
- A measuring cylinder to measure out appropriate volumes of acid and alkali.

- A polystyrene cup with a lid that you can do the neutralisation reaction in and it be reasonably well insulated.
- A beaker and some cotton wool so you can insulate the reaction further.
- A thermometer to measure the temperature of the reaction.
- A stopwatch to measure the time.

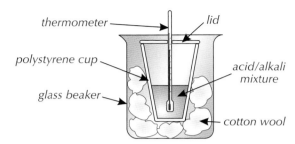

Figure 1: *Diagram of the equipment needed for this investigation.*

2. Describing the method

Once you've written your equipment list, you should then write down exactly what you're going to do, listing the steps in the order that you're going to do them. Here's an example of a method.

Example

1. Use a measuring cylinder to measure out 30 cm³ of 0.2 mol/dm³ sulfuric acid (H_2SO_4) and place the sulfuric acid in a polystyrene cup.

2. Put the polystyrene cup into a beaker and surround it with cotton wool for insulation.

3. Use another measuring cylinder to measure out 30 cm³ of 0.5 mol/dm³ potassium hydroxide (KOH).

4. Use a thermometer to measure the starting temperatures of the acid and the potassium hydroxide.

5. If the acid and the alkali are at the same temperature, pour the potassium hydroxide into the sulfuric acid. If they're not the same, put them in a water bath and when they are the same temperature, mix them together.

6. Put a lid on the polystyrene cup, place a thermometer in the mixture through a hole in the lid and start the stopwatch.

7. Watch the thermometer for 5 minutes and record the highest temperature reached by the reaction in that time.

8. Calculate the temperature change of the reaction by subtracting the starting temperature of the acid and alkali away from the maximum temperature reached by the reaction.

9. Repeat the experiment with 0.4 mol/dm³, 0.6 mol/dm³, 0.8 mol/dm³ and 1.0 mol/dm³ acid.

10. Repeat the whole experiment two more times and average the results.

3. Controlling the variables

To make your experiment a **fair test** you need to make sure you control all of the variables. In your method, you will probably be asked to explain how you're going to do this in order to make sure your experiment is a fair test.

Tip: There's more on fair tests and controlling variables on pages 7-8.

> **Example**
>
> In this experiment, you're helping to make it a fair test by making sure the starting temperatures of the acid and the alkali are the same, by insulating the reaction to minimise heat loss to the surroundings and by using the same volume of acid and alkali each time the experiment is repeated.

Things that you might need to watch out for completely depend on the experiment — use your common sense to make sure that anything that might affect the result is kept the same.

4. Hazards

There will always be hazards associated with any experiment. In your plan you should identify these hazards and say how you're going to reduce the risk.

> **Example**
>
> In this neutralisation reaction, the main hazards are the sulfuric acid and the potassium hydroxide. Sulfuric acid and potassium hydroxide are corrosive and will burn the skin, so when doing this experiment safety goggles and gloves should be worn to protect the skin and eyes.

There are lots of other hazards that you might need to watch out for. See page 9 for more on hazards.

***Figure 2**: Students wearing safety goggles.*

Method selection

During your research you will have investigated at least two methods that you could have used. You may be asked to explain why you've chosen the method you have. Think about things like equipment choices, whether it is practical to do in class, how long it'll take to do and anything else that made you choose it.

Preliminary investigations

If you've done any preliminary investigations (or trial runs) you should make sure you can explain how they helped you to come up with your method. Trial runs are useful for working out what range of variables would be best to use and the intervals between the variables.

Tip: See pages 8-9 for more information on trial runs and why they are useful.

> **Example**
>
> In this experiment, a trial run could have been useful for two reasons:
>
> - To work out what concentrations and volumes of acid and alkali are needed to get a sensible temperature change. This would involve testing a range of concentrations/volumes to see which ones give a good temperature difference.

- To work out how long you need to monitor the temperature for. For example, you could use a variety of acid concentrations and record how long it takes for the reactions to reach their maximum temperature. If they all reach their maximum temperature in under 5 minutes, then 5 minutes is a sensible amount of time to monitor the temperature for.

Table of results

In this part of the test, you will also need to draw a table of results that you can fill in when you do the experiment. There are a few things to remember when drawing tables of results:

Tip: You don't have to draw your table of results by hand — you can use a computer if you'd prefer.

- Make sure you include enough rows and columns to record all of the data you need to. You might also want to include a column for processing your data (e.g. working out an average).

- Make sure you give each column a heading so you know what's going to be recorded where.

- Make sure you include units for all your measurements.

Here's an example of a jolly good table for results.

Tip: Your table of results won't look exactly like this one. For example, you might need more or less rows and columns depending on what kind of data you're collecting.

Example

Conc. of acid (mol/dm³)	Repeat	Starting temp. (°C)	Maximum temp. (°C)	Temperature change (°C)	Average temperature change (°C)
0.2	1				
	2				
	3				
0.4	1				
	2				
	3				
0.6	1				
	2				
	3				
0.8	1				
	2				
	3				
1.0	1				
	2				
	3				

4. Doing the Experiment

If your plan isn't too outrageous, you'll then get to actually do the experiment you've planned. So grab your safety goggles and your lab coat...

Good laboratory practice

When it comes to actually doing the investigation, you might be allowed to do the one you planned, or you might be given another method to use by your teacher. When you're doing your experiment it's important that you use good laboratory practice. This means working safely and accurately. To ensure you get good results, make sure you do the following:

- Measure out all your quantities carefully — the more accurately you measure things the more accurate your results will be.

- Try to be consistent — for example, if you need to stir something, stir every sample for the same length of time.

- Don't let yourself get distracted by other people — if you're distracted by what other people are doing you're more likely to make a mistake or miss a reading.

As you're going along, make sure you remember to fill in your table of results — it's no good doing a perfect experiment if you forget to record the data.

> **Tip:** If you're given an alternative method it doesn't necessarily mean your method was bad — it could be that your teacher thinks there are too many different methods in the class or doesn't have the right equipment for you.

Processing your results

Once you've got your data you might need to process it. This could involve calculating a mean (by adding all your data together and dividing by the number of values) or working out a change in something (by subtracting the start reading from the end reading).

Then you'll need to plot your data on a graph. It's up to you what type of graph you use. See pages 12-14 for more information on how to draw a good graph.

> **Tip:** See page 12 for more on processing your results and calculating averages.

> **Tip:** Your graph will be marked along with your exam papers so make sure it's nice and neat and all your axes are properly labelled.

Things to think about

As you're doing the experiment there are some things you need to think about:

- Is the equipment you're using good enough?
- Is there anything you would have done differently if you could do the experiment again?
- Have you got any anomalous results and if so can you think what might have gone wrong?
- Do the results you've got support your initial hypothesis?

These are all things that you could get asked about in the second part of your ISA so it's a good idea to think about them while the experiment is still fresh in your mind.

Figure 1: *A student working in a laboratory.*

5. Section 2 of the ISA test

Once you've done your experiment and processed the results it's time for the final part of your controlled assessment — Section 2 of the ISA test.

Making conclusions

In Section 2 of the ISA test you will be asked to draw conclusions about your data. You could be asked what your data shows, or whether it supports your initial hypothesis. When drawing conclusions it's important to back them up with data from your results. You should describe the general trend in the data but also quote specific numerical values.

> ### Example
>
> **Do your results support your initial hypothesis?**
>
> Yes, my results do support my initial hypothesis because the temperature change increased as the concentration of acid increased. For example, when using 0.2 mol/dm^3 acid the temperature only rose by 2 °C, when using 1.0 mol/dm^3 acid the temperature rose by 13 °C. So increasing the concentration of the reactants increased the heat energy given out by the reaction.

Comparing results

In Section 2 of the test you will probably be asked to compare your results with the results of other people in your class. This lets you see what similarities or differences there are between sets of results, and allows you to determine if your results are reproducible. If you got similar results to someone else doing the same experiment then your experiment is reproducible. If everyone doing the experiment got different results to you, your results aren't reproducible. It's OK to say your results aren't reproducible, though you should try to suggest why they weren't. And as always, back up anything you say by quoting some data.

Improving your method

In this part of the assessment, you might be given the opportunity to evaluate the experiment — in other words say how you would improve the experiment if you did it again.

> ### Example
>
> - You could say that it would be better to use equipment with a higher resolution (e.g. 0.1 °C instead of 1 °C), so you could detect smaller changes and get more precise results.
>
> - You could say that you'd repeat the results more times to increase the repeatability and accuracy of the results.
>
> - You could say that you'd use a better technique (e.g. using a water bath to keep all the reactants at the same temperature) to help make sure your experiment was a fair test.

Anomalous results

You could be asked whether or not there are any anomalous results in your data. Anomalous results are results that don't seem to fit with the rest of the data. If you're asked about anomalous results make sure you quote the result and explain why you think it is anomalous.

> **Example**
>
> I think the measurement that the temperature change for 0.8 mol/dm³ acid was only 4 °C was an anomalous result because it doesn't seem to fit with the rest of the data (it's too low).

If you don't have any anomalous results, that's fine — just make sure you explain why you're sure none of your results are anomalous.

> **Example**
>
> I don't think there were any anomalous results in my data because an anomalous result is one that doesn't seem to fit with the rest of the data and all of my data points were very close to the line of best fit when plotted on a graph.

Tip: You could also be asked to suggest a reason for an anomalous result — e.g. in this case the thermometer might not have been submerged in the reaction mixture.

Analysing other data sources

In this final part of the controlled assessment you won't only get asked about your own data. You'll also be given some case studies to look at and be asked to analyse that data as well. You could be asked to compare this data to your own data and point out similarities and differences. Or you could be asked whether this data supports or contradicts your hypothesis.

As with making conclusions about your own data, when you're answering questions about these secondary sources it's crucial that you quote specific pieces of data from the source. You shouldn't blindly trust the data in these sources either — you should think as critically about this data as you did about your own data. Don't assume that it's better than yours and be on the look out for mistakes.

Exam Tip
The important thing when analysing other data sources is to read the question carefully and make sure you answer it — don't just describe the data without referring back to the original question.

Applying your results to a context

Another thing you could be asked to do is explain how your results can be applied to a particular context. This means thinking of a practical application of what you've found out. You should have done some research on this in the planning part of the controlled assessment. You can use the notes you made then to help you answer questions like this.

> **Example**
>
> I found that increasing the reactant concentration increases the heat energy given out in an exothermic reaction. Applying this to the context of hand warmers — if the hand warmers are too hot, you can decrease the temperature of them by decreasing the concentration of the reactants in them. If the hand warmers are too cold, you can increase the temperature of them by increasing the concentration of the reactants in them.

1. The Exams

Unfortunately, to get your GCSE you'll need to sit some exams. And that's what these pages are about — what to expect in your exams.

Assessment for GCSE Chemistry

To get your GCSE Chemistry you'll have to do some exams that test your knowledge of chemistry and How Science Works. All the content that you need to know is in this book — there's even a dedicated How Science Works section on pages 2-16.

You'll also have to do a Controlled Assessment (also known as an 'ISA'). There's more about this on pages 277-287.

The exams

You'll sit three separate exams — remember that you could be asked questions on How Science Works in any of them. You're allowed to use a calculator in all of your GCSE Chemistry exams, so make sure you've got one.

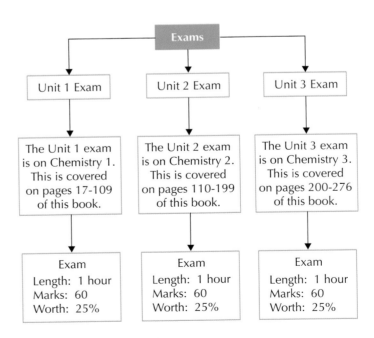

Other GCSE Science qualifications

GCSE Science A

If you're taking GCSE Science A, your exams will cover everything in Chemistry 1 (as well as Biology 1 and Physics 1). All of the chemistry that you'll need to study for GCSE Science A is covered in the Chemistry 1 sections of this book (see pages 17-109).

GCSE Additional Science

If you're taking GCSE Additional Science, your exams will cover everything in Chemistry 2 (as well as Biology 2 and Physics 2). All of the chemistry that you'll need to study for GCSE Additional Science is covered in the Chemistry 2 sections of this book (see pages 110-199).

GCSE Further Additional Science

If you're taking GCSE Further Additional Science, your exams will cover everything in Chemistry 3 (as well as Biology 3 and Physics 3). All of the chemistry that you'll need to study for GCSE Further Additional Science is covered in the Chemistry 3 sections of this book (see pages 200-276).

Exam Tip
Remember, whichever science GCSEs you're taking, any exam could include questions on How Science Works.

Controlled assessment (ISA)

As well as your exams, you'll have to do a controlled assessment. The controlled assessment involves a test made up of two sections, which will be based on a practical investigation that you've researched, planned and carried out.

Exam Tip
It doesn't matter which exams you're taking — <u>everyone</u> has to do a controlled assessment.

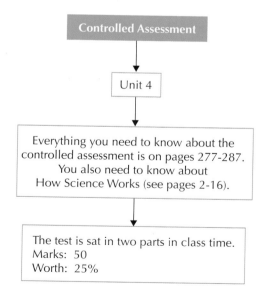

Controlled Assessment

Unit 4

Everything you need to know about the controlled assessment is on pages 277-287. You also need to know about How Science Works (see pages 2-16).

The test is sat in two parts in class time.
Marks: 50
Worth: 25%

Exam Tip
As well as the test, you'll have to do some research and carry out a practical investigation for your controlled assessment.

2. Exam Technique

Knowing the science is vitally important when it comes to passing your exams. But having good exam technique will also help. So here are some handy hints on how to squeeze every mark you possibly can out of those examiners.

Time management

Exam Tip
If a question is only worth 1 mark, don't waste time writing more than you need to.

Good time management is one of the most important exam skills to have — you need to think about how much time to spend on each question. Check out the length of your exams (you'll find them on page 288 and on the front of your exam papers). These timings give you about 1 minute per mark. Try to stick to this to give yourself the best chance to get as many marks as possible.

Don't spend ages struggling with a question if you're finding it hard to answer — move on. You can come back to it later when you've bagged loads of other marks elsewhere. Also, you might find that some questions need a lot of work for only a few marks, while others are much quicker — so if you're short of time, answer the quick and easy questions first.

> **Example**
>
> The questions below are both worth the same number of marks but require different amounts of work.
>
> **1** **(a)** Give the names of the **two** main elements found in steel.
>
> *(2 marks)*
>
> **2** **(a)** Balance the equation shown below for the reaction between aluminium and hydrochloric acid.
>
> $$......Al \quad + \quad ......HCl \quad \rightarrow \quad ......AlCl_3 \quad + \quad ......H_2$$
>
> *(2 marks)*
>
> Question 1 (a) only asks you to write down the names of two elements — if you can remember them this shouldn't take you too long.
>
> Question 2 (a) asks you to balance an equation — this may take you longer than writing down a couple of names, especially if you have to have a few goes at it before finding the answer.
>
> So, if you're running out of time it makes sense to do questions like 1 (a) first and come back to 2 (a) if you've got time at the end.

Exam Tip
Don't forget to go back and do any questions that you left the first time round — you don't want to miss out on marks because you forgot to do the question.

Making educated guesses

Make sure you answer all the questions that you can — don't leave any blank if you can avoid it. If a question asks you to tick a box, circle a word or draw lines between boxes, you should never, ever leave it blank, even if you're short on time. It only takes a second or two to answer these questions, and even if you're not absolutely sure what the answer is you can have a good guess.

Look at the question below.

1 (a)   Which of the metals below are alloys? Tick **two** boxes.

Cupronickel ☐   Manganese ☐

Zinc ☐   Bronze ☐

(2 marks)

Say you knew that zinc was an element, and that cupronickel contained copper and nickel, but weren't sure about the other two metals.

You can tick cupronickel — you know it's an alloy. If zinc is an element itself, it can't be an alloy of more than one element, so leave that box blank. That leaves you with manganese and bronze. If you're not absolutely sure which is an alloy and which isn't, just have a guess. You won't lose any marks if you get it wrong and there's a 50% chance that you'll get it right.

Command words

Command words are just the bits of a question that tell you what to do. You'll find answering exam questions much easier if you understand exactly what they mean, so here's a brief summary of the most common ones:

Command word:	What to do:
Give / Name / State / Write down	Give a brief one or two word answer, or a short sentence.
Complete	Write your answer in the space given. This could be a gap in a sentence or table, or you might have to finish a diagram.
Describe	Write about what something's like, e.g. describe the trend in a set of results.
Explain	Make something clear, or give the reasons why something happens. The points in your answer need to be linked together, so you should include words like because, so, therefore, due to, etc.
Calculate	Use the numbers in the question to work out an answer.
Suggest	Use your scientific knowledge to work out what the answer might be.
Compare	Give the similarities and differences between two things.
Evaluate	Give the arguments both for and against an issue, or the advantages and disadvantages of something. You may also need to give an overall judgement.

Some questions will also ask you to answer 'using the information provided' (e.g. a graph, table or passage of text) — if so, you must refer to the information you've been given or you won't get the marks.

3. Question Types

If all questions were the same, exams would be mightily boring. So really, it's quite handy that there are lots of different question types. Here are just a few...

Quality of written communication (QWC)

All of the exams you take for GCSE Chemistry will have at least one 6 mark question that assesses your quality of written communication — this just means that the examiner will assess your ability to write properly. This may seem like a bit of a drag, but you will lose marks if you don't do it. Here are some tips on how to get all the marks you can...

- Make sure your scribble (sorry, writing) is legible.

- Be careful with your spelling, punctuation and grammar — they need to be accurate.

- Make sure your writing style is appropriate for an exam. You need to write in full sentences and use fairly formal language. For example, the sentence "cooking in vegetable oil rather than water improves the flavour of food" is an appropriate style. "Vegetable oil makes food taste dead good" isn't — it's too informal.

- Organise your answer clearly. The points you make need to be in a logical order.

- Use specialist scientific vocabulary whenever you can. For example, if you're describing how poly(ethene) was made you'd need to use scientific terms like polymer and monomer. You also need to use these terms correctly — it's no good knowing the words if you don't know what they mean.

You'll be told which questions will be used to assess the quality of your written communication. On the front of your exam paper it will say something like 'Question 2 should be answered in continuous prose' — and that's the question where your writing will be assessed. There'll also be a reminder when you get to the question itself. It'll say something like:

In this question you will be assessed on the quality of your English, the organisation of your ideas and your use of appropriate specialist vocabulary.

Calculations

Questions that involve a calculation can seem a bit scary. But they're really not that bad. Here are some tips to help you out...

Showing working

The most important thing to remember is to show your working. You've probably heard it a million times before but it makes perfect sense. It only takes a few seconds more to write down what's in your head and it might stop you from making silly errors and losing out on easy marks. You won't get a mark for a wrong answer but you could get marks for the method you used to work out the answer.

Exam Tip
You'll need to use black ink or a black ball-point pen to write your answers, so make sure that you've got a couple ready for the exam.

Exam Tip
Make sure you write enough to get all the marks that are available. QWC questions are worth six marks, so a one sentence answer won't be enough — you'll need to write at least a paragraph or two.

Exam Tip
You should really be doing these things all the way through your exam — they're just particularly important on the QWC questions, so it's worth taking special care with them there.

Units

You must always give units for your answers. You may be given the units at the end of the answer line — if you are, make sure your answer is in those units.

Units of volume

Volume can be measured in dm³ and cm³ — you need to be able to convert between these units.

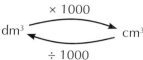

$$dm^3 \xrightleftharpoons[\div 1000]{\times 1000} cm^3$$

Examples

Write 7 dm³ in cm³.

- To convert 7 dm³ into cm³ you need to multiply by 1000.

$$7 \text{ dm}^3 \times 1000 = 7000 \text{ cm}^3$$

Write 0.3 cm³ in dm³.

- To convert 0.3 cm³ into dm³ you need to divide by 1000.

$$0.3 \text{ cm}^3 \div 1000 = 0.0003 \text{ dm}^3$$

Some measuring equipment uses litres — fortunately, litres are the same as dm³ (and ml are the same as cm³).

Units of energy

Energy can be measured in J, kJ and calories. You need to be able to convert between these units too.

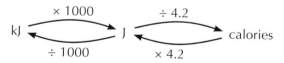

$$kJ \xrightleftharpoons[\div 1000]{\times 1000} J \xrightleftharpoons[\times 4.2]{\div 4.2} calories$$

Examples

Write 69 kJ in J.

- To convert 69 kJ into J you need to multiply by 1000.

$$69 \text{ kJ} \times 1000 = 69\,000 \text{ J}$$

Write 399 J in calories. (1 calorie = 4.2 J)

- To convert 399 J into calories you need to divide by 4.2.

$$399 \text{ J} \div 4.2 = 95 \text{ calories}$$

Write 1500 calories in kJ. (1 calorie = 4.2 J)

- To convert 1500 calories into J, you need to multiply by 4.2.

$$1500 \text{ calories} \times 4.2 = 6300 \text{ J}$$

- Then, to convert 6300 J into kJ, you need to divide by 1000.

$$6300 \text{ J} \div 1000 = 6.3 \text{ kJ}$$

Figure 1: *A calculator. Under the pressure of an exam it's easy to make mistakes in calculations, even if they're really simple ones. So don't be afraid to put every calculation into the calculator.*

Exam Tip
Practice conversions like these over and over again — it'll make your exams a lot less stressful if it's second nature.

Exam Tip
You <u>don't</u> need to remember that 1 calorie = 4.2 J. If you're asked to do a conversion between calories and joules in the exam, you'll be given this information in the question.

Exam Tip
A calorie is bigger than a J, so the number gets smaller when you convert from J to calories — each unit is worth more, so there are fewer of them.

Formula triangles

Formula triangles are extremely useful tools for lots of tricky maths problems.

If three things are related by a formula like this: $n = c \times v$ or like this: $c = \dfrac{n}{V}$

...then you can put them into a formula triangle like this:

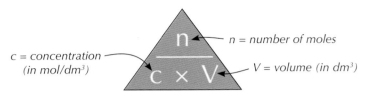

c = concentration (in mol/dm³)

n = number of moles

V = volume (in dm³)

Figure 2: The formula triangle for $n = c \times V$.

- If there are two terms multiplied together in the formula then they must go on the bottom of the formula triangle (so the other one goes on the top).

- If there's one term divided by another in the formula then the one on top of the division goes on top in the formula triangle (and so the other two must go on the bottom — it doesn't matter which way round).

- To use the formula triangle, put your thumb over the thing you want to find and write down what's left showing. This gives you your formula (for example $c = n \div V$).

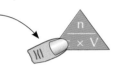

- Then put in the values for the other two things and work out the thing you don't know.

Example

If you want to find number of moles, but you only have this formula:

relative formula mass (M_r) = mass in grams (m) ÷ number of moles (n)

...then you can turn it into a formula triangle.

- As m is divided by n, m goes on top, leaving $n \times M_r$ on the bottom:

- Covering n leaves $m \div M_r$.

- So, number of moles = mass in grams ÷ relative formula mass.

Standard form Higher

You need to be able to work with numbers that are written in standard form. Standard form is used for writing very big or very small numbers in a more convenient way. Standard form must always look like this:

This number must always be between 1 and 10.

This number is the number of places the decimal point moves.

$$A \times 10^n$$

You can write numbers out in full rather than in standard form by moving the decimal point. Which direction to move the decimal point, and how many places to move it, depends on the value of 'n'. If 'n' is positive, the decimal point needs to move to the right. If 'n' is negative the decimal point needs to move to the left.

Examples

Here's how to write out 9.3×10^4 in full.

- Work out which way the decimal point needs to move, by looking at the 'n' number. Here it's a positive number (4) so the decimal point needs to move to the right.

- Then count the number of places the decimal point has to move to the right. In this example it's four:

$$9.3 \times 10^4 = 9\ 3\ 0\ 0\ 0.$$

- So 9.3×10^4 is the same as 93 000.

Here's how to write out 5.6×10^{-5} in full.

- 'n' is a negative number (−5) so the decimal point needs to move to the left.

- Count five places to the left.

$$5.6 \times 10^{-5} = .0\ 0\ 0\ 0\ 5\ 6$$

- So 5.6×10^{-5} is the same as 0.000056.

Exam Tip
You need to add a zero into any space left by the decimal point moving.

The key things to remember with numbers in standard form are...

- When 'n' is positive the number is big. The bigger 'n' is, the bigger the number is.

- When 'n' is negative the number is small. The smaller 'n' is (the more negative), the smaller the number is.

Example

Put the numbers below in size order, from smallest to largest:

$$1.0 \times 10^8 \qquad 3.0 \times 10^5 \qquad 5.0 \times 10^{-7} \qquad 4.5 \times 10^5$$

- 5.0×10^{-7} is the only number where 'n' is negative, so this is the smallest number.

- 1.0×10^8 has the biggest value of 'n' (8) so this is the largest number.

- 'n' is 5 in both 3.0×10^5 and 4.5×10^5. So to work out which number is bigger you need to look at the rest of the number. 4.5 is bigger than 3.0, so 4.5×10^5 is bigger than 3.0×10^5.

So, from smallest to largest the numbers are:

$$5.0 \times 10^{-7} \qquad 3.0 \times 10^5 \qquad 4.5 \times 10^5 \qquad 1.0 \times 10^8$$

Exam Tip
If you need to do any rough work, do it in the exam paper booklet. If you don't want it to be marked then cross it out before handing your paper in.

Answers

Chemistry 1

Chemistry 1.1 The Fundamental Ideas in Chemistry

1. Atoms and Elements
Page 19 — Fact Recall Questions
Q1 E.g. atoms have a small nucleus surrounded by electrons. The nucleus is in the middle of the atom and contains protons and neutrons. The electrons occupy shells around the nucleus.
Q2 a) +1
   b) 0
   c) −1
Q3 The number of protons in its nucleus.
Q4 An element is a substance that only contains one type of atom.
Q5 There are about 100 elements.

Page 19 — Application Questions
Q1 One type of atom.
Q2 47
Q3 34
Q4 The atoms contain different numbers of protons so they are atoms of different elements.
Q5 a) +17
   b) −1
   c) The particle has an overall charge so it is not an atom.

2. The Periodic Table
Page 22 — Fact Recall Questions
Q1 The number of protons in an atom.
Q2 The total number of protons and neutrons in an atom.
Q3 They have the same number of electrons in their outer shell.
Q4 They each have one electron in their outer shell.
Q5 The noble gases.
Q6 They have a stable arrangement of electrons. / They have a full outer shell.

Page 22 — Application Questions
Q1 Metals — any three elements from the left side of the purple line on the periodic table on page 20.
   Non-metals — any three elements from the right side of the purple line on the periodic table on page 20.
Q2 Beryllium, magnesium, calcium, strontium, barium, radium.
Q3 a) S
   b) Cl
   c) K

Q4 a) 20
   b) 29
   c) 5
Q5 a) 80
   b) 39
   c) 4
Q6 a) 11
   b) 11
   c) $23 - 11 =$ **12**
Q7 a) 26
   b) 26
   c) $56 - 26 =$ **30**
Q8 5
   Nitrogen and arsenic are in the same group (Group 5) so must have the same number of electrons in their outer shells.

3. Electron Shells
Page 24 — Fact Recall Questions
Q1 An energy level.
Q2 2 electrons
Q3 8 electrons
Q4 8 electrons
Q5 The one closest to the nucleus. / The one with lowest energy level.

Page 24 — Application Questions
Q1 Neon
Q2 Carbon
Q3 Sulfur
Q4

Q5

Q6 2, 8, 5
Q7 2, 8, 2

4. Compounds
Page 28 — Fact Recall Questions
Q1 An ion is a charged particle.
Q2 Positive ions.
Q3 Negative ions.
Q4 Ionic bonding.
Q5 Covalent bonding.

Page 28 — Application Questions

Q1 One carbon atom and one oxygen atom.

Q2 One hydrogen atom, one nitrogen atom and three oxygen atoms.

Q3 D

D is a compound because it contains atoms of different elements chemically joined together. A and C only contain atoms of one element, so can't be compounds. B contains atoms of different elements, but there are no bonds between the atoms.

Q4 Negative ions.

Q5 Lose electrons.

Q6 Positive ions.

Q7 Gain electrons.

Q8 Ionic bonding.

Magnesium is a metal and oxygen is a non-metal, so the bonding in magnesium oxide is ionic bonding.

Q9 Covalent bonding.

Sulfur and oxygen are both non-metals, so the bonding in sulfur dioxide is covalent bonding.

5. Equations
Page 32 — Application Questions

Q1 a) Iron sulfate and copper.
 b) Copper sulfate and iron.
 c) copper sulfate + iron → iron sulfate + copper

Q2 a) copper + oxygen → copper oxide
 b) $127 + 32 = $ **159 g**

No atoms are lost or made during a chemical reaction, so the total mass at the end of a reaction is the same as the total mass at the start of the reaction.

Q3 $68 - 56 = $ **12 g**

The total mass of nitrogen and hydrogen must equal the mass of ammonia produced.

Q4 a) sodium hydroxide + hydrochloric acid →
 sodium chloride + water
 b) Total mass of reactants = $80 + 73 = 153$ g.
 $153 - 36 = 117$ g. So **117 g** of sodium chloride are formed.

Q5 a) $Cl_2 + 2KBr \rightarrow Br_2 + 2KCl$
 b) $2HCl + Mg \rightarrow MgCl_2 + H_2$
 c) $C_3H_8 + 5O_2 \rightarrow 3CO_2 + 4H_2O$
 d) $Fe_2O_3 + 3CO \rightarrow 2Fe + 3CO_2$

Q6 $H_2SO_4 + 2LiOH \rightarrow Li_2SO_4 + 2H_2O$

Pages 34-35 — Chemistry 1.1
Exam-style Questions

1 a) i) non-metals *(1 mark)*
 ii) compounds *(1 mark)*
 b) i) carbon monoxide + oxygen → carbon dioxide *(1 mark)*
 ii) Two molecules of carbon monoxide *(1 mark)* react with one molecule of oxygen *(1 mark)* to form two molecules of carbon dioxide *(1 mark)*.

c)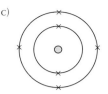

(1 mark for drawing six electrons, 1 mark for placing two in the first shell and four in the second shell.)

2 a)

Atomic number	13
Mass number	27
Number of protons	13
Number of electrons	13
Number of neutrons	14

(1 mark for each correct answer.)

 b) i) $2Al + 6HCl \rightarrow 2AlCl_3 + 3H_2$
 (1 mark for correctly balancing the left hand side of the equation. 1 mark for correctly balancing the right hand side of the equation.)
 ii) Mass of reactants: $135 + 547.5 = 682.5$ g *(1 mark)*
 Mass of hydrogen: $682.5 - 667.5 = $ **15 g** *(1 mark)*

Remember — the total mass of the products is the same as the total mass of the reactants.

 iii) covalent bonding *(1 mark)*
 c) i) Group 7 *(1 mark)*
 ii) Chlorine and bromine both have the same number of electrons in their outer shell / both have 7 electrons in their outer shell *(1 mark)* so react in a similar way *(1 mark)*.
 iii) Argon is a noble gas / is in Group 0 *(1 mark)*. This means it has a full outer shell of electrons / a stable arrangement of electrons so it is unreactive *(1 mark)*.

Chemistry 1.2 Limestone and Building Materials

1. Limestone and Other Carbonates
Page 38 — Fact Recall Questions

Q1 Calcium carbonate/$CaCO_3$.

Q2 calcium carbonate → calcium oxide + carbon dioxide
 $CaCO_3 \rightarrow CaO + CO_2$

Q3 A metal salt, carbon dioxide and water.

Q4 calcium sulphate/$CaSO_4$.

Q5 Calcium oxide

Q6 If you make a solution of calcium hydroxide in water (called limewater) and bubble gas through it, the solution will turn cloudy if there's carbon dioxide in the gas. The symbol equation is as follows:
 $Ca(OH)_2 + CO_2 \rightarrow CaCO_3 + H_2O$

Page 38 — Application Questions

Q1 zinc carbonate → zinc oxide + carbon dioxide

Q2 a) Magnesium chloride
 b) $MgCO_3 + 2HCl \rightarrow MgCl_2 + CO_2 + H_2O$

2. Using Limestone
Page 40 — Fact Recall Questions
Q1 a) To make cement, powdered limestone is heated in a kiln with clay.
b) To make mortar you add water and sand to cement.
c) To make concrete you add sand and aggregate to cement.

Q2 Any two from: e.g. Concrete can be poured into moulds to make blocks or panels that can be joined together. / Using concrete is a cheap and easy way of constructing buildings. / Concrete doesn't rot when it gets wet. / Concrete is fire-resistant. / Concrete is resistant to corrosion.

Q3 Any two from: e.g. Limestone is used to make dyes, paints and medicines. / Limestone products can be used to neutralise acidic soils (e.g. by farmers). / Acidity in lakes and rivers caused by acid rain can be neutralised by limestone products. / Limestone can be used in power station chimneys to neutralise sulfur dioxide (a cause of acid rain).

Q4 a) Any three from: e.g. Quarrying makes big, ugly holes in the landscape. / Quarrying processes make lots of noise and dust in quiet, scenic areas. / Quarrying destroys the habitats of animals and birds. / Quarries cause increased traffic (usually lorries), which causes more noise and pollution. / Waste materials produce unsightly tips.
b) E.g. Limestone quarries and associated businesses provide jobs for people and bring more money into the local economy. This can lead to local improvements in transport, roads, recreation facilities and health, which local people can benefit from.

Q5 E.g. Concrete is quite unattractive as a building material. / Concrete has low tensile strength and can crack.

Page 41 — Application Question
Q1 a) E.g. Richard should use concrete in his garage. It is hard-wearing and cheap. A more attractive floor that was as hard-wearing (marble) would be very expensive. Wood wouldn't be a good choice as it's not as hard-wearing as the other materials.
b) E.g. Richard could use wood flooring in his conservatory. It is attractive but not as expensive as marble. Concrete, although cheaper, would be an unattractive choice. Wood is less hard-wearing than concrete or marble but will be suitable for use indoors.

For this question the reasons that you use to support your floor choices might be a bit different from the ones shown above, or you might have picked different materials than the ones shown above. That's fine as long as you've supported your answers with good reasons.

Chemistry 1.3 Metals and Their Uses

1. Metal Ores
Page 42 — Fact Recall Questions
Q1 A metal ore is a rock which contains enough metal to make it profitable to extract the metal from it.

Q2 If the market price of a metal falls, it might cost more to extract the metal than would be gained from selling it. So the amount of metal extracted would fall. If the market price of the metal increased then more of the metal might be extracted from its ore, as more money could be made from it.

Q3 Any two from: reduction / electrolysis / displacement reactions.

2. Extracting Metals from Rocks
Page 44 — Fact Recall Questions
Q1 a) Electrolysis
b) Reduction
Q2 More reactive.
Q3 Oxygen
Q4 They have many stages and use a lot of energy.
Q5 Any two from: e.g. aluminium, magnesium, calcium, sodium, potassium.

Page 44 — Application Question
Q1 a) Reduction with carbon.
b) Electrolysis
c) Reduction with carbon.
d) Electrolysis

3. Extracting Copper
Page 47 — Fact Recall Questions
Q1 Smelting
Q2 a) The positive electrode.
b) Electrons are pulled off copper atoms at the positive electrode.
c) The negative electrode.
Q3 a) Bioleaching and phytomining.
b) E.g. The methods are less damaging to the environment. / The methods are cheaper.
Q4 a) A displacement reaction.
b) E.g. Scrap iron is very cheap.
c) Iron sulfate and copper.

4. Impacts of Extracting Metals
Page 49 — Fact Recall Questions
Q1 E.g. Mining metal provides materials to make useful products. / Mining provides local people with jobs. / Mining brings money into the area which means services such as transport and health can be improved.

Q2 E.g. Mining causes noise / scarring of the landscape / loss of habitats / release of gases such as CO_2 and SO_2 / contribution to acid rain, global dimming and climate change.

Q3 E.g. Mining requires energy, which usually comes from burning fossil fuels. This releases carbon dioxide and sulfur dioxide, which contribute to acid rain and climate change.

Q4 a) Recycling metal saves energy because it only uses a small fraction of the energy needed to mine and extract new metal.

   b) Any three from: e.g. conserves fossil fuels / saves money (on energy costs) / conserves metal resources / reduces the amount of rubbish being sent to landfill.

Page 49 — Application Question
Q1 a) i)

	Tonnes of waste metal to landfill	Cost (£)
Year 1	15 000	1 725 000
Year 2	12 000	1 380 000

   ii) The council would save £1 725 000 – £1 380 000 = **£345 000**.

   b) E.g. by recycling more metal.

5. Properties and Uses of Metals
Page 52 — Fact Recall Questions
Q1 B

Q2 a) E.g. electrical wiring.

   b) Any two from: e.g. They are strong/hard to break. / They can be bent into different shapes. / They are good conductors of heat.

Q3 They are strong and have low density/are lightweight.

Q4 It can be bent into different shapes (like pipes) and doesn't react with water.

Q5 It's not too bendy, it's light and it doesn't react with water.

Q6 Metals can corrode when exposed to air and water. Metals can also suffer from metal fatigue which can cause them to break.

Page 52 — Application Question
Q1 E.g. Rachel should buy an aluminium frame. Aluminium has a very low relative density so it's very lightweight. It's also highly resistant to corrosion so won't corrode when it gets wet, and it's quite strong. It isn't the cheapest type (steel) but it isn't the most expensive either (titanium). Titanium shares similar properties to aluminium but it's more expensive.
For this question you might have chosen a different type of frame that Rachel should buy. That's fine as long as you've backed up your choice with good reasons.

6. Alloys
Page 55 — Fact Recall Questions
Q1 About 96%

Q2 It contains impurities that make it brittle.

Q3 In pure iron atoms are arranged regularly in layers that can slide over each other. This makes pure iron soft and bendy.

Q4 Carbon

Q5 Stainless steel

Q6 As a pure metal it is too soft for many uses.

Q7 a) Copper and tin.

   b) Copper and nickel.

Q8 It's too soft.

Page 55 — Application Questions
Q1 High-carbon steel could be used (as it's a very hard, inflexible type of steel).

Q2 Stainless steel could be used (as it is resistant to corrosion).

Pages 57-60 — Chemistry 1.2-1.3
Exam-style Questions
Q1 a) i) E.g. alloys are mixtures of two or more metals *(1 mark)*, or a mixture of a metal and a non-metal *(1 mark)*.

     ii) Iron *(1 mark)*

     iii) Harder *(1 mark)*

   b) E.g. It is easily shaped *(1 mark)*.

   c) i) E.g. aluminium is resistant to corrosion *(1 mark)*.

     ii) E.g. aluminium has a low density, which means that it is lightweight *(1 mark)*.

     iii) E.g. pure aluminium is too soft *(1 mark)*.

     iv) Aluminium is extracted by electrolysis *(1 mark)* which requires lots of energy *(1 mark)*.

Q2 a) i) E.g. calcium oxide and water *(1 mark)*.

     ii) $CaO + H_2O \rightarrow Ca(OH)_2$ *(1 mark for correct left-hand side of equation. 1 mark for correct right-hand side.)*

   b) i) Limewater *(1 mark)*.

     ii) The solution of calcium hydroxide would go cloudy *(1 mark)*.

     iii) $Ca(OH)_2 + CO_2 \rightarrow CaCO_3$ *(1 mark)* $+ H_2O$ *(1 mark)*.

   c) i) Calcium hydroxide increases soil pH *(1 mark)*.

     ii) A neutralisation reaction *(1 mark)*.

     iii) The liming took place in May/June *(1 mark)* as after this month the soil pH increased steadily *(1 mark)*.

Q3 a) $CuCO_3$ *(1 mark)*

   b) i) Thermal decomposition *(1 mark)*

     ii) Carbon dioxide/CO_2 *(1 mark)*

   c) Electrolysis *(1 mark)*

   d) i) E.g. chalcopyrite is a low-grade copper ore *(1 mark)*. To extract copper from a low-grade ore is very expensive using the method outlined in the diagram *(1 mark)*.

ii) E.g. bioleaching could be used to extract copper from chalcopyrite *(1 mark)*. Bioleaching is less damaging to the environment *(1 mark)* and is also cheaper *(1 mark)* than the method outlined above.

e) i) E.g. copper is a good conductor of electricity *(1 mark)* and can be drawn out into wires *(1 mark)*.

ii) E.g. Plumbing/pipes *(1 mark)*.

Q4 a) clay *(1 mark)*, sand *(1 mark)*, aggregate *(1 mark)*, concrete *(1 mark)*.

b) i) Iron oxide is heated in the blast furnace *(1 mark)* with carbon *(1 mark)*. The iron oxide is reduced to iron *(1 mark)*.

ii) It contains impurities *(1 mark)*.

iii) E.g. gold *(1 mark)*. Gold is unreactive *(1 mark)*.

c) i)

Statement	Env. Impact Tick (✓)
Jobs are created in the local area.	
Traffic to and from the mine/ quarry causes pollution.	✓
Habitats are destroyed.	✓
Dust from the site can cause health problems for local people.	

(1 mark for each correct tick.)

ii) E.g. mining and quarrying requires lots of energy that comes from burning fossil fuels *(1 mark)*. This releases the greenhouse gas carbon dioxide into the atmosphere *(1 mark)*.

Chemistry 1.4 Crude Oil and Fuels

1. Fractional Distillation of Crude Oil
Page 63 — Fact Recall Questions
Q1 A substance made from two or more elements or compounds that aren't chemically bonded to each other.

Q2 A hydrocarbon is a molecule that only contains hydrogen and carbon.

Q3 Fractional distillation

Q4 Near the top.
Compounds with a small number of carbon atoms have low boiling points so they condense near the top of the fractionating column where it is cooler.

Page 63 — Application Questions
Q1 a) Butane
Butane condenses at the lowest temperature because it has the smallest number of carbon atoms.

b) Tetracontane
Tetracontane has the largest number of carbon atoms so it will condense at a high temperature near the bottom of the fractionating column.

Q2 a) Petrol
The fractionating column is hottest at the bottom and coolest at the top, so the fraction with the lowest boiling temperature range will be removed at the top. This is petrol.

b) i) 125 °C
ii) Naphtha
The boiling point of octane is within the boiling temperature range of naphtha, so octane will be found in naphtha.

2. Properties and Uses of Crude Oil
Page 65 — Fact Recall Questions
Q1

$$H-\overset{\displaystyle H}{\underset{\displaystyle H}{C}}-H$$

Q2 Propane

Q3 Because all of the atoms in alkanes have formed bonds with as many other atoms as they possibly can. / Because alkanes don't contain any carbon-carbon double bonds. / Because alkanes only contain single carbon-carbon bonds.

Q4 The shorter the molecules (the shorter the carbon chains) the more flammable the alkane is. / The longer the molecules (the longer the carbon chains) the less flammable the alkane is.

Page 65 — Application Questions
Q1 The general formula of an alkane is C_nH_{2n+2}, so if octane has 8 carbon atoms, it must have $(2 \times 8) + 2 = 18$ hydrogen atoms. So the chemical formula of octane is $\mathbf{C_8H_{18}}$.

Q2 As hexadecane has long carbon chains, it will be very viscous. Its viscosity makes it suitable for use as a lubricant.

3. Environmental Problems
Page 69 — Fact Recall Questions
Q1 a) Carbon dioxide and water (vapour).
b) E.g. carbon monoxide, carbon particulates, unburnt fuel.

Q2 Sulfur dioxide

Q3 When the fuel burns at a high temperature.

Q4 a) Sulfur dioxide and oxides of nitrogen.
b) Any two from: e.g. It can cause lakes to become acidic and many plants and animal may die as a result. / It can kill trees. / It can damage limestone buildings or stone statues.
c) E.g. The sulfur impurities can be removed from fuel before it is burnt. / Harmful gases can be removed from fumes before they are released into the atmosphere. / The use of fossil fuels could be reduced.

Q5 a) Global warming is the increase in the average temperature of the Earth.
b) E.g. It could cause other types of climate change such as changing rainfall patterns. / It could cause severe flooding due to melting of the polar ice caps.

Q1 a) Yes — burning hexadecane as a fuel will contribute to climate change because one of the products is carbon dioxide which causes global warming.

b) Yes — if the hexadecane contains sulfur impurities, sulfur dioxide may be produced which could cause acid rain / if the hexadecane is burnt at high temperatures, nitrogen oxides could be produced which could cause acid rain.

Q2 This is global dimming — it could be caused by particles of soot and ash that are released into the atmosphere when fossil fuels are burned. These particles could reflect sunlight back into space or could help produce more clouds that reflect the sunlight back into space.

Q3 $C_5H_{12} + 8O_2 \rightarrow 5CO_2 + 6H_2O$

Q4 $2C_6H_{14} + 13O_2 \rightarrow 12CO + 14H_2O$

4. Alternative Fuels

Page 71 — Fact Recall Questions

Q1 A renewable fuel made from plant material. Examples include ethanol and biodiesel.

Q2 Advantages: e.g. Ethanol is carbon neutral. / The only products produced when ethanol burns are carbon dioxide and water. / Ethanol is a renewable fuel. / Growing crops for ethanol provides jobs.
Disadvantages: e.g. Engines need to be converted before they can use ethanol fuels. / Ethanol fuel isn't widely available. / If demand for ethanol increases, farmers may switch to growing crops for ethanol instead of crops for food and food prices could increase.

Q3 Vegetable oils (e.g. rapeseed oil and soy bean oil).

Page 71 — Application Questions

Q1 The company could use biodiesel to run their vans, rather than diesel.

You couldn't give using ethanol or hydrogen gas as an answer to this question because the company would have to replace their vans with vans that are adapted to use ethanol or hydrogen gas as fuel.

Q2 a) The energy to make the hydrogen comes from burning fossil fuels and burning fossil fuels releases carbon dioxide and other pollutants.

b) They could use electricity from a renewable energy source (e.g. solar power) to make their hydrogen.

Pages 73-74 — Chemistry 1.4
Exam-style Questions

1 a) i) The crude oil is heated so that it evaporates *(1 mark)*. The vaporised gases rise up the fractionating column and cool gradually *(1 mark)*. As they cool they condense *(1 mark)*. Different compounds condense at different temperatures and so they are separated *(1 mark)*.

ii) They have short carbon chains. / They have low boiling points. *(1 mark)*

b) How to grade your answer:
0 marks:
No environmental impacts are given.
1-2 marks:
Brief description of one or two environmental impacts.
3-4 marks:
Several environmental impacts are clearly described. The answer has some structure and spelling, grammar and punctuation are mostly correct. Some specialist terms are used.
5-6 marks:
Several environmental impacts are described in detail. The answer has a logical structure and uses correct spelling, grammar and punctuation. Relevant specialist terms are used correctly.

Here are some points your answer may include:
Burning petrol releases carbon dioxide which contributes to global warming.

If the petrol has sulfur impurities in it, sulfur dioxide might form when the petrol burns and this contributes to acid rain.

If the fuel is burnt at very high temperatures, oxides of nitrogen may be formed and this contributes to acid rain.

If there is not enough oxygen available when the fuel is burnt carbon particulates may be produced and released into the atmosphere. These contribute to global dimming.

2 a) Any two from: e.g. Fossil fuels are non-renewable so they will eventually run out. / Burning fossil fuels contributes to global warming. / Burning fossil fuels contributes to global dimming. / Burning fossil fuels can lead to the production of acid rain. / Burning fossil fuels damages the environment. *(1 mark for each correct answer, maximum 2 marks)*

b) i) Because the CO_2 released when ethanol is burnt was taken up by the plants as they grew *(1 mark)*.

ii) Any two from: e.g. ethanol is not widely available. / Engines need to be converted before they will work with ethanol fuels. / People have concerns that using ethanol as a fuel may lead to increased food prices. *(1 mark for each correct answer, maximum 2 marks)*

c) i) Sulfur dioxide can cause acid rain *(1 mark)* so a fuel that produces less sulfur dioxide will be better for the environment *(1 mark)*.

ii) Positive: e.g. Growing crops for biodiesel is labour intensive *(1 mark)*, so provides jobs for local people *(1 mark)*.
Negative: e.g. If there is increased demand for biodiesel, farmers may switch to growing crops for biodiesel and fewer crops will be grown for food *(1 mark)*, so food will become more expensive *(1 mark)*.

3 a) C_nH_{2n+2}

If you're asked to give the general formula of the alkanes in the exam make sure you use upper case letters for the C and the H and lower case letters for the n and 2n + 2 — you could lose marks if you don't.

b) i) Decane because it has the longest carbon chains *(1 mark)*.

ii) Propane because it has the shortest carbon chains *(1 mark)* so has the lowest boiling point *(1 mark)*.

c) i) $C_7H_{16} + 11O_2 \rightarrow 7CO_2 + 8H_2O$
(3 marks for correct answer, otherwise 1 mark for correct formulae on the left-hand side, 1 mark for correct formulae on the right-hand side, 1 mark for balancing the equation).

ii) If there is not enough oxygen *(1 mark)*.

iii) If the heptane is burned at a very high temperature *(1 mark)* nitrogen in the air will react with oxygen in the air to form nitrogen oxides *(1 mark)*.

4 a) E.g. because the only product when hydrogen is burnt is water. / Because burning hydrogen does not produce carbon dioxide. *(1 mark for any correct answer)*.

b) i) E.g. the hydrogen is difficult to store. / You still need to use energy from other sources to make the hydrogen. / Hydrogen is highly flammable so could cause explosions. *(1 mark for each correct answer, maximum 2 marks)*

ii) E.g. They could use biodiesel *(1 mark)*. Biodiesel is carbon neutral / produces less sulfur dioxide / produces less carbon particulates / is a renewable resource so is better for the environment *(1 mark)*. Biodiesel can be mixed with ordinary diesel fuel/doesn't require engines to be converted so it would be cheaper than hydrogen gas *(1 mark)*.

Chemistry 1.5 Other Useful Substances from Oil

1. Cracking Crude Oil
Page 76 — Fact Recall Questions
Q1 a) Cracking is the process used to break long-chain hydrocarbons down into smaller ones. It is useful because shorter-chain hydrocarbons are usually more useful than longer-chain hydrocarbons.

b) E.g. fuel and making plastics.

Q2 A thermal decomposition reaction.

Q3 a) The long-chain hydrocarbon is heated so that it vaporises. The vapour is then passed over a powdered aluminium oxide catalyst at a temperature of about 400-700 °C. The long-chain molecules will crack on the surface of the catalyst.

b) By mixing the vaporised hydrocarbon with steam at a very high temperature.

Q4 E.g. alkanes and alkenes.

2. Using Crude Oil
Page 78 — Fact Recall Questions
Q1 E.g. lots of energy is released when they burn / they burn cleanly / they are a reliable source of energy.

Q2 a) E.g solar power / wind power / nuclear power / tidal power / biofuels.

b) E.g. everything is already set up for using crude oil. / Crude oil fractions are often more reliable. / It will take time to adapt things so that renewable energy sources can be used on a large scale.

Q3 E.g. oil spills can happen when the oil is being transported. / Burning oil releases gases that contribute to global warming/global dimming/acid rain.

Q4 E.g. new oil reserves have been discovered in the last 40 years. / Technology has improved which means we can now extract oil that was too difficult or too expensive to extract 40 years ago.

Q5 E.g. crude oil is non-renewable and alternative fuels for transport are available, so stopping using crude oil for transport would mean we could keep the crude oil for things that it's essential for, like making chemicals and medicines.

3. Alkenes and Ethanol
Page 80 — Fact Recall Questions
Q1

Q2 Because more atoms can be added to them — they contain a double bond that can open up, allowing the two carbon atoms to bond with other atoms.

Q3 a) Technique 1: By hydrating ethene with steam in the presence of a catalyst.
Technique 2: By fermenting sugars.

b) E.g. making ethanol from ethene is cheap at the moment, but ethene comes from crude oil which is a non-renewable resource so when the crude oil starts to run out it will become very expensive. Ethanol made by hydration also occurs at a high temperature
Making ethanol by fermentation requires lower temperatures and simpler equipment and uses less energy than making ethanol from ethene. Sugars are also a renewable resource that won't run out so the production of ethanol by fermentation should remain cheap. But the ethanol produced by fermentation isn't very concentrated and it needs to be purified. Plus, growing more crops to make sugars for ethanol could lead to more deforestation.

Page 80 — Application Questions

Q1 Bottle A contains propene because the solution turned bromine water colourless.
Bottle B must therefore contain propane.

Q2 C
You can tell that C is the alkene because it's the only one that contains just carbon and hydrogen atoms AND has twice as many hydrogen atoms as carbon atoms.

4. Using Alkenes to Make Polymers
Page 83 — Fact Recall Questions

Q1 Many small alkene monomers are joined together to form long-chain polymers.

Q2 E.g. the monomers that the polymer is made from and the conditions (temperature and pressure) of the polymerisation reaction.

Q3 It gets softer as it gets warmer, so a memory foam mattress will mould to your body shape when you lie on it.

Q4 a) Biodegradable means the material can be broken down by microorganisms.
b) Non-biodegradable

Q5 Polymers are made from crude oil. Crude oil is non-renewable so the price of crude oil, and therefore the price of polymers, will increase when the crude oil reserves start to run out.

Page 83 — Application Questions

Q1 Poly(chloroethene)

Q2 a) b)

Q3 a) b)

Page 85 — Chemistry 1.5
Exam-style Questions

1 a)

(1 mark for drawing the carbon-carbon double bond correctly, 1 mark for drawing the four single bonds correctly)

b) i) Ethene is an alkene *(1 mark)*.
ii) Long chain hydrocarbons are vaporised *(1 mark)* and passed over a catalyst *(1 mark)* at a high temperature *(1 mark)* so that thermal decomposition takes place *(1 mark)*. / Long chain hydrocarbons are vaporised *(1 mark)*, mixed with steam *(1 mark)* and heated to a very high temperature *(1 mark)* so that thermal decomposition takes place *(1 mark)*.
iii) Ethanol *(1 mark)*.

2 a) i) C_nH_{2n} *(1 mark)*
You can only have the mark for this question if the C and the H are capital letters and the n and the 2n are written as subscript. cnh2n and CNH2N are not correct answers.

---

ii) Alkenes are unsaturated *(1 mark)* because they contain a double bond that can open up allowing the two carbon atoms to bond with other molecules *(1 mark)*.
iii) Add some of the solution to bromine water *(1 mark)*. If the bromine water turns from orange to colourless, alkenes are present *(1 mark)*.

b) i) Poly(propene) / polypropene *(1 mark)*
ii) Lots of propene molecules *(1 mark)* join together to form long chains *(1 mark)*.

c) Polymers are non-biodegradable / aren't broken down by micro-organisms *(1 mark)*, so if they are put into a landfill site they'll still be there years later *(1 mark)*.

Chemistry 1.6 Plant Oils and Their Uses

1. Plant Oils
Page 88 — Fact Recall Questions

Q1 a) The olives are crushed. The crushed plant material is then pressed between metal plates to squash the oil out.
b) E.g. using a centrifuge / using distillation.

Q2 E.g. (steam) distillation

Q3 Vegetable oils contain useful nutrients.

Q4 a) Food cooks quicker in vegetable oil than in water because vegetable oils have higher boiling points than water, so they can cook food at a higher temperature.
b) E.g. cooking with vegetable oil gives food a different flavour/makes the flavour more intense.
c) E.g. using oil to cook food increases the energy we get from eating it/makes the food more fattening/ makes us more likely to put on weight.
We all need energy, and vegetable oils are really energy rich. But that's the reason that you have to be careful not to eat too much of them — they can be really fattening.

Q5 a) Vegetable oils are suitable for use as fuels because they can provide a lot of energy.
b) E.g. biodiesel

2. Unsaturated Oils
Page 90 — Fact Recall Questions

Q1 An unsaturated oil contains double bonds between some of the carbon atoms in its carbon chain. A saturated oil doesn't contain any carbon-carbon double bonds.

Q2 Add some bromine water to the oil. If the mixture turns colourless then the oil is unsaturated.

Q3 a) nickel, 60 °C
b) E.g. spreads/margarines / baking cakes and pastries

Q4 Saturated fats increase the amount of cholesterol in the blood, which can block up the arteries and increase the risk of heart disease. Unsaturated fats reduce blood cholesterol.
Remember, unsaturated fats are the good ones and saturated fats are the bad ones. Don't get them mixed up.

Page 90 — Application Question
Q1 a) Sample X, because hydrogenated oils have higher melting points than unsaturated oils.
  b) Sample Y
  Hydrogenating oils gets rid of double bonds. The natural oil will have more double bonds than the hydrogenated oil, so it will also have a higher degree of unsaturation.
  c) The bromine water would be decolourised because sample Y contains unsaturated fats.

3. Emulsions
Page 93 — Fact Recall Questions
Q1 No — oils will not dissolve in water.
Q2 a) E.g.

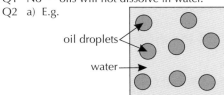

  b) E.g. the oil-in-water emulsion will be thicker.
Q3 a) Any two from: E.g. salad dressing / mayonnaise / ice cream / whipped cream / milk.
  b) E.g. moisturising cream / cosmetics / paints
Q4 a) An emulsifier is a substance that stops an emulsion from separating out.
  b) Advantage — e.g. emulsifiers stop emulsions from separating out and this gives them a longer shelf-life. / Emulsifiers allow food companies to produce food that's lower in fat but that still has a good texture.
  Disadvantage — e.g some people are allergic to certain emulsifiers.
Q5 a) Hydrophilic head / Hydrophobic tail
  b) E.g. emulsifier molecules have a hydrophilic end that's attracted to water and a hydrophobic end that's attracted to oil. When you shake oil and water together with an emulsifier, the oil forms droplets, surrounded by a coating of emulsifier with the hydrophilic bit facing outwards. Other oil droplets are repelled by the hydrophilic bit of the emulsifier, while water molecules surround it. So the emulsion won't separate out.

Page 93 — Application Questions
Q1 a) Put the oil and the water in a flask/bottle, seal it and shake well.
  b) Kevin's method. An emulsion of oil and water will be thicker than either oil or water. So an emulsion will coat the salad leaves better.
Q2 To act as an emulsifier, molecules of Polysorbate 80 must have a hydrophilic end and a hydrophobic end.

Page 95 — Chemistry 1.6
Exam-style Questions
1 a) E.g. to stop it separating out / to make it more stable *(1 mark)*.
  b) i) Washing-up liquid and mustard *(1 mark)*
    You need both things here to get the mark.
    ii) The emulsions in tubes B and E took much longer to separate out than the other tubes *(1 mark)*. This means that the test substances in tubes B and E must be making the emulsion more stable *(1 mark)*.
2 a) E.g. the seeds could be crushed and the oil pressed out of them *(1 mark)*.
  Any sensible method would get you a mark here.
  b) E.g. saturated fats increase the amount of cholesterol in the blood, which can lead to heart disease *(1 mark)*. Cottonseed oil contains more saturated fat than olive oil, so it is less healthy *(1 mark)*.
  c) E.g. food will cook faster in oil than in water. / Cooking with vegetable oil gives food a different flavour. / Cooking in oil makes flavours seem more intense. / Using oil to cook food increases the energy you get from eating it *(1 mark)*.
  d) React the oil with hydrogen/hydrogenate the oil *(1 mark)* in the presence of a nickel catalyst *(1 mark)* at about 60 °C *(1 mark)*.

Chemistry 1.7 Changes in the Earth and its Atmosphere

1. Plate Tectonics
Page 98 — Fact Recall Questions
Q1 a) Scientists thought that the mountains formed due to the surface of the Earth shrinking as the Earth cooled down after it was formed.
  b) Scientists now think that the Earth's crust is made up of tectonic plates and that mountains are formed when these tectonic plates collide.
Q2 Wegener's theory of continental drift says that there used to be just one supercontinent (called Pangaea) and that this supercontinent broke apart into smaller chunks which gradually drifted apart to form the continents we know today.
Q3 E.g. there may have been land bridges between the continents that allowed animals to walk from one continent to another.

2. The Earth's Structure
Page 101 — Fact Recall Questions
Q1 The crust.
Q2 The mantle has all the properties of a solid except that it can flow very slowly.
Q3 Iron and nickel.
Q4 Convection currents in the mantle.
Q5 Very slowly — speeds of a few cm per year.
Q6 At the boundaries between tectonic plates.
Q7 E.g. exactly when the earthquake will happen, exactly where the earthquake will happen and how strong the earthquake will be.

Page 101 — Application Questions

Q1 a) The mini-earthquakes could be a sign that the volcano is about to erupt.

b) E.g. The mini-earthquakes could be a false alarm and evacuating is very expensive/inconvenient.

Q2 Earthquakes occur when tectonic plates suddenly move, so they often occur at boundaries between tectonic plates. Palmdale is located on the boundary between two tectonic plates and so it will get lots of earthquakes.

3. The Evolution of the Atmosphere
Page 104 — Fact Recall Questions

Q1 Nitrogen and oxygen

Q2 The early atmosphere was probably mostly carbon dioxide with virtually no oxygen. There may also have been water vapour and small amounts of methane and ammonia.

Q3 When the Earth began to cool, the water vapour in the air condensed to form the Earth's oceans.

Q4 Green plants and algae absorb carbon dioxide and use it in photosynthesis.

Q5 It has been locked away in sedimentary rocks and fossil fuels or it has dissolved in the oceans.

Q6 a) Carbon dioxide (CO_2)

b) The oceans are absorbing more carbon dioxide which is causing them to become more acidic.

Q7 Fractional distillation

Page 105 — Application Questions

Q1 a) The concentration of water vapour in the atmosphere decreased from about 25% 4.5 billion years ago to virtually 0% 4 billion years ago. This is because 4.5 billion years ago the Earth began to cool and the water vapour in the atmosphere condensed to form the Earth's oceans.

b) E.g. the concentration of carbon dioxide in the early atmosphere was initially high but decreased due to it dissolving in the oceans and being absorbed by plants and green algae. So the red/dotted line, which starts high and then decreases must represent carbon dioxide.
The concentration of oxygen in the early atmosphere was initially low but increased due to plants and green algae producing oxygen during photosynthesis. So the green/dashed line, which starts low and then increases must represent oxygen.

Q2 a) The pH of the oceans has decreased. The rate at which the pH of the oceans was decreasing got faster.

b) E.g. humans are burning more fossil fuels which is leading to an increase in the concentration of CO_2 in the atmosphere. As a result, the oceans are absorbing more CO_2 from the atmosphere and this is causing them to become more acidic/decrease in pH.

c) E.g. the increase in the acidity of the oceans could be harmful to wildlife. / Eventually the oceans won't be able to absorb any more CO_2, so there

will be even more CO_2 in the atmosphere, which could result in more global warming.

4. Life on Earth
Page 106 — Fact Recall Questions

Q1 According to the primordial soup theory, life first began when lightning struck, causing a chemical reaction between the gases in the Earth's atmosphere (nitrogen, hydrogen, ammonia and methane). This reaction resulted in the formation of amino acids that later combined to produce organic matter, which eventually evolved into living organisms.

Q2 E.g. because life began a very long time ago and there is no evidence left today of the earliest forms of life. / Because we can't be certain under what conditions life began. / Because we don't have the capabilities to test many of the theories of how life began.

Pages 108-109 — Chemistry 1.7
Exam-style Questions

1 a)

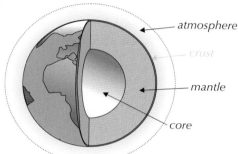

(1 mark for each correct label)

b) i) Any two from: e.g. similar fossils were found on the opposite sides of oceans. / The coastlines of Africa and South America seem to match, as if they once fitted together. / Matching layers have been found in rocks in different continents. / Fossils have been found in places where the current climate would have killed them off. *(1 mark for each correct answer, maximum 2 marks)*

ii) E.g. Wegener's explanation of how the continents moved was not very convincing and other scientists had shown that it couldn't be correct. / A lot of Wegener's evidence could be explained by the existence of land bridges between the continents, which was the accepted theory at the time.
(1 mark for any correct explanation)

c) i) Radioactive decay *(1 mark)*

ii) Most tectonic plates move very <u>slowly</u> *(1 mark)*, at a rate of a few <u>centimetres</u> *(1 mark)* per year.

d) X drawn anywhere along the plate boundary *(1 mark)*. X drawn somewhere opposite the area affected by the tsunami *(1 mark)*.

2 a) Nitrogen *(1 mark)*

b) i) Volcanoes *(1 mark)*

ii) Any two from: e.g. lots of the carbon dioxide
     was absorbed by the oceans. / Some carbon
     dioxide was absorbed by plants and algae
     when they evolved. / The carbon dioxide was
     locked away in sedimentary rocks/fossil fuels.
     *(1 mark for each correct answer,
     maximum 2 marks)*
c) E.g. the increased concentrations of carbon
    dioxide is causing global warming *(1 mark)*.
    Increased concentrations of carbon dioxide mean
    the oceans are absorbing more carbon dioxide and
    becoming more acidic *(1 mark)*.
d) E.g. one theory is that lightning *(1 mark)* caused
    a chemical reaction between nitrogen, hydrogen,
    ammonia and methane in the atmosphere *(1 mark)*
    leading to the formation of amino acids which
    came together to form organic matter *(1 mark)*.

Chemistry 2

Chemistry 2.1 Structure and Bonding

1. Bonding in Compounds
Page 110 — Fact Recall Questions
Q1 A compound is a substance that's formed when atoms
    of two or more elements are chemically combined.
Q2 E.g. covalent bonding and ionic bonding.
Q3 So that they can have a full outer shell of electrons/a
    stable electronic structure/the electronic structure of a
    noble gas.
Q4 By atoms sharing electrons.

2. Ionic Bonding
Page 115 — Fact Recall Questions
Q1 Ionic bonding is a strong electrostatic attraction
    between oppositely charged ions that holds ions in
    an ionic compound together.
Q2 Group 6 and Group 7.
Q3 Positively charged ions.
Q4 They gain electrons.
Q5 1^+
Q6 1^-
Q7 a)

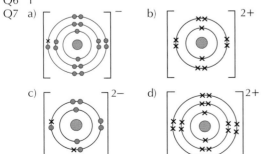

*It doesn't matter if you've used dots AND crosses to show
the electrons in the ions, or if you've used all dots or all
crosses. The important thing is that you've got the right
number of electrons.*

Q8 An ionic compound is a giant structure made of ions.
    The ions are held together in a lattice by electrostatic
    forces of attraction acting in all directions.

Page 115 — Application Questions
Q1 a) Rb^+
    b) Br^-
    c) Ba^{2+}
    d) S^{2-}
Q2 a) Sodium loses one electron to form Na^+ ions.
        Bromine gains one electron to form Br^- ions.
        $(+1) + (-1) = 0$, so the charges are balanced with
        one ion of each and the formula is **NaBr**.
    b) Calcium loses two electrons to form Ca^{2+} ions.
        Fluorine gains one electron to form F^- ions.
        $(+2) + (-1) + (-1) = 0$, so the charges are balanced
        with one ion of calcium and two ions of fluorine.
        So the formula is CaF_2.
    c) Sodium loses one electron to form Na^+ ions.
        Oxygen gains two electrons to form O^{2-} ions.
        $(+1) + (+1) + (-2) = 0$, so the charges are balanced
        with two ions of sodium and one ion of oxygen.
        So the formula is Na_2O.
    d) Calcium loses two electrons to form Ca^{2+} ions.
        Oxygen gains two electrons to form O^{2-} ions.
        $(+2) + (-2) = 0$, so the charges are balanced with
        one ion of each and the formula is **CaO**.
Q3 a) K^+ ions and I^- ions.
    b) $(+1) + (-1) = 0$, so the charges are balanced with
        one ion of each and the formula is **KI**.
    c) E.g. potassium has one electron in its outer shell
        and iodine has seven electrons in its outer shell.
        When they react, the electron in the outer shell
        of the potassium atom is transferred to the iodine
        atom. A positively charged potassium ion and a
        negatively charged iodide ion are formed. They
        both have full outer shells of electrons.
Q4 E.g. magnesium has two electrons in its outer shell.
    Chlorine has seven electrons in its outer shell. When
    they react, the magnesium atom gives up its outer
    electrons and forms an Mg^{2+} ion. Chlorine atoms
    accept one electron each to form Cl^- ions. Chloride
    ions and magnesium ions have stable electronic
    structures. Because the magnesium ions and chloride
    ions are oppositely charged they are strongly attracted
    to each other, and this strong electrostatic attraction,
    known as ionic bonding, holds them together in the
    ionic compound magnesium chloride.

3. Covalent Bonding
Page 119 — Fact Recall Questions
Q1 A shared pair of electrons.
Q2 a) Hydrogen chloride
    b) Water
Q3 a)

b)

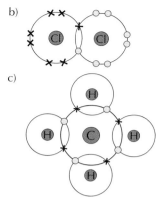

c)

Q4 a) Cl—Cl

b)
```
       H
       |
   H—N—H
```

c) O = O

Q5 Two pairs of electrons shared between two atoms.
Q6 E.g. silicon dioxide and diamond.

Page 119 — Application Questions
Q1 'A' has seven electrons in its third shell, so needs one more to have a full outer shell. Hydrogen has one electron in its outer shell, so needs one more to have a full outer shell. Hydrogen and element A both share one of their electrons so that both atoms have a full outer shell, forming a single covalent bond.
Q2 a) Molecule A contains a double bond — there are two pairs of electrons shared between two atoms in this molecule.
There are actually two double bonds in molecule A.
b) O = C = O

4. Metallic Bonding
Page 120 — Fact Recall Questions
Q1 Metals are giant structures, with atoms arranged in a regular pattern.
Q2 Electrons that aren't associated with a particular atom or bond — they're free to move through the whole structure.
Q3 a) Electrostatic forces.
b) Electrostatic forces exist in a metal because there are delocalised electrons and positive metal ions.

Chemistry 2.2 Structure, Properties and Uses of Substances

1. Ionic Compounds
Page 122 — Fact Recall Questions
Q1 High melting points. The electrostatic forces of attraction between the ions in an ionic compound are very strong, so it takes a lot of energy to overcome this attraction and melt the compound.

Q2 When ionic compounds are dissolved in water the ions separate and are free to move in solution, so they can carry an electric current.

2. Covalent Substances
Page 125 — Fact Recall Questions
Q1 A molecule made up of only a few atoms.
Q2 Covalent bonding.
Q3 Any three from: e.g. hydrogen / chlorine / hydrogen chloride / methane / ammonia / water / oxygen.
Q4 The forces of attraction between the molecules/ intermolecular forces are very weak. So the molecules are easily parted from one another — little energy is needed to break them.
Q5 Diamond has a giant structure where all the carbon atoms are bonded to each other by strong covalent bonds. Lots of energy is required to overcome these bonds and melt diamond.
Q6 b) and c)
Q7 It can conduct heat and electricity.

Page 125 — Application Questions
Q1 It is very hard.
Q2 The layers in graphite can slide over each other so it is slippery.
Q3 a) B
b) C
c) A

3. Metallic Structures
Page 126 — Fact Recall Questions
Q1 The atoms in metals are arranged in layers that are able to slide over each other. This allows the metal to be bent.
Q2 Metals have delocalised electrons that are able to move through the whole structure. They carry heat energy, allowing the metal to conduct heat.
Q3 Alloys are made from more than one element, so they contain atoms of different sizes. The atoms of the element that is added to the metal distort the layers of metal atoms, making it more difficult for them to slide over each other.

4. New Materials
Page 129 — Fact Recall Questions
Q1 c)
Q2 E.g. nitinol.
Q3 1–100 nanometres across.
Q4 E.g. new industrial catalysts / highly specific sensors / strong, light building materials / new cosmetics / lubricant coatings / in electric circuits for computer chips / delivering drugs into the body / reinforcing materials (e.g. graphite in tennis rackets).
Q5 B
Fullerenes are based on hexagonal rings of carbon atoms.
Q6 E.g. new industrial catalysts / lubricant coatings / delivering drugs into the body / reinforcing materials (e.g. graphite in tennis rackets).

5. Polymers
Page 132 — Fact Recall Questions
Q1 A thermosetting polymer.

Q2 A thermosoftening polymer.

Q3 Thermosetting polymers have strong cross-links between the polymer chains. These forces are difficult to overcome so thermosetting polymers are strong, hard and rigid. The intermolecular forces between the polymer chains in thermosoftening polymers are much weaker. There are no cross-links, between the chains and the forces are easily overcome, so thermosoftening polymers melt easily and can be remoulded.

Q4 E.g. the reaction conditions. / The temperature at which the polymer was formed. / The pressure at which the polymer was formed. / The catalyst used when the polymer was formed.

Q5 E.g. low density (LD) polythene and high density (HD) polythene.

It doesn't matter whether you've put polythene or poly(ethene) here — both are correct.

Page 132 — Application Questions
Q1 A thermosetting polymer. E.g. kitchenware such as ladles and spatulas needs to be able to withstand heat without melting. Thermosetting polymers don't melt when heated, so melamine resin is likely to be a thermosetting polymer.

Q2 A thermosoftening polymer. E.g. thermosoftening polymers soften when they are heated and can be remoulded.

Q3 a) E.g. expanded polystyrene. The polymer will need to be able to absorb shocks to protect the glassware, and be lightweight so that it can be moved around easily.

b) E.g. poly(methyl methacrylate). The polymer needs to be transparent so that the spectators can see through it and shatter-resistant so that it doesn't break if it gets hit.

c) E.g. expanded polystyrene. The polymer needs to be a poor conductor of heat so that it traps heat inside the house.

d) E.g. polyvinyl chloride. The polymer needs to be rigid so that it can hold its shape and strong so that it can carry the material that flows through it.

Pages 134-136 — Chemistry 2.1-2.2
Exam-style Questions

1 a)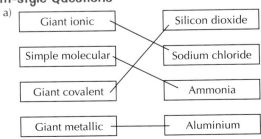

(1 mark for each correct line drawn).

b) i) Simple molecular *(1 mark)*.
   ii) Giant metallic *(1 mark)*.
   iii) Giant covalent *(1 mark)*.
   iv) Giant ionic *(1 mark)*.

2 a) i) Covalent bonding *(1 mark)*.
   ii) Chlorine is made of simple molecules *(1 mark)* and so the intermolecular forces between molecules are weak *(1 mark)*. This means not much energy is needed to overcome them/ chlorine has a low boiling point *(1 mark)*.

b) i) Lithium loses one electron *(1 mark)* and chlorine gains one electron *(1 mark)*. This happens so that both lithium and chlorine can achieve a full outer shell of electrons/stable electronic structure *(1 mark)*.

   ii)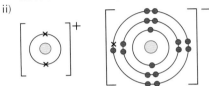

(1 mark for correct electron arrangement for a sodium ion, 1 mark for correct electron arrangement for a chloride ion. 1 mark for both charges shown correctly.)

   iii) LiCl *(1 mark)*.

Lithium loses one electron so has a charge of +1, chlorine gains one electron so has a charge of −1. (+1) + (−1) = 0, so only one of each ion is needed to balance out the charges.

c) Lithium chloride is an ionic compound so consists of oppositely charged ions held together by strong electrostatic forces *(1 mark)*. A lot of energy is required to overcome these forces and melt the compound *(1 mark)*.

3 a) Thermosoftening polymer *(1 mark)*.

You're told that polycaprolactone melts so it must be a thermosoftening polymer — thermosetting polymers don't melt when they're heated.

b) i) When a covalent bond forms, atoms share a pair of electrons *(1 mark)* so that they've both got full outer shells of electrons/stable electronic structures *(1 mark)*.

   ii) Polycaprolactone has weak intermolecular forces between its polymer chains *(1 mark)*. It's these forces that need to be overcome to melt the polymer, and not much energy is required to do this *(1 mark)*.

c) Thermosetting polymers contain cross-links between polymer chains *(1 mark)* so they do not soften when they are heated *(1 mark)*. This means they cannot be melted down and made into new shapes *(1 mark)*.

d) E.g. silicon dioxide / graphite / diamond *(1 mark)*

a) How to grade your answer:

0 marks:
No relevant details of the arrangement of atoms or bonding in diamond or graphite are given.

1-2 marks:
Brief description of the arrangement of atoms or the bonding in both substances, or the arrangement of atoms and the bonding in one substance.

3-4 marks:
The arrangement of atoms and the bonding in diamond and graphite are described. The answer has some structure and spelling, grammar and punctuation are mostly correct. Some specialist terms are used.

5-6 marks:
The arrangement of atoms and the bonding in diamond and graphite are described in detail. The answer has a logical structure and uses correct spelling, grammar and punctuation. Relevant specialist terms are used correctly.

Here are some points your answer may include:

In diamond each carbon atom forms four covalent bonds.

This makes diamond a hard, rigid, giant covalent structure.

In graphite, each carbon atom only forms three covalent bonds.

This results in layers of carbon atoms.

The layers are held together by weak intermolecular forces/aren't covalently bonded to each other.

The layers can slide over each other making graphite soft and slippery.

b) Carbon nanotubes have different properties to bulk carbon *(1 mark)*. Carbon nanotubes contain carbon atoms arranged into hexagons *(1 mark)*.
A nanoparticle is made out of a few hundred atoms, not thousands, and carbon nanotubes have a high surface area to volume ratio. Unfortunately, if you've ticked more than 2 boxes for this question you can't have any marks.

5   a) The electrons in the outer shells of silver atoms are delocalised *(1 mark)*, so they are free to move throughout the whole metal, carrying electric charge *(1 mark)*.
   b) i) Diagram B — sterling silver is an alloy so contains atoms of different elements *(1 mark)*.
      ii) Sterling silver is harder — in pure silver the atoms are arranged in layers that can slide over each other making the metal soft *(1 mark)*. In sterling silver other atoms have been added that disrupt the layers, preventing them from sliding over each other *(1 mark)*.

Chemistry 2.3 Quantitative Chemistry and Analysis

1. Atoms and Isotopes
Page 138 — Fact Recall Questions
Q1   a) The atomic number tells you how many protons there are in the atom.
   b) The mass number tells you the total number of protons and neutrons in the atom.
Q2   Subtract the atomic number from the mass number.
Q3   a) 1
   b) very small
   c) 1
Q4   Isotopes are different atomic forms of the same element, which have the same number of protons but a different number of neutrons.

Page 138 — Application Questions
Q1   a) 8 protons, 8 neutrons
   b) 13 protons, 14 neutrons
   c) 23 protons, 28 neutrons
   d) 47 protons, 61 neutrons
Q2   A is the isotope.
You know A is the isotope because it has the same number of protons (17) but a different number of neutrons (20 as opposed to 18).

2. Relative Formula Mass
Page 140 — Fact Recall Questions
Q1   The mass of atoms of that element measured relative to atoms of carbon-12.
Q2   If more than one stable isotope of an element exists, the relative atomic mass of that element is the average relative atomic mass of all the isotopes, taking into account how much of each isotope there is.
Q3   By adding together the relative atomic masses of all the atoms in the compound.
Q4

$$\text{Number of moles} = \frac{\text{Mass in g (of element or compound)}}{M_r \text{ (of element or compound)}}$$

Page 141 — Application Questions
Q1   a) 9
   b) 31
   c) 65
   d) 63.5
Q2   a) $16 \times 2 = \mathbf{32}$
   b) $39 + 16 + 1 = \mathbf{56}$
   c) $1 + 14 + (3 \times 16) = \mathbf{63}$
   d) $40 + 12 + (3 \times 16) = \mathbf{100}$
Q3   a) A_r of K = 39
      moles = mass ÷ A_r = 19.5 ÷ 39 = **0.5 moles**
   b) M_r of NaCl = 23 + 35.5 = 58.5
      moles = mass ÷ M_r = 23.4 ÷ 58.5 = **0.4 moles**
   c) M_r of SO_2 = 32 + (2 × 16) = 64
      moles = mass ÷ M_r = 76.8 ÷ 64 = **1.2 moles**
   d) M_r of $CuSO_4$ = 63.5 + 32 + (4 × 16) = 159.5
      moles = mass ÷ M_r = 31.9 ÷ 159.5 = **0.2 moles**

Q4　a)　A_r of Ni = 59
　　　　mass = moles × A_r = 0.8 × 59 = **47.2 g**
　　b)　M_r of MgO = 24 + 16 = 40
　　　　mass = moles × M_r = 0.5 × 40 = **20 g**
　　c)　M_r of NH_3 = 14 + (3 × 1) = 17
　　　　mass = moles × M_r = 1.6 × 17 = **27.2 g**
　　d)　M_r Ca(OH)$_2$ = 40 + (2 × (16 + 1)) = 74
　　　　mass = moles × M_r = 1.4 × 74 = **103.6 g**

3. Formula Mass Calculations
Page 144 — Fact Recall Questions
Q1　% mass = $\dfrac{A_r \times \text{No. of atoms}}{M_r} \times 100$

Q2　The simplest possible whole number ratio of atoms of each element within that compound.

Q3　List all the elements in the compound and write their experimental masses underneath them. Divide each mass by the A_r of that element. Take the numbers you end up with and divide each of them by the smallest number. If any of your answers are not whole numbers, multiply everything up to get the lowest possible whole number ratio.

Page 144 — Application Questions
Q1　a)　A_r of H = 1
　　　　M_r of HCl = 1 + 35.5 = 36.5
　　　　% mass of hydrogen = (1 ÷ 36.5) × 100 = **2.7%**
　　b)　A_r of Na = 23
　　　　M_r of NaOH = 23 + 16 + 1 = 40
　　　　% mass of sodium = (23 ÷ 40) × 100 = **57.5%**
　　c)　A_r of Al = 27
　　　　M_r of Al_2O_3 = (2 × 27) + (3 × 16) = 102
　　　　% mass of aluminium = ((2 × 27) ÷ 102) × 100
　　　　= **52.9%**
　　d)　A_r of O = 16
　　　　M_r of Cu(OH)$_2$ = 63.5 + (2 × (16 + 1)) = 97.5
　　　　% mass of oxygen = ((16 × 2) ÷ 97.5) × 100
　　　　= **32.8%**

Q2

N	O
5.6	12.8
$\dfrac{5.6}{14} = 0.4$	$\dfrac{12.8}{16} = 0.8$
$\dfrac{0.4}{0.4} = 1$	$\dfrac{0.8}{0.4} = 2$

The empirical formula is NO_2.

Q3

C	H
80	20
$\dfrac{80}{12} = 6.67$	$\dfrac{20}{1} = 20$
$\dfrac{6.67}{6.67} = 1$	$\dfrac{20}{6.67} = 3$

The empirical formula is CH_3.

Q4

C	H	O
10.8	2.4	9.6
$\dfrac{10.8}{12} = 0.9$	$\dfrac{2.4}{1} = 2.4$	$\dfrac{9.6}{16} = 0.6$
$\dfrac{0.9}{0.6} = 1.5$	$\dfrac{2.4}{0.6} = 4$	$\dfrac{0.6}{0.6} = 1$
3	8	2

The empirical formula is $C_3H_8O_2$.

Q5

Fe	O	H
52.3	44.9	2.8
$\dfrac{52.3}{56} = 0.93$	$\dfrac{44.9}{16} = 2.8$	$\dfrac{2.8}{1} = 2.8$
$\dfrac{0.93}{0.93} = 1$	$\dfrac{2.8}{0.93} = 3$	$\dfrac{2.8}{0.93} = 3$

The empirical formula is FeO_3H_3 or Fe(OH)$_3$.

4. Calculating Masses in Reactions
Page 147 — Application Questions
Q1　$2KBr + Cl_2 \rightarrow 2KCl + Br_2$
　　M_r of 2KBr = 2 × (39 + 80) = 238
　　M_r of 2KCl = 2 × (39 + 35.5) = 149
　　238 g of KBr reacts to give 149 g of KCl
　　(÷ 238) 1 g of KBr reacts to give 0.626 g of KCl
　　(× 36.2) 36.2 g of KBr reacts to give **22.7 g** of KCl

Q2　$6HCl + 2Al \rightarrow 2AlCl_3 + 3H_2$
　　M_r of 6HCl = 6 × (1 + 35.5) = 219
　　M_r of $2AlCl_3$ = 2 × (27 + (3 × 35.5)) = 267
　　219 g of HCl reacts to give 267 g of $AlCl_3$
　　(÷ 219) 1 g of HCl reacts to give 1.22 g of $AlCl_3$
　　(× 15.4) 15.4 g of HCl reacts to give **18.8 g** of $AlCl_3$

Q3　$CaCO_3 + H_2SO_4 \rightarrow CaSO_4 + H_2O + CO_2$
　　M_r of $CaCO_3$ = 40 + 12 + (3 × 16) = 100
　　M_r of $CaSO_4$ = 40 + 32 + (4 × 16) = 136
　　100 g of $CaCO_3$ reacts to give 136 g of $CaSO_4$
　　(÷ 100) 1 g of $CaCO_3$ reacts to give 1.36 g of $CaSO_4$
　　(× 28.5) 28.5 g of $CaCO_3$ reacts to give **38.8 g** $CaSO_4$

Q4　$HNO_3 + KOH \rightarrow KNO_3 + H_2O$
　　M_r of KOH = 39 + 16 + 1 = 56
　　M_r of KNO_3 = 39 + 14 + (3 × 16) = 101
　　56 g of KOH reacts to give 101 g of KNO_3
　　(÷ 101) 0.554 g of KOH reacts to give 1 g of KNO_3
　　(× 25.0) **13.9 g** of KOH reacts to give 25.0 g of KNO_3

Q5　$C_2H_4 + H_2O \rightarrow C_2H_6O$
　　M_r of C_2H_4 = (2 × 12) + (4 × 1) = 28
　　M_r of C_2H_6O = (2 × 12) + (6 × 1) + 16 = 46
　　28 g of C_2H_4 reacts to give 46 g of C_2H_6O
　　(÷ 46) 0.609 g of C_2H_4 reacts to give 1 g of C_2H_6O
　　(× 60) **36.5 g** of C_2H_4 reacts to give 60.0 g of C_2H_6O

Q6　$2Fe_2O_3 + 3C \rightarrow 4Fe + 3CO_2$
　　M_r of $2Fe_2O_3$ = 2 × ((2 × 56) + (3 × 16)) = 320
　　M_r of 4Fe = 4 × 56 = 224
　　320 g of Fe_2O_3 reacts to give 224 g of Fe
　　(÷ 224) 1.429 g of Fe_2O_3 reacts to give 1 g of Fe
　　(× 32.0) **45.7 g** of Fe_2O_3 reacts to give 32.0 g of Fe

5. Percentage Yield

Page 150 — Fact Recall Questions

Q1 The yield is the amount of product formed in a reaction.

Q2 The percentage yield is the amount of product produced in a reaction, given as a percentage of the predicted yield.

Q3 $\% \text{ yield} = \dfrac{\text{actual yield}}{\text{predicted yield}} \times 100$

Q4 E.g. The reaction could be reversible. / Some of the product may be lost when it is separated from the rest of the reaction mixture. / There may be some unexpected reactions happening that are using up some of the reactants.

Q5 If the percentage yield is high then fewer resources will be used/less chemicals will be wasted.

Page 150 — Application Questions

Q1 This reaction is reversible, so the yield will not be 100% because there will always be some product converting back to reactants.

Q2 E.g. the new method has a higher percentage yield than the old method, so it will use up less resources/ waste less chemicals and produce less waste. The new method also works at a lower temperature, so it will save energy, using less fuel and creating less pollution.

Q3 $\% \text{ yield} = (28.6 \text{ g} \div 34.6 \text{ g}) \times 100 = \textbf{82.7\%}$

Q4 $\% \text{ yield} = (33.4 \text{ g} \div 41.9 \text{ g}) \times 100 = \textbf{79.7\%}$

Q5 $\% \text{ yield} = (10.3 \text{ g} \div 15.2 \text{ g}) \times 100 = \textbf{67.8\%}$

Q6 $\% \text{ yield} = (4.27 \text{ g} \div 8.45 \text{ g}) \times 100 = \textbf{50.5\%}$

6. Chemical Analysis

Page 153 — Fact Recall Questions

Q1 Put spots of the food colouring on a pencil baseline on some filter paper. Put the paper in a beaker with some solvent, making sure that the baseline is kept above the level of the solvent. The solvent seeps up the paper, taking the dyes with it. Different dyes form spots in different places.

Q2 Any three from: E.g. They are very sensitive/can detect very small amounts of substance. / They are very fast. / The tests can be automated. / They are very accurate.

Q3 A gas is used to carry the mixture through a column packed with solid material. Different substances in the mixture travel through the column at different speeds, so they are separated.

Q4 The relative molecular mass of each of the substances separated in the gas chromatography column.

Page 153 — Application Questions

Q1 C: Three or more — there are 3 spots so there must be at least 3 dyes. But if two different dyes have travelled similar distances their spots could have joined together, so there could be more than 3 dyes.

Q2 a) 4

You know there are 4 compounds in the substance because there are 4 peaks on the chromatogram.

b) 8 minutes

Pages 155-156 — Chemistry 2.3
Exam-style Questions

1 a) i) M_r of $Na_2CO_3 = (2 \times 23) + 12 + (3 \times 16) = 106$
      (1 mark)
      moles = mass $\div M_r = 25 \div 106 = \textbf{0.24 moles}$
      (1 mark)

   ii) E.g. M_r of $Na_2CO_3 = 106$ (see above)
       M_r of $2NaOH = 2 \times (23 + 16 + 1) = 80$
       106 g of Na_2CO_3 reacts to give 80 g of NaOH
       1 g of Na_2CO_3 reacts to give 0.755 g of NaOH
       25 g of Na_2CO_3 reacts to give **18.9 g** of NaOH
       (2 marks for correct answer, otherwise 1 mark for some correct working)

   b) i) % yield = (actual yield $\div$ predicted yield) $\times$ 100
          = (10.4 $\div$ 18.9) $\times$ 100
          = **55%**
          (2 marks for correct answer, otherwise 1 mark for writing out the percentage yield calculation correctly)

   If you used the value of 22.4 g as the expected yield, you should get a percentage yield of 46.4%. Give yourself full marks if you got this answer.

   ii) E.g. some sodium hydroxide will be lost when the solution is filtered to remove the calcium carbonate *(1 mark)*.

   iii) If the percentage yield of a reaction is low, lots of reactants/chemicals/resources will be wasted / the reaction will be unsustainable *(1 mark)*.

2 a) i) $(3 \times 1) + 31 + (4 \times 16) = 98$ *(1 mark)*

   ii) On the gas chromatography read-out there is a peak with the same retention time as phosphoric acid (about 10 minutes) *(1 mark)*. On the mass spectrometry read-out there is a molecular ion peak with the same M_r as phosphoric acid (98) *(1 mark)*.

   b) % mass = $((A_r \times \text{no. of atoms}) \div M_r) \times 100$
      % mass of carbon = $((12 \times 4) \div 133) \times 100$
      = **36.1%**
      (2 marks for correct answer, otherwise 1 mark for some correct working)

   c)

C	H	O
4.8	1.2	3.2
$\dfrac{4.8}{12} = 0.4$	$\dfrac{1.2}{1} = 1.2$	$\dfrac{3.2}{16} = 0.2$
$\dfrac{0.4}{0.2} = 2$	$\dfrac{1.2}{0.2} = 6$	$\dfrac{0.2}{0.2} = 1$

   The empirical formula is C_2H_6O.
   (3 marks for correct answer, otherwise 1 mark for dividing the masses by the A_rs and 1 mark for finding the ratio 2:6:1)

   d) E.g. instrumental methods are more sensitive. / Instrumental methods can be used with very small amounts of sample. / Instrumental methods are much faster than manual methods. / Instrumental methods can be automated. / Instrumental methods are more accurate than manual methods. *(1 mark)*

Chemistry 2.4 Rates of Reaction

1. Rate of Reaction
Page 160 — Fact Recall Questions
Q1 The two particles must collide with sufficient energy.

Q2 If you increase the concentration of the reactants, the particles will be closer together and so collisions between the particles will be more likely. More frequent collisions means a faster rate of reaction.

Q3 Increasing the temperature increases the frequency of collisions because the particles are moving faster. It also increases the energy of the collisions because the particles are moving faster, so more particles collide with enough energy to react.

Q4 A catalyst is a substance that can increase the rate of a reaction without being changed or used up during the reaction.

Q5 a) E.g. a catalyst increases the rate of a reaction so more product can be produced in the same length of time, which saves money. / Catalysts can allow reactions to work at lower temperatures, which saves energy and money. / Catalysts don't get used up in reactions, so once you've got them you can use them over and over again.

b) E.g. catalysts can be very expensive to buy. / Different reactions require different catalysts. / Catalysts can be poisoned by impurities, so they stop working.

Page 160 — Application Questions
Q1 E.g. the reaction was slowest with the marble chips and fastest with the powdered chalk. This is because the powdered chalk has a much larger surface area than the marble chips. This larger surface area means that there are more collisions between the reacting particles and so the rate of reaction is faster.

Q2 a) At a higher temperature, the rate of reaction will be faster. If the rate of reaction is faster, the factory can produce more product in the same amount of time.

b) E.g. they could use a catalyst. / They could increase the concentration of the reactants.

2. Measuring Rates of Reaction
Page 163 — Fact Recall Questions

Q1 $$\text{Rate of reaction} = \frac{\text{Amount of reactant used or product formed}}{\text{Time}}$$

Q2 E.g. observe a mark through the solution and time how long it takes for the mark to disappear. The quicker the mark disappears, the quicker the reaction.

Q3 a) E.g. gas syringes are usually quite precise and they don't release the gas into the room, which is useful if the gas produced is poisonous. But you can only use this technique to measure the rate of reactions where one of the products is a gas and if the reaction is too vigorous the plunger could blow out of the end of the syringe.

b) E.g. the student could measure the change in mass of the reaction using a mass balance.

Page 163 — Application Questions
Q1 E.g. by directly measuring the amount of carbon dioxide produced over time using a gas syringe. / By measuring the decrease in mass of the reactants as carbon dioxide is given off using a mass balance. *You can use either of these methods for this reaction because one of the products of the reaction is a gas — carbon dioxide. You can tell this from the equation for the reaction that you're given in the question.*

Q2 E.g. by putting a mark behind the solution and timing how long it takes for the mark to disappear. *One of the products of this reaction is a solid ($Mg(OH)_2$), which means it will form as a precipitate in the solution.*

Q3 $4.3 \text{ cm}^3 \div 5.0 \text{ s} = \textbf{0.86 cm}^3\textbf{/s}$

Q4 $34.31 \text{ g} - 32.63 \text{ g} = 1.68 \text{ g}$
$1.68 \text{ g} \div 8.0 \text{ s} = \textbf{0.21 g/s}$

3. Rate of Reaction Graphs
Pages 165-166 — Application Questions
Q1 Reaction A — reaction A has the steepest curve at the beginning of the reaction. The higher the temperature, the faster the rate of reaction and the steeper the curve.

Q2 Reaction C — reaction C has the shallowest curve at the beginning of the reaction. The lower the concentration of the acid, the slower the rate of reaction and the shallower the curve.

Q3 a) and b)

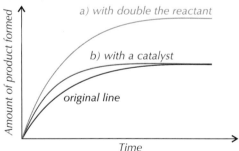

4. Rate of Reaction Experiments
Page 170 — Fact Recall Questions
Q1 E.g. react hydrochloric acid with marble chips. Measure the volume of carbon dioxide produced with a gas syringe. Take readings at regular intervals. Repeat the experiment with crushed marble chips and powdered chalk. The powdered chalk, which has the largest surface, will produce the fastest rate of reaction. The marble chips, which have the smallest surface area, will produce the slowest rate of reaction.

Q2

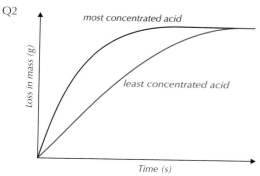

To get this question right you need to draw two curves that start and finish in the same place. The steeper curve should be labelled as the more concentrated acid and the shallower curve should be labelled as the least concentrated acid.

Q3 E.g. the reaction between sodium thiosulfate and hydrochloric acid produces a yellow sulfur precipitate. To measure the rate of the reaction you could put a mark behind the solution and time how long it takes for the mark to disappear.

Chemistry 2.5 Exothermic and Endothermic Reactions

1. Energy Transfer in Reactions

Page 174 — Fact Recall Questions

Q1 a) An exothermic reaction is a reaction that transfers energy to the surroundings.
b) E.g. combustion / neutralisation / some oxidation reactions.

Q2 a) Because endothermic reactions absorb energy from the surroundings.
b) E.g. endothermic reactions are used in some sports injury packs.

Q3 If a reaction is exothermic in the forward direction it must be endothermic in the reverse direction, so the reverse reaction must absorb heat from the surroundings.

Pages 175-176 — Chemistry 2.4-2.5 Exam-style Questions

1 a) E.g. measuring the decrease in mass as the CO_2 is given off using a mass balance **(1 mark)**.
b) i) 14 minutes **(1 mark)**
You can tell that the reaction finished after 14 minutes because this is how long it took for the graph to level off.
ii) 12 cm³ of CO_2 was produced in the first 2 minutes, so the rate of reaction was
$12 \div 2 = $ **6 cm³/min**.
(2 marks for correct answer, otherwise 1 mark for dividing a volume read from the graph by a time read from the graph).
iii) As the reaction progresses, the reactants get used up, so the concentration of the reactants decreases **(1 mark)**. This means there are fewer collisions between the reacting particles **(1 mark)**.

c)

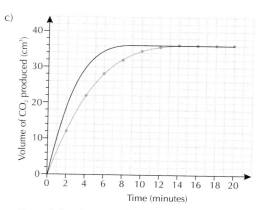

(1 mark for the curve being steeper than the original curve, 1 mark for the curve ending at the same level as the original curve).

2 a) i) A catalyst is a substance that can speed up the rate of a reaction, without being changed or used up **(1 mark)**.
ii) Advantages: e.g. using a catalyst increases the rate of reaction, so more product can be produced in the same amount of time. / Using a catalyst means the reaction will work at a lower temperature, so energy costs can be reduced. / Using a catalyst means the reaction will work at a lower temperature, which is good for sustainable development.
(1 mark for each, maximum 2 marks).
Disadvantages: e.g. catalysts are expensive to buy. / Catalysts only work with one reaction. / Catalysts can be poisoned by impurities.
(1 mark for each, maximum 2 marks).
If you get a question asking you to discuss the advantages and disadvantages of something, make sure you talk about both. You won't be able to get full marks on the question if you only talk about advantages or only talk about disadvantages.
b) i) Increasing the pressure will increase the rate of reaction **(1 mark)**.
ii) At higher pressures, the reactant molecules are closer together **(1 mark)**, so there will be more frequent collisions between the reacting particles **(1 mark)**.

3 a) exothermic **(1 mark)**
b) i) The reaction is reversible **(1 mark)**, so the solid sodium acetate trihydrate that is formed when the hand warmer is activated can be converted back into sodium acetate trihydrate solution **(1 mark)**.
ii) The conversion of sodium acetate trihydrate solution to solid sodium acetate trihydrate is exothermic, so the reverse reaction (the conversion of solid sodium acetate trihydrate back to sodium acetate trihydrate solution) must be endothermic **(1 mark)**. This means the hand warmer could be reset by heating it **(1 mark)**.

Chemistry 2.6 Acids, Bases and Salts

1. pH and Neutralisation
Page 179 — Fact Recall Questions
Q1 E.g. pH is a measure of how acidic or alkaline a solution is.
Q2 pH 7
Q3 a) pHs greater than 7.
    b) E.g. an alkali is soluble in water. A base can be either soluble or insoluble in water.
    c) $H^+_{(aq)}$ ions make solutions acidic and $OH^-_{(aq)}$ ions make them alkaline.
    It's important that you mention that the ions are aqueous. It is only in this state that they can affect the pH of a solution.
Q4 (aq)
Q5 a) Water/$H_2O_{(l)}$.
    b) $H^+_{(aq)} + OH^-_{(aq)} \rightarrow H_2O_{(l)}$

Page 179 — Application Questions
Q1 a) Acidic
    b) Alkaline
Q2 a) pH 6
    b) Blue
Q3 a) Gas
    b) Liquid
    c) Aqueous
    d) Solid
Q4 a) Neutralisation
    b) Water/H_2O.

2. Making Salts
Page 183 — Fact Recall Questions
Q1 a) acid + metal $\rightarrow$ salt + hydrogen
    b) Some metals are too reactive to use (e.g. sodium) / Some metals are not reactive enough (e.g. copper).
    Only one example metal is required for this question.
Q2 a) Bases
    b) acid + metal hydroxide $\rightarrow$ salt + water
Q3 a) Nitric acid/HNO_3
    b) E.g. It is used as a fertiliser. / It is used to supply nitrogen to plants.
Q4 $NH_{3(aq)} + HNO_{3(aq)} \rightarrow NH_4NO_{3(aq)}$

Page 183 — Application Questions
Q1 a) $SnSO_{4(aq)}$
    b) Hydrogen gas/H_2
Q2 hydrochloric acid + magnesium hydroxide $\rightarrow$ magnesium chloride + water
Q3 a) Iron sulfate.
    b) Calcium chloride.
Q4 a) Copper nitrate.
    b) Potassium sulfate.
Q5 a) $2HCl_{(aq)} + Mg_{(s)} \rightarrow MgCl_{2(aq)} + H_{2(g)}$
    The salt is magnesium chloride.
    b) $HNO_{3(aq)} + NaOH_{(aq)} \rightarrow NaNO_{3(aq)} + H_2O_{(l)}$
    The salt is sodium nitrate.

3. Methods for Making Salts
Page 186 — Fact Recall Questions
Q1 An indicator.
Q2 E.g. first, heat the solution to evaporate most of the water from the salt solution to make it more concentrated. Then leave the rest of the water to evaporate very slowly at room temperature. This process is called crystallisation.
Q3 a) A precipitation reaction.
    b) E.g. to remove ions from solutions. / To remove poisonous ions from drinking water. / To remove calcium and magnesium ions from drinking water. / To remove unwanted ions from sewage (effluent).

Page 186 — Application Questions
Q1 a) hydrochloric acid + tin $\rightarrow$ tin chloride + hydrogen
    b) E.g. put the hydrochloric acid in a beaker. Then add the tin and stir. Keep adding the tin until it is in excess. Then filter out the excess tin to get the salt solution ($SnCl_2$) using filter paper and a filter funnel. Finally, you can use crystallisation to get pure crystals of $SnCl_2$ by evaporating water from the solution.
Q2 E.g. you can't produce magnesium carbonate by reacting magnesium sulfate and sodium sulfate because there's no source of the carbonate ion.

Pages 188-189 — Chemistry 2.6
Exam-style Questions
Q1 a) i) A base *(1 mark)*
        ii) Neutral *(1 mark)*
        iii) An acid *(1 mark)*
    b) i) Hydrogen ions/H^+ ions *(1 mark)*
        ii) Potassium hydroxide *(1 mark)*
        iii) E.g. Niall could add universal indicator to the solution *(1 mark)*. When the indicator turns green this shows that the solution has become neutral and the reaction has finished *(1 mark)*.
        iv) $H^+_{(aq)} + OH^-_{(aq)} \rightarrow H_2O_{(l)}$
        (1 mark for correct equation, 1 mark for correct state symbols).
Q2 a) i) acid + metal oxide $\rightarrow$ salt + water
        (1 mark for each correct product).
        ii) A neutralisation reaction *(1 mark)*.
    b) i) Magnesium chloride *(1 mark)*.
        ii) E.g. the reaction will be finished when all the acid has been neutralised and no more magnesium oxide/MgO will react *(1 mark)*. At this point you'll be able to see the excess magnesium oxide/MgO in the solution *(1 mark)*.
        iii) E.g. first filter the solution to remove the excess magnesium oxide/MgO *(1 mark)*. Then evaporate most of the water from the salt solution by heating it up *(1 mark)*. Then leave the remaining water to evaporate slowly at room temperature *(1 mark)*.

Q3 a) i) $Ba(OH)_2 + 2HCl \rightarrow BaCl_2 + 2H_2O$
        (1 mark for correct reactants and products, 1 mark for balancing the equation)
     ii) An alkali is a substance with a pH greater than 7/a base *(1 mark)* that is soluble in water *(1 mark)*.
     iii) E.g. barium is too reactive. / Barium reacts explosively with acid. / The reaction would be too dangerous *(1 mark)*.
    b) i) Sulfuric acid/H_2SO_4 *(1 mark)*.
     ii) E.g. so that you can separate the barium sulfate from the excess barium chloride at the end of the reaction *(1 mark)*.
     iii) E.g. to remove poisonous ions such as lead from drinking water. / To remove calcium and magnesium ions from drinking water. / To remove unwanted ions during the treatment of effluent (sewage) *(1 mark for each answer, maximum of 2 marks)*.

Chemistry 2.7 Electrolysis

1. Electrolysis — The Basics
Page 193 — Fact Recall Questions.
Q1 a) It breaks down into the elements it's made from.
    b) Electrolysis
Q2 Because they contain free ions.
Q3 Electrons are taken away from negative ions at the positive electrode. As the ions lose electrons they become atoms or molecules and are released.
Q4 Positive ions.
Q5 Reduction is a gain of electrons.
Q6 The negative electrode.
Q7 Bromine will form.

Page 193 — Application Questions
Q1 a) (Molten) zinc chloride.
    b) The positive electrode.
    c) The chloride ions lose one electron each (they are oxidised) and form chlorine molecules.
    d) They are reduced.
Q2 Potassium bromide solution contains hydrogen ions, from the water in the solution. Potassium is more reactive than hydrogen so the potassium ions stay in solution and the hydrogen ions are reduced to form hydrogen gas.
Q3 a) $2Br^- \rightarrow Br_2 + 2e^-$ / $2Br^- - 2e^- \rightarrow Br_2$ and $2H^+ + 2e^- \rightarrow H_2$
    b) $Cu^{2+} + 2e^- \rightarrow Cu$ and $2O^{2-} \rightarrow O_2 + 4e^-$ / $2O^{2-} - 4e^- \rightarrow O_2$

2. Electrolysis of Sodium Chloride
Page 195 — Fact Recall Questions
Q1 Chlorine and hydrogen.
Q2 E.g. to make soap.
Q3 Hydrogen
Q4 Hydrogen

Q5 The sodium ions remain in solution because they're more reactive than hydrogen. Hydroxide ions from water are also left behind. This means that sodium hydroxide is left in the solution.

3. Electrolysis of Aluminium Ore
Page 196 — Fact Recall Questions
Q1 It allows the aluminium oxide to be melted at a lower temperature, which saves energy, making the process cheaper and easier.
Q2 a) Oxygen
    b) Aluminium
Q3 The oxygen that is produced at the positive electrode reacts with the carbon in the electrode. This reaction produces carbon dioxide.

4. Electroplating
Page 198 — Fact Recall Questions
Q1 A process that uses electrolysis to coat the surface of one metal with another metal.
Q2 E.g. copper and silver.
Q3 E.g. decorating other metals. Making objects conduct electricity better.

Page 199 — Chemistry 2.7
Exam-style Questions
1   a) Copper chloride solution *(1 mark)*.
    b) i) Water *(1 mark)*
     ii) Each copper ion gains two electrons/is reduced *(1 mark)* and becomes a neutral copper atom *(1 mark)*.
     iii) The hydrogen ions stay in solution *(1 mark)* because copper is less reactive than hydrogen *(1 mark)*.
    You can look up how reactive copper is compared to hydrogen using the reactivity series. There's one on page 43, and you'll be given one in the exam too.
    c) i) E.g. the production of bleach / the production of plastics *(1 mark)*.
     ii) $2Cl^- \rightarrow Cl_2 + 2e^-$ *(1 mark for $2Cl^-$, 1 mark for $2e^-$.)*
2   a) Electroplating *(1 mark)*
    b) The ring *(1 mark)*.
    c) Silver nitrate solution *(1 mark)*.
    d) Oxidation is the loss of electrons *(1 mark)*.

Chemistry 3

Chemistry 3.1 The Periodic Table

1. History of the Periodic Table
Page 202 — Fact Recall Questions
Q1 Their relative atomic masses.
Q2 a) He noticed that every eighth element has similar properties and arranged the elements in rows of seven so that elements with similar properties were aligned in columns/groups.
b) Any two from: e.g. some of his groups contained elements that didn't have similar properties. / Some of his groups contained a mixture of metals and non-metals. / He didn't leave any gaps in the table for elements that hadn't been discovered yet.
Q3 a) To leave space for undiscovered elements.
b) The gaps in Mendeleev's table predicted the properties of elements not discovered at the time. The gaps were filled when new elements were discovered.
Q4 According to atomic number/proton number.
Q5 a) E.g. there wasn't much evidence to suggest that elements really did fit together in that way.
b) Protons, neutrons and electrons were discovered and the periodic table matched up very well to what was discovered about the structure of the atom.

2. Trends in the Periodic Table
Page 205 — Fact Recall Questions
Q1 The number of electrons in the outer shell of an atom of the element.
Q2 Because the outer electron is further away from the nucleus and there is more shielding/there are more inner electrons between the outer electrons and the nucleus.
Q3 E.g. caesium is below lithium in Group 1. As you move down the group, the combination of increased distance from the nucleus and increased shielding means that the outer electron is more easily lost, because there's less attraction from the nucleus holding it in place. So caesium is more reactive than lithium.
Q4 E.g. fluorine is above iodine in Group 7. As you move up the group, the combination of decreased distance from the nucleus and decreased shielding means that the outer electron shell is more likely to gain an electron — there's more attraction from the nucleus pulling electrons into the atom. So fluorine is more reactive than iodine.

Page 205 — Application Questions
Q1 a) 5   b) 6   c) 1
   d) 4   e) 2   f) 7
   The number of electrons in the outer shell of an element is the same as its group number in the periodic table.

Q2 Calcium is more reactive. This is because calcium is further down the group, so is larger than magnesium and it's outer electrons are further from the nucleus and more shielded. This means the attraction between the outer electrons and the nucleus is weaker so the two outer electrons are easier to lose.
Q3 Oxygen is more reactive. This is because oxygen is further up the group, so it is smaller than sulfur and its outer electrons are closer to the nucleus and less shielded. This means the attraction between the outer electron shell and the nucleus is stronger so it gains electrons more easily.

3. Group 1 — The Alkali Metals
Page 208 — Fact Recall Questions
Q1 Group 1.
Q2 Low density
Q3 Reactivity increases down Group 1.
Q4 Those at the bottom of Group 1.
Q5 a) ionic bonds
b) Any two from: e.g. they are white. / They are solids. / They are soluble. / They dissolve in water to give colourless solutions.
Q6 a) Alkali metal + water → metal hydroxide + hydrogen
b) Alkaline

Page 208 — Application Questions
Q1 a) Potassium
b) Rubidium
Q2 a) Lithium
b) Potassium
Q3 An ionic compound.
   The alkali metals always form ionic compounds when they react with non-metals.
Q4 $2Li_{(s)} + 2H_2O_{(l)} \rightarrow 2LiOH_{(aq)} + H_{2(g)}$

4. Group 7 — The Halogens
Page 211 — Fact Recall Questions
Q1 At the top of Group 7.
Q2 The melting points of the halogens increase as you move down Group 7.
Q3 1^- / -1
Q4 Ionic bonding.

Page 211 — Application Questions
Q1 a) Chlorine
b) Fluorine
Q2 a) Iodine
b) Bromine
Q3 a) Yes
b) No
c) No
d) Yes
Q4 a) $Cl_{2(g)} + 2KI_{(aq)} \rightarrow I_{2(aq)} + 2KCl_{(aq)}$
b) $Br_{2(g)} + 2NaI_{(aq)} \rightarrow I_{2(aq)} + 2NaBr_{(aq)}$
c) $F_{2(g)} + 2LiCl_{(aq)} \rightarrow Cl_{2(aq)} + 2LiF_{(aq)}$

5. Transition Elements

Page 214 — Fact Recall Questions
Q1 In the centre block (between Group 2 and Group 3).
Q2 Any two from: e.g. they don't react as vigorously with water or oxygen/they are less reactive. / They are denser. / They are stronger. / They are harder. / They have higher melting points.
Q3 E.g. they act as catalysts.

Page 214 — Application Questions
Q1 Metal B is denser and has a higher melting point than metal A, so metal A must be potassium and metal B must be zinc.

Transition elements (like zinc) are usually denser and have higher melting points than Group 1 metals (like potassium).
Q2 Transition elements are relatively unreactive and form colourful compounds, so metal Y (which reacts with oxygen slowly and produces a red compound) is most likely to be a transition metal.

Pages 216-217 — Chemistry 3.1
Exam-style Questions
1 a) i) The elements were listed in order of atomic mass *(1 mark)*. Then they were arranged in rows of seven *(1 mark)*, so that elements with similar properties were aligned in columns/groups *(1 mark)*.
　　ii) E.g. some of the groups contained elements that didn't have similar properties. / Some of the groups contained mixtures of metals and non-metals. / There were no gaps in the table for undiscovered elements.
　　　　(1 mark for any correct answer)
　b) E.g. Mendeleev and Newlands' tables were similar because they both put elements in order of atomic mass *(1 mark)*. Mendeleev and Newlands' tables were different because Mendeleev left gaps for undiscovered elements whereas Newlands didn't *(1 mark)*.
　c) Elements are arranged in order of atomic number/proton number, not relative atomic mass *(1 mark)*.
　d) i) 6 electrons *(1 mark)*
　　The number of electrons in the outer shell of an element is the same as its group number in the periodic table.
　　ii) Selenium is below sulfur in Group 6 *(1 mark)*. This means that selenium is larger than sulfur/its outer electron shell is further from the nucleus *(1 mark)*, so the forces attracting electrons are weaker/more shielded by inner electrons *(1 mark)* and it is harder for selenium to gain electrons *(1 mark)*.
2 a) i) A transition metal *(1 mark)*.
　　ii) Any two from: e.g. copper will be less reactive/react less vigorously with water or oxygen. / Copper will be denser. / Copper will be stronger. / Copper will be harder. / Copper will have a higher melting point.
　　　　(1 mark for each correct answer, maximum 2 marks)

b) Because copper can form more than one type of ion (a Cu^+ ion or a Cu^{2+} ion) *(1 mark)*.
c) i) The halogens *(1 mark)*
　ii) Fluorine *(1 mark)*
Boiling point increases down Group 7, so an element with a lower boiling point than chlorine must be above chlorine in Group 7. Fluorine is the only element above chlorine in Group 7 so the answer must be fluorine.
d) Nothing would happen *(1 mark)* because chlorine is more reactive than bromine *(1 mark)*.
3 a) i) The reactivity of the alkali metals increases down the group *(1 mark)*.
　　ii) Atoms get larger down the group/the outer electron is further from the nucleus *(1 mark)*, so the forces attracting electrons are weaker/more shielded by inner electrons *(1 mark)* and therefore outer electrons are lost more easily *(1 mark)*.
　b) i) Hydrogen *(1 mark)*
　　ii) A metal hydroxide is formed in the reaction *(1 mark)*, which dissolves in the water to give an alkaline solution *(1 mark)*.
　c) i) Ionic bonding *(1 mark)*
　　ii) Displacement *(1 mark)*

Chemistry 3.2 Water

1. Hard and Soft Water
Page 220 — Fact Recall Questions
Q1 Calcium ions and magnesium ions.
Q2 a) The dissolved calcium ions and magnesium ions in the water react with the soap to make insoluble scum.
　b) Use more soap (than you'd need to use with soft water to form a lather).
Q3 E.g. the calcium ions (Ca^{2+}) in hard water are good for the development and maintenance of healthy teeth and bones. / Hard water reduces the risk of developing heart disease.
Q4 a) Temporary and permanent.
　b) Temporary hard water.
　c) Temporary hard water.
　d) E.g. scale reduces the efficiency of heating systems.
Q5 a) HCO_3^-
　b) The hydrogencarbonate ions decompose to produce carbonate ions (CO_3^{2-}). These ions can then combine with calcium and magnesium ions to form precipitates.
Q6 E.g. adding sodium carbonate (Na_2CO_3). The added carbonate ions react with Ca^{2+} or Mg^{2+} ions to make an insoluble precipitate of calcium carbonate or magnesium carbonate. / Running water through ion exchange columns. The columns have lots of sodium ions (or hydrogen ions) and 'exchange' them for calcium or magnesium ions in the water that runs through them.

Page 220 — Application Questions

Q1 a) E.g. soap will lather more easily in soft water than hard water, so she will need to use less of it for cleaning. This will save money on soap costs. / With soft water she won't get scale formation in pipes and appliances. This means they will run efficiently and cost less money than if they were scaled up.

b) E.g. Sharon will no longer gain the health benefits associated with hard water — Ca^{2+} ions help keep bones and teeth healthy and reduce the risk of developing heart disease.

Q2 E.g. Mike could boil the water samples. Samples of permanent hard water will remain clear. Samples of temporary hard water will become cloudy as magnesium and calcium precipitates form.

2. Investigating Water Hardness
Page 222 — Fact Recall Questions

Q1 a) A titration.

b) E.g. a burette, a conical flask, a rubber bung, a stand for holding the burette, water samples and a soap solution.

Q2 E.g. if bubbles cover the surface of the liquid for at least 30 seconds then it is a lasting lather.

Page 223 — Application Questions

Q1 a) Sample C. Very little soap is needed to get a lasting lather and boiling the water has no impact on the amount of soap needed to do this.

b) Sample A. All of the hardness is removed by boiling, so it must have been temporary hard water. You can tell all the hardness is removed by boiling because a very small amount of soap solution is needed to form a lasting lather after boiling (the same amount as needed for the distilled water, which contains no hardness), but much more is needed before boiling.

c) Samples B and D. You can tell this because some hardness remains after these samples have been boiled — they need more soap to get a lasting lather than the distilled water sample (which is soft).

d) B, D, A, C

Q2

Water sample	Volume of soap solution needed to give a good lather (cm³)	
	Using unboiled water	Using boiled water
Distilled	1	1
Tap	16	9
Bottled	8	1

3. Water Quality
Page 226 — Fact Recall Questions

Q1 1: screening
2: filtration
3: sterilisation

Q2 E.g. silver and carbon.

Q3 a) i) E.g. fluoride
ii) E.g. It can help prevent tooth decay.

b) E.g. Chlorine and fluoride have both been linked to causing cancer.

Q4 a) Distillation
b) Lots of energy is needed to boil the water.

Page 226 — Application Questions

Q1 E.g. when chlorine is added to water, toxic by-products can be generated which might contribute to cancer. Treatment with UV light doesn't add any chemicals to the water.

Q2 E.g. a filter that contains silver.

Q3 Distillation

Page 228 — Chemistry 3.2
Exam-style Questions

Q1 a) E.g. poisonous salts *(1 mark)* and microbes *(1 mark)*.

b) E.g. carbon / silver *(1 mark)*.

c) How to grade your answer:
0 marks:
No advantages or disadvantages are given.
1-2 marks:
Brief description of one or two advantages or disadvantages.
3-4 marks:
Some advantages and disadvantages are clearly described. The answer has some structure and spelling, grammar and punctuation are mostly correct. Some specialist terms are used.
5-6 marks:
Several advantages and disadvantages are described in detail. The answer has a logical structure and uses correct spelling, grammar and punctuation. Relevant specialist terms are used correctly.

Here are some points your answer may include:
Adding fluoride to drinking water can help to reduce tooth decay.
Adding chlorine to drinking water kills microbes and helps to prevent disease.
Studies have linked adding chlorine to water with an increase in certain cancers. Chlorine can react with other natural substances in water to produce toxic by-products which some people think could cause cancer.
In high doses fluoride can cause cancer and bone problems in humans.
Some people don't think it's right to 'mass

medicate' — people can choose whether to use a fluoride toothpaste, but they can't choose whether their tap water has added fluoride.

Levels of chemicals added to drinking water need to be carefully monitored. In some areas the water may already contain a lot of fluoride, so adding more could be harmful.

Q2 a) Scum *(1 mark)*

b) i) Some of the soap reacts with the hard water to form scum, so more is needed to form a lather *(1 mark)*.

ii) Hard water can form scale on the inside of pipes, boilers and other appliances, such as kettles *(1 mark)*. This scale reduces the efficiency of heating systems and appliances, which means they cost more to run *(1 mark)*.

Chemistry 3.3 Energy Change

1. Energy in Reactions

Page 232 — Fact Recall Questions

Q1 An endothermic reaction takes in energy from the surroundings. An exothermic reaction gives out energy to the surroundings.

Q2 a) Endothermic
   b) Exothermic

Q3 During an exothermic reaction, the energy released in bond formation is greater than the energy used in breaking old bonds. The energy that is left over is released into the surroundings as heat.

Q4 Energy change =
Energy of bond breaking − Energy of bond making

Page 232 — Application Questions

Q1 Energy used in bond breaking =
$(2 \times 436) + 498 = 1370$ kJ/mol
Energy released in bond making =
$(4 \times 464) = 1856$ kJ/mol
Energy change = $1370 - 1856 =$ **−486 kJ/mol**

Q2 Energy used in bond breaking =
$(2 \times ((3 \times 413) + 358 + 464)) + (3 \times 498) = 5616$ kJ/mol
Energy released in bond making =
$(2 \times (2 \times 805)) + (4 \times (2 \times 464)) = 6932$ kJ/mol
Energy change = $5616 - 6932 =$ **−1316 kJ/mol**

Q3 a) Energy used in bond breaking
= $(4 \times 413) + (4 \times 242) = 2620$ kJ/mol
Energy released in bond making
= $(4 \times 346) + (4 \times 431) = 3108$ kJ/mol
Energy change = $2620 - 3108 =$ **−488 kJ/mol**

b) Exothermic — the energy change is negative, so energy is being released to the surroundings.

2. Energy Level Diagrams

Page 235 — Fact Recall Questions

Q1 E.g.

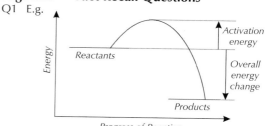

Q2 For exothermic reactions, the reactants have more energy than the products so the energy level diagram starts high and finishes lower than where it started. For endothermic reactions, the products have more energy than the reactants so the energy level diagram starts low and finishes higher than where it started.

Q3 a) Catalysts speed up reactions by providing a different pathway for the reaction that has a lower activation energy.

b) E.g. if a catalyst is used the difference between the energy of the reactants and the highest point reached by the curve will be smaller.

Page 235 — Application Question

Q1 a) Exothermic
   b) Endothermic

3. Measuring Energy Transfer

Page 238 — Fact Recall Questions

Q1 Joules

Q2 a) E.g. measure out both solutions and record their temperature. Check that they are the same temperature. Mix the solutions in a polystyrene cup and stir well. Take the temperature of the mixture every 30 seconds and record the highest temperature it reaches.

b) E.g. use a polystyrene cup. Put the polystyrene cup used into a beaker of cotton wool to give more insulation. Put a lid on the cup.

Q3 Q is the energy transferred, m is the mass of water being heated, c is the specific heat capacity of water and ΔT is the change in temperature.

Page 238 — Application Questions

Q1 $Q = mc\Delta T = 200 \times 4.2 \times 33 =$ **27 720 J**

Q2 Temperature change $(\Delta T) = 55 - 12.5 = 42.5$ °C
$Q = mc\Delta T = 120 \times 4.2 \times 42.5 = 21\ 420$ J
If 0.6 g of kerosene releases 21 420 J of energy, then 1 g of kerosene will release:
$(21\ 420/0.6) \times 1 =$ **35 700 J**

4. Energy from Hydrogen

Page 240 — Fact Recall Questions

Q1 E.g. burning fossil fuels contributes to global warming/climate change. Fossil fuels are non-renewable/will eventually run out.

Q2 hydrogen + oxygen → water

Q3 A fuel cell is an electrical cell that's supplied with a fuel and oxygen and uses energy from the reaction between them to generate electricity.

Q4 a) The only product when hydrogen burns in air is water, so it is very clean.

b) Any two from: e.g. hydrogen is a gas so takes up lots of space when it's stored. / Hydrogen is very explosive so it's difficult to store safely. / Energy from another source is needed to make the hydrogen and this could come from fossil fuels.

Pages 242-243 — Chemistry 3.3

Exam-style Questions

1 a) The formation of ammonia is exothermic because the reactants are at a higher energy on the energy level diagram than the products *(1 mark)*.

b) i) Energy used in bond breaking =
945 + (3 × 436) = 2253 kJ/mol *(1 mark)*
Energy released in bond making =
2 × (3 × 391) = 2346 kJ/mol *(1 mark)*
Energy change = 2253 – 2346 = **–93 kJ/mol** *(1 mark)*

ii)

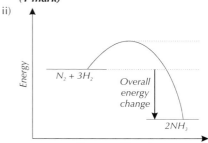

(1 mark)

c)

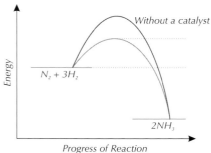

(1 mark)

2 a) i)

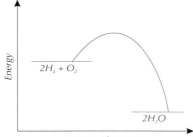

(1 mark for labelling the axes correctly, 1 mark for having the energy of the reactants higher than the energy of the products, 1 mark for drawing a correctly shaped curve)

ii) This reaction gives energy out to the surroundings because more energy is released forming the bonds in the products *(1 mark)* than is absorbed breaking the bonds in the reactants *(1 mark)*.

b) E.g. burning hydrogen only forms water/doesn't produce any pollutants *(1 mark)*.

c) E.g. electrolysis uses a lot of energy/electricity *(1 mark)*. This energy/electricity is usually generated by burning fossil fuels *(1 mark)*.

3 a) Temperature change = 90.3 – 21.4 = 68.9 °C *(1 mark)*
Energy released = 50 × 4.2 × 68.9 = 14 469 J *(1 mark)*
Mass of propane used = 34.56 – 34.04 = 0.52 g *(1 mark)*
If 0.52 g of propane released 14 469 J of energy then 1 g of propane releases:
(14 469 ÷ 0.52) × 1 = **27 825 J** *(1 mark)*
The formula that you should be using here is $Q = mc\Delta T$. It says that energy released (Q) is equal to the mass of water (m) multiplied by the specific heat capacity of water (c) and the temperature change (ΔT).

b) Not all the energy from the fuel is used to heat the water *(1 mark)*. Some energy is lost to the surroundings *(1 mark)*.

Chemistry 3.4 Further Analysis and Quantitative Chemistry

1. Titrations

Page 246 — Fact Recall Questions

Q1 a) The end-point is the exact point when all the alkali (or acid) in the flask has been neutralised.

b) The indicator changes colour.

Q2 The acid should be added a drop at a time and the flask should be swirled regularly.

Q3 Universal indicator changes colour gradually. For a titration you need an indicator that will give you a definite colour change so you can see the exact point when the alkali is neutralised by the acid (or vice versa).

Q4 E.g. wear safety goggles / dilute the acid and alkali.

Page 246 — Application Question

Q1 a) E.g. a pipette.

b) i) Titration 1: $75.35 - 35.15 =$ **40.20 cm³**
Titration 2: $70.20 - 30.05 =$ **40.15 cm³**
Titration 3: $90.00 - 49.70 =$ **40.30 cm³**

ii) $40.20 + 40.15 + 40.30 = 120.65$
$120.65 \div 3 =$ **40.22 cm³**

c) Red

The indicator would be in the flask with the alkali, so would be yellow to begin with. When all the alkali is neutralised the indicator would turn red.

2. Titration Calculations

Page 250 — Fact Recall Questions

Q1 a) 1 dm³
b) 1000 cm³

Q2 Number of moles = concentration (mol/dm³) × volume (dm³)

Q3 Concentration (mol/dm³) = number of moles ÷ volume (dm³)

Q4 Mass in grams = moles × relative formula mass

Page 250 — Application Questions

Q1 M_r of HCl = $1 + 35.5 = 36.5$
Mass in grams = moles × relative formula mass
$= 1.50 \times 36.5 = 54.8$ g
So the concentration is **54.8 g/dm³**.

Q2 a) Number of moles = concentration (mol/dm³) × volume (dm³)
Number of moles = $0.500 \times 0.0350 =$ **0.0175**

b) $NaOH + HCl \rightarrow NaCl + H_2O$
1 mole of HCl is needed to neutralise 1 mole of NaOH, so **0.0175 moles** of HCl is needed to neutralise 0.0175 moles of NaOH.

c) Concentration (mol/dm³) = number of moles ÷ volume (dm³)
Concentration (mol/dm³) = $0.0175 \div 0.0250$
= **0.700 mol/dm³**

Q3 a) Volume of NaOH in dm³ = $25.0 \div 1000$
$= 0.0250$ dm³
Number of moles = concentration (mol/dm³) × volume (dm³)
Number of moles = $0.750 \times 0.0250 =$ **0.01875**

b) $NaOH + HCl \rightarrow NaCl + H_2O$
1 mole of HCl is needed to neutralise 1 mole of NaOH, so **0.01875 moles** of HCl is needed to neutralise 0.01875 moles of NaOH.

c) Volume of HCl in dm³ = $37.5 \div 1000$
$= 0.0375$ dm³
Concentration (mol/dm³) = number of moles ÷ volume (dm³)
Concentration (mol/dm³) = $0.01875 \div 0.0375$
= **0.5 mol/dm³**

Q4 Volume of NaOH in dm³ = $20.0 \div 1000$
$= 0.0200$ dm³
Number of moles = concentration (mol/dm³) × volume (dm³)
Number of moles NaOH = $1.00 \times 0.0200 = 0.0200$
$2NaOH + H_2SO_4 \rightarrow Na_2SO_4 + 2H_2O$

1 mole of H_2SO_4 is needed to neutralise 2 moles of NaOH so $0.0200 \div 2 = 0.0100$ moles of H_2SO_4 is needed to neutralise 0.0200 moles of NaOH.
Volume of H_2SO_4 in dm³ = $27.5 \div 1000 = 0.0275$ dm³
Concentration (mol/dm³) = number of moles ÷ volume (dm³)
Concentration of H_2SO_4 = $0.0100 \div 0.0275$
= **0.364 mol/dm³**

Q5 a) Volume of HNO_3 in dm³ = $25.0 \div 1000$
$= 0.0250$ dm³
Number of moles = concentration (mol/dm³) × volume (dm³)
Number of moles HNO_3 = 0.500×0.0250
$= 0.0125$
$NaOH + HNO_3 \rightarrow NaNO_3 + H_2O$
1 mole of NaOH is needed to neutralise 1 mole of HNO_3 so 0.0125 moles of NaOH is needed to neutralise 0.0125 moles of HNO_3.
Volume of NaOH in dm³ = $43.7 \div 1000$
$= 0.0437$ dm³
Concentration (mol/dm³) = number of moles ÷ volume (dm³)
Concentration of NaOH = $0.0125 \div 0.0437$
= **0.286 mol/dm³**

b) M_r of NaOH = $23 + 16 + 1 = 40$
Mass in grams = moles × relative formula mass
$= 0.286 \times 40 = 11.44$ g
So the concentration is **11.44 g/dm³**

3. Tests for Ions

Page 254 — Fact Recall Questions

Q1 a) Green
b) Lilac
c) Crimson

Q2 a) Calcium, aluminium and magnesium.
b) Aluminium (hydroxide).

Q3 Carbon dioxide.

Q4 Add dilute nitric and then silver nitrate solution. If a cream precipitate forms then the solution must contain bromide ions.

Q5 Sulfate ions.

Page 254 — Application Questions

Q1 Calcium carbonate.
The red flame in the flame test shows that there are calcium ions in the compound. The limewater turning cloudy shows that carbonate ions are present.

Q2 Copper(II) sulfate.
Copper ions react with sodium hydroxide to form a blue precipitate. The white precipitate formed after barium chloride and acid are added shows that there are sulfate ions.

Q3 He should add sodium hydroxide solution to test for iron(II) ions. If the sample is iron(II) chloride solution a green precipitate will form. He should add dilute nitric acid followed by silver nitrate solution to test for chloride ions. If the sample is iron(II) chloride solution a white precipitate will form.

Pages 256-257 — Chemistry 3.4
Exam-style Questions

1 a) i)   Burette *(1 mark)*.
      ii) The indicator will change colour when all
           the sodium hydroxide solution has reacted
           (1 mark), so the student will be able to see the
           end-point of the reaction *(1 mark)*.
      iii) E.g. so that she doesn't miss the end-point of
           the reaction / so that she doesn't add more acid
           than is needed to neutralise the alkali *(1 mark)*.
   b) i)   E.g. it lets you see whether your results are
           repeatable / so you can calculate a mean result
           / it lets you spot any anomalous results / it
           improves the accuracy of your result *(1 mark)*.
      ii) E.g. the concentration of the acid / the
           concentration of the alkali / the indicator used /
           amount of indicator used *(1 mark)*.
      iii) Volume of acid used in titration 1:
           $78.65 - 46.20 = 32.45$ cm^3
           Volume of acid used in titration 2:
           $87.00 - 54.45 = 32.55$ cm^3
           Volume of acid used in titration 3:
           $71.00 - 38.70 = 32.30$ cm^3 *(1 mark)*
           Average volume of acid:
           $(32.45 + 32.55 + 32.30) \div 3 = $ **32.43 cm^3**
           (1 mark)

2 a) i)   Volume of acid (dm^3) $= 37.6 \div 1000 = 0.0376$
           Number of moles = concentration (mol/dm^3) $\times$
           volume (dm^3)
           Moles of H$_2$SO$_4$ $= 0.500 \times 0.0376$ *(1 mark)*
           $=$ **0.0188** *(1 mark)*
      ii) H$_2$SO$_4$ + 2KOH $\rightarrow$ K$_2$SO$_4$ + 2H$_2$O *(1 mark)*
      iii) 1 mole of sulfuric acid reacts with 2 moles
           of potassium hydroxide, so 0.0188 moles
           of sulfuric acid reacts with $0.0188 \times 2 = $
           0.0376 moles of potassium hydroxide *(1 mark)*.
           Volume of KOH (dm^3) $= 25.0 \div 1000 = 0.0250$
           Concentration (mol/dm^3) = number of moles $\div$
           volume (dm^3)
           Concentration of KOH $= 0.0376 \div 0.0250$
           (1 mark)
           $=$ **1.50 mol/dm^3** *(1 mark)*.
   b) A white precipitate is formed *(1 mark)*.
   *Dilute hydrochloric acid followed by barium chloride solution
   is the test for sulfate ions. Sulfuric acid contains sulfate
   ions, so you'd expect to see a white precipitate forming.*

3 a) Sodium ions *(1 mark)* and aluminium ions
      (1 mark).
      *The yellow flame in the flame test indicates that there are
      sodium ions. A white precipitate that forms when sodium
      hydroxide solution is added to a solution of the powder, and
      then dissolves when excess sodium hydroxide solution is
      added, shows that there are aluminium ions.*
   b) Carbonate ions *(1 mark)*.
      *When hydrochloric acid is added to a carbonate, carbon
      dioxide is formed. Carbon dioxide turns limewater cloudy.*
   c) Baking powder contains carbonate ions.
      Carbonates react with acid to produce carbon
      dioxide. The fizzing is the carbon dioxide being
      released *(1 mark)*. Barium chloride tests for sulfate
      ions. No precipitate is formed, so there are no
      sulfate ions in the baking powder *(1 mark)*.

Chemistry 3.5 The Production of Ammonia

1. Reversible Reactions
Page 261 — Fact Recall Questions
Q1 a) None of the reactants or products can escape.
   b) It will reach a state of equilibrium.
Q2 The rates of the forward and reverse reactions are the
   same.
Q3 The exothermic direction is favoured.
Q4 How many molecules are on each side of the
   equation/How much volume is on each side of the
   equation.

Page 261 — Application Questions
Q1 a) i) The exothermic/reverse reaction.
      ii) NH$_4$Cl$_{(s)}$/ammonium chloride.
   b) i) The endothermic/forward reaction.
      ii) NH$_{3(g)}$/ammonia and HCl$_{(g)}$/hydrogen chloride
Q2 a) The left side.
   b) E.g. the yield of sulfur trioxide (SO$_3$) increases.
   c) E.g. the yield of sulfur trioxide (SO$_3$) decreases.
   d) i) The yield of SO$_3$ would increase.
      ii) The overall rate of reaction would decrease/the
          reaction would slow down.
   *This one's a bit tricky. The forward reaction is exothermic,
   so decreasing the temperature increases the rate of
   the forward reaction <u>relative to</u> the rate of the reverse
   reaction. But decreasing the temperature slows down
   both reactions — so the <u>overall</u> rate of the reaction
   decreases.*
Q3 a) Andrew decreased the temperature.
   b) Andrew would need to raise the temperature.

2. The Haber Process
Page 264 — Fact Recall Questions
Q1 a) Nitrogen/N$_2$ and hydrogen/H$_2$.
   b) E.g. nitrogen is obtained from the air. Hydrogen
      can be obtained from natural gas (methane).
Q2 nitrogen + hydrogen $\rightleftharpoons$ ammonia
Q3 Iron
Q4 A temperature of 450 °C and a pressure of 200
   atmospheres.
Q5 a) They are recycled.
   b) The ammonia gas is cooled in a condenser and
      turns from a gas into a liquid. The liquid ammonia
      is then drained out of the reaction vessel.

Page 264 — Application Question

Q1 a) E.g. higher pressure favours the forward reaction of the Haber process, as there are fewer molecules on the right-hand side of the equation. This increases the yield of ammonia.

b) E.g. using a lower temperature favours the exothermic forward reaction (so it increases the yield of ammonia. Using a lower temperature also saves energy, making it more environmentally friendly and cheaper.

c) E.g. using a lower temperature means a lower rate of reaction. This means it takes longer for the product to be made.

Page 266 — Chemistry 3.5
Exam-style Questions

Q1 a) Nitrogen *(1 mark)* hydrogen *(1 mark)*.

For this question it doesn't matter which way round you have given the answers.

b) 200 atm *(1 mark)*

c) iron *(1 mark)*

d) i) 450 °C *(1 mark)*

ii) A low temperature results in a low rate of reaction/A relatively high temperature gives a faster rate of reaction *(1 mark)*. It's better to get a lower yield more quickly than a high yield very slowly *(1 mark)*.

Q2 a) This would decrease the yield of ethanol *(1 mark)* because increased temperature favours the reverse (endothermic) reaction *(1 mark)*.

b) This would increase the yield of ethanol *(1 mark)* because increased pressure favours the reaction that produces fewer molecules of gas (the right-hand side of the equation) *(1 mark)*.

Chemistry 3.6 Alcohols, Carboxylic Acids and Esters

1. Alcohols

Page 269 — Fact Recall Questions

Q1 $C_nH_{2n+1}OH$

Q2 E.g. they are flammable, they dissolve completely in water to give neutral solutions and they react with sodium to give hydrogen and alkoxides.

Q3 Any two from: e.g. for making alcoholic drinks. / As industrial solvents. / For making perfumes/aftershave lotions. / To clean paint brushes. / As fuels.

Page 269 — Application Question

Q1 c), d) and e) are all alcohols.

You can tell c) and d) are alcohols because they both have an -OH group. You can tell e) is an alcohol because its name ends in '-ol'.

2. Carboxylic Acids

Page 272 — Fact Recall Questions

Q1 –COOH

Q2 Methanoic acid, ethanoic acid and propanoic acid.

Q3 carbon dioxide

Q4 They only partially ionise in water.

Q5 a) E.g. using microbes and using oxidising agents.

b) ethanol + oxygen → ethanoic acid + water

c) E.g. making vinegar.

Page 272 — Application Questions

Q1 a), d) and e) are all carboxylic acids.

You can tell a) and e) are carboxylic acids because they both have a –COOH group. You can tell d) is a carboxylic acid because its name ends in '-oic acid'.

Q2 E.g.

You could have drawn this molecule slightly differently (for example, if you'd put some of the carbons in side chains). The most important things to get right here though are the 5 carbon atoms and the –COOH group.

Q3 Hydrochloric acid is a strong acid that fully ionises in water. Ethanoic acid is a weak acid that only partially ionises in water, so fewer H^+ ions will be released and the solution will have a higher pH than a solution of hydrochloric acid that's the same concentration.

3. Esters

Page 274 — Fact Recall Questions

Q1

Q2 a) an alcohol

b) an acid catalyst/concentrated sulfuric acid.

Q3 '-oate'

Q4 Ethanol and ethanoic acid.

Q5 Any two from: e.g. they have pleasant smells/smell sweet. / They are volatile. / They are flammable. / They don't mix very well with water. / They are soluble in alcohols/organic solvents.

Q6 a) Any two from: e.g. to make perfumes. / To make flavourings. / In ointments. / As solvents in paint/ink/glue/nail varnish removers.

b) E.g. inhaling the fumes from some esters irritates mucous membranes in the nose and mouth. / Esters are very flammable which makes them quite dangerous. / Some esters are toxic.

Page 276 — Chemistry 3.6
Exam-style Questions

1   a) i) ethanol *(1 mark)*
       ii) an ester *(1 mark)*
    b) Ethanoic acid has a higher pH because it is a
        weak acid, whereas hydrochloric acid is a strong
        acid *(1 mark)*. This means that ethanoic acid only
        partially ionises in water and releases fewer H^+
        ions than hydrochloric acid, which fully ionises in
        water *(1 mark)*.

2   a) i) It has an –OH functional group *(1 mark)*.
       ii) pH 7 *(1 mark)*
    All alcohols dissolve in water to form neutral solutions
    (solutions with a pH of 7).
    b) $2C_5H_{11}OH + 15O_2 \rightarrow 10CO_2 + 12H_2O$
        (1 mark for correct reactants and products,
        1 mark for correctly balancing the equation)
    c) hydrogen gas *(1 mark)*

3   a)
$$
\begin{array}{c}
\text{H} \\
| \\
\text{H--C--OH} \\
| \\
\text{H}
\end{array}
$$
            (1 mark)

    b) How to grade your answer:
        0 marks:
        No reasons are given why ethanol is the best fuel
        to use.
        1-2 marks:
        Brief statement of one or two reasons why ethanol
        is the best fuel to use.
        3-4 marks:
        Three or four reasons why ethanol is the best fuel
        to use are stated clearly. The answer has some
        structure and spelling, grammar and punctuation
        are mostly correct. Some specialist terms are used.
        5-6 marks:
        Five or six reasons why ethanol is the best fuel to
        use are stated clearly. The answer has a logical
        structure and uses correct spelling, grammar and
        punctuation. Relevant specialist terms are used
        correctly.
        Here are some points your answer may include:
        Although methanol is cheaper than ethanol, it
        produces less energy per litre.
        This makes it less efficient as a fuel.
        Methanol is also more toxic than ethanol.
        This makes it more difficult to transport and store
        safely.
        Although propanol and butanol produce more
        energy per litre than ethanol, making them more
        efficient, they are much more expensive.
        Propanol and butanol are also more harmful
        to health than ethanol, making them harder to
        transport and store safely.

Glossary

A

Accurate result
A result that is very close to the true answer.

Acid
A substance with a pH of less than 7 that forms H^+ ions in water.

Activation energy
The minimum amount of energy that particles must have in order to react.

Alcohol
A compound that contains an –OH functional group.

Alkali
A base that dissolves in water and forms OH^- ions in solution.

Alkali metal
An element in Group 1 of the periodic table. E.g. sodium, potassium etc.

Alkane
A saturated hydrocarbon with the general formula C_nH_{2n+2}. E.g. methane, ethane, propane etc.

Alkenes
A group of unsaturated hydrocarbons that contain a carbon-carbon double bond and have the general formula C_nH_{2n}. E.g. ethene, propene etc.

Alloy
A metal that is a mixture of two or more metals, or a mixture involving metals and non-metals.

Anhydrous
Doesn't contain any water molecules.

Anomalous result
A result that doesn't seem to fit with the rest of the data.

Atmosphere
The layer of air that surrounds the Earth.

Atmospheric pollution
Pollution caused by releasing harmful gases into the atmosphere, such as CO_2, sulfur dioxide and methane.

Atom
A neutral particle made up of protons and neutrons in the nucleus, with electrons surrounding the nucleus.

Atomic number
The number of protons in the nucleus of an atom. It's also known as proton number.

B

Base
A substance with a pH of more than 7.

Bias
Prejudice towards or against something.

Biodegradable
Can be broken down by microorganisms.

Biodiesel
A type of biofuel produced from vegetable oils.

Biofuel
A type of renewable fuel that is produced from plants and waste. E.g. ethanol or biodiesel.

Bioleaching
The process by which copper is separated from copper sulfide using bacteria.

Bond energy
The amount of energy required to break a bond (or the amount of energy released when a bond is made).

C

Calorimetry
A technique used to measure the energy content of fuels or foods. The substance is burnt and the flame is used to heat a set volume of water. The temperature change can be used to calculate the energy released.

Carbon neutral fuel
A fuel is carbon neutral if it absorbs as much CO_2 from the atmosphere (when it's grown) as it releases when it's burned.

Carboxylic acid
A compound that contains a –COOH functional group.

Catalyst
A substance that can speed up a reaction without being changed or used up in the reaction.

Categoric data
Data that comes in distinct categories. E.g. type of fuel or metals.

Climate change
Any change in the Earth's climate. E.g. global warming, changing rainfall patterns etc.

Collision theory
The theory that in order for a reaction to occur, particles must collide with sufficient energy.

Complete combustion
When a fuel burns in plenty of oxygen. The only products are carbon dioxide and water.

Compound
A substance made up of atoms of at least two different elements, chemically joined together.

Condensation
The process where a gas changes into a liquid.

Continental drift
The movement of the Earth's continents.

Continuous data
Numerical data that can have any value within a range. E.g. length, volume or temperature.

Control experiment
An experiment that's kept under the same conditions as the rest of the investigation, but doesn't have anything done to it.

Control group
A group that matches the one being studied, but the independent variable isn't altered. It's kept under the same conditions as the group in the experiment.

Control variable
A variable in an experiment that is kept the same.

Core
The innermost layer of the Earth, thought to be made of iron and nickel.

Correlation
A relationship between two variables.

Covalent bond
A chemical bond formed when atoms share a pair of electrons to form molecules.

Covalent substance
A substance where the atoms are held together by covalent bonds.

Cracking
The process that is used to break long-chain hydrocarbons down into shorter, more useful hydrocarbons.

Crust
The thin, outer layer of the Earth (the bit that we live on).

Crystallisation
The formation of solid crystals as water evaporates from a solution. For example, salt solutions undergo crystallisation to form solid salt crystals.

Delocalised electron
An electron that isn't associated with a particular atom or bond and is free to move within a structure.

Dependent variable
The variable in an experiment that is measured.

Direct proportionality
When a graph of two variables is plotted and the variables increase or decrease in the same ratio.

Discrete data
Numerical data that can be counted in chunks with no in-between value. E.g. number of people.

Displacement reaction
A reaction where a more reactive element replaces a less reactive element in a compound.

Distillation
A way of separating a liquid out from a mixture. You heat the mixture until the bit you want evaporates, then cool the vapour to turn it back into a liquid.

Distillation (of water)
A process where water is boiled to make steam and then the steam is condensed and collected. It is used to make pure water.

Double covalent bond
Two pairs of electrons shared between two atoms.

Electrolysis
The process of breaking down a substance using electricity.

Electrolyte
A liquid used in electrolysis to conduct electricity between the two electrodes.

Electron
A subatomic particle with a relative charge of –1. Electrons are located in shells around the nucleus.

Electron shell
A region of an atom that contains electrons. It's also known as an energy level.

Electronic structure
The number of electrons in an atom (or ion) of an element and how they are arranged.

Electroplating
A process that uses electrolysis to coat the surface of a material with a metal.

Element
A substance that is made up of only one type of atom.

Empirical formula
A chemical formula showing the simplest possible whole number ratio of atoms in a compound.

Emulsifier
A substance that can be added to an emulsion to make it more stable and stop it from separating out.

Emulsion
A mixture made up of lots of tiny droplets of one liquid suspended in another liquid.

Endothermic reaction
A reaction which takes in energy from the surroundings.

Energy level
A region of an atom that contains electrons. It's also known as an electron shell.

Energy level diagram
A graph that shows how the energy in a reaction changes as the reaction progresses.

Equilibrium
A state that occurs during a reversible reaction in a closed system when the amounts of reactants and products reach a certain balance and stay there.

Ester
A compound that contains a –COO– functional group.

Evaporate
To change from a liquid into a gas.

Evaporation
The process where a liquid changes into a gas.

Exothermic reaction
A reaction which transfers energy to the surroundings.

Fair test
A controlled experiment where the only thing that changes is the independent variable.

Flame test
A chemical test used to identify metal ions by the colour of the flame produced when a substance is held in a Bunsen burner flame.

Flammability
How easy it is to ignite a substance.

Fossil fuel
A fuel that is produced over millions of years from the buried remains of plants and animals. The fossil fuels are coal, oil and natural gas. They're non-renewable resources that we burn to generate electricity.

Fraction
A group of hydrocarbons that condense together when crude oil is separated using fractional distillation. E.g. petrol, naphtha, kerosene etc.

Fractional distillation
A process that can be used to separate the substances in a mixture according to their boiling points.

Fuel cell
An electrical cell that's supplied with fuel and oxygen and uses energy from the reaction between them to generate electricity.

Fullerene
A nanoparticle made from carbon. Its structure is based on hexagonal rings of carbon atoms.

Functional group
A group of atoms that are responsible for the chemical properties of a compound. E.g. the –OH group in an alcohol).

G

Gas chromatography
A technique that can be used to separate and identify the compounds in a mixture.

Global dimming
The decrease in the amount of sunlight reaching the Earth's surface due to an increase in the amount of particulate carbon in the atmosphere.

Global warming
The increase in the average temperature of the Earth.

Group
A column in the periodic table that contains elements with similar properties.

H

Haber process
A process used to make ammonia by reacting nitrogen with hydrogen.

Half equation
An equation that shows the reaction that takes place at an electrode during electrolysis.

Halide ion
An ion with a –1 charge formed when a halogen atom gains an electron. E.g. Cl⁻, Br⁻ etc.

Halogen
An element in Group 7 of the periodic table. E.g. chlorine, bromine etc.

Hard Water
Water that contains high levels of dissolved compounds, usually containing calcium ions and magnesium ions.

Hazard
Something that has the potential to cause harm. E.g. fire, electricity, etc.

Homologous series
A group of chemicals that react in a similar way because they have the same functional group. E.g. the alcohols or the carboxylic acids.

Hydrated
Chemically combined with water molecules.

Hydrocarbon
A compound that is made from only hydrogen and carbon.

Hydrogenation
The addition of hydrogen to a compound.

Hydrophilic
Attracted to water (water loving).

Hydrophobic
Attracted to oil or repelled by water (water hating).

Hypothesis
A possible explanation for a scientific observation.

I

Incomplete combustion
When a fuel burns but there isn't enough oxygen for it to burn completely. Products can include carbon monoxide and carbon particulates. Also known as partial combustion.

Independent variable
The variable in an experiment that is changed.

Indicator
A substance that changes colour above or below a certain pH.

Instrumental methods
Analytical techniques that use machines.

Intermolecular force
A force of attraction that exists between molecules.

Ion
A charged particle formed when one or more electrons are lost or gained from an atom or molecule.

Ionic bonding
A strong attraction between oppositely charged ions.

Ionic compound
A compound that contains positive and negative ions held together in a regular arrangement (a lattice) by electrostatic forces of attraction.

Ionic lattice
A closely-packed regular arrangement of ions held together by electrostatic forces of attraction.

Ionisation
The formation of ions, often by removing one or more electrons, but also when an ionic compound dissolves in water.

Isotopes
Different atomic forms of the same element, which have the same number of protons but a different number of neutrons.

J

Joules
The standard unit of energy.

L

Lather
The bubbles that are produced when you mix soap with water.

Limewater
A solution of calcium hydroxide in water. When carbon dioxide is bubbled through it the solution turns cloudy.

Linear relationship
When a graph of two variables is plotted and the points lie on a straight line.

M

Macromolecule
A large molecule made up of a very large number of atoms held together by covalent bonds.

Mantle
The layer of the Earth between the crust and the core. It has all the properties of a solid but can flow very slowly.

Mass number
The total number of protons and neutrons in an atom.

Mean (average)
A measure of average found by adding up all the data and dividing by the number of values there are.

Mixture
A substance made from two or more elements or compounds that aren't chemically bonded to each other.

Mole
A unit of amount of substance — one mole of a substance is the relative formula mass of that substance in grams.

Molecular formula
A chemical formula showing the actual number of atoms of each element in a compound.

Molecule
A particle made up of at least two atoms held together by covalent bonds.

Monomer
A small molecule that can be joined together with other small molecules to form a polymer.

Monounsaturated fat
A fat that contains just one carbon-carbon double bond.

N

Nanoparticle
A tiny particle, made up of a few hundred atoms, that is between 1 and 100 nm in size.

Negative correlation
When one variable decreases as another variable increases.

Negative ion
A particle with a negative charge, formed when one or more electrons are gained.

Neutralisation
The reaction between acids and bases that leads to the formation of neutral products — usually a salt and water.

Neutron
A subatomic particle with a relative charge of 0 and a relative mass of 1. Neutrons are located in the nucleus of an atom.

Noble gases
The elements in Group 0 of the periodic table.

Non-renewable energy resource
An energy resource that is non-renewable will run out one day. It will run out more quickly the more we use it to generate electricity.

Nucleus
The central part of an atom or ion, made up of protons and neutrons.

O

Ore
A rock that contains enough metal to make it profitable to extract.

Oxidation
A reaction where electrons are lost.

P

Paper chromatography
A technique that can be used to separate and identify dyes.

Partial combustion
When a fuel burns but there isn't enough oxygen for it to burn completely. Products can include carbon monoxide and carbon particulates. Also known as incomplete combustion.

Percentage yield
The amount of product formed in a reaction, given as a percentage of the predicted amount of product.

Period
A row in the periodic table. Elements in a period all have the same number of electron shells.

Periodic table
A table of all the known elements, arranged so that elements with similar properties are in groups.

Permanent hardness
A type of water hardness that can't be removed by boiling the water.

pH scale
A scale from 0 to 14 that is used to measure how acidic or alkaline a solution is.

Predicted yield
The amount of product you would expect to be formed in a reaction. Also known as theoretical yield.

Primordial soup theory
A theory that suggests life started when lightning caused gases in the atmosphere to react and form amino acids, which then formed organic matter.

Polymer
A long chain molecule that is formed by joining lots of smaller molecules (monomers) together.

Polymerisation
The process of joining lots of small molecules (monomers) together to form a much longer molecule (a polymer).

Polyunsaturated fat
A fat that contains more than one carbon-carbon double bond.

Positive correlation
When one variable increases as another variable increases.

Positive ion
A particle with a positive charge, formed when one or more electrons are lost.

Precipitate
A solid that is formed in a solution during a chemical reaction.

Precipitation
A reaction that takes place in aqueous solution and leads to the formation of an insoluble precipitate.

Precise result
When all the data is close to the mean.

Prediction
A statement based on a hypothesis that can be tested.

Product
A substance that is formed in a chemical reaction.

Proton
A subatomic particle with a relative charge of +1 and a relative mass of 1. Protons are located in the nucleus of an atom.

Proton number
The number of protons in the nucleus of an atom. It's also known as atomic number.

Random error
A small difference in the results of an experiment caused by things like human error in measuring.

Range
The difference between the smallest and largest values in a set of data.

Reactant
A substance that reacts in a chemical reaction.

Reactivity series
A list of elements arranged in order of their reactivity. The most reactive elements are at the top and the least reactive at the bottom.

Reduction
A reaction where electrons are gained.

Relative atomic mass (A_r)
The average mass of the atoms of an element measured relative to the mass of one atom of carbon-12. The relative atomic mass of an element is the same as its mass number in the periodic table.

Relative molecular mass (M_r)
All the relative atomic masses of the atoms in a molecule added together.

Reliable result
A result that is repeatable and reproducible.

Renewable energy resource
An energy resource that is renewable won't run out, no matter how much we use it.

Repeatable result
A result that will come out the same if the experiment is repeated by the same person using the same method and equipment.

Reproducible result
A result that will come out the same if someone different does the experiment, or a sightly different method or piece of equipment is used.

Resolution
The smallest change a measuring instrument can detect.

Reversible reaction
A reaction where the products of the reaction can themselves react to produce the original reactants.

Saturated
A molecule that contains only single bonds.

Scale
A white, chalky deposit made of calcium and magnesium carbonates. It is formed when temporary hard water is heated.

Shape memory alloy
A material that can be bent out of shape but will return to its original shape when its heated.

Shielding
When electrons from inner electron shells block the nuclear charge, reducing the attraction between the nucleus and outer electron shells.

Simple molecule
A molecule made up of only a few atoms held together by covalent bonds.

Single covalent bond
A pair of electrons shared between two atoms.

Smart material
A material that has properties that change in response to external stimuli, like heat or pressure.

State symbols
The letter or letters in brackets that are placed after a substance to show what physical state it is in. E.g. gaseous carbon dioxide is shown as $CO_{2(g)}$.

Strong acid
An acid that fully ionises when it is dissolved in water. E.g. hydrochloric acid.

Subatomic particle
Particles that are smaller than an atom. Protons, neutrons and electrons are all subatomic particles.

Successful collision
A collision between particles that results in a chemical reaction.

Systematic error
An error that is consistently made every time throughout an experiment.

Tectonic plates
The huge chunks of crust and upper part of the mantle that float on the mantle below.

Temporary hardness
A type of water hardness that can be removed by boiling the water. This type of water hardness causes scale.

Theoretical yield
The amount of product you would expect to be formed in a reaction. Also known as predicted yield.

Theory
A hypothesis which has been accepted by the scientific community because there is good evidence to back it up.

Thermal decomposition
A reaction where one substance chemically changes into at least two new substances when it's heated.

Thermosetting polymer
A polymer that has cross-links between its chains.

Thermosoftening polymer
A polymer made of individual tangled polymer chains, with no cross-links between them.

Titration
A type of experiment that you can use to find the concentration of a solution. One solution is added to a known volume of another until the reaction is complete.

Transition metals
The metal elements found in the central block of the periodic table.

Trial run
A quick version of an experiment that can be used to work out the range of variables and the interval between the variables that will be used in the proper experiment.

Universal indicator
A combination of dyes which gives a different colour for every pH on the pH scale.

Unsaturated
A molecule that contains at least one double bond.

Valid result
A result that answers the original question.

Variable
A factor in an investigation that can change or be changed.
E.g. temperature or concentration.

Viscosity
How runny or gloopy a substance is.

Volatile
Will easily turn from a liquid to a gas.

Weak acid
An acid that only partially ionises when it is dissolved in water.
E.g. ethanoic acid.

Yield
The amount of product made in a reaction.

Z

Zero error
A type of systematic error caused by using a piece of equipment that isn't zeroed properly.

Acknowledgements

Photograph acknowledgements

Cover Photo **Charles D. Winters**/Science Photo Library, p 3 **Gustoimages**/Science Photo Library, p 4 **Philippe Plailly**/Science Photo Library, p 5 **Philippe Plailly**/Science Photo Library, p 6 **Frank Zullo**/Science Photo Library, p 7 **Andrew Lambert Photography**/Science Photo Library, p 8 **Robert Brook**/Science Photo Library, p 9 **Tony McConnell**/Science Photo Library, p 10 **Rosenfeld Images Ltd**/Science Photo Library, p 11 **Martyn F. Chillmaid**/Science Photo Library, p 16 **PR. M. Brauner**/Science Photo Library, p 18 Science Photo Library, p 21 **Andrew Lambert Photography**/Science Photo Library, p 22 (top) **Aaron Haupt**/Science Photo Library, p 22 (bottom) **Chris Martin-Bahr**/Science Photo Library, p 25 (top) Science Photo Library, p 25 (middle) **Andrew Lambert Photography**/Science Photo Library, p 25 (bottom) **Martyn F. Chillmaid**/Science Photo Library, p 35 **Andrew Lambert Photography**/Science Photo Library, p 38 **Andrew Lambert Photography**/Science Photo Library, p 39 **Ria Novosti**/Science Photo Library, p 40 (top) **Martin Bond**/Science Photo Library, p 40 (bottom) **Martin Bond**/Science Photo Library, p 42 **Ben Johnson**/Science Photo Library, p 46 **Dirk Wiersma**/Science Photo Library, p 48 **Patrick Dumas/Eurelios**/Science Photo Library, p 50 **Philippe Psaila**/Science Photo Library, p 51 **Custom Medical Stock Photo**/Science Photo Library, p 53 **David Guyon**/Science Photo Library, p 54 **Martin Bond**/Science Photo Library, p 57 **Christophe Vander Eecken/Reporters**/Science Photo Library, p 61 **Paul Rapson**/Science Photo Library, p 65 **Martyn F. Chillmaid**/Science Photo Library, p 67 (top) **Simon Fraser**/Science Photo Library, p 67 (bottom) **Adam Hart-Davis**/Science Photo Library, p 68 **Bjorn Svensson**/Science Photo Library, p 70 **Ashley Cooper, Visuals Unlimited**/Science Photo Library, p 71 **Martin Bond**/Science Photo Library, p 75 **Paul Rapson**/Science Photo Library, p 76 **Paul Rapson**/Science Photo Library, p 77 (top) **Richard Folwell**/Science Photo Library, p 77 (bottom) **Andy Levin**/Science Photo Library, p 79 **Jerry Mason**/Science Photo Library, p 83 **Victor de Schwanberg**/Science Photo Library, p 86 **Sheila Terry**/Science Photo Library, p 87 **David Munns**/Science Photo Library, p 90 **Paul Rapson**/Science Photo Library, p 91 (left) **Martyn F. Chillmaid**/Science Photo Library, p 91 (right) **Martyn F. Chillmaid**/Science Photo Library, p 92 **Martyn F. Chillmaid**/Science Photo Library, p 97 **Sinclair Stammers**/Science Photo Library, p 99 **Theodore Clutter**/Science Photo Library, p 100 **Ria Novosti**/Science Photo Library, p 101 **Bernhard Edmaier**/Science Photo Library, p 103 **Andrew Lambert Photography**/Science Photo Library, p 104 **Steve Allen**/Science Photo Library, p 114 **Charles D. Winters**/Science Photo Library, p 119 **Andrew Lambert Photography**/Science Photo Library, p 124 (middle) **Lawrence Lawry**/Science Photo Library, p 124 (bottom) **Scientifica, Visuals Unlimited**/Science Photo Library, p 127 (top left) **Charles D. Winters**/Science Photo Library, p 127 (top middle) **Charles D. Winters**/Science Photo Library, p 127 (top right) **Charles D. Winters**/Science Photo Library, p 127 (bottom) **Pascal Goetgheluck**/Science Photo Library, p 129 **Friedrich Saurer**/Science Photo Library, p 130 **Victor de Schwanberg**/Science Photo Library, p 136 (left) **Pasieka**/Science Photo Library, p 136 (right) **Natural History Museum, London**/Science Photo Library, p 140 **Martyn F. Chillmaid**/Science Photo Library, p 141 **Andrew Lambert Photography**/Science Photo Library, p 145 **Andrew Lambert Photography**/Science Photo Library, p 149 **Martyn F. Chillmaid**/Science Photo Library, p 151 **Andrew Lambert Photography**/Science Photo Library, p 152 **Mark Sykes**/Science Photo Library, p 161 **Martyn F. Chillmaid**/Science Photo Library, p 162 **Andrew Lambert Photography**/Science Photo Library, p 163 **Andrew Lambert Photography**/Science Photo Library, p 167 **Trevor Clifford Photography**/Science Photo Library, p 168 **Andrew Lambert Photography**/Science Photo Library, p 170 **Charles D. Winters**/Science Photo Library, p 172 **Martyn F. Chillmaid**/Science Photo Library, p 173 **Andrew Lambert Photography**/Science Photo Library, p 174 **Martyn F. Chillmaid**/Science Photo Library, p 177 **Andrew Lambert Photography**/Science Photo Library, p 178 **Martyn F. Chillmaid**/Science Photo Library, p 180 **Charles D. Winters**/Science Photo Library, p 185 (top) **Martyn F. Chillmaid**/Science Photo Library, p 185 (bottom) **Martyn F. Chillmaid**/Science Photo Library, p 186 **Massimo Brega, The Lighthouse**/Science Photo Library, p 195 **Trevor Clifford Photography**/Science Photo Library, p 197 **Sam Ogden**/Science Photo Library, p 200 Science Photo Library, p 201 **Ria Novosti**/Science Photo Library, p 206 **Martyn F. Chillmaid**/Science Photo Library, p 207 (top) **Martyn F. Chillmaid**/Science Photo Library, p 207 (bottom) **Martyn F. Chillmaid**/Science Photo Library, p 208 **Martyn F. Chillmaid**/Science Photo Library, p 209 **Andrew Lambert Photography**/Science Photo Library, p 210 **Andrew Lambert Photography**/Science Photo Library, p 212 **Klaus Guldbrandsen**/Science Photo Library, p 213 **Martyn F. Chillmaid**/Science Photo Library, p 219 (top) **Sheila Terry**/Science Photo Library, p 219 (bottom left) **Martyn F. Chillmaid**/Science Photo Library, p 219 (bottom right) **Martyn F. Chillmaid**/Science Photo Library, p 221 **Charles D. Winters**/Science Photo Library, p 225 **Adam Hart-Davis**/Science Photo Library, p 228 **John Heseltine**/Science Photo Library, p 230 **E. R. Degginger**/Science Photo Library, p 232 **Charles D. Winters**/Science Photo Library, p 236 **Martyn F. Chillmaid**/Science Photo Library, p 239 **GIPhotostock**/Science Photo Library, p 240 (top) **Friedrich Saurer**/Science Photo Library, p 240 (bottom) **GIPhotostock**/Science Photo Library, p 244 **GIPhotostock**/Science Photo Library, p 245 (top) **Jerry Mason**/Science Photo Library, p 245 (bottom) **Andrew Lambert Photography**/Science Photo Library, p 251 (all five photographs) **Andrew Lambert Photography**/Science Photo Library, p 253 (top) **Andrew Lambert Photography**/Science Photo Library, p 253 (bottom) **Charles D. Winters**/Science Photo Library, p 260 **Deloche**/Science Photo Library, p 264 **Robert Brook**/Science Photo Library, p 268 **Charles D. Winters**/Science Photo Library, p 269 (top) **Martyn F. Chillmaid**/Science Photo Library, p 269 (bottom) **Roger Job/Reporters**/Science Photo Library, p 271 **Andrew McClenaghan**/Science Photo Library, p 273 **Martyn F. Chillmaid**/Science Photo Library, p 277 **Martyn F. Chillmaid**/Science Photo Library, p 283 **Andrew Lambert Photography**/Science Photo Library, p 285 Science Photo Library, p 293 **Photostock-Israel**/Science Photo Library.

Index

CATB41